MW01231224

Exploring Positive Psychology

Exploring Positive Psychology

*The Science of Happiness
and Well-Being*

**ERIK M. GREGORY AND
PAMELA B. RUTLEDGE**

An Imprint of ABC-CLIO, LLC

Santa Barbara, California • Denver, Colorado

Copyright © 2016 by ABC-CLIO, LLC

All rights reserved. No part of this publication may be reproduced, stored in a retrieval system, or transmitted, in any form or by any means, electronic, mechanical, photocopying, recording, or otherwise, except for the inclusion of brief quotations in a review, without prior permission in writing from the publisher.

Library of Congress Cataloging-in-Publication Data

Names: Gregory, Erik M., author. | Rutledge, Pamela B., author.
Title: Exploring positive psychology : the science of happiness and
    well-being / Erik M. Gregory and Pamela B. Rutledge.
Description: Santa Barbara : Greenwood, 2016. | Includes bibliographical
    references and index.
Identifiers: LCCN 2016015544 | ISBN 9781610699396 (alk. paper) |
    ISBN 9781610699402 (ebook)
Subjects: LCSH: Positive psychology. | Happiness. | Well-being.
Classification: LCC BF204.6 .G74 2016 | DDC 150.19/88—dc23
LC record available at https://lccn.loc.gov/2016015544

ISBN: 978-1-61069-939-6
EISBN: 978-1-61069-940-2

20 19 18 17 16   1 2 3 4 5

This book is also available as an eBook.

Greenwood
An Imprint of ABC-CLIO, LLC

ABC-CLIO, LLC
130 Cremona Drive, P.O. Box 1911
Santa Barbara, California 93116-1911
www.abc-clio.com

This book is printed on acid-free paper ∞

Manufactured in the United States of America

Erik:
For Rictor, Elfie, Miriam, and the Harvard Humanist Hub community

Thanks to Joe, Kelly, and Ligia for their support and enthusiasm; Marissa
Herzog for helping us put this all together; and to Pamela Rutledge,
a wonderful colleague and friend.

Pam:
For Katie and Elizabeth

Thanks to my parents Cathie and Syd, for always seeing the rich
narrative in life; my husband John Rutledge for his continued
support and encouragement; Marissa Herzog for her attention
to detail; and to Erik Gregory, who continues to open new
doors and say "come on in!"

Contents

Preface   ix

1   An Introduction to Positive Psychology   1

2   Strengths   24

3   Flow   49

4   Resilience   69

5   Mindfulness   101

6   The Neuroscience of Positive Psychology   125

7   Storytelling and Positive Psychology   154

8   Positive Psychology in the Real World   181

9   The Road to Happiness   209

10 Finding Your Place within the World of Positive Psychology   230

Glossary   249

References and Further Reading   259

Index   273

Preface

Happiness is produced not so much by great pieces of good fortune that seldom happen as by little advantages that occur every day.

—Benjamin Franklin

It should not come as a surprise that North Americans have embraced positive psychology, with its emphasis on self-betterment, and made the pursuit of happiness an industry unto itself. In 2013, over 50 million inspirational books, self-help books, and how-to books were purchased in the United States, ringing up over $11 billion in sales. Happiness is so part of the very fabric of the United States that it is written as a right in the Declaration of Independence, which emphasizes the pursuit of "life, liberty, and happiness." Today much of this pursuit of happiness in fact fuels the U.S. economies and others in the form of consumerism created by industries that ceaselessly promote the consumption of goods as the road to well-being.

The study of well-being is an age-old pursuit. The philosophers of ancient Greece believed happiness arose through a life of freedom where basic needs were met and individuals had time for intellectual reflection. Aristotle argued that happiness is the "supreme good," and all else man did in life was in pursuit of attaining happiness. Cicero said, "There is no fool who is happy, and no wise man who is not." Happiness was seen as above passion and material rewards.

Epicurus claimed that happiness was the result of a simple life that included tranquility and peace of mind. He believed that the wise individual takes delight in the present and faces the future without fear. And the Stoics believed that happiness was the attainment of noble characteristics such as the wisdom to know between good and bad, right and wrong.

Today, the question of well-being continues to play a central role in our personal lives and in the life of modern science. Researchers have a wealth of data regarding individual physical and material well-being, yet despite all of this data, there are just the beginnings of an understanding of why some people seem to experience a life with more well-being than others.

In his 1992 book *The Pursuit of Happiness: Discovering the Pathway to Fulfillment, Well-Being, and Enduring Personal Joy*, David G. Myers beautifully captures the dilemma our society faces today in trying to understand well-being. He wrote:

> For never has a century known such abundance, or such massive genocide and environmental devastation.
>
> Never has a culture experienced such comfort and opportunity, or such widespread depression.
>
> Never has a technology given us so many conveniences, or such terrible instruments of degradation and destruction.
>
> Never have we been so self-reliant, or so lonely.
>
> Never have we seemed so free, or our prisons so overstuffed.
>
> Never have we had so much education, or such high rates of teen delinquency, despair, and suicide.
>
> Never have we been so sophisticated about pleasure, or so likely to suffer broken or miserable marriages.

In a meta-analysis of studies examining well-being, Myers found a number of popular notions about what it takes to be happy dispelled. These *myths* include:

- That few people are genuinely happy
- That wealth buys well-being
- That tragedies or traumatic events destroy happiness
- That happiness springs from memories of intense, if rare, positive experiences
- That teens and elderly are the unhappiest populations
- That one gender is happier than the other

If these are the myths about happiness, then what do we know about well-being? In the past 20 years, there has been a great deal of research on this very question. Positive psychologists have largely been leading the way in asking questions about positive traits, fostering excellence, subjective well-being, resiliency, life satisfaction—and have done so with the use of the scientific method in order to understand the complexity of human behavior. Seligman and Csikszentmihalyi (2000), leaders in the field of positive psychology, wrote, "Psychology is not just the study of pathology, weakness, and damage; it is also the study of strength and virtue . . . treatment is not just fixing what is broken; it is nurturing what is best."

Psychology has traditionally looked at diseases such as anxiety and depression as real and human strengths as simply coping mechanisms. Positive psychologists study the building blocks of characteristics such as courage, for-giveness, optimism, hope, and joy so that there can be a greater understanding of how to promote that which is healthy in human beings and to collect a set of psychological tools in which to treat the number of individuals seeking mental health services.

Positive psychologists examine preventive factors that promote positive human functioning and provide information to scientists and practitioners not only as a means of bettering understanding of human behavior, but also as a means of improving the mental health of the public.

The academic psychology literature has traditionally focused on issues of anxiety and depression 100 times more than the journal articles on the top-ics of joy and well-being. Positive psychologists such as Seligman argue that this orientation has left psychology "blind" to individual growth, mastery, and insight that human beings are able to harness in order to overcome the pain and setbacks of life. Seligman believes that by building "psychological muscles" through positive psychology research, one can create a public health promotion of the mind and prevent problems before they occur. Certainly he recognizes that human limitations exist, but he argues that individuals can function optimally within those limits.

Tal Ben-Shahar, a positive psychologist and author of the best-selling book *Happier* (2007), describes positive psychology as the bridge between the ivory tower and the main street—between the rigor of academe and the fun of the self-help movement. With this text, we aim to position ourselves between those points.

In this text, we will review the different approaches to positive psychology with a focus on understanding how the activities, thoughts, and feelings of an individual in his or her everyday life can allow for a greater understanding of characteristics that promote well-being.

The text is arranged to help you understand the theory and practice of pos-itive psychology for the 21st century, including chapters that review the sem-inal material of positive psychology; sidebars that give you highlights about important thinkers and ideas in positive psychology; case studies that give you actual examples of applied positive psychology; and "life strategy" com-ponents that will support your own movement toward resilient behavior.

It is our goal to integrate the study of courage, hope, optimism, and resiliency (tenets of positive psychology) to promote that which is best in humankind.

CHAPTER 1

An Introduction to Positive Psychology

It may be unusual to begin an introduction to positive psychology of what positive psychology is not, but it is important to clarify this first as the field of psychology is often confused for the power of positive thinking movement. Positive thinking is the idea that if you *think* positively life will *be* positive. While there is a small element of this in positive psychology as you will learn (optimists tend to have more resiliency), the field of positive psychology is about understanding human strengths such as courage, hope, optimism, and resiliency.

Historically, the field of psychology took a medical model toward the research and practice of psychology. In Western medicine, one sees a doctor when ill. The physician examines that which is wrong and works toward correcting it with various scientific interventions. Psychology followed this model by examining that which was wrong in human behavior in order to correct it. It missed an essential element, however: that which is right in human behavior.

THE PURSUIT OF HAPPINESS

The study of well-being is an age-old pursuit. The philosophers of ancient Greece believed happiness arose through a life of freedom where basic needs were met and individuals had time for intellectual reflection. Aristotle argued that happiness is the "supreme good," and all else man did in life was in pursuit of attaining happiness. Cicero said, "There is no fool who is happy, and no wise man who is not." Happiness was seen as above passion and material rewards.

Today, the question of well-being continues to play a central role in our personal lives and in the life of modern science. For the past 20+ years, researchers have begun to create a picture and understanding of why some people seem to experience a life with more well-being than others. Positive psychologists have led the way in asking questions about positive traits, fostering excellence, subjective well-being, resiliency, and life satisfaction—and have done so with the use of the scientific method in order to understand the complexity of human behavior (Seligman & Csikszentmihalyi, 2000). Seligman and Csikszentmihalyi, leaders in the positive psychology movement, wrote, "Psychology is not just the study of pathology, weakness, and damage; it is also the study of strength and virtue . . . treatment is not just fixing what is broken; it is nurturing what is best" (the term "positive psychology" was first used by Abraham Maslow, a humanistic psychologist known for his "hierarchy of needs" model that moved individuals to realizing their full potential).

Both Seligman and Csikszentmihalyi argued that positive psychology needed to be based on good science. This meant running scientific studies that could be replicated by other scientists to reveal facts about healthy human behavior. This is important to emphasize as science is different from someone's beliefs or hunches about a topic. For example, if you believe that Echinacea (a plant extract) will cure colds and has cured your colds, that may indeed be true for you. This, however, cannot be generalized to a larger population unless testing is completed on a group of people who have cold and are given Echinacea versus a "control group" who have colds but are not given Echinacea.

THE SCIENTIST-PRACTITIONER MODEL

Positive psychology also embraces the scientist-practitioner model. In other words, once theories have established some significant outcomes (such as the usefulness of keeping gratitude journals), practitioners, such as therapists or clinicians, can ask their patients to engage in such an activity to improve the patients' well-being. In turn, practitioners who have hands-on interaction with patients can provide feedback to researchers about the actual application of the theory.

Around the world and across culture, gender, and religious beliefs, we find constructions of what it means to be happy. "Happiness" is a slippery term as it can mean many different things to different people. In fact, individuals socially construct what it means to be happy or lead a good life. This means that as a social group, over time we explicitly or implicitly agree upon what terms such as "good," "bad," "happy," "sad," "success," or "failure" mean. This allows a group of people to jointly create an understanding of the world around them.

For example, in the middle of the last century, it was considered socially shameful to have a child out of "wedlock." Many young women who became pregnant out of marriage were hidden away or, in many cases, sent away for nine months to be removed from the stigma associated with this belief. Today, the social construction of marriage and what is appropriate in and out of marriage has changed a great deal. We are seeing new constructions of family between non-married couples and same-sex couples. Other examples of social construction is the understanding of gender. Consider the way much of society shares a definition of what it means to be a boy or a girl right down to identifying blue for boys and pink for girls (although this was originally pink to signify male "royalty" and blue female "serenity" in Victorian times). When boys or girls, and men or women, step out of their prescribed gender roles by taking on the other gender's stereotype behavior, people feel uncomfortable, some to the point of persecuting those who have stepped out of these socially prescribed contracts (see the film *Boys Don't Cry*).

Hence, social and cultural development shifts over time and changes the way we define aspects of society, including an understanding of what it means to live a good life. At the basis of understanding what it means to live a healthy and happy life are the foundations of hope, courage, optimism, and the pursuit of happiness. In what follows, these four cornerstones of positive psychology are reviewed.

CORNERSTONES OF POSITIVE PSYCHOLOGY

Hope

Hope is about realizing the goals, dreams, and objectives that we have in life. One of the earliest researchers of hope is Charles R. Snyder who generated "Hope Theory." In this theory, he argues that individuals will use their strengths to determine how to achieve the outcomes that they desire. Thus there must not only be will to get to the end of the rainbow, but also action and strategy. Snyder believes that hope is part of a cognitive/motivational system that goes beyond good feelings and instead is generated from thinking and assessing how to move toward one's hoped-for goal.

Thanks to researchers in positive psychology, hope can now be better defined and measured. With a definition of hope as not only being emotion but also a cognitive process as well, hope includes aspects of motivation, optimism, sense of self, and self-efficacy. These include the following:

- Having goals: These goals can be short-term or long-term and should be important enough that they stay with your thoughts. There should be some challenge associated with your goal. If it is too easy, you will have completed the objective already and there is no need for the goal.
- Ways of getting to your goals: A plan is required that makes it possible for you to reach your goal. It may not be easy, but there is a potential path for you to take through actions with which you can start. There is often not just one route to achieving your goals and hence surfacing many options will provide an alternative route so that when one gets blocked, there are still options to maintaining a hoped-for outcome.
- You can do it: An individual needs to have a sense that through one's own ability, the goal can be achieved. There is a cause-and-effect mechanism that leads step by step toward the goal with small rewards as you move toward your ultimate goal.
- Higher hope, higher outcome: The greater one's sense of hope, the greater the performance outcomes athletes find, and those who have higher hope when it comes to standardized achievement tests (not intelligent tests) do better as well.

- Higher self-worth leads to higher levels of goal: Those with a higher sense of self-worth tend to have a greater belief in reaching goals, even when setbacks occur. This group tends to focus on what can be done to meet their objectives rather than what cannot.

- Optimism: As reviewed in this chapter, optimism is the perception that one can move toward one's goals. This is distinct from hope. Hope is the concrete establishment of goals and consideration of how to reach those goals. Optimistic people, however, tend to be more hopeful people, and more hopeful people tend to be optimists.

- Self-efficacy: This emerges from Albert Bandura's models of self-efficacy discussed in this text. Self-efficacy is one's belief that successful outcomes can be achieved through one's ability. In other words, one can control or influence his or her own motivation, behavior, and interpersonal behavior to achieve various goals in life.

A distinction does indeed exist between those who are considered "high-hope" people and those who are considered "low-hope" people. High-hope people pursue goals with an emotional and physical energy and in the process often generate more goals and generally recover from obstacles in their path more quickly. They also seek out feedback to assess and reassess the strategies toward meeting their goals. In addition, high-hope people create relationships with other people creating networks that provide a greater chance of successful outcomes.

Low-hope people tend to carry more self-doubt, have lower levels of tolerance for frustration, and may withdraw when obstacles are placed in their path. They are less likely to manage ambiguous situations and are often not open to generating or surfacing additional goals during the process.

Moving toward change through hope requires motivation. Motivation is often defined by the energy an individual is willing to expend in order to satisfy a need or desire. Often motivation may be reinforced by achieving a desired outcome. For example, a high school student may be motivated to work during the summer at a job that is not very interesting in order to buy a car in the fall. Therefore, motivation reflects an expectation of a positive outcome. Motivation is often used within leadership or management by creating goals and a vision that the employee chooses to follow in order to attain a collective good or reward. Hence, motivation requires not only a goal as in hope but also inspiration. People do not want to be told what to do necessarily when it comes to moving toward a goal, but instead they want to be inspired, shown, led, or supported.

Despite the best intentions of setting goals (take into consideration the many goals generated at the New Year that are often not followed through), many find the commitment to a goal fades over time. The more complex or difficult the goal, the less hope some feel in attaining the goal. Therefore goal setting may need to be broken down to allow for successes at various milestones that maintain motivation. Thus, the ultimate goal seems more attainable over time.

Goals that are intrinsically (meaning something that comes from within) created are more likely to be followed than goals that are enforced upon one from the outside (extrinsically). This is not to say that extrinsic goals cannot be integrated into intrinsic goals, but starting from within makes the pursuit of the goal a value in itself rather than pursuing for an external reward. Building hope, whether individually or within an organization, is always more effective than taking a fear-based approach, which tends to immobilize one from reaching established goals. Individuals who work toward a goal through a hope pathway rather than a fear pathway (a do-this-or-else approach) tend to have more willpower and energy in attaining established goals.

Martin Seligman argues that negative, depressing narratives and outlooks that lack a sense of hope are ubiquitous in today's culture, limiting us to what we think we can change and that we cannot. Maintaining a cynical or pathological view of the world is not useful for the human psyche. Albert Bandura is a recognized expert on self-efficacy and he also sees that psychological theories have traditionally "grossly overpredict(ed) psychopathology." In particular the cultural sense of hopelessness these theorists believe comes from the likes of Sigmund Freud and John Bowlby, who maintained that if a child has an impoverished childhood he or she will have an impaired life. Thus, widespread poverty of opportunity leads to a cynical society that in turns leads to hopelessness.

Research shows the contrary, however, where in fact many children while having suffered from exposure to crime, poverty, violence, or deprivations have moved to having good jobs and healthy partnerships (and do not fall into the justice system as is often predicted). These individuals maintained a sense of hope for a better future and most likely benefited from the concurrent sense of resilience that came with it. This speaks for the adaptability of individuals to change no matter what the circumstances, and current research reflects that the plasticity of the brain over the lifespan changes.

Society celebrates those who have been resilient and hopeful in the face of adversity. Much of our heroic folklore in the past and our Hollywood movies of today reflect such themes.

In many world traditions, hope is the force that moves people toward change and light. The hero's journey is based on Joseph Campbell's (refer to *The Power of Myth* by Joseph Campbell) argument that all stories have a hero who must face obstacles to achieve his outcome and the journey is done for the sake of hope and attaining a better outcome for the world. Most world religions give a lot of attention and time to hope as it moves individuals, groups, communities, and states toward something better than it is today. It is a motivating force that shifts people into useful action.

Within Greek mythology, for example, the first woman in creation, Pandora, was given a box that was not to be opened (Pandora's Box or Pandora's Jar). Naturally, her curiosity got the better of her and she opened the container, releasing all the evils of the world, including hate, pain, violence, and starvation. Pandora quickly realized what happened and closed the box keeping inside only hope. Hope for something better is something that is very much part of the human condition as it provides the spirit that is needed to work toward change.

CASE STUDY: DELIVERING HAPPINESS AT ZAPPOS

Since its founding in 1999, Zappos has changed how people think about buying shoes. More profoundly, however, Zappos has changed how companies think about doing business. Under the leadership of CEO Tony Hsieh, Zappos has become synonymous with "wow" customer service and is one of the most frequently cited examples of a values-oriented company that combines, in Hsieh's words, "profits, passion and purpose."

The idea for Zappos.com came when founder Nick Swinmurn spent a day searching unsuccessfully through several stores to find a pair of Airwalk desert boots. Buying shoes shouldn't be that hard, he thought, why not start an online shoe store?

Swinmurn had little success finding an investor because no one believed you could sell shoes online, until he met Tony Hsieh. Hsieh was a 24-year-old serial entrepreneur. Hsieh had gone from one "crazy" idea to another, such as starting a worm farm when he was 8 years old to, most recently, co-founding an Internet advertising cooperative that was sold to Microsoft for $295 million.

Hsieh brought more than money to the Zappos venture. He viewed a values-driven culture as the top priority, believing that if you managed to get the culture right, things like great customer service and an enduring brand would naturally follow. It was the core values of the culture that created a sense of community and purpose that promoted employees believing in what they're doing so that they were always excited to come to work.

Hsieh says that as the company grows, it becomes even more important to explicitly define the values that drive their culture, brand, and business strategies.

The core values also power Zappos's legendary customer service. Beyond their 365-day return policy, Zappos routinely "surprises" customers with free upgraded overnight shipping. Zappos also has no-script call centers with no time limit per call, and its customer service reps are empowered to create "wow" service in whatever way they can, such as sending flowers to a customer whose mother just died or overnighting a pair of free shoes to the Best Man who had forgotten his shoes for the wedding. Zappos routinely gives its employees brief questionnaires to monitor the health of the company culture.

Positive Psychology and Zappos

Zappos now sees its brand promise as "delivering happiness," recognizing that the contact they have with every person, from employee and customer to vendor, has the ability to create positive emotion through the sense of connection, regard, and appreciation. (Note: See the section on positive psychology and the brain to read about the neural impact of positive emotions and the way positivity spreads across networks.)

> **CASE STUDY (Continued)**
>
> Zappos's core values exemplify positive psychology tenets, such as purpose, meaning, individual agency, control, feedback, and authentic connection. Zappos recognizes that people spend a lot of time at work, so rather than addressing work–life separation, or work–life balance, they argue in favor of work–life integration, so that work becomes a way to express higher qualities, connect with people you care about, and do something that you feel matters.

The theme remained central to later monotheistic beliefs. The universal theme of hope in world faiths and belief systems reflects the following:

- The future can be better than the present through combined efforts.
- Attaining ideals to which people strive to live requires the hope that they can be met.
- Hope requires generating action in order to move toward the ideal.
- Hope takes place within a context of values, beliefs, attitudes, and culture.
- Community brings to awareness the need for hope in order to create constructive change.

Themes of hope that provide resiliency in life are part of the daily stories that are told in cultures around the world. There are the stories of individuals who may have experienced poverty, war, divorce, alcoholism, mental illness, or violence and who move forward to stable and "normal" lives. Other people may find a family member or friend who admirably models another way of living despite setbacks, and for others it may simply be a genetic predisposition that provides a greater ability to move forward from terrible challenges or experiences. What is clear is that individuals who had some sense of self-reliance, hope, and some feeling of agency are able to move on to a better way of living. Positive psychologists work to understand how hope helps individuals and groups overcome adversity.

Recent research is also uncovering that the traditional focus on pathology, such as within therapy or the criminal justice system, does not lead to healthier individuals or improved outcomes. For example, more than 50 percent of adolescents who worked with social welfare services in which resources are constrained and the presenting pathology takes precedence were found not to have successful adult lives including personality problems, lack of minimal education, lower wages, and more dysfunctional relationships. The researchers suggest that youth need to have an opportunity to meet pro-social expectations in order to find greater hope in life. Negative life experiences apparently beget more negativity, while the experience of positive experiences through social networks provides hope and resiliency.

ADAPTATION AND SUCCESS

Adaptation is the key to success in the 21st century given the many changes and challenges that exist at an ever faster pace. Consider evolutionary biology. If an organism exists and there is a huge impact on it, say, a meteor that creates a change to extremely high temperatures all of a sudden, the organism may continue to try to live as if nothing has changed and will eventually go extinct. Or the organism can adapt by eventually creating a shell, changing its living location, or hiding in water. In other words, it adapts to the change and not only survives but also hopefully thrives. This ability to adapt is what has made human beings successful as a species.

This same principle is being applied to organizational change and leadership. If organizations do not change to the needs of their consumers, they would also go extinct. This was readily seen by the impact Amazon.com has had on the way people buy their goods. Companies such as Circuit City and Borders Books did not make the shift to online sales quickly enough, instead holding on to their traditional models of sales and eventually going out of business (or becoming extinct).

Similarly leaders must adapt to the challenges, needs, and priorities of the world around them and help their followers hold steady through these changes to be able to come out having adapted successfully. Too much change too quickly is overwhelming for individuals and groups and often creates a pushback to a default way of being. For many, the safety and security of the default position are more important than the disequilibrium that change brings. Yet without disequilibrium, we do not change. In fact, it isn't so much the change that people dislike, but it is the sense of loss that comes with that change.

In the past 100 years humans have adapted to a whole new way of living with the introduction of commercial flying, automobile travel, electricity, Internet, communication shifts, and countless other shifts so much so that our great-grandparents may have difficulty in understanding the current world around them. Change is a given in our world. We must learn to adapt ourselves, our families, our communities, and our governments in order to address the quickly changing world in the 21st century.

Dwelling on the negative does indeed impact one's sense of hopefulness. Seligman and his colleagues found that individuals who came to terms with past grievances, hurts, and trauma typically do not dwell on a negative past. Focusing on one's bad lot in life, shortcomings, bad luck, or hard life circumstances does nothing but make one assume a negative mood, have lower energy levels, and leads to a sense of helplessness.

Positive psychologists instead endorse focusing as constructively and purposefully on the future as possible. This may not be achieved independently and individuals may take the help of parents, friends, teachers, or thera-pists. The theories of Seligman's "Learned Optimism" and Albert Bandura's "Self-Efficacy" have been well researched and demonstrate that one's cogni-tive approaches to setbacks make a difference in feeling hopeful or hopeless.

Positive modeling is key to learning the skill of turning to hope in adverse situations. This, in addition to having a social network that reminds one of possibilities rather than limitations, is critical. Ideally, learning pro-social skills should be included in the curriculum of every elementary school as much as verbal and quantitative skills are emphasized.

The Theory and Practice of Hope

Martin Luther King Jr. had a dream and had hope. He hoped for an end to segregation in the United States that was legal in many parts of the country. There were restrooms for white people and others for *colored* people, as there were drinking fountains that were for white people and for *colored* people. Beginning in the 1950s this Baptist minister engaged as a civil-rights activ-ist. In pursuit of his dream he was also assaulted, arrested, and yet found a way to deliver his famous "I Have a Dream" speech to over 250,000 people in Washington, D.C. King said that he wanted African Americans to have the same rights as promised in the Constitution and the Declaration of Inde-pendence. In that speech he emphasized that he had not lost hope. He said: "I say to you today, my friends, so even though we face the difficulties of today and tomorrow, I still have a dream. It is a dream deeply rooted in the American dream . . . that one day this nation will rise up and live out the true meaning of its creed: 'we hold these truths to be self-evident, that all men are created equal.'"

His hope was to see a country that was not separated based on race. His plan for that goal was to mobilize people to support him; he wrote five books on the subject and traveled six million miles over an 11-year period, presenting over 2,500 speeches protesting inequality and injustice. He followed Gandhi's approach to nonviolent protest and lived to see the passing of the 1964 Civil Rights Act. At the age of 35, King Jr. received the Nobel Peace Prize for his work in the civil-rights movement. He gave the entire prize money to further support his work.

In 1968 he was assassinated on the balcony of his motel room in Mem-phis, Tennessee, where he was scheduled to march with striking sanitation workers.

Courage

Aristotle believed that courage is so important that it is the "first of human virtues because it makes all others possible." Today courage is considered another cornerstone for positive psychology. Recent research has led neurosci-entists to better understand how courage works in the brain so that the individ-ual is better able to face fears and navigate difficult decision making. Courage is not only about managing fear but also about understanding tolerance for risk or uncertainty. There are five major aspects of courage that must be culti-vated to become more courageous. These are the following:

- Vulnerability: While this may sound counterintuitive to some, vulnerabil-ity allows one to move away from always being defensive (trying to show the world how together you are when you may not be) in which feelings of unworthiness may be hidden, creating a life based on the fear that others may find out about this secret. People maintain a number of defenses to protect their ego, but those defenses only work for so long and may or may not be effective. In order to grow and develop courageousness, one must take risks and allow others to see the real person behind the defenses. While a prescrip-tion to open oneself to fear or even criticism of the self may sound difficult, it helps shift the energy placed into being something that we are not to some-thing that we are more of authentically. When the alignment between who we are and how we are in the world merges, people report a far greater sense of well-being and confidence.

- Surfacing fears: Oftentimes people tend to avoid their fears or push them away. However, as part of the movement toward being honest with oneself, identifying one's fears is an important step. Denying one's fears takes one away from courage. Everyone, no matter how he or she may present to the world, has anxieties, limitations, and protective psychological layers devel-oped over years. The key is to identify one's fears and then work through them. One must surface these fears, look at them, and then consider how you want to proceed in life without them. Other researchers argue that facing your fear is critical as well. For the individual who has fear of public speaking, it is important to get training in public speaking and get in front of various audi-ences to desensitize one to such fears. Exposure therapy does the same thing. For those fearful of spiders or snakes, a therapist may first ask you to think about the animal and identify your internal reactions. With time an aquar-ium with a spider or snake may be brought into treatment to view it from a distance with the goal over time of being able to be in the same room with the animal or near it (even touch it) with the fear response no longer being triggered. Such exposure reduces your response to fear over time and can be applied to many things that are feared in life.

- Reframe your thinking: Researchers have found that if you expect negative outcomes in a situation, you most likely will realize them. Shifting one's thinking toward how adversity or setbacks can be addressed rather than their impossibility. Even visualizing a successful outcome or providing yourself with some self-encouragement can change the outcomes (as is the case for professional athletes who perform better when engaging in reframing and positive self-talk). This will not fix all situations, but it certainly can be a step toward more constructive outcomes.

- Address the stress: In the 21st century, people are reporting higher levels of stress and anxiety. Managing stress is a key quality to life when so many demands and uncertainties exist. Stress can result from feeling overwhelmed, which then triggers the fear that one's hoped-for outcomes will not be suc-cessful, oftentimes leading to depression and anxiety. To better face challenge with courage, it is important to practice self-care. Exercise, meditation, or breaks to breathe deeply can reset one to better handle daily stressors of life and build that courage muscle.

- Practice, practice, practice: Moving out of one's default way of being takes a lot of fortitude. Often one feels more comfortable staying in what is familiar, despite it being less than ideal or perhaps even destructive, than making change. It isn't change that is so difficult for people, but rather the loss of what is known. Heroism is defined by moving beyond what is familiar and stepping into the fear or unknown. It does not need to grandiose. Facing each day with its uncertainty can be an act of courage. The trade-off of trying to remain in what is familiar and safe, while not bad, does not necessarily expand our ability to meet intense challenges as they arise, whether threatening, frightening, intimidating, disorienting, and endangering. Oftentimes through practice the terror lessens, and the courage grows. Try to be an everyday hero to yourself.

Courage is often synonymous with strength, bravery, and power. Courage, however, originally had a very different meaning. It comes from the French *cour*, which means the heart. Courage is about the heart that of course pumps blood throughout the body to maintain bodily life. Traditionally, the heart has also represented where our feelings originate. In order to maintain the heart of oneself or those we love, we may be called upon to be courageous in protecting and defending those in our life. It also takes courage to follow our passions in life despite the voices around us telling us to do something different. In the same way, the courage of one's convictions is critical to having a guiding philosophy in life.

C.G. Jung wrote, "Man cannot stand a meaningless life." In order to make meaning of one's life, it takes courage to identify what is important to one, pursue it, fail once or twice, try again, and fall back upon one's feelings of courage as need to move forward. Ludwig van Beethoven had a difficult life, for example, and often fought depression and loneliness. Music was his life and when he learned at the age of 28 of his impending deafness, he fell into despair. Nonetheless, his courage and fortitude seemed to have served him well as he engaged himself in composing while deaf until his death at 57. Had he stayed within his despair, he would not have provided the world with the gift of his compositions that we have today.

Courage comes in all shapes and sizes. Take the story of Irena Sendlerowa (later Sendler) and what has become to be known as the "Jar Project." Sendler was one of the many courageous people of World War II who risked their lives in the protection of other lives. Irena Sendler was trained as both a social worker and nurse. In 1939, the Nazis invaded Poland. Life became increasingly worse for Jews as a result. Irena Sendler did all that she could to smuggle food and provide shelter for Jews despite the possibility of being shot on the spot for doing so. In 1940, she witnessed many orphaned children left behind when their parents were taken by force to the ghettos. Irena Sendler organized herself and others to help the orphaned children and began to create false documents to save Jewish families. Her group created over 3,000 such documents.

Sendler did this as she knew the fate of the Jews who had been rounded up. She and her group of 10 began in earnest to smuggle children out of the ghetto. The team was able to rescue 2,500 children through many ingenious means. Entering the ghetto as a nurse or social worker, Sendler would smuggle children out by hiding them under a stretcher of an ambulance; escaping through sewer pipes or secret underground passages; hiding the children in a sack, trunk, or suitcase and taking the children out of the ghetto; and having children pretend to be very ill so that they could be removed from the ghetto. The children would then be hidden away through a network of collaborators including the help of many Christian orphanages. While the children were given new identities, Sendler felt it was important to be able to reunite the children with remaining families after the war. Therefore, she kept the real names of the children on a thin tissue paper, placed it in a jar, and buried it in her backyard.

Sendler was captured, tortured, and had both of her legs broken by the Nazis. She was sentenced to death and only the bribing of the executioner let her escape and go into hiding for the rest of the war. After the war, she rededicated herself to reuniting the children with their families but most of the families had been killed at the Treblinka concentration camp. Sendler died in 2008 at the age of 98.

Without courage, one may be without a sense of agency, self, or ability. In the *Wonderful Wizard of Oz* (Baum, 1900/1996) and later the classic film *The Wizard of Oz* (1939), the character of the Cowardly Lion seeks courage as he finds himself fearful and therefore less of a brave lion. In both versions (the book and film), the lion continually demonstrates his courage, which he does not believe he has, during his journey to Oz to meet the wizard. In the text, the wizard gives the lion a potion to drink to realize his courage; in the film the lion is given a medal of courage to demonstrate the courage already inside him as evidenced by his journey to meet the wizard. The lion in both cases realizes his courage through bringing it forth in times of challenge during the hero's journey he had with Dorothy, Toto, and the Tinman on their Journey to Oz. He flexes his courage muscle over time to find courage in himself and never needed a potion (or medal) in the end to signify its existence.

Many people often seek help when they are feeling *dis*couraged. They need to be reminded or *en*couraged to rediscover the courage within them. A therapist, for example, will work with a client to discover his or her internal courage and to rebound to health pulling upon strengths the client may have forgotten or overlooked (in other words, using the tenants of positive psychology).

Ultimately, courage contributes to the ability to bounce back from adverse situations. It develops an ability to persevere in the face of adversity with the hope of creating something better.

Optimism

In his research on helplessness and learned optimism, Martin Seligman argues that how an individual approaches the world through thoughts,

ED DIENER AND THE MEANING OF HAPPINESS

In everyday language, many use the term "happy" to describe a positive emotional state. Positive psychologists such as Ed Diener, however, have asked what does being "happy" really mean? Researchers in positive psychology have worked to determine if one's way of understanding happiness, or well-being, is the same as someone else's within and across cultures. Diener developed numerous theories about happiness and well-being.

For example, Diener examined the relationship between income and well-being. He found that after a certain threshold of income, in which one can procure shelter, food, and access to a basic level of education and health care, people are not happier with more wealth. In fact, in a study of the wealthiest individuals in the United States, the level of greater happiness was not significant.

Diener also argued that happiness is mostly genetically determined and that human beings live within a "set level" of happiness. This means that humans have evolved to be happy and that trauma and other horrible life events upset happiness temporarily and then we return to our "set level" of well-being.

Diener found that there are many qualities and characteristics of what makes one happy. He concluded that levels of happiness are something that are subjectively rated, so if you think you are happy, you are happy. This was termed "subjective well-being," or SWB, which simply means a subject's happiness is assessed by asking how happy he or she is.

Diener (1999) asked Americans to rate their happiness on a scale of 1 to 10. He found that one in three people in the United States responded as being "very happy"; and only one in ten claimed they were "not too happy." The majority of respondents rated themselves as "pretty happy." This approach was replicated in countries around the world to find how citizens rated their subjective well-being. One outcome of the study revealed that people across cultures with the greatest levels of self-reported happiness and lowest levels of depression had ongoing and strong attachments to family and friends.

In his book *Happiness: Unlocking the Mysteries of Psychological Wealth* (2008) Diener distills the following four central qualities for a happy life that he collected from over 25 years of his research.

1. Psychological wealth is more important than financial wealth.

2. Happiness not only makes one feel good but also contributes to daily well-being with friends, work, and one's health.

3. It is important to set realistic expectations about happiness and being happy is not the default way of being at all times.

4. Thinking in a happy framework helps make one's daily life happier.

THE LIFE ORIENTATION TEST (LOT)-REVISED

Psychologists don't all agree on the best way to define and measure some of the constructs central to positive psychology. Optimism is one of the big ones. Often, the differences in definition lie in the theoretical foundations theorists and researchers use to formulate their models.

Psychologists Scheier and Carver introduced their version of an optimism index in 1985. Called the Life Orientation Test (LOT, later revised to the briefer LOT-R), their assessment tool is based on expectancy-value theory. Expectancy-value theory says that people are motivated by the pursuit of goals. Goals are defined as desirable future states or, more simply stated, as things we want to do in the future. The motivation comes from identifying our goals in combination with our expectations about whether or not we can actually achieve them. This goal and expectation relationship creates a cognitive framework, or schema, that filters how we feel about the future. The LOT-R measures whether an individual has an optimistic schema about the future based upon his or her goals and expectations of success. The questionnaire is made up of 10 questions that try to identify how we view the future. For example, questions look at things like whether or not you believe that if things can go wrong they will, or whether you consistently have an optimistic and hopeful view of their future.

The questions on the LOT-R have been empirically validated, which means they have been tested to make sure that they are reliably measuring what the researchers think they are. In the case of the LOT-R, they have been shown to be consistent across demographics and many cultures.

Across an extensive body of research, Carver and Scheier have demonstrated that basic dispositional optimism creates a psychological foundation that has a significant impact on an individual's life and how he or she approaches adversity. Researchers have applied the LOT-R assessment to many situations where people are facing challenges as an indicator of how these individuals will adjust. This allows practitioners to determine who will need additional support and be proactive in their interventions. The LOT-R has consistently shown the ability to identify coping skills and the ability to maintain a positive balance of emotions under times of challenge and duress. Higher scores on the LOT-R have been related to a number of positive health outcomes, including better recovery from coronary bypass surgery, coping with AIDS, and sticking with rehabilitation treatment for substance abuse.

Scheier and Carver's model has been very influential because the findings relating optimism to positive health outcomes have been consistently strong. This link reinforces the power of replacing some therapies that suppress optimism with positive visualizations of future outcomes.

feelings, and actions that markedly influence the way in which the individual both experiences and explains the world. Seligman in particular has spent the past 30 years looking at how optimistic thoughts can influence the well-being of an individual and how pessimistic thoughts can lead to depression. An optimist may explain the experiences of the world in terms that are more self-efficacious, which in turn influences his or her thoughts, feelings, or action. These thoughts, feelings, and actions in turn influence the experience of the individual. This looping mechanism can function at higher and lower levels depending on the spectrum of an individual's explanatory style.

A pessimist is defined as an individual who tends to "believe bad events will last a long time, will undermine everything they do, and [bad events] are their own fault"; he defines optimism as an individual who "believes defeat is a temporary setback . . . that defeat is not their fault: circumstances, bad luck, or other people brought [the circumstances] about" (Seligman).

Researchers have found that optimists have different coping skills than pessimists when confronting challenging situations. Optimists use more problem-focused coping strategies, acceptance, use of humor, and positive reframing when confronted with challenges. Pessimists tend to cope through denial, and disengaging from the situation at hand.

The coping tendencies of optimists include the following:

- Information seeking
- Active coping and planning
- Positive reframing
- Seeking benefit
- Use of humor
- Acceptance

The coping tendencies of pessimists include the following:

- Suppression of thoughts
- Giving up
- Self-distraction
- Cognitive avoidance
- Focus on distress
- Overt denial

Optimists tend to do better than pessimists in stressful situations and cope with these events in ways that provide a more proactive approach to problems as reviewed earlier. Some researchers have raised concerns that optimists may be more prone to engaging in risky behaviors because of their investment in a good outcome however,

A study on the differences between the expected outcomes of optimists and pessimists found that positive belief in one's capabilities is beneficial. In fact, moderate and high expectations of success were linked to increased performance, and an ability to tackle difficult problems more effectively. Negative expectations offered the opposite results in that they led to poor performance and a greater tendency to feel as a failure.

Optimists will approach misfortune as a temporary setback and limited to a particular situation, whereas pessimists believe misfortune is their own fault and that it will affect all that they do. There have been many studies that have shown that pessimists give up more easily when confronted with challenges and get depressed more often.

Most individuals that experience some sort of failure will feel a sense of helplessness. For optimists this experience is short-lived and creates a positive resiliency for the individual to continue with life in other domains. For pessimists, the explanatory style tends to maintain helplessness for longer periods of time and casts a shadow on current events and future ones.

Optimism can be considered a hidden asset that we need to bring forward and nurture. When it comes to aging in a healthy way, optimistic attitudes tend to have a strong impact. George Valliant's text *Aging Well: Surprising Guideposts to a Happier Life* (2008) examined 800 people from adolescence to old age encompassing more than 50 years of life. Valliant and his team found that healthy and successful aging was best determined by the coping skills individuals developed over time to address life's challenges. In this study, five main coping strategies surfaced that were a common denominator among those who aged well. These include the following:

- Altruism: Doing something for someone else solely for that person rather than the benefit to oneself

- Constructive distraction: Focusing energy on enjoyable outcomes such as creating, reading, or exercise

- Replacement: Putting to the side challenges and upsets rather than burying them in oneself

- Humor: Finding the lighter side of problems

- Planning: Looking at the future with hope for positive change

The healthier group avoided perfectionism and instead focused on taking smaller steps toward their goals. This is particularly important as perfectionists tended to give up more easily if they could not achieve the outcomes that they wanted with 100 percent success.

Optimists in this group tended to create a visualization of what a happier outcome would be and then "stretched" themselves toward putting into place means of achieving that picture.

Finally, the members of this group viewed adversity in life as temporary and not something that reflected a bad aspect of their selves, but rather something that emerged externally that was beyond their control. Optimists then found opportunities to make change. Pessimists, on the other hand, saw adversity as unchangeable, global, and personal. Researchers find that many optimists are born with their attitude. The good news is that optimism can be learned by practicing resiliency and creating a context for that resiliency to grow.

- Avoid negative contexts: Some people like to focus on the worst of things and some organizations are negative environments in which to work. It is important to find the company of people who demonstrate some optimism and resiliency in their lives and to find work contexts in which the good can help to outweigh the negative.

- Understand your own strengths: Many people are quick to point out their weaknesses but often forget to celebrate and cultivate their strengths. Thus, it is important to focus on what assets you have and to employ them in daily life.

- Practice self-care: For some this may mean engaging in spiritual venues; for others it may mean meditating or exercising; for others it may mean taking a nap or reading a good book.

- Know that you cannot control outcomes: When reflecting on what wisdom they would impart to younger generations, many respondents reported that it is critical to learn what one can influence, and to understand what one cannot. When setbacks arise, determine what ability one has for making changes and what will simply stay as it is.

- Reframe the picture: Looking at the situation from another perspective or lens always provides options and ideas that may have been overlooked.

- Try an optimistic explanatory style: Often by changing the language used to describe adversity, one can improve psychologically. Understand that the situation is not what you wanted to have happened, but ask what you can do with the possibilities to change it for the better over time.

- Get out of your own way: Study after study in positive psychology demonstrates that when we are self-conscious we are not at our best; however, when we are taking ourselves outside of a focus on the self in the service of others, we tend to feel much better. Meet with friends, cultivate a hobby, or volunteer to see how it impacts your sense of well-being.

Anne Frank and the Practice of Optimism

Anne Frank's diary while in hiding from the Nazis during World War II is an international testament to hope and optimism in the face of horror. While sadly Anne Frank died of typhoid in a concentration camp, her two years of hiding in the attic of the family home with seven others was made tolerable by her optimistic view of the world despite her circumstances that were recorded in her writing. The Frank family fled Germany due to growing anti-Semitism, and Anne's father, Otto, started a business in the Netherlands. While the Netherlands hoped to stay out of the war, they were soon occupied by Germany and severe restrictions were placed on Jews.

The Frank family had tried to emigrate to both the United Kingdom and the United States; however, both attempts failed. Therefore, as the threat of violence and deportation against Jews grew, the Franks decided to go into hiding in the attic of a home behind Otto's place of business. The business colleagues of Otto Frank helped the family hide and provide them with resources and news.

ROBERT BISWAS-DIENER, THE INDIANA JONES OF POSITIVE PSYCHOLOGY

CNN dubbed Robert Biswas-Diener the "Indiana Jones of Positive Psychology." This is largely due to Diener's travels around the world researching how happiness is understood and constructed across cultures.

Biswas-Diener's research reflects that many people have a tendency to go on "autopilot" and move through the motions of life without really being engaged with activities leading to feelings of being "stuck." Diener argues that in order to be happier, individuals need to "wake themselves up" and be more mindful about one's activities. He and his father, Ed Diener (see sidebar), found that overall people have a tendency to be mildly happy most of the time.

Biswas-Diener finds that travel provides an opportunity to shake oneself out of ruts. What one takes for granted in one's everyday life such as smells, foods, mailboxes, and a laundry list of other ways of living suddenly is recast and one has to look at the world through a non-assumptive lens. He believes that one doesn't necessarily need to travel the world to get this wake-up call, but one can proactively work toward finding "luster" in everyday life. Being curious and asking questions is key to this approach. Learning something new or taking a creative approach to the tried and true allows one to find a greater sense of happiness in daily life.

Biswas-Diener supports positive coaching, which helps individuals and organizations move to greater well-being. He advocates the following steps:

- Examine strengths (go beyond the weaknesses).
- Harness positivity (focusing on positive emotions in daily life).
- Diagnose positively (asking what is going on right here).
- Assess positively (use positive psychology assessment tools for assessment).

Biswas-Diener argues that happiness is not a place but a process. He advocates the collection of experiences in life rather than material "things."

Biswas-Diener is an editorial board member of the *Journal of Happiness Studies* and *Journal of Positive Psychology*. He co-founded the Strengths Project charity. This organization focuses on helping "underprivileged individuals and groups realize their strengths to enhance quality of life and build on their life circumstances." He argues that strengths are potentials that can be learned rather than simply characteristics or traits.

Just before going into hiding, Anne received a diary for her birthday. This diary proved to be a great source of comfort and distraction while in hiding. She began to write short stories, and collected her thoughts and feelings while hiding in what became to be known as the "secret annex."

The Minister of Education at the time made an appeal for people to keep war diaries. Hence, Anne edited her diary and in her optimism edited it for use in her career as a future journalist and expected her diary to be made into a future novel.

One can imagine how difficult life was for those hiding in the small secret annex. They lived in ongoing fear of being discovered, could never go outside, and had to be very quiet during the day to not be heard by those working in the warehouse below them. No light could come in the windows and no toilets could be flushed during the day. Anne found resilience in writing in her diary.

She created an imaginary friend called Kitty to whom she wrote in her diary about her life, feeling alone, and her frustration with her family members.

The family was discovered 25 months after the Nazis entered the secret annex. The Gestapo had discovered them from an anonymous tip whose identity to this day remains uncertain. The family was sent to concentration camps. Anne and her sister died of typhus in Bergen-Belsen after being separated from their mother, who died of starvation in Auschwitz, and their bodies were thrown into a mass grave. A few weeks later, the British liberated the camp. Otto Frank survived Auschwitz when the Soviets liberated that camp.

A friend of the Frank family, Miep Gies, had saved Anne's diary and gave it to Otto Frank in hopes that Anne's dream of being a published author could be realized through this diary. According to the Anne Frank Center, since the diary was published in 1947, over 30 million copies have been sold in 67 languages. The diary remains one of the most powerful testaments of courage, hope, and optimism in the face of adversity during the Holocaust. Here are some quotes from Anne Frank:

Optimism in the Face of Horror

I have often been downcast, but never in despair; I regard our hiding as a dangerous adventure, romantic and interesting at the same time. In my diary I treat all the privations as amusing. I have made up my mind now to lead a different life from other girls and, later on, different from ordinary housewives. My start has been so very full of interest, and that is the sole reason why I have to laugh at the humorous side of the most dangerous moments.

—Anne Frank

Optimism as a Way of Surviving

Everyone has inside of him a piece of good news. The good news is that you don't know how great you can be! How much you can love! What you can accomplish! And what your potential is!

—Anne Frank

Optimism as Hope

Because paper has more patience than people.

I don't want to have lived in vain like most people. I want to be useful or bring enjoyment to all people, even those I've never met. I want to go on living even after my death!

—Anne Frank

Happiness

Happiness is a psychological concept that joins other interests of positive psychology such as morality, resiliency, courage, and hope that may at times be difficult to define yet are widely used and understood. Positive psychologists have moved toward defining happiness as "subjective well-being" (SWB), which reflects a person's own assessment of his or her life satisfaction as well as having more positive emotions over negative emotions. Other positive psychologists define happiness as having three parts: pleasure, engagement, and meaning. Pleasure reflects the positive emotions of happiness. Engagement refers to the "good life" of connection to work, family, friends, and activities. Meaning reflects the cultivation and use of strengths in contribution for something greater than the self. These three factors are critical to happiness and people around the world tend to emphasis engagement and meaning as the biggest contributors to being happy in life.

There have been several approaches to understanding happiness, and many of these studies have found that most of all, an individual's personal resources such as intelligence, health, attractiveness, income, and education are the most important individual difference variables to happiness. These variables influence an individual's social competence that in turn improves the individual's ability to develop relationships, which is central to well-being. An early study on happiness found that only 10 percent of the variance in happiness is due to demographic factors such as age, gender, and socioeconomic status.

Overall an individual's temperament (whether it is from nature or nurture), cognitive abilities, goals, culture, and coping skills have a far greater mediating influence of life events and their effects on an individual's sense of well-being. This is not to say that nothing can change an individual's sense of well-being and that one is either genetically born predisposed to subjective well-being or is not. What is known is that a happy person in today's Western society has a profile of a positive temperament, a resilient ability to look on the positive more than the negative, does not focus on bad circumstances, lives in an economically developed society where food and shelter are not the focus of one's primary efforts, has friends, and is able to make progress toward reaching his or her goals.

Contrary to popular cultural opinion, happiness is not about feeling good all the time. Researchers have found a greater sense of subjective well-being in those who tend to *hold steady* rather than have great highs (and consequent drops from those highs). When asked about what makes life happy, people typically respond without mentioning mood. Instead they reference aspects of their life that feel meaningful such as family, friends, work, and hobbies. Moreover, those who are focused on "feeling good" tend to sabotage feelings of wellness as such a focus removes one from everyday happy experiences and puts too much emphasis (and work) on satisfaction of feeling good all the time.

Researchers asked the rich of the rich (such as Bill Gates, Warren Buffet, and Oprah Winfrey) about their levels of happiness and compared them to those of the general population. The findings revealed that being very wealthy is not statistically significant when it comes to greater happiness. In fact, once one earns an income that provides food, shelter, and a sense of security that allows one to meet expenses, additional income does not make one happier. However, most people will report that additional income will make them happier. If they attain the higher income, their expectations shift to adjust to that level of income and then they find themselves back to the level of happiness they were before with the continued belief that the next level of income will do the trick. Buying new consumer goods provides a temporary euphoria, but in fact, those who spent money on experiences with friends and family found the most sustaining feeling of happiness.

The so-what of happiness as we know it today is the combination of subjective well-being level (satisfaction with you or your life) and with more positive emotions over negative emotions on a daily basis. While happiness is largely determined by genetics, one can cultivate happier mood states by creating a steady experience of well-being from day to day rather than searching for hits of high happiness from time to time.

There are a number of common beliefs about happiness that have been verified and refuted by research: Happiness is not related to age or there is no time in life where individuals are markedly happier than other years. In a survey of 169,776 people across 16 nations, knowing an individual's age did not give insight into his or her sense of well-being. Emphasis on what was important to the individual did vary with age however.

It turns out that the most concrete contributor to happiness is adaptation. Researchers found that money, social skills, and intelligence were predictive of subjective well-being only if they were relevant to how a person structured his or her life and personal goals. Essentially, happiness increases not from passive experiences, but rather from involvement in valued activities and the progress of working toward one's goals. Individuals judge their subjective well-being by the balance of their positive and negative emotions. Positive emotions, they argue, are an overall indication of optimal being.

Individuals who are resilient are considered to be able to recover more quickly and efficiently from stressful experiences. In fact, individuals who experienced more positive emotions over time became also more resilient over time to adversity. This upward spiral enhanced coping skills over time. This finding suggests that positive emotions, although often temporary, may have a cumulative effect and positive long-term consequences for the well-being of an individual.

Technology and Understanding Happiness

The Experience Sampling Method (ESM) was used in a study of adolescents to determine where they report the greatest sense of self-reported happiness or well-being. An application (app) downloaded to each of their phones was scheduled to ring at seven random times during the day over the course of the week. The adolescents were to stop what they were doing at that time and complete a brief survey of their actions, feelings, and thoughts at that particular time. The data was then uploaded after each entry for analysis. The findings were consistent with other types of research. Adolescents reported the greatest sense of well-being when with other people. More importantly, as other research demonstrated, a lack of self-consciousness allows for greater sense of happiness or well-being. Adolescents reported the least sense of well-being when they were comparing their looks, for example, with others or were thinking about how they came across to others. For those with eating disorders, this was the most likely time they would focus on restricting or purging.

As social creatures, we are built to have interpersonal interactions. Across cultures self-consciousness or being in a state of comparing oneself to others tends to move one away from feelings of well-being. Humans are also creative beings. It is important to be engaged in activities such as hobbies or work that allows one to use his or her skills against a challenge that has been coined "flow." Many people find that volunteering or doing work in the service of others promotes a sense of greater well-being. While many in today's world find it difficult to complete all that is needed on a daily basis, considering a few hours of contributing to community may be a better way to happiness than a few hours of television (where researchers find that people's mood is lowered after viewing over a period of time).

RESILIENCY: BRINGING THE CORNERSTONES TOGETHER

The four cornerstones of positive psychology lead to a house built on resiliency. The combination of courage, hope, optimism, and happiness allows one to bounce back from setbacks, stress, severe accidents, traumas, and other life challenges. It is the ability to come through adversity and rebuild one's life. This is not to say that as a resilient person one does not experience sadness, anger, upset, or grief in such circumstances, but instead that one is able to move through adversity or setbacks and on the other hand able to continue with daily life.

Resilience can be learned either through life circumstances that provide greater wisdom and insight into having to manage crises, or through communities that support the individual through difficult times including friends, family, and other significant relationships. In fact, across all cultures and traditions, there are communal ways of addressing tragedy in life through various rituals. Consider neighbors bringing food over for families that have had a setback or grieving together at a memorial service when a loved one passes. This type of support, reassurance, and caring for each other improves the ability of individuals and groups to move through challenging times.

Resiliency allows one to bounce back after adverse life circumstances. This is learned early in life. Take, for example, a child who falls and skins his knee. The parent teaches resiliency by picking the child up, brushing him off, and, despite the tears, moving him on with reassurance that the child is going to be OK. The parent who catastrophizes the situation by focusing on the hurt, the potential danger of infection, as well as admonishing the child to be more careful may create a state of anxiety and fear instead.

Being resilient doesn't mean going through life without experiencing stress and pain. People feel grief, sadness, and a range of other emotions after adversity and loss. The road to resilience lies in working through the emotions and effects of stress and painful events. Resilience develops as people grow up and gain better thinking and self-management skills and more knowledge. Resilience also comes from supportive relationships with parents, peers, and others, as well as cultural beliefs and traditions that help people cope with the inevitable bumps in life.

There is no single way that one reacts to stress or trauma and the coping mechanisms involved are as diverse as those who experience such pain. However, key qualities to nurturing resilience in oneself and others include the following:

- Have a support network: Having good relationships is the most important factor in being resilient. Whether this is family, friends, or a community group, it is important to have people who care about you and will provide support and insight. Developing a support network of course requires social skills such as good communication skills, listening, and a sense of confidence.

- Avoiding catastrophizing situations: Just because you had this setback or challenge does not mean that all things in life will be this way.

- Accept change: Change is an inherent aspect of life (e.g., taxes and death). Try to influence that which you can, and work toward accepting that which cannot be changed.

- Practice self-care: In times of crisis we may forgo exercise and eating well. This time, however, is when one need to do those things that help one physically and emotionally. Seek out activities that may reconnect you with joy and meaning.

- Engagement: Try other practices such as being outside, practicing meditation, or visiting a faith-related services.

Human beings have been so successful because as a species due to adaptation within all sorts of climates and geographic challenges around the planet. Part of that success is the human ability to recover from setbacks in life and in fact move forward with a sense of hope and meaning. There are many people who have been exposed to the horrors of war, lost a loved one, been in a traumatizing experience (such as a car accident), or had to deal with serious illness.

Reaching out to others in times of distress is critical to one's ability to move forward. In a 2006 study, 3,000 nurses with breast cancer had four times a greater likelihood to survive if that nurse had 10 or more friends. A strong social network is critical when dealing with disease, illness, and death. Human beings are social creatures and while some may prefer the company of more people over less or vice versa, ultimately the isolated human being does not function in a healthy way emotionally and physically.

CHAPTER 2

Strengths

You don't have to be a superhero to have strengths (there is more about super-heroes later in this chapter). Positive psychology includes not only the understanding of the pathology of individuals (as was the traditional training for clinical psychology) but also individual strengths that provide psychological fortitude. Some individuals may rely on optimistic explanatory styles; others may turn to forgiveness, gratitude, faith, or some philosophical meaning of life to find support during painful, difficult, and trying times. These approaches pull on the strengths most people have from which to draw.

From positive psychology research, it is known that those who feel a sense of agency in the world will find opportunities or answers to move forward; those who feel a sense of hopelessness or helplessness in the world tend to not do as well. For example, positive psychologists wanted to understand why two people who faced the same challenge or setback in life would emerge from it very differently, perhaps one moving on with his or her life and the other retreating into a world of depression or anxiety. While researchers found that a great deal of this had to do with genetics, they learned it wasn't the full story. It turns out that the attachments and models of resilient behavior had in childhood are critical to resiliency.

In meta-studies (studies that aggregate individual studies) researchers find that strengths such as courage, hope, altruism, optimism, emotional intelligence, honesty, forgiveness, and gratitude are psychological buffers that help individuals bounce back from life's upset and best of all these can be learned. In this chapter, knowledge about strengths is reviewed and understood through strengths-based approaches to counseling, teaching and learning, leadership, and archetypal narrative. The latter topic, archetypal narrative, is included as central to understanding strengths given that human beings are meaning-making creatures and have drawn from stories throughout human history. For example, the past civilizations' mythologies were stories to explain natural phenomenon and disasters. In fact, strengths-based narratives are critical to finding a sense of meaning and purpose in life that support psychological needs such as community, safety, security, independence, and competency.

Today, strengths are generally classified across cultural groups thanks to the work of the researchers at the University of Pennsylvania. They include:

- Emotional strengths: Finding meaning in life, insight, optimism, perseverance
- Character strengths: Honesty, courage, hope, integrity
- Relationship strengths: Creating strong relationships with others, communication of feelings, cooperation, compassion, forgiveness, empathy
- Educational strengths: Analytical and cognitive ability, creative problem solving, reasoning, formal and informal education levels

Strengths-based psychology is credited to Donald O. Clifton. He established the firm of Selection Research Inc. in 1969, which was later acquired by the Gallup organization, including the famous 177-item Clifton StrengthsFinder assessment that reflects individual talents.

Clifton started his work to address the need to find the right people for the right jobs following the influx of returning soldiers into the workforce after World War II. He was also passionate for people's voices to be heard and hence the numerous polls that the Gallup organization continues to do to the present time.

Clifton wrote:

> From this point of view, to avoid your strengths and to focus on your weaknesses isn't a sign of diligent humility. It is almost irresponsible. By contrast the most responsible, the most challenging, and, in the sense of being true to yourself, the most honorable thing to do is face up to the strength potential inherent in your talents and then find ways to realize it.

Strengths-based approaches are applicable across fields and cultures. For example, in one Gallup survey of 10 million people surveyed over 10 years, the Gallup organization found that only one-third of the respondents believed that they ideally engaged in work. The researchers found that when a manager actively focused on an employee's strengths the chance that the employee was disengaged from work was only 1 percent; this in contrast to the manager who ignores employees and then may find that 40 percent of his or her employees are disengaged from work.

In 2002, the American Psychological Association (APA) gave Clifton a Presidential Commendation as the Father of Strengths-Based Psychology. The APA stated, "An educator, thought leader, inventor, and entrepreneur, Clifton is remembered for his unusual ability to bring out the best in people and help individuals and organizations achieve outstanding results."

Clifton crafted three major themes in examining strengths-based psychology:

- Strengths can be identified.
- The greatest individual growth comes from expanding on one's strengths.
- Individuals can build strengths-based organizations for greater success.

Strengths create virtues, and virtues create strengths, which often are essential to the path of happiness and well-being. One's character is based on virtues (qualities that reflect the essence of who we are). Virtues and sins have been studied for millennial. For example, Christianity's virtues reminded followers of human's tendency to "sin." These sins became very popular in the 14th century as it became fashionable to use them as themes in paintings (often underwritten by the Catholic Church). The sins were first established in Latin as SALGIA (the first letters of the seven deadly sins), which were superbia, avaritia, luxuria, invidia, gula, and ira. We know them in English as pride, sloth, greed, wrath, lust, envy, and gluttony.

In the poem "Psychomachia" (*Battle* or *Contest of the Soul*), Aurelius Clemens Prudentius, a Spanish Christian governor in 410 AD, wrote about the clash between good and evil. In the poem, Prudentius established the seven heavenly virtues that stand in contrast to the seven deadly sins.

- Chastity versus lust: Chastity reflects maintaining good health and hygiene; abstaining from sexual contact before marriage; being pure of thought; and not being taken by temptation or corruption.

- Temperance versus gluttony: Temperance reflects restraint, justice, and the practice of self-control. It also emphasizes the balance between the focus on self and the focus on community and that the rights and needs of others hold importance in society.

- Charity versus greed: Charity is about generosity, self-sacrifice, and demonstrating kindness and love to others.

- Diligence versus sloth: Diligence emphasizes good work ethics; careful with one's thoughts and actions; and not giving up in the face of setbacks.

- Patience versus wrath: Patience to face difficult situations with dignity and time; willingness to forgive; and an effort to create healthy community and bonds.

- Kindness versus envy: Compassion and caring for others through friendship or support and in turn those actions inspire kindness in others.

- Humility versus pride: Respect, modesty, and not making oneself all important.

CHARACTER VIRTUES AND STRENGTHS

As the 21st century continues to try to address issues of environmental, political, social, and economic challenges that are more severe and intense than ever before, the concept of virtuous behavior has garnered more attention (this was once the purview of religious or spiritual organizations whose documents Seligman and Peterson closely studied and included in their inventory).

Peterson and Seligman wrote *Character Strengths and Virtues: A Handbook and Classification* (2004), which examines strengths as "the psychological ingredients, processes or mechanisms that define virtues."

The authors reviewed 2,500 years of written records that reflected positive traits, including virtues and strengths from philosophy, the Bible, the Koran, Confucian and Taoist writings, and Buddhist and Hindu teachings to create a sophisticated taxonomy.

The Values in Action (VIA) Inventory of Strengths is a survey that assesses your major strengths. The VIA Institute on Character is a nonprofit organization that was developed in 2001 to utilize science and practice to "fill the world with greater virtue via wisdom, courage, humanity, justice, temperance, and transcendence."

Hence virtues are excellent aspects of the self; the combination character strengths describe virtue. Virtues are positive characteristic traits that reflect, for example, value and principles. Virtues are nurtured by family, community, and effort. One may consider virtues as the foundation upon which courage, hope, optimism, and resiliency are built. Virtues that are fundamental and that are emphasized in many societies around the world include:

- Service: Contributing to the well-being of others
- Discipline: Defining goals and working toward them despite distraction
- Gratitude: Recognizing daily that for which we celebrate and are thankful
- Kindness: Caring or concern for another individual
- Creativity: Solving problems creatively and developing unique understandings of approaches to one's environment
- Trust: An investment in another to support one and doing no harm

In examining the six major virtue categories outlined by Peterson and Seligman, one can see how character strengths emerge. For example, below is the virtue of courage. Courage is largely defined as pursuing one's convictions in the face of challenge. This results in strengths such as bravery, diligence, or integrity.

The VIA survey has been taken by over 3 million people worldwide. The VIA Classification of Character Strengths has six "virtue" categories and 24 specific strengths as follows:

1. Wisdom and Knowledge: creativity, curiosity, judgment and open-mindedness, love of learning, perspective
2. Courage: bravery, perseverance, honesty, zest
3. Humanity: capacity to love and be loved, kindness, social intelligence
4. Justice: teamwork, fairness, leadership
5. Temperance: forgiveness and mercy, modesty and humility, prudence, self-regulation
6. Transcendence: appreciation of beauty and excellence, gratitude, hope, humor, religiousness and spirituality

Together, these strengths and virtues bring together people, community, states, and countries across cultures around the world.

The StrengthsFinder assessment includes 34 themes in its most recent iteration. The data that the Gallup researchers collected indicated to them that identifying talents, or strengths, allowed for the greatest opportunity to excel. Just as Peterson and Seligman created six themes, the StrengthsFinder identifies five major themes that reflect individual strengths. The Clifton StrengthsFinder (StrengthsFinder 2.0, 2013, which includes a code for taking the assessment) includes 34 themes.

This strengths-based approach to traits and characteristics is being applied to many other domains, including leadership, counseling, and teaching.

STRENGTHS-BASED LEADERSHIP

The 21st century is faced with social, economic, environmental, and political challenges. Leaders are needed to mobilize resources for socially constructive change. The 20th-century approach to leadership and management often failed. Strengths-based leadership has been introduced to address some of the needs of today's world.

From the field of positive psychology, a strengths-based approach to leadership, or positive leadership, has emerged. Strengths-based leadership looks at that which is working well or is an asset and capitalizes on it. For example, research reflects that within organizations or groups the potential of individual contribution is typically underutilized. Rather than trying to fix individuals or groups, leaders are understanding that focusing on strengths, passions, and possibilities will yield far more useful results. This approach moves the leader into giving power back to followers.

Leadership is unique from management in that leaders must have followers to create change and to adapt to the needs of newly formed contexts. Management works to improve efficiencies from within and while some technical changes are required as managers, it is not about moving systems to another level of functioning as with leadership.

When Gallup asked followers what was most important to them in a leader (from a survey of 10,000 people), followers reported the following:

- Trust: Followers believe a leader and find that leader good, reliable, and predictable (the leader will do as she or he says).

- Compassion: Followers want leaders who show some caring for them. Followers who feel that their leaders care tend to stay and put in more effort. Most people in today's harried environments still want to find a human connection and understanding.

- Stability: In environments where there is too much disequilibrium, followers tend to suffer from both psychological and physical symptoms. Having a leader who holds things steady is critical for followership. Of course some instability is required to make change, but too much of it leads to lack of solidity and confidence.

- Hope: Hope has been discussed in detail in this book so far, but it is important to stress that followers want to know that there is direction, guidance, and change for the better coming. Hope leads to optimism, which is far better than environments without hope that run into despair and being "stuck."

Research shows repeatedly that people perform best when they work within their areas of strengths (and hence the importance of individuals knowing their own strengths). Those who do not work in their areas of strengths are engaged only 9 percent of the time, whereas those who are utilizing their strengths are engaged 74 percent of the time. Moreover, those followers who have some degree of control over their work or time find greater motivation in their work, work harder, and produce higher-quality work.

Kim Cameron, a leader in positive leadership research and practice, writes positive leadership is "the ways in which leaders enable positively deviant performance, foster an affirmative orientation to organizations, and engender a focus on virtuousness and the best of human behavior." According to Cameron, positive leadership promotes three main orientations:

1. Positive deviance: Leaders want followers to move away from the norm and engage in approaches that bring greater energy, insight, and ability to attain high levels of achievement. Leaders facilitate moving away from default ways of doing or thinking to reveal new (and positive) ways of working.

2. Affirmative bias: This is a leader's focus on the strengths and talents of followers that enables followers to thrive and flourish despite challenges to change. It stresses the tenets of positive psychology such as the promotion of courage, hope, and optimism.

3. Leadership for good: Leaders have an opportunity to unveil the natural inclination of followers to do good work and contribute in a healthy and happy manner. This is not to dismiss the difficulties that exist in the world; rather, it provides a path to reflecting that which is best in individuals and groups. It leads individuals to a level of intrinsic motivation and doing a task for the sake of wanting to do the task rather than a strong external motivator such as fear or anxiety.

There is a marked difference between leadership, power, and authority. Twenty-first-century (good) leaders engage stakeholders to move toward socially constructive outcomes. Those who use power or an authoritarian approach insist that followers do as the leader requires and such regimes emphasize that serious repercussions will follow such as personal or professional harm if not followed as required.

Those organizations or systems that embrace aligning employee strengths and skills with the right work engagements find increased productivity and happier and healthier communities (see Chapter 3). Facebook is a good example of such an organization. Facebook takes a unique approach to hiring employees. The company recruits the best and brightest, oftentimes without any particular position in mind, instead allowing the employee to match his or her skills with ongoing projects. In addition, every year, Facebook engineers are rotated to pursue a different project, thereby creating new challenges for the engineers.

Strengths-based leadership has the following qualities:

- Matches challenges and skills: Leaders examine the skill set of individuals and align those skills with the needs of a project. The leader will periodically assess the challenges and skills and reconfigure teams for a greater opportunity at successful outcomes. The leader thus creates a more creative and innovative environment.

- Creates diversity of all kinds: Leaders need varying perspectives to avoid their own "blind spots." Diversity of talents, people, passion, gender, age, and culture provides an opportunity to avoid single-minded thinking and rather embraces multiple perspectives and strengths. High-technology companies have been leading the charge with these models and have had many successful outcomes.

- Is trustworthy: Leaders who create transparency don't play favorites and promote a culture of trust in which followers are heard, have a voice, and find that they have the healthiest work environment.

- Allows strengths to emerge: Leaders often fall into the trap of shifting into a managerial role telling people what to do and how to do it. No one wants to be told what to do; rather, followers want to be inspired, shown, and motivated. The leader creates an environment in which followers are empowered to bring forth insight and creativity; the leader also allows for healthy conflict in order to surface important ideas. Such a leader is not afraid of allowing differing perspectives and strong opinions.

- Avoids the default: Leaders realize that maintaining default behavior can be seductive. Most people prefer what is known than having to change and move into the unknown. The strengths-based leader will not accept the theme of "this is how it always has been done," but rather brings people into the disequilibrium that is required of change.

In *Strengths-Based Leadership* (2008), researchers and authors Tom Rath and Barry Conchie found four major domains of leadership strength, which they labeled as executing, influencing, relationship building, and strategic thinking. Their descriptions are as follows:

- Executing: Mobilizing resources for change and achieving results through organization and action

- Influencing: Engaging and influencing leaders and stakeholders both within and without a system to move toward the needed change

- Relationship building: Bringing and holding a team together

- Strategic thinking: Looking at what is possible rather than that which is impossible and gathering data to bring insight into their strategies

What Does Positive Leadership Look Like?

Leadership can be defined as mobilizing resources for socially constructive change outcomes. Of course there are good leaders and bad leaders that followers may choose. In the bad leader category, individuals such as Hitler and Stalin turned to authoritarian leadership to mobilize resources for destruction.

Positive leaders work toward promoting individuals and organizations by looking at what is working well; that which is life giving (and depleting); and how to inspire and promote creativity and extraordinary performance for outcomes that provide an atmosphere of not just surviving but thriving, growing, and flourishing.

Leaders at Google, for example, are constantly looking at how to redefine the workplace to promote creativity for new product lines, lower worker burn-out, and challenge employees to develop their skill set. At Google, employees are given 20 percent of their work time to pursue a project of their own that may provide some insight for new direction for the company.

Chade-Meng Tan was an engineer at Google who used his 20 percent time at Google to examine how to make work environments healthier. He mobilized the resources he was given to speak with leaders in mind-body medicine, including Daniel Goleman (emotional intelligence) and Jon Kabat-Zinn. He used validated science-based practices to create his course, which was so successful at Google that his model is now being used by organizations and individuals around the world (Tan, Goleman, & Kabat-Zinn, 2012). Tan reflected the work of a positive leader by examining how obstacles could be removed from individual and group work to have healthier and more successful outcomes (while reducing stress at the same time).

Strengths-Based Leadership and the Military

The U.S. military has been at the forefront in understanding strengths-based leadership in order for commanders and soldiers to work together optimally. The military's approach to strengths-based leadership is to construct a positive collaborative or team environment; promote the self-development of followers; and encourage the growth of followers through mentoring, coaching, and matching skills to challenges.

In this approach, strengths are identified and then examined for improvement. Formal processes are used, such as assessments, as well as more informal self-reflective exercises. Rather than force someone to do something that they do not like or may not have an aptitude toward, the military moves soldiers to engaging in tasks that reflect talents. As a result, the military has found followers have greater energy, performance, and engagement, and lose track of time when absorbed in a challenging assignment (this is called "Flow," which is discussed in Chapter 3). Ultimately, this approach sets up soldiers for success, rather than failure.

The other critical component of this military model is to provide individualized feedback. This applies to both the leader and the follower. Individuals are often unclear about their strengths and weaknesses and benefit tremendously from an outside mirror in the form of feedback. This feedback may take place with a counselor, coach, or peer. The point is to shine light in areas that may be dark. Feedback must be authentic, specific, and precise. Such work increases the insight both personally and professionally for those engaging in it.

This model also emphasizes the importance of a positive climate. There are many systems that have become "toxic" where those within the system feel anxious, depressed, frustrated, and hopeless and helpless. Turning around such a system is a very difficult task. However, putting into place factors that create a positive climate is useful for all involved both within the system and outside of it.

The qualities most identified with promoting a positive climate include listening by the leader, allowing followers to voice their perspectives without fear of fallout, and the leader modeling a healthy emotional state for others to follow. This includes how to address stress, anxiety, and conflict when they arise. Leaders in such a model also reflect appreciation, humility, respect, and support. Human beings across cultures want to feel being an important part of a system and seen as something more than a cog in the machinery. While this makes intuitive sense, it is sadly not often practiced.

Finally, strengths-based leaders create engaging learning environments. This means that the method of operation is not business as usual but is open to adaptation and flexibility to changing circumstances and contexts. Allowing followers to improve their skill set against different challenges creates the greatest sense of well-being for followers. Facebook, for example, has a *hackathon* session from time to time to surface new ideas and change the duties of the engineers in order to keep engagement and stimulation high.

Research from the military reveals that this model improves organizational morale and well-being.

In summary, the military's current approach to strengths-based leadership is as follows:

- Identify talents and areas for growths for followers.
- Provide individualized feedback.
- Utilize followers' strengths.
- Create a positive climate.
- Demonstrate authentic investment and caring for followers.
- Provide followers with opportunities to learn and grow (empowerment).

STRENGTHS-BASED COUNSELING

Focusing on strengths has found a place in counseling and therapeutic practice as well. In strengths-based approaches to counseling, the aim is to identify and emphasize strengths and not focus only on diagnosing problems (or deficits). This is not entirely new to practitioners but is now becoming more formalized. Research shows that individuals are eager to recognize their own strengths, but often do not see them without the insight of others. By having a therapist identify with the client strengths, there is a "self-righting" tendency, according to researchers, that humans have and thus the client can start moving to an improved way of daily living. The strengths-based approach allows the client to reframe their situations that moves the client away from hopelessness to understanding what aspects of life can be shifted and changed creating hope instead. Hope in turn creates a positive reinforcement as behavior and cognitive changes start to be put into place. Essentially, changing the clients perceptions from what is wrong to what also includes what is right can change the client's reality with a new interpretation of events.

Hence, the client reframing the situation with the support of the therapist is the primary therapeutic intervention. A shift onto the assessment of the client's qualities, characteristics, skills, and relationships is critical to this approach to therapy. According to White and Epston's strengths-based intervention (1990), there are five critical steps to change:

- Externalize the issue: The challenge is not the person but outside of the person.
- Attach a name to the issue: Providing a clinical diagnosis is necessary for practice, however, for the client reframe the diagnosis so that it is something that can be external to the client's identity. For example, for someone who is obsessive compulsive about order, the label could be "triggered by mess."
- Support identifying strengths and resources: Work with the client to identify personal resources as well as supports in the client's network. Also recall when the issue was not dominating the client's life and what abilities were employed to keep that issue from impacting daily life.
- Identify strengths to address the issue: Clients can generate personal strengths to start managing the issue.
- Encourage the client to make an effort to consider change by deploying personal strengths. This must be authentic so that the client feels a sense of personal ability and respect.

Strengths-based approaches are not limited to the therapeutic realm. In teaching and learning, strengths-based models for the 21st century are working to engage students in their studies and prepare for an information-based age.

What Does Strengths-Based Counseling Look Like?

Josiah (not the actual name of the client) visited a social worker to address ongoing anxiety and depression. He thought that he had put his childhood behind him and the violent family dynamics in which he grew up. His father was an alcoholic and family members never knew when the father, while inebriated, would express his angry and violent side or when he would be tired and simply go to sleep. Josiah described life as if he was always walking on egg shells. When his father screamed, shouted, or hit, Josiah would hide under his bed and tremble. He created an imaginary and safe life for himself under the bed with friends (his toys) who were kind and nurturing. His mother and sister were unable to protect themselves or Josiah from the father's outburst.

At school, he would boast of how successful and strong his father was. At 16, his sister left the family to stay with an Aunt. This left only Josiah and his mother at home. Josiah felt a great deal of resentment toward his mother for not divorcing his father. At 16, Josiah also left the family to stay with his sister and never had contact with his father again. His father committed suicide five years after Josiah moved out, and he had only intermittent contact with his mother.

Josiah had first seen a counselor during college where he reported feeling anxious and depressed and unable to make deep romantic contacts. He was prescribed medication and while this helped him, he continued to struggle with feelings of worthlessness and anger.

After college, Josiah took a job in IT and was referred to a strengths-based social worker by a friend who appreciated this professional's approach to making change. The social worker explored Josiah's history with him and recognized the depression and anxiety that he was facing were likely rooted in an unpredictable and unsafe environment where Josiah never felt a strong attachment to either of his parents. She, however, also pointed out that Josiah got himself through that terrible situation by imagining a better life; pretending he had a better family; and when he could, he took the opportunity to move into his sister's house, which was a more stable environment for him. Upon hearing how he did mobilize resources as a child to do the best he could with the circumstances within which he lived, Josiah physically dropped his shoulders and cried. He had had, for the first time, pointed out to him that he had strengths that he did not realize and that he was in a very difficult and troubling situation. This was not the end of his therapeutic journey, but it was the beginning of Josiah's understanding the strengths he employed, without his realization, that served him well as a child but perhaps were no longer serving him as needed as an adult. Had the social worker focused only on Josiah's deficiencies, he may not have made the therapeutic changes as readily as he had with the insight of the strengths that he possessed and could deploy as he moved forward.

STRENGTHS-BASED TEACHING AND LEARNING

Strengths-based approaches can be applied to many settings, including teaching and learning. In strengths-based education both students and teachers are assumed to have talents that can be utilized for successful instruction and learning.

In the 20th century many economies were agriculturally based, including the United States. The model of the teacher as the expert and the student as novice prevailed. Education was based on the so-called three "Rs": reading, writing, and arithmetic. Students were expected to utilize quantitative and verbal skills as the primary "intelligences" for learning.

However at the end of the 20th century, agriculture was less dominant as the main economic mainstay in the United States, and the world had changed tremendously given technological advances and the emergence of competing world economies. However, educators found that students had become good at memorizing material, but not always good at applying the concepts to real-world situation. A famous study at MIT found that students who were able to do well on theoretical exam questions were not able to translate that knowledge into practical applications outside of the classroom. In other words, they had become good test-takers, which was exactly what the educational system had required of them.

The 21st century is an exciting time of change for education as technology is available to learn online, and the costs of education have sparked a national debate about its costs and benefits.

At Harvard University, Howard Gardner reignited the consideration of the many ways in which people learn through his theory of multiple intelligence.

Gardner developed a primary set of intelligences that he argued are different ways in which individuals understand the world around them. Some may indeed approach learning through verbal and qualitative methods, but others may have a kinesthetic (movement) intelligence that allows them to pursue dancing or sports; others may understand the world through musical intelligence and so forth. It was clear that our educational systems were not always providing opportunities for individuals to express those strengths but instead were teaching to exam scores. This was often a deficit-based model in which the student's deficiencies needed to be remediated. While it is important to learn the basic tools to participate in society, this model did not always recognize the individual talents for learning and achievement and that teaching could incorporate these intelligences (often in combination) for more useful outcomes.

Strengths-based education assumes that emphasizing one's talents will lead to greater success rather than trying to overcome deficiencies or weaknesses. A parallel process emerges in which the educator identifies teaching strengths in order to help students identify and apply their strengths in learning to acquire the necessary academic knowledge and skills as well as creative problem-solving skills.

Strengths, or intelligences, are based on each student's unique talents and is built upon what comes naturally as the best. Traditional measures of ability, such as IQ or SAT scores, reflect more global levels of strengths and are not always useful in understanding specifically what a student can do. In turn, these natural strengths can be applied to academic challenges.

What Does Strengths-Based Teaching and Learning Look Like?

Mei was a bright 10-year-old girl in Hawaii's public school system. She was attentive and loved working with others. She was a natural and nurturing leader on the classroom and on the playground, adhering to rules of fairness and safety. Despite this, her new fourth-grade teacher simply could not keep Mei and many of the other students in the classroom seated at their individual desks. Mei would often get up to consult with her classmates or share a story and she complained that sitting at her individual desk was boring and lonely. Next door, the other fourth-grade teacher had decided to create learning pods (six students whose desks were brought together as a team with a pod name and a weekly team leader) to create a collaborative learning environment. Given that human beings are social animals and that we learn from one another, this teacher also argued that pods better reflected not only human nature but the collaborative culture of Hawaii. To her credit, Mei's teacher decided to run "an experiment" and put her students into pods as well. While many students who had not experienced this format before were a bit thrown off, the effort was a great success at the end of the year and for Mei included. The pod approach allowed students to work together, create a group identity, as well as a group statement of values (no cheating, being cooperative, etc.). Moreover, students could better express themselves across various ways of learning through the revised curriculum Mei's teacher included that promoted a 21st-century approach to teaching and learning that went beyond just

CASE STUDY: POSITIVE PSYCHOLOGY AND THE AUTOMOTIVE INDUSTRY

Toyota Motor Company was created in Japan in 1933. The Toyoda Automatic Loom Company (for textiles) created a new motor division under the management of the founder's son. Later, the new Toyota corporation was created. Toyota created a company philosophy that states "do the right thing for the company, its employees, the customer and the society as a whole." Today Toyota is a worldwide leader in automobile sales with its 200 millionth vehicle produced in 2012, making it, at that time, the global leader in car sales. Much of its success is based on the Toyota operation strategy that emphasizes an employee participation culture.

At Toyota, employees are required to participate in the Total Productive Maintenance (TPM) program that promotes ongoing skill training, feedback from employees to report on how to improve equipment and make it more reliable, and open communication between operators and engineers. Toyota even trains personnel to be able to do routine maintenance on their cars in order for them to understand the product and its engineering. In return, Toyota has asked for employee loyalty, which it has cultivated over the years. Employees at Toyota report greater work satisfaction than other companies such as GM and Ford.

Employee participation is promoted through:

- Quality circles in which employees from across the company and divisions work together to consider continuous quality issues
- Suggestion programs in which employees are encouraged to present ideas for improvements
- Incentive programs in which employees are rewarded for efficiency, creativity, and development

Another auto manufacturer, Volvo, saw its quality decrease and employee absenteeism increase in the 1990s. This impacted the bottom line of Volvo. The management hired many consulting firms that provided numerous and detailed technical suggestions (solutions such as improving the efficiency of the assembly line or putting into place better orientation and training). Despite these expensive consulting projects, Volvo continued to experience challenges. Volvo finally brought in positive psychologists to assess the situation. The recommendation: allow assembly line workers to rotate their responsibilities when constructing the vehicles, and provide more training for employees and a greater sense of control over their work. It perhaps sounded too easy for Volvo but to their credit they gave it a try. Soon they found productivity and quality up, and absenteeism down. As Toyota has done for years, Volvo shifted to allowing employees to have more ownership and agency in their work and provided employees with increased challenges to their skills. Thus, rather than working on attaching a door to the skeleton of the vehicle day in and day out, employees would be trained to not only attach doors effectively but also to work on many parts

CASE STUDY (Continued)

of the auto's assembly, thus creating job variety. In order to achieve this challenge, Volvo had to create additional skills training for the employees. If this sounds familiar, it should. This is the application of flow theory to the manufacturing assembly line (see sidebar and chapter). Employees were also to stop the assembly line, without disparagement, to alert supervisors of manufacturing concerns or to suggest ideas to improve some portion of the work being done.

The example of Volvo demonstrates that after mastering a certain skill set, repeating that application (such as attaching doors every day) becomes boring. Certainly the assembly line can be sped up if all workers have mastered their specialized skills, but this may lead to anxiety if there are too many vehicles passing by for the team to do a quality job. Allowing for a mix of challenges (one week doors; another week engine installation) allows for the development of skills and new challenges that keeps employees alert and engaged. Moreover, rather than being a cog in the machinery, empowering employees to have a voice in the work that they do provides agency and insight into opportunities for development or improvement. When employees feel more engaged in their work, they also feel more optimistic and energized, and hence, companies often find a decrease in absenteeism.

Volvo also faced an adaptive challenge. They needed to change the culture, values, attitudes, and beliefs of what it meant to work at Volvo. Technical fixes, while important, were not the entire answer to creating effective change. The company also needed to understand human behavior and create the environment in which people can not only work but also thrive.

Toyota continues to emphasize and reemphasize core values (in particular after recent quality control issues that led to massive recalls and fines). These include:

- Kaizen: An environment in which companies and employees proactively work to improve the manufacturing process to increase employee involvement and customer satisfaction

- Jikoda: Automation with a human touch

- Andon: Employees are asked to detect defects, stop the assembly line, and help correct the condition.

- A pull system: Employees are encouraged to gather wisdom through ongoing training to improve the manufacturing process.

- Quality awards: This is an incentive for worldwide Toyota manufacturing plants to be the best in manufacturing quality vehicles.

For the 21st century, it is useful to incorporate the theories and practice of positive psychology to organizational structure and flow for not only improved and engaged work environments for employees but also for the well-being of organizations. Many factories and organizations, however, have been slow to change despite the promise of better outcomes.

verbal and quantitative skills, but also included learning that utilized movement, art, and music (from Howard Gardner's multiple intelligence theory of understanding).

From Talent to Strengths

In the strengths-based model, talents are assumed not always to be known to the student because they are a natural part of that student. Here is a breakdown of the strengths and talent dynamic:

- Each individual has various talents.
- Groups of talents create strengths.
- The utilization of combined talents can lead to successful outcomes.
- Many people are not aware of their talents.
- Talents are often defined and limited by culture.
- Awareness of talents allows an individual to develop them (or dismiss them).
- When talents are developed and used as strengths, there is a greater outcome of success and fulfillment.
- Identifying talent requires discovery, practice, and feedback.

Thus rather than trying to fix what is deficient or asking a person to become or act like another person, one's current ability and potential is maximized. In other words the focus is on strengths, and weaknesses are managed so as not to be detrimental.

Within an academic setting, a strengths-based approach is to identify educational indicators (from positive psychology), including hope, well-being, engagement, optimism, and resiliency as well as accrediting requirements such as retention rates, instructor academic training, credits, and costs.

There are five principles of strengths-based education: They include:

- Student and educator measurement: Alongside critical data such as academic and behavioral data (campus safety, on- and off-campus living opportunities, attendance, etc.), additional data examining positive variables provide a larger picture of academic opportunity and success. In other words, having additional data about strengths and potential strengths provides an opportunity to build contexts in which greater academic may be achieved.

- Personalizing learning by having students take ownership: Students in this model are expected to set goals based on their strengths to achieve more successful outcomes both personally and academically. Ideally, educators would personalize the learning and provide regular feedback to the student on the movement along the student's and educator's goals for that student. This is not too different from the traditional tutor model of the United Kingdom in which a student meets regularly with a tutor to review work and academic progress.

- Creating a community of learning: Donald O Clifton argued that "strengths develop best in response to other human beings." People do not learn in isolation. We watch others, we model their behavior, and we rely on experts to support our journey from novice to greater ability. As students gain expertise, they in turn can share this knowledge and talent with others in, for example, a mentoring role. In today's world, collaborative work is necessary, and therefore, it is critical to move beyond just an individual focus on achievement. By leveraging the expertise of others, one also gains greater perspective on some of the sophisticated challenges in the 21st century. No one person can have all the answers.

- Integrating learning both within and without the learning environment: Oftentimes, education is compartmentalized rather than integrated. It is critical in this model to help students create a link between strengths and personal and academic goals. The ultimate purpose of strengths-based education is to motivate students based on the psychological needs of competence, autonomy, and relatedness.

- Applying strengths: Students need venues in which to experiment and try out their identified strengths in a chemistry lab, computer lab, internships, assistantships, or extracurricular activities. Students should have the opportunity to practice and engage their learning in new experiences and identifying their own efficacy or problem-solving skills.

A strengths-based approach to education assumes that educators and students have talents that can lead to successful learning. The students' strengths, or talents, are the basis for this achievement, and students are then taught to apply talents to different areas of learning and development. Overall, this approach involves educators identifying their own strengths and developing and applying them to support students to do the same in learning.

Researchers have demonstrated that strengths-based learning has the following student impact:

- Increased awareness of talents
- Increased personal and academic confidence
- Increased motivation to do well
- Increased investment in the future
- Better interpersonal connections
- Movement toward greater authenticity

RAIDERS OF THE LOST ARK: THE STRENGTH OF ARCHETYPES

Joseph Campbell is a well-known anthropologist and mythologist from the United States. He did a great deal of research and writing in comparative religions and is perhaps best known for his "hero's journey" philosophy. He is also known for an oft-repeated phrase that is abridged from his work: "Follow your bliss."

As a child, Campbell spent time in New York City museums and had a special passion for Native American culture. In particular, he was taken by this culture's mythology and reviewed closely varying tribal myths and legends. Later, as he began to expand his interest to other cultures, he was struck at the themes of such stories that exist wherever man establishes himself.

LIFE STRATEGY: CULTIVATING YOUR STRENGTHS

People have many types of intelligence. Often colleges and universities focus on quantitative and verbal intelligences. However, people have a variety of ways of understanding the world and using a variety of intelligences in developing their strengths.

Howard Gardner identified nine original intelligences: musical–rhythmic, visual–spatial, verbal–linguistic, logical–mathematical, bodily–kinesthetic, interpersonal (or emotional intelligence), intrapersonal, spiritual, and naturalistic. Gardner argues that one intelligence should not be singled out, but rather cultivating multiple intelligences provides one with the greatest strengths.

In his book *Frames of Mind*, Gardner writes: "Intelligence is the capacity to do something useful in the society in which we live. Intelligence is the ability to respond successfully to new situations and the capacity to learn from one's past experiences."

Donald O. Clifton is considered the father of Strengths Psychology, and others would say the "grandfather" of positive psychology. He created the 177-item Clifton StrengthsFinder to reflect individual talents, which was quickly used across industries and countries. Clifton founded the organization that was the precursor to the famous Gallup Organization, which today focuses on understanding and assessing human behavior.

Today over 2 million people have taken the revised Gallup StrengthsFinder assessment. The assessment provides one with a report of five major strengths from a list of 34 and the ways in which those strengths can be deployed. The Gallup StrengthsFinder 2.0 assessment can be completed online at www.strengthsfinder.com.

Recognizing strengths requires self-reflection and feedback. The Reflected Best Self Exercise, by Robert Quinn, Jane Dutton, Gretchen Spreitzer, and Laura Morgan Roberts, requires emailing individuals from an immediate circle of friends, family, and colleagues, and asking them to write a story about when they saw you at your best. The collection of these stories surfaces patterns that allow you to identify your strengths. You can do the Reflected Best Self Exercise by following the instructions below:

1) Identify five to seven people in your circle who know you in different domains of your life. Ask them to write a story about when they saw you at your best and to send the story to you within a week's time.

2) Assess for patterns in the feedback you get from all the stories you have received. Create a list of common themes of strengths and the settings in which these strengths were seen.

3) Now piece together the stories and create your own strengths story from the information that you have gathered.

4) Create a plan of how to put the strengths that emerged into action in both your personal and professional life.

CHRIS PETERSON: A TRIBUTE TO A PIONEER

Chris Peterson was one of the founders and leading figures in the field of positive psychology. Garrulous, generous, and larger than life, he was a professor of psychology and organizational behavior at the University of Michigan and co-founder of Michigan's Positive Psychology Center. He was one of the most frequently cited psychologists in the world in the last 20 years, devoting his efforts to the establishment and growth of positive psychology as a legitimate field of study, by asking the simple question: what makes life worth living?

Among his many contributions, Peterson was a member of the Positive Psychology Steering Committee, a member of the board of directors of the Gallup Organization Positive Psychology Institute, co-author of *Character Strengths and Virtues*, author of the best-selling *A Primer in Positive Psychology,* and lead scientist in the development of the Values in Action (VIA) Classification system. The VIA was a hallmark project in positive psychology because it was the first rigorous effort to describe, classify, measure, and validate important character strengths. The project resulted in the *VIA Survey of Signature Strengths*, an assessment tool taken by millions of people around the world. (See the sidebar on the VIA for a more detailed description.)

Peterson is noted for his academic work on the study of optimism, health, character, and well-being. In the 1980s, Peterson and colleagues published groundbreaking research showing the relationship between optimism and good health. His work identified the complexity of optimism, showing that different pathways of optimism correlated with different types of impact. Peterson researched variations on optimism such as immunological strength, the absence of negative mood, and health-promoting behaviors, and categorized these differences into what he called "little optimism" and "big optimism." His work showed that the pathway of major diseases, such as AIDS and cancer, could be better predicted by big optimism that works through the immune system and mood, whereas the likelihood of disease onset and traumatic injuries was more likely influenced by little optimism that manifested through behavior and concrete lifestyle choices.

Beyond his profound academic influence, Peterson was an extraordinary man and had widespread personal impact as someone who walked the talk, applying positive psychology in his daily life. He was known to students and colleagues by his trademark phrase "Other People Matter." This personal mantra made such a mark on so many that it headlined a tribute to his life and work in the *Journal of Applied Psychology* in 2013. He died in 2012.

It was when Campbell studied Eastern Philosophy that he decided to reject his Catholic upbringing and decided to retreat to a remote area outside of New York City, where he spent up to nine hours each day reading over a period of five years. It is during this time that Campbell formulated his ideas and theories about life. *The Hero with a Thousand Faces* (1949) was a culmination of his writing, reading, and thinking, in which he argued that myths, regardless from which culture, follow the use of archetypal patterns.

Campbell worked to bring together the theories of Sigmund Freud and Carl Jung. Jung was a student of Freud's who later turned away from his teacher's theories to examine the collective unconscious (certain patterns of instincts, cognitive orientation, recollections, and experiences that are common to all human beings). These are ingrained patterns in human experience. In order to create an understanding and discussion about this abstract concept, Jung looked to archetypes for making the understanding and discussion more open.

The word "archetype" comes from the Ancient Greek *archein* meaning "original or old," and *typos*, which means "model or type." Hence, in combination the term means an "original pattern" or template of which people, objects, or concepts are born and emulated.

Jung expanded the concept of archetype by arguing that there are universal, mythic characters that exist within the collective unconscious of human beings. Archetypes represent fundamental themes of experience and evoke deep emotions.

Jung wrote, "The term 'archetype' is often misunderstood as meaning certain definite mythological images or motifs, but these are nothing more than conscious representations. Such variable representations cannot be inherited. The archetype *is a tendency to form such representations* of a motif—representations that can vary a great deal in detail without losing their basic pattern."

Archetypes are common to all mankind but are further shaped by context such as personality, culture, and experience. Jung moved away from the theory of human psychological development referred to as tabula rasa, or blank slate in English, which posited that individual knowledge comes from experience in life. This of course did not explain instinctual behavior that we have as humans. Jung instead argued that evolution created pre-established patterns and experience was responsible for giving that framework existence and meaning. Thus, the archetype is a possibility of what exists for the individual and the individual must fill this empty archetypal framework over the course of human development.

Jung described a number of archetypal figures, including themes we refer to in everyday life. They include:

- The Self: Reflects the integrated or unified personality of a person.
- The Trickster: Is seen in many forms such as an animal, spirit, or joker. The Trickster plays tricks and challenges social norms to bring to light new ways or ideas. In the process, however, the trickster can create challenges in the form of confusion, jokes, or riddles. The Trickster may also create self-doubt so that the individual does not take the risks needed in life to create change.
- The Wise Old Man: The older leader (sometimes on top of a mountain or hill) who may act as a mentor or a source of good advice and judgment.
- The Wise Old Woman: The counterpart to the wise old man and represents the wisdom of nature and nurture (the negative archetype of the wise old woman is the witch).

- The Shadow: One's dark side and those aspects of oneself that we prefer not to acknowledge.
- The Hero/Heroine: Individual who faces a dangerous challenge and who must engage in courage, hope, and optimism as well as self-sacrifice to reach the outcome of the challenge's journey. The anti-hero is an archetype that does not have character or culturally celebrated traits such as honesty, compassion, and honor.

Campbell wrote: "A hero ventures forth from the world of common day into a region of supernatural wonder: fabulous forces are there encountered and a decisive victory is won: the hero comes back from this mysterious adventure with the power to bestow boons on his fellow man." It is said that there are 13 archetypal Hollywood stories that are reconfigured and distributed in various forms with differing heroes, wise leaders, shadowy characters, and anti-heroes. Campbell focused on the hero's journey as life presented individuals with challenges that required heroic approaches.

Campbell studied Eastern and Western religions and argued that beneath the surface they had the same themes. In fact, he looked at the world's rituals, Gods, and beliefs, and understood them as varying masks all representing truth that man will not ever quite learn or reach. In other words, all of man's religions, spiritual interests, and philosophies are differing means to asking the same questions about the unknown.

Consider the fairy tales from childhood (bring to mind *Little Red Riding Hood*, or *Jack and the Beanstalk*, for example) as well as modern-day stories such as *Raiders of the Lost Ark*, *Star Wars*, and *Lord of the Rings*. And most recently, add to that the narratives and themes of video games such as "Lara Croft" series, or *Call of Duty*. All of these stories have a hero in which everyday events are changed due to call to some sort of challenge or quest. This requires the hero to leave the familiar and venture into the unfamiliar. There are obstacles in the journey that are often overcome with the help of a sage; the hero continues to a more challenging aspect of his quest with carry tests in which he must use might, magic, or muscle to reach the object of the journey. Upon attaining the object, the hero is transformed from whom he was at the beginning of the journey and attains "liberation" from the previous changes that bound him (Campbell, 2008).

Themes from positive psychology, including courage, hope, optimism, and resiliency, reflect the elements of a hero's journey. Without the characteristics and qualities that come from positive psychology, the hero is unable to complete his journey.

Jung created 12 major archetypes on which Campbell later expanded. These archetypes represent basic orientations to life alongside a set of values, meanings, beliefs, and attitudes. It is a combination of these archetypes that both men argued created personality. These archetypes (or also egos) include:

- The Innocent: This archetype reflects faith and optimism. The core desire of the innocent is to get to an ideal realm or utopia. The Innocent may emerge in literature as someone naïve, romantic, mystical, or saint-like.

- The Everyman: This archetype reflects the girl-next-door narrative in literature and film. The everyman is humble, realistic, and a good friend and citizen.

- The Hero: This archetype is reflected as the superhero, warrior, cowboy, and dragon slayer. The hero is a team player and must check his arrogance in being all powerful. The hero proves his competency through strength and courage.

- The Caregiver: This archetype is the parent, helper supporter, angel, or fairy godmother. The caregiver wants to protect and care for others.

- The Explorer: Indiana Jones from *Raiders of the Lost Ark* represents the explorer archetype best. The explorer is the rugged individual who will not be contained in any formal way. The explorer escapes boredom by seeking out adventure. This archetype follows instincts and comes to a better understanding of the self and the world through the adventure that is pursued.

- The Rebel: James Dean's famous film *Rebel without a Cause* personifies the rebel archetype. This is the outlaw, misfit, and revolutionary who pushes against social norms, often with outrageous actions that are sometimes for good outcomes and sometimes for evil.

- The Lover: This archetype reflects the partner, spouse, love interest, or pal. This archetype creates connections that go deep and are often intimate. The Lover represents passion, gratitude, and appreciation.

- The Creator: This archetype is found in the characters of the artist, inventor, dreamer, musician, or writer. This archetype reflects imagination and the ability to take ideas and images and put them into the world.

- The Sage: This archetype seeks the truth through knowledge and learning. This is a very often used archetype in the form of the detective, scholar, expert, or teacher. The Sage is wise and knowing.

- The Jester: This archetype reflects a desire to live in the moment and with joy. The Jester is also called the fool, joker, or trickster, and creates joy through comic acts or jokes.

- The Magician: This magical archetype creates change and transformation. The Magician focuses on making dreams reality. Some cultures refer to the Magician as the Medicine Man or Shaman.

- The Ruler: This archetype pursues power, success, fame, and fortune as the major motivation in life. This archetype is reflected as royalty, politicians, and some leaders.

Archetypes are the bases for today's superheroes who represent strength and resiliency in the face of obstacles and evil. Finding your superhero archetype may provide an opportunity to consider how to embrace positive psychology and its tenets for yourself.

The Archetypal Superhero

Many consider superheroes a product of modern-day Hollywood with more and more superhero film and variations on the theme being released each year. However, superhero themes have been part of human storytelling forever.

HAPPINESS SET POINT

A common argument against much of the work in positive psychology is that happiness is an innate trait, something you are born with that can't be changed. The famous studies of Minnesota twins published by Lykken and Tellegen (1996) estimated that while happiness or subjective well-being (SWB) varies over a lifetime; each person has a happiness level or "happiness set point" that is approximately 80 percent explained by heredity. The remaining 20 percent is something individuals have more ability to influence.

In support of the set point theory, research also shows that the emotional impact of both positive and negative life events mostly disappears in as little as three months. For example, in a well-known 1978 study, Brickman, Coates, and Janoff-Bulman (1978) found that lottery winners were not any happier than paraplegic accident victims and, in fact, the lottery winners took less enjoyment from minor pleasures. Research such as this led social science researchers to assume that people always return to a relatively stable "happiness set point," even after extreme changes in life events. Our brains habituate to new things, so the elation over the big lottery win fades as we adapt over time.

More recent findings, however, are causing researchers to challenge these earlier assumptions and to think about the set point as having more flexibility. Advances in research have suggested that the impact of genetics on happiness may be weaker than the original studies suggested as scientists have a much better understanding of how the environment continually interacts with biology. Researchers also demonstrated that a different sample of lottery winners actually did have an increase in well-being. They measured on average 1.4 points higher on a 36-point scale over a year and a half after the win. In another study, people suffering a disability experienced a drop in their satisfaction score. The more severe the disability, the lower the score measured. The researchers are careful to note that these findings don't imply that people with disabilities are depressed or miserable. People do adapt, just not in the way that a strict set point theory would dictate.

This turns out to be good news. Researchers like Sonia Lyubomirsky argue that people can also intentionally increase their happiness through the conscious application of the positive interventions such as counting blessings, reframing events, and performing acts of kindness.

Strengths-based qualities are manifested in today's action heroes and superheroes. The action hero uses cunning, might, and ability to defeat the villain; the superhero engages special powers to do social good.

In the United States, the first truly 20th-century superheroes emerged during the Great Depression of the 1920s and 1930s. During this time, as funding was cut dramatically, police forces dwindled in the face of soaring organized crime.

Dr. Fury was introduced in 1928 with a gun, fedora, and trench coat to support the police and battle organized crime on the streets of Chicago. This was the beginning of the "good" vigilante. Soon thereafter, other characters were introduced such as the Black Shadow and Lady Mercy, both of whom had strength and wits. Later, the *Human Fly* emerged who relied on special high-technology weapons to combat crime and protect community and family from evil and violence.

Meanwhile, Superman was created in 1933 by the team of Jerry Siegel and Joe Schuster. The comic book creation was rejected for five years by publishers that scoffed at a man who was "faster than a speeding bullet." It was not until DC Comics bought the series in 1938 that Siegel and Schuster's invention, a hero with a blue costume, red cape, S shield on his chest, with an origin story of being raised as Clark Kent in Kansas, became a national phenomenon. By 1940, Superman had become a radio show, cartoons, toys, and a Macy's balloon. Many believed that Superman was so popular because he was a regular man in everyday life and resonated with newly arrived immigrants who were looking for the American Dream.

With Superman's tremendous success, DC Comics had commissioned Bob Kane and Bill Finger to create another superhero. They created Bruce Wayne, a billionaire who had been subjected to seeing his parents' murder and wanted to avenge their deaths. Unlike Superman, Wayne's alter ego, at that time called *Bat-Man* (and later simply *Batman*), had inventions and gadgets to battle evil. *Batman* became equally successful to *Superman*.

As America was pulled into World War II a new group of superheroes was introduced. The first female superhero was created by William Moulton Marston, who was a member of the Massachusetts bar, held a doctorate in psychology from Harvard University, and invented the lie detector.

Marston's creation, Wonder Woman debuted in 1941. Other superheroes who were created to fight the enemies of the United States during World War II included Namor, who fought the Japanese; and the new Human Torch joined Wonder Woman, Superman, and Batman's new sidekick Robin to fight the Axis powers. Captain America debuted at this time as well giving Hitler a punch in the face on the cover of the first comic book who became the leader in "fighting the good fight."

After World War II, most of the superheroes disappeared. Westerns, mysteries, and romances supplanted these heroes. It wasn't until the late 1950s that updated superheroes were introduced, including Aquaman, Green Lantern, and Atom. These new heroes, during the Cold War, created the Justice League of America. This renewed interest led to the additional creations in the 1960s of Iron Man, Thor, and the Hulk. But no one topped Superman in wide appeal until 1966 when Spiderman was introduced.

During the Nixon-era Watergate scandal, Captain America shared the U.S. disillusionment with government and politics and stopped calling himself Captain America and instead took the moniker Nomad (the man without a country).

Peter Parker was a bright young man who while on a school field trip received a bite from a radioactive spider. The atomic power from the bite gave him super powers. The creators reflected society's love and fear of atomic

THE FUN THEORY

How do we make positive media? The same way we encourage positive behavior. We quit looking for what's wrong and start making more of what's right. This isn't as easy as it sounds because we tend to focus on the negative, rarely equating media with positive potential. There is a negative bias in the research, as scholars tend to gravitate toward society's concerns around the potential for harmful impact, from commercialism to stereotyping to unrealistic standards of beauty.

The perceptions of negative messaging is so ingrained that even public service announcements are negative. Campaigns, such as those trying to combat AIDS, obesity, smoking or drunk driving, target negative consequences of such behaviors in spite of the fact that a meta-analysis of 94 studies found that positive messages, those showing a gain rather than a loss, were more successful in promoting illness prevention behaviors (Gallagher & Updegraff, 2012).

The tides are finally changing. The Internet has created a new sensibility, empowering people to do all kinds of things, from starting online businesses to posting cat videos. Advertising is starting to respond. Where ads used to be designed to point out our failings—not fashionable enough, sweet-smelling enough or rich enough—or scare us to death, there is a trend now toward a different type of media content. A new host of companies are replacing the "hard sell" with positive messages where media is designed to inspire, entertain, and empower.

Volkswagen, for example, created a campaign called the "Fun Theory," to see if fun could change people's behavior for the better. They created, and then filmed, events that targeted recycling, climbing stairs rather than escalators, and using trash bins rather than littering.

In one event, Volkswagen turned a subway staircase in Stockholm into a giant piano keyboard to encourage people to take the stairs. Not only did 66 percent more people take the stairs in the subway, the video received over 20 million views on YouTube.

This is applied positive psychology. Volkswagen tackled issues by making them fun at the decision or trigger points, where someone is able to make a choice.

power at that time. In 1965, Spiderman ranked alongside Bob Dylan and Che Guevara as revolutionary icons according to *Esquire* magazine's reader poll.

In 1978 *Superman* came to film with Christopher Reeves and since then superhero films have dominated the cinema with successful box office results. In the 1990s old comic books started trading and selling at extraordinarily high prices, bringing a renewed push for publishing comic books back into fashion. With the worldwide success of the X-Men in 2000, superheroes were clearly here to stay expanding their appeal and access beyond print, television, and film, to phones, tablets, and video gaming. Today, the superheroes of DC and

Marvel Comics dominate film screens around the world bringing in billions of dollars in ticket sales. Jung and Campbell would not be surprised: they would see archetypes being created for modern tastes and understanding.

Following is a sampling of the superheroes from the 20th and 21st centuries with their individual strengths. Take a look at how they compare to Jung's 12 archetype models:

- Ironman—creativity
- Batman—athleticism
- Wolverine—rebel
- Jean Grey (X-Men)—caregiver
- Professor X—sage
- Wonder Woman—ruler or royalty
- Superman—advocate/protector
- Mister Fantastic—intellectual

CONCLUSION

This chapter reviewed the importance of understanding individual and group strengths that can be applied to many fields including counseling, teaching, and leadership. It is important to examine that which is working well in order to leverage those aspects for the possibility of more successful and productive outcomes.

In particular, the importance of understanding one's own strengths through assessment, narrative, or archetype is critical. Without insight, it is difficult to promote and nurture that which is best for one or a system. The diversity of strengths have been celebrated throughout mankind's history. Written records go back to the Greek Gods; later Jung formalized 12 major archetypes that are shared across cultures as inherent human themes, and Campbell shaped the model of the hero's journey to understand how heroes exist in everyday life as all people are faced with challenges in life.

Modern archetypal heroes in the form of superheroes whose stories are found across all types of media today reflect the way the 20th and 21st centuries have viewed vulnerability and strength in society and how the leverage of those strengths, despite hidden weakness, does create positive social outcomes.

CHAPTER 3

Flow

Flow is defined as activities in which there is a match between high challenge and high skills. The outcome of Flow is that the ego, or self-consciousness, disappears. After the experience of Flow, people report feeling stronger and more vital. It is the experience of being so absorbed in a task that one loses track of time. It is within Flow experiences that people across cultures report having the greatest sense of well-being.

Typically, when individuals reach this point of concentration, they describe a feeling of being "ecstatic" (from the Greek "to step to the side"), that is, stepping out of the ordinary routine of life and experiencing something that is vital and different, often referred to as ecstasy. In his work on Flow, Mihaly Csikszentmihalyi points out that the only remaining architecture we know of from past cultures are their symbols of "ecstasy"—such as the temples, sports arenas, and theaters of the ancient Greeks, Mayans, Egyptians, and Chinese. Much as seeing a moving or playing video games today, these places were an opportunity for individuals to step out of everyday life and experience something different.

People who experience Flow do not necessarily need enormous arenas in which to do so. An opportunity for action that is in balance with the ability to act (the match of skills and challenges) can produce a Flow experience. If one considers any sort of game or art form, there is a match of skill to a challenge (in sports, for example, one wants to play an equally skilled opponent so as to be challenged and not to be bored). The experience of such engagement, ecstasy, or Flow creates a condition where people feel a sense of peacefulness and a decrease in anxiety and depression. Csikszentmihalyi argues that worries disappear because the individual does not have the information-processing capacity to both focus on the task at hand and to worry. This results from the concentration taking place when one is challenged, skills are in balance, goals are clear, and feedback is present. Flow researchers have found that the worst moments in an individual's day-to-day life are when he or she is self-conscious.

When challenge and skills are out of balance, life can feel unsatisfying to those who feel overwhelmed (the challenges of life exceed the individual's time or skills), which results in anxiety and stress, and those who feel "underwhelmed" (the challenges of life do not engage an individual's time or skills) and therefore, the individual becomes bored and anxious.

THE CONDITIONS OF A FLOW EXPERIENCE

Flow is universal and applies to individuals regardless of socioeconomic status (SES), education, and gender. Csikszentmihalyi and his colleagues collected over 8,000 interviews from individuals around the world, including Japan, Korea, India, Europe, and the United States, to determine the universality of the Flow experience and its characteristics. These researchers found that indeed there were constant characteristics of the Flow experience. Generally, the experience of Flow took place when an individual enjoyed the task at hand and the task was being pursued for its own sake and not for an external reward (intrinsic motivation). The conditions of the Flow experience are as outlined below (adapted from Csikszentmihalyi, 1997):

- Goals are clear: An individual is aware of what he or she wants to do.
- Immediate feedback: An individual knows how well he or she is doing at any moment.
- Skills match challenges: The skill level of an individual is in balance with the task at hand.
- Concentration is deep: The individual focuses all attention on the task at hand.
- Problems are forgotten: The individual is able to dismiss irrelevant stimuli that may interfere with concentration.
- Control is possible: A feeling of mastery is gained.
- Self-consciousness disappears: An individual feels able to transcend the limits of the ego.
- The sense of time is altered: An individual either loses track of time or time seems to pass with rapidity.
- The activity is intrinsically rewarding: The experience is worth engaging in for its own sake.

Optimal experiences such as Flow provide a sense of well-being after they occur. Outside of Flow one may feel very content such as when one is eating a good meal or reading a book, but such states of happiness are dependent on external circumstances rather than internal ones.

Flow experience is important to development because one must continue learning in order to achieve Flow experiences. If one is in "control," one may feel satisfied but not very involved. For this individual, increasing challenges would create a more optimal experience for living or working. Skill development is important for individuals who may be in a state of "arousal" characterized by involvement but not exactly strong or happy experience.

According to Csikszentmihalyi, when a sample of Americans were asked, "Do you ever get involved in something so deeply that nothing else seems to matter, and you lose track of time?" about 20 percent of the respondents reported this experience as occurring frequently, and 15 percent of the respondents reported this experience occurring seldom. Researchers have found this frequency to be consistent with populations measured around the world.

FLOW THEORY AND COUNSELING

The goal from a Flow theory orientation to counseling and education is to assist individuals in the development of the self in order to attain increasing levels of emotional and cognitive complexity. Rathunde (1988) outlines five cornerstones that increase an individual's optimal development in terms of Flow theory. They include:

1. Clear goals: Clients who create clear and attainable goals are cognitively ordering their experience and consciousness. As goals are set and eventually met, new and more complex goals are formed. Those clients without clear goals tend to be vulnerable to anxiety and boredom. Much like Vygotsky's (1978) *zone of proximal development*, an individual masters skills and then jumps to the next level of challenge to attain the next level of skills. This cycle builds a positive sense of self such as resilience and characteristics such as initiative, responsibility, and commitment. Many clients come to counseling when their skills do not measure the challenges they face, and they may experience anxiety, depression, or detachment. Narrative can be an effective way of helping the client establish goals. Through the use of stories, films, literature, and other art forms, the counselor can expose the client to creating a story about his or her goal setting that includes a protagonist (the client), challenges, and avenues to resolution. Included in this is the development of skills that the counselor can create via an appropriate structure for the client, such as modeling of homework assignments, in order for the client to better meet the challenges of his or her objectives.

2. Developing "centeredness": The term "being centered" has been used a great deal in popular psychology; however, in this case it refers to an awareness of one's physical and emotional states. Oftentimes a client seeking counseling is in a state of chaos and is unable able to cope with the immediate situation. Flow theory emphasizes the importance of being aware of one's activities and states of being with attention to detail. This "centering" or awareness of one's inner and outer states is important to develop a sense of insight, creativity, problem solving, and attentiveness—all characteristics of the larger positive psychology hallmarks.

   The counselor can help the individual bring order to the internal state of chaos through various therapies, including art therapy, play therapy, and music therapy as examples. These approaches create a context in which the client can find a means of using creativity to help the client express his or her awareness. Encouraging hobbies, or assigning them as homework, may be an effective means to encourage the client to focus their minds and work toward achieving Flow states. Reading, gardening, sewing, and running are all possible pursuits to fulfill this goal.

Flow theory counseling also lends itself well to the practices of meditation, yoga, or guided imagery. All of these approaches help the client order his or her thoughts and in the process learn methods to "control impulses, delay gratification, and regulate emotions."

3. Intrinsic motivation: This is the key to optimal experience psychology. As discussed earlier, feedback as an activity taking place is important in achieving Flow. This helps the individual gauge how well he or she is doing. For a client, it is important that the counselor provide regular feedback and to outline the options and possible consequences of actions that an individual pursues. The purpose is to help the client internalize the ability to self-monitor (independent feedback) his or her actions and emphasizes the importance of applying skills to a task at hand.

4. Commitment: In a Flow theory model, clients will pursue individual goals if the counselor is able to maintain a therapeutic alliance that is based on Carl Rogers's tenets of "accurate empathy, non-possessiveness, warmth, and genuineness." This alliance seems to be therapeutic in itself. Clients absorb this trust and then be able to make a commitment to their individual objectives with greater enthusiasm, optimism, and resilience.

5. Focus on the self: It is through the development of the complexity of the self that an individual is able to maintain greater mental stability and health by being able to address challenges with the appropriate set of individual skills. Typically, the self is poorly developed, according to psychodynamic therapists, because of a deficit in the family where the child is not supported with developmental tasks.

According to Csikszentmihalyi, the self develops complexity from the parallel processes of differentiation and integration. Differentiation is important for an individual to be individuated from the parents and to establish a unique and separate identity of the self. Integration is the reach beyond the self to create attachments with others and form cognitive reasoning (such as the formation of ideas that rely on information from the outside world). Counseling from a Flow theory perspective works toward the integration of these processes with an outcome emphasis on developing self-confidence, independence, optimism, and initiative. Group counseling has been especially effective in encouraging the development of both processes as Yalom (1995) has established by encouraging "altruism, universality, and existential issues."

Intrinsic Motivation

It is important to distinguish extrinsic and intrinsic motivation. Extrinsic motivation refers to activities that are justified by the consequent rewards such as prestige, power, and money. Intrinsic motivation, in contrast, refers to activities that are pursued because it is worthwhile to the individual and does not require any other incentives. A person gardens, sings, or runs because the quality of these experiences provides a certain satisfaction. The voluntariness variable reflects extrinsic and intrinsic motivation with the question of whether the participant wanted to pursue the activity by choice or had to engage in the activity.

Intrinsic motivation is key to the creative, problem-solving process. A frequently cited study by Harvard Business School faculty member Teresa Amabile (1983) asked 95 participants to create various works under varying conditions. Under one scenario, the participants were told they could produce a work in any way they wished; in another scenario the participants were told that their work would be evaluated for its creativity by a panel of experts.

Those participants who were prompted to be creative were less likely to produce creative work than those who were given their own choice of pursuits. In another variation, a group of participants were promised a reward for their creative works. This group produced less creative results than those who were not promised a reward. The conclusion is that individuals are more likely to be creative in situations where the individual is intrinsically motivated rather than extrinsically motivated.

Intrinsic rewards are often a more powerful motivator of behavior than extrinsic ones. Individuals are more likely to engage in an activity or perform an activity well if they enjoy what they are doing. An activity is fundamentally changed with the introduction of extrinsic rewards. This means that individuals find internal rewards for engaging in certain activities. In attempting to define these rewards, Flow theory has entered the picture. The rewards of intrinsically motivated behavior include a sense of control, clear perception of feedback, the merging of action and awareness, a loss of self-consciousness, and a feeling of euphoria.

Psychological well-being (measured in terms of happiness) results from an individual's ability to perceive intrinsic rewards in everyday life situations. Individuals who perceive their lives to be intrinsically motivated are overall happier people. That is, positive affect is accompanied by intrinsically rewarding experiences because the action is a fulfillment of the individual's desires.

Csikszentmihalyi asserts, "The best moments in our lives are not the passive, receptive, relaxing times . . . the best moments usually occur if a person's body or mind is stretched to its limits in a voluntary effort to accomplish something difficult and worthwhile. Optimal experience is thus something we make happen."

No individual route to Flow is better than another. The Flow experience depends on the person and the context in which various Flow experiences can take place. Researchers knows that Flow experiences lead to a greater sense of reported individual well-being. These positive emotions are more important than previously thought. Positive psychologists have found that the experience of positive states is key to overall well-being. Some positive emotional states are outside of oneself or passive in nature (such as attending a party or sharing a joke with someone). Flow experiences are more inner experiences. Flow, as mentioned earlier, requires one to do something for the sake of doing it (intrinsic motivation), which proactively challenges one's skill set.

Positive psychologists have found a number of reasons for individuals to engage in Flow experiences for greater overall health and well-being. These include:

- A sense of control: Albert Bandura demonstrated that a sense of control or autonomy is critical to well-being. This includes the opportunity to make decisions and choices in life. Flow provides a sense of control alongside a loss of self-conscious thinking.

- Loss of self-consciousness: One of the greatest ways of moving into losing a sense of well-being is being self-conscious. This is often reflected in comparing oneself to others, critical self-talk, and spending time in the mirror. Flow experiences release one from negative thoughts and provide a sense of freedom as the mind directs attention to the task at hand. Self-consciousness or negative thinking takes one out of a Flow experience.

- Expertise: Flow experiences provide an opportunity to move from one skill level to the next. Those who are video gamers enjoy mastering a skill set in the game and then going to the next level of difficulty. Some psychologists report that it takes 10,000 hours of practice to really master a discipline. The route to those 10,000 hours can be rewarding.

- Integration and confidence: Flow leads to a sense of achievement through mastery that creates a sense of pride and accomplishment for one. You may advance in your talents as a musician or craftsman and that feels unique and good. Flow also creates a sense of integration that brings together thoughts, feelings, and actions. This promotes a sense of harmony for oneself and in one's interactions with others.

FLOW AND EDUCATION

Research reflects that most students in U.S. classrooms live between anxiety (the challenges that they face exceed their skill set) and boredom (the challenges that they face are lower than their skill level). A longitudinal study of 526 high school students examined how adolescents spent their time in school and where they reported the greatest sense of engagement (where their skills were in balance with the classroom challenges). Fifty percent of the respondents reported that courses were boring and one-third reported that playing around was the only way to get through the school day. Students who graduated from high school successfully reported a greater sense of the daily school experience as engaging. Students who reported high levels of boredom and anxiety are at risk for not completing highs school, and for those students who are eager for a greater challenge in the learning environment and do not find it, a great deal of potential is lost.

These researchers found that students were more engaged in the teaching and learning when engaged in individual or group work that called for creative problem solving and the application of recently learned skills. Students reported that they were least engaged when listening passively to a lecture, watching a film, or completing exams. These results reflect an ongoing adherence to an agrarian model of teaching and learning, as mentioned earlier, of the teacher as expert and the student as novice. The novice in this model memorizes and regurgitates material.

Today, we live in an information age and hence teaching and learning is adapting to a new way of understanding the world. This includes the support of Flow experiences in which the student can engage in activities that work to challenge and existing skill level and move that skill level to the next step.

Teachers are learning to let go of some of the instructional control and to let the learning take many shapes and forms. The classroom in which the following qualities are present can promote Flow experiences:

- Concentration: A student must be in a strong state of concentration and engagement in an activity. The ability to focus on getting into a Flow state for challenging tasks is critical for deeper teaching and learning.

- Interest: Topics that intrigue and interest a student are more likely to elicit a Flow response. Interest is the first ingredient of Flow and moves a task from being outwardly motivated toward inwardly motivated. With curiosity, students will engage in the learning more through reading, collaboration, and writing.

- Enjoyment: Providing students with challenging learning tasks can in fact be fun for students. There is an opportunity to creatively engage in the material as skills are developed. In hindsight, students report a feeling of accomplishment and satisfaction with such learning models.

Ultimately, it is the students' experience of a sense of control and feelings of relevance to an activity that contribute to the experience of Flow in an educational setting. Student disengagement comes from many things, but research reflects that a "lack of challenge or meaning" is the typical reason that most students find non-academic pursuits to elicit more positive emotions than academic pursuits, indicating the importance of extracurricular activities for students as well as a shift from the traditional lecture format of today's classrooms.

Educators can prime the classroom for Flow experiences by creating learning environments that are engaging and enjoyable experiences. Instructors should continue to provide constructive feedback alongside an assessment of student work to create the framework for intrinsic motivation. This may promote students owning goal setting and activity choice. An overly controlled environment of emphasizing deadlines, grades, and performance reduces the creativity that comes with Flow experiences as well as interest and motivation. Today's learners seem to succeed most when engaged in cognitive and emotionally engaging topics, which for the teacher is not always easy to create, but critical to optimal learning experiences.

New Ways of Learning for the 21st Century

When it comes to optimal learning experiences, educators are reassessing teaching and learning in the information age. This means different ways of engaging the learner to master material and to promote creative problem-solving skills. Online learning has shifted the face of traditional on-site learning

CASE STUDY: EXPERIENCE SAMPLING METHODOLOGY IN POSITIVE PSYCHOLOGY RESEARCH

The Experience Sampling Methodology (ESM) is used for a variety of research across many fields but its roots are firmly planted within positive psychology. ESM is a tool to understand the daily lived experiences of individuals. Researchers, for example, interested in learning about how major events influence the health and well-being of an individual day-to-day have utilized ESM to assess how daily stressors affect the mood of an individual over a period of time.

There are numerous ways to use ESM to study ongoing behavior. Participants' reports are dependent (or contingent) on one of the following:

- Signal contingent—The participant is signaled via a pager, watch, or mobile phone within a period of time during the day to record items such as mood, thoughts, or feelings.
- Interval contingent—The participant is assigned a time to report items such as when waking up or before bed.
- Event contingent—The participant records information whenever a key event occurs such as feeling depressed, or the onset of headaches.

Keep in mind that ESM data is self-reported and therefore subjective. Nonetheless, it provides a snapshot of participants' daily lived lives, which is more immediate than asking participants to recall an event after it happens.

In one ESM study, Shifren (1996) followed the daily lived experiences of individuals with Parkinson's disease. He found that more optimistic individuals saw themselves as needing less daily assistance and on those days when the participant felt more optimistic the following day the individual perceived the illness as less severe.

Affleck, Tennen, and Apter (2001) examined the daily symptoms, mood, and functioning of individuals suffering from rheumatoid arthritis. Participants in this study reported their pain intensity, mood, and limitation of activities due to pain for 75 days. The results revealed that those participants who were more optimistic construed more benefits from their illness, had a higher average positive daily mood, and reported less limitation of activities due to pain.

In another study of the daily experiences of individuals with rheumatoid arthritis, asthma, and fibromyalgia, Affleck, Tennen, and Apter (2001) concluded that pessimism was a predictor of daily sadness, and optimism was a predicator of daily happiness. The mood-regulating function of optimism

CASE STUDY (Continued)

did not change the patients' experience of pain, but it did contribute to pain-coping strategies that helped improve overall mood.

In the analysis of self-reports on the studies of women with bulimia, ESM studies examined the interaction between the individual and the situation. Researchers found in the analysis of self-reports that the cognitive and emotional state of women with bulimia reflected low moods followed with a dissociative period of binging, and then followed by a return of control with a concurrent feeling of shamefulness and guilt.

ESM studies have also been useful in examining what makes for a healthy relationship. Kirchler (1988) studied 21 couples and found that happier couples were better able to evaluate one another's moods and needs. These couples also spent more time together, more time talking with one another, felt stronger when together, spoke of more personal matters, and experienced a balance of power when together.

In organizational settings, ESM has been used to develop a larger picture of how varying contexts influence individual's lives. Managerial science has used ESM to evaluate employees' time use and productivity. For example, ESM research in organizations' settings has found that workers report working 65 percent of the time on the job. The other 35 percent of the employee's time is divided between eating and non-work-related activities such as conversations with co-workers, or on the telephone with family and friends.

A great deal of ESM research has focused on understanding adolescents and the experience of education in their lives. Studies of adolescents from around the world indicate that schooling is among the least rewarding experiences in adolescents' lives in that these students report low motivation and high rates of boredom. This may be due to instructors and students not understanding or listening to one another. In a corresponding study, the researcher signaled teachers and students at the same time in order to understand the levels of concentration and mood of both groups during the school day. He found that of the 20 hours spent each week in the classroom, only 4 hours were spent listening to the teacher and 5 hours were spent listening to others or in discussion.

An ESM study in the Netherlands examined the daily lives of individuals experiencing stress and psychopathology (DeVries, 1992). Participants were individuals who were experiencing depression, stress, anxiety, drug abuse, and schizophrenia. The study ran for six days with ten random signals sent per participant per day. The self-report form asked about symptoms, mental state, and the context in which the report took place. This gave the researcher a closer picture and story of the daily lived lives of those with mental illness.

models. Harvard University and the Massachusetts Institute of Technology have collaborated to create EdX, which provides an opportunity for students of all ages and backgrounds to access lectures outside of the Cambridge, Massachusetts, area. A similar Stanford University business course was streamed to over 100,000 participants around the world. Perhaps this is a sign of a more democratic approach to top education. The learner still needs access to a computer and Internet service and from there may participate from wherever he or she may be in the world.

While online learning was at first questioned by traditional academicians, research after research reflects that there is only one difference between the learning online versus on-site: the shy learner tends to participate more in the online learning environment.

Introducing interactive learning (where students can take quizzes during a lecture to reflect understanding and learning), multimedia, and a focus on both individual and group work make learning more engaging for today's student. In 2012, President Obama declared that low-cost online learning was the model of education for the future of the United States. Optimal learning continues to evolve in this very exciting time for education.

FLOW AND NEUROBIOLOGY

Studies by scientists internationally have reflected that Flow is beyond subjective reports and is reflected in the neurobiology of the brain. Flow in fact shifts the standard way the brain functions from fast-moving beta waves to a far slower pace associated with daydreaming and deep sleep. Scientist believe that this "re-combinatory" state (a state in which the individual takes new information and combines it with existing information) enhances creativity and hence problem solving with greater insight.

Moreover, Flow temporarily deactivates the prefrontal context (the area of the brain that contains higher cognitive functioning) that reduces self-consciousness, a key to entering Flow experiences. Thus, as the self-monitoring aspect of the brain is quieted the inner critic many carry around has nothing to say for that time. The removal of critical thoughts allows the individual to discover new insights and imagine novel ways of approaching a challenge.

Finally, the brain also releases neurochemicals such as norepinephrine, dopamine, endorphins, anandamide, and serotonin, all related to feelings of well-being, pleasure, and enhanced performance.

Flow, the Brain, and Magnetic Resonance Imaging

Richard Davidson, PhD, runs the Center for Investigating Healthy Minds at the University of Wisconsin-Madison. He uses magnetic resonance imaging to determine how experiences such as meditation or Flow impact the brain and change the way the brain (and, hence, the individual) functions. In 1992, the Dalai Lama challenged Dr. Davidson to understand how neuroscience could inform well-being. The Dalai Lama has always argued that a main motivation of human beings is to "overcome suffering and find happiness" and that meditation was a path to this objective.

Davidson's research on emotion and the brain included peering into the brain of the Dalai Lama and other practitioners of meditation using medical technology that reflects how the brain lights up in varying ways when one is happy, sad, contentedness and other emotional states. Davidson believed that individuals can learn about happiness, well-being, and compassion in the same way individuals learn sports, academics, or music. He sees the pursuit of well-being as skill development and has been able to demonstrate scientifically that with training the brain does change.

In 2014, Davidson traveled to Davos, Switzerland's, Economic Forum, to challenge leaders and CEOs to consider the role that happiness plays. He presented his famous study in which research participants were each given $100. One group had to spend the money on themselves; the other group was to spend money on others. When the participants were assessed afterward for their levels of happiness, Davidson and his team found that those who gave their money away were significantly happier than those who used the money for themselves.

FLOW AND MUSIC

Many musicians will describe being in "rapture" when performing or practicing. They may begin a piece only to be shaken out of this Flow state by the applause of the audience or some other distraction. Playing music takes a great deal of concentration as the musician interprets the notes to the instrument and then combines these streams often to be in sync with other instruments, for example, within an orchestra.

In a recent study (2013) of pianists, researchers found that 91 percent of the pianists reported being in a Flow state. The gender, age, or number of years playing the piano had no impact on whether one could enter a Flow state or not. Rather, the amount of practice in which the pianist engaged tended to indicate the probability of Flow. In addition, the style of music, researchers found, tended to elicit greater engagement in Flow. In this study, the Romantic style characterized by Chopin was most frequently associated with a Flow state; the works of Beethoven and Debussy followed as second and third place.

Csikszentmihalyi's study into engaged states or optimal experiences started with artists. In particular, he assessed how composers would be able to maintain long sessions of work with intense focus often losing sense of time. One composer reported starting his work in the morning only to look up and find it dark outside as evening had arrived.

The quality of the work created within Flow states can be varied as this is not as important as the investment in the music and the challenge to one's existing musical talent. Musicians reported, as others who leave Flow states, that boredom, anxiety, room temperature, or noise will take them out of the Flow state. Musicians describe Flow as a "laser-like" concentration in which other aspects of consciousness disappear and one's action and awareness for the task at hand merge. Amiable's research found that Flow states also improve individual creativity. This is why painters, musicians, and other artists can spend hours in a studio without with engagement and concentration.

FLOW AND SPORTS

Athletics, throughout history and across cultures, have served to promote the movement of the body and the competition of sport. Those who engage in kinesthetic activities have always reported that the greatest motivator is the experience that it provides. From runners, to swimmers, and tennis and soccer, participants get into the zone when they feel there is a sense of control, a great awareness of how to move the body to achieve the movement necessary, and a loss of focus on the outside world and rather just on the task at hand. These Flow experiences once again take life from the ordinary to the engaged and extraordinary: a primary motivator for many athletes besides the benefits of health and strength. When researchers asked participants to recall a time when one was totally involved in a task and when there were feelings of being strong and positive, a majority of the respondents named sports.

Those who engage in sports are keen on pursuing further engagement for the peak experiences that Flow in such activities brings. There is a sense of exhilaration, loss of fear, and focused concentration. Athletes from various sports describe Flow using a number of terms, including "focused," "switched on," "super alive," "unbeatable," "tuned in," and "nothing else matters."

Athletes describe Flow more often than the general population, in part because the athlete is pushing toward his or her bodily limits to achieve greater ability. While winning may be the goal for some athletic teams, often the athlete reaches being "in the zone" because it is an experience that he or she wants to achieve for its own sake and not always for the prize that may come from winning. In fact, athletes who focus too much on the outcome tend to perform less well. While the practice may not always feel enjoyable, the participation in sports overall has to be in order for Flow to be experienced.

FLOW AND HOBBIES

Many of our parents and grandparents nurtured hobbies. From model trains, to sewing, gardening, or craft making. Today, between work, family, and commuting many feel that there is less time to include hobbies in life. Hobbies are important to engage individuals in activities that are interesting. Moreover, it makes one feel good.

Hobbies enhance creativity and sharpen one's focus. Researchers find that hobbies promote a sense of self and as a result, self-confidence as well as counter burns out.

For some, taking a class in an area of interest can be a hobby. A hobby should be an active endeavor, however, rather than a passive one. Today, many people have chosen watching television as a way to fill spare time. While television may be relaxing, it is not the same as a hobby. Csikszentmihalyi found that:

Hobbies are about two and a half-times more likely to produce a state of heightened enjoyment than TV does and active games and sports about three times more.

According to a Kaiser Family Foundation study (2010) Americans now spend 11 hours per day, on average, consuming media. This includes waking up and listening to the radio or television, to seeing billboards on the way to work and reading the news on the computer. A growing trend found in media consumption is multitasking in which, for example, an individual texts while watching television or a film on a tablet.

Television viewing allows for relaxation and then boredom or upward comparison in which the viewer compares his or her life to those featured on television programs and feels less good about life. It may take some creativity in finding a hobby that you want to spend time with, but research shows that it is well worth one's time to go back to what previous generations knew and enjoyed: hobbies make life more enjoyable and enhance the quality of life outside of the hobby with which one engages.

Almost 50 percent of employees in the United States and the United Kingdom report low satisfaction with work–life balance and many seek stress relief from the demands of 21st-century life. Engaging in hobbies, and hence engaging in Flow, can be a one of the best non-pharmaceutical and simple approaches to reducing stress. Here are some hobbies people use to reduce stress:

- Reading: Books can provide a platform for both relaxation and engagement. Readers report less stress after learning about other experiences, realities, or even fantasy.

- Writing: Many who keep journals or are asked to write a paper, for example, can enter a state of Flow. The self-reflection and individual expression is healthy for one too.

- Exercise: The body enjoys both the physical and neurochemical aspects of exercise. Challenging oneself to attain greater strength of aerobic capacity is a useful challenge to one's existing physical skill set.

- Gardening: Many gardeners report starting work in their garden only to find the sun setting as if only moments passed. The preparing of soil, nurturing of plants, and physical exercise involved makes this hobby a wonderful choice for many.

- Volunteering: Besides being one of the best ways to move away from self-consciousness and be in service of others, volunteering allows one to engage in activities in which he or she is passionate about and one that often comes with challenging circumstances. Volunteers who work with agencies that build homes for those who don't have one, for example, work collaboratively with a team and learn new skills. These groups of volunteers regularly report losing track of time in the construction of such homes.

- Dancing: Learning new types of dance requires whole brain thinking that translates into movement. Becoming an expert in tango, square dancing, or the waltz provides creativity, physical movement, and engagement.

Internationally, researchers find that creating time for hobbies stimulates the brain associated with creativity and a sense of well-being. This in turn can contribute to an individual's sense of confidence and agency. It may be time to make an old tradition once again new.

FLOW AND CREATIVITY

A lot about creativity is being written today, in part because creativity is key to addressing some of the social challenges faced in the 21st century and to creating a better world, whether politically, socially, environmentally, or economically.

Creativity can be summed up as finding novel approaches and connections between ideas and way to address challenges in work and life. Sometimes the connections seem unrelated only to generate a new solution. Creativity is about thinking and producing solutions. Rollo May, in his book *Courage to Create*, wrote:

> Creativity is the process of bringing something new into being. Creativity requires passion and commitment. It brings to our awareness what was previously hidden and points to new life. The experience is one of heightened consciousness: ecstasy.

Researchers find that positive emotions promote creativity; and negative emotions tend to hinder the creative process, especially those associated with anger and sadness. It is a sense of lifelong curiosity and inquiry that promotes creativity. In particular those who seek new ideas and perspectives tend to be more creative and resilient individuals who report overall greater well-being and happiness. There are ways in which individuals can promote creativity. These include:

- Strengths awareness: As reviewed in the previous chapter, knowing your talents and strengths is critical in order to practice and apply these assets.

- Be curious: Creative people are curious people who don't assume that they have all the answers. Learning and inquiring contributes to lifelong learning and well-being.

- Challenges: Whereas Flow requires a match between challenges and skills (and then challenges just exceeding skills), creativity requires novel approaches to new or unique challenges.

- Knowledge: It never hurts to learn more so that one is informed with greater perspectives and data in which to approach a challenge and make connections between various domains.

- Pay attention: As described with mindfulness (next), it is important to focus on the task at hand and become absorbed within it. Try to minimize distractions, reduce multitasking, and concentrate on the issue at hand.

- Teamwork: Working with others brings varying perspectives and ideas to the table as long as one is open to listening to and understanding them. Often in such settings additional ideas surface that leads to greater creative directions.

In a world in which people are under severe time pressure, creativity is less pervasive. The "go, go, go" mentality of 21st-century life does not provide an ideal context for creativity. Nor do emotions such as fear and anxiety. When joy and happiness are emotional states individuals are more likely to generate creative thinking, and more creative moments in life create a greater sense of well-being and happiness.

FLOW AND MINDFULNESS

Mindfulness is another way of describing awareness and being "awake" or conscious. Awareness and focus can be developed through mindfulness training (see "apps" by Jon Kabat-Zinn in the Google Play or iTunes store as well as his text for easy training support). Zinn describes mindfulness as paying attention in a special or particular way. This means paying attention with purpose, in the present moment, with nonjudgment. Researchers have demonstrated that mindfulness enhances Flow experiences. For example, sports psychologists are training athletes in mindfulness, which promotes concentration and optimal performance. When the athlete's focus moves to other thoughts, this serves as a distraction and interferes with the competition at hand. The key, whether for athletes, musicians, or hobbyists, is to bring the mind to the present. This is not always easy given the years of training many have had of anticipating future events. It is, however, critical to nurturing greater experiences in daily life.

In today's world, many people report that they are on automatic pilot: going through the motions of life without being aware of what and how things are being done. That, on top of a culture that celebrates multitasking, and many people are running on mindlessness rather than mindfulness. Mindlessness takes one away from the present moment as life's daily demands pile up. This leads to a sense of frustration and living life without feeling engaged in it.

In fact, many people are not in the present moment. They think about past events or future concerns that often include a healthy serving of self-criticism or internal judging.

Some may assume that mindfulness is for the wise man on the mountaintop. In fact, it is accessible for everyone and the benefits of mindfulness and meditation continue to be scientifically validated to reduce stress and increase concentration and substantiate its usefulness because, as in Flow, the brain slows down and stops processing information as immediately in its regular form. This is in part due to the frontal lobe of the brain (responsible for reasoning, planning, and self-consciousness) is quieted; the parietal lobe (where sensory information about the world is processed) slows down; the thalamus (where deeper sensory information is processed) has less information coming to it to address; and the reticular function of the brain (where incoming stimuli are processed and prepares the individual to be ready to quickly respond to threats in the environment) is less aroused.

A study at the Massachusetts General Hospital found that 40 minutes of daily meditation thickens parts of the cerebral cortex (responsible for attention

EXPERIENCE SAMPLING METHODOLOGY

In understanding the dynamics of well-being, it is important to use a methodology that can reflect such dynamics in everyday life situations. Experience sampling methodology (ESM) is a research procedure that examines what people think, feel, and do in their daily lives. This approach asks participants to provide self-reports in a systematic fashion, at random or specific times, which provides a snapshot of an individual's daily experiences.

Diary use or journaling has provided a means of examining the reflection of an individual's public and private life. These studies have given insight into the places and activities in which an individual may spend his or her time.

Today, researchers from a number of disciplines are taking another direction in evaluating the quality of life with insight into how certain contexts or situations affect individual experience and well-being. The shift has been necessary as researchers have found that instruments such as questionnaires, surveys, and interviews do not always provide an adequate reflection of daily lived experiences.

The recollection of events people provide may not reflect the truth of those events, but rather a narrative construction. There is also the issue of the "recency" effect with retrospective studies. It has been proven that an individual's recent experiences have a greater impact on recall than more distant experiences.

ESM is used as a way of surmounting the methodological limitations of other research procedures. Instead of traditional survey methods that rely on retrospective data or reconstruction by research participants, ESM collects immediate self-reports on the actions, thoughts, and feelings of an individual somewhat like a snapshot of one's daily life. This method is able to capture mood states in a generally unobtrusive manner while individuals go about their daily life activity. Therefore, the researcher has a valid and reliable procedure that can be used within the ecological contexts of people's daily experiences. Additionally, this methodology does not rely on a single assessment, but rather repeated measurements across a period of time. This repeated sampling of an individual's experience allows the collection of small events to be woven into a tapestry that allows for insight into a greater dynamic process.

In the past, pagers were used to alert the user up to eight times a day to stop what they were doing and complete a written survey of their actions, thoughts, and feelings at that time. Today, with smartphone technology, applications can be written that alert the user to complete a survey on the phone itself. The data is then uploaded (rather than manually entered, as with past methods) for immediate analysis. ESM harnesses technology to provide qualitative data that provide interesting insights into human behavior.

GROSS NATIONAL HAPPINESS INDEX

You may have heard the economic term GDP (gross domestic product) on television, the news, or your economics class. The GDP reflects the amount a country produces over a designated amount of time. The GDP is typically used to determine the economic well-being of a country with the idea that the larger the GDP, the larger the economy and hence the stronger the position one has in the world. The GDP is calculated by estimating all the output of a country (consumer, investment, and government spending) minus the amount of imports coming in.

In 1972, the former king of Bhutan (Jigme Singye Wangchuck) established the concept of a "National Happiness Index," which would instead measure the combined levels of citizen happiness to determine the health of a country. Hence, instead of measuring economic output, countries would measure such qualities as access to clean water and air, education, and health care. Qualities of environmental protection and longevity were included as well. Recently the prime minster of Bhutan stated, "The GNH is more focused on creating the right conditions that can lead people to fulfilling, and hopefully, happy lives" (Martin, 2016).

The four pillars upon which the Happiness Index is based include:

- Sustainable and equitable economic development
- Preservation and promotion of culture
- Environmental conservation
- Good governance

These pillars are further subdivided into nine domains such as education, health, and living standards.

Over the years, Canada, France, and Britain have added qualities of happiness to their GDP indices. So intrigued by this concept, the National Geographic Society with the leadership of Dan Buettner pursued a five-year study to find what makes a country happy and which are the happiest countries. In 2010, the National Geographic Society released their study and found that the happiest places in the world are Denmark, Singapore, Mexico, and California. What made these places so happy? The researchers found that the indicators for happiness within a country or state had to do with the quality of your community, workplace, and social life; financial life; home; and self. The better your social life, the more satisfied with your job, the greater financial security you had, and the increased safety you had for yourself and family created the greatest sense of happiness for the citizens of happy places. Today, the World Happiness Report made up of a consortium of universities and economic institutes publishes the happiest and saddest places on earth every year.

MIHALY CSIKSZENTMIHALYI AND FLOW THEORY

Mihaly Csikszentmihalyi, considered one of the fathers of positive psychology, was born in Hungary and came to the United States at age 22. He had a multifaceted career in journalism and art before studying human development. He coined the phrase "flow" as the matching of skills and challenges such that one becomes so absorbed in a task, one loses track of time. Through this research, he found that Flow experiences take place across cultures and reflect where people will report the greatest sense of well-being.

Csikszentmihalyi observed athletes and musicians in Flow states where the former referred to the state as "in the zone" and the latter as "rapture." People have Flow experiences across the world. Such experiences may emerge from a hobby, or a pursuit to be more talented or expert within a discipline, sport, crat, or profession.

Csikszentmihalyi uses playing tennis as an example of Flow. If you play with someone who is a novice (and you are fairly good), you eventually become bored because your skills are far higher than the challenge available to you on the court. If you play with a Wimbledon professional, you get anxious because your skills cannot match the big challenge you face. Ultimately, to find a Flow state you want to play with someone whose skills are well matched to yours or slightly higher so that there is a good balance between challenge and skills.

The conditions of Flow include:

- Goals are clear.
- Immediate feedback—an individual knows how well he or she is doing at any moment.
- Skills match challenges.
- Concentration is deep.
- Problems are forgotten.
- Control is possible—a feeling of mastery is gained.
- Self-consciousness disappears.
- The sense of time is altered—an individual either loses track of time or the activity is intrinsically rewarding—the experience is worth engaging in for its own sake.

Csikszentmihalyi also advocated the use of collecting data on people's everyday actions and emotions as "daily lived snapshots." He used ESM to capture the real-time feelings, thoughts, and experiences of individuals using pagers to notify people randomly throughout the day to stop what they were doing and complete a survey. This approached yielded data that proved to be more insightful than some surveys that asked people to think back to an experience in the past and report it in the present. Today, applications (apps) on smartphones can easily gather such lived data for researchers' studies. After leaving the University of Chicago, Csikszentmihalyi started the first doctoral program in Positive Psychology at Claremont Graduate University.

and sensory information processing). In another study by the University of California, San Francisco, teachers were taught meditation techniques to use for 30 minutes or less per day. These teachers had the equivalent mood improvement of those who only took anti-depressants.

After six to eight weeks of mindful meditation practice, individuals are better focused, are less anxious, are more creative, are more compassionate, remember things better, and have less stress, all without any pharmaceutical intervention.

Mindfulness studies, as reviewed in this text, continue to demonstrate the elasticity of the brain and how meditation and daily awareness of one's actions can improve well-being.

In today's world most people find their mind filled with a focus on past events or hoped for future events. This is often referred to as the Monkey Brain in which our brain jumps from topic to topic, thought to thought taking one away from being present to what exists in the moment.

Beginning meditators in fact have difficulty sitting still as their brain continues to monkey around creating distraction and perhaps anxiety and stress. The beginning meditator is asked to allow those thoughts to come into awareness and then to let them go.

After becoming more acquainted with mindfulness and practicing, individuals find that meditating clears the mind, provides an opportunity to reset, gain greater energy and clarity from life's daily demands, and improves overall a sense of contentment and happiness. Meditators must challenge themselves to use the skills that they learn to sit with regularity to gain the most benefit. They enter a Flow state in which there is intense focus and an experience of losing track of time. Moreover, meditators find that they can invoke a return to a sense of tranquility under duress by engaging in breathing exercises or useful visualizations.

Meditation is an inexpensive approach to a scientifically validated approach to increasing the quality of day-to-day life and provides an opportunity for Flow experience as icing on the cake.

PROMOTING FLOW IN DAILY LIFE

Individuals across cultures and backgrounds report Flow experiences. There are three universal conditions for an individual to enter a state of Flow. These include:

- Goals: Whether you are learning how to play an instrument, become a better goalie, or become a more sophisticated painter, there needs to exist a motivation to one's efforts. Ideally, this motivation comes from with you (you want to achieve a goal for the sake of achieving it rather than some external reward).

- Balance: If one's challenge is too great in comparison to where his or her skills are now, he or she experiences anxiety. The challenge and skills should be closely in balance. If the skills are too sophisticated for the challenge, boredom ensues.

- Feedback: Clear, immediate feedback is essential whether it comes from outside or from one's own assessment. For example, a computer programmer may see the creation of code and execution of a program take place while working; the musician may find improvement in the piece played; and the athlete may find greater endurance or strength.

From these three major conditions for Flow experiences, what follows are approaches to promoting more Flow in life:

- Set realistic goals.
- Focus on the task at hand rather than multitask or be distracted by interruptions.
- Those who have the confidence that a goal can be achieved through effort tend to find Flow more readily.
- Feedback of some sort is important for both improvement and maintenance of Flow. This feedback may be in the form of an individual assessment by someone or the feedback that is evident as one engages in the task more and more (progress, change, understanding, development, etc.).
- As skills are developed, move the challenge up a notch.

CHAPTER 4

Resilience

Resilience is often conceptualized as the ability to bounce back from adversity, but in fact, resilience is defined in a variety of ways in the psychological literature. It is a repertoire of thoughts and behaviors that reflect a rainbow of perspectives, starting with the absence of pathology at one end through the resumption of healthy functioning at the center to the pot of gold—flourishing under adversity—at the other end of the spectrum. As this metaphor suggests, many positive psychology concepts aren't discrete. They overlap and interact with many others. Researchers and theorists attempt to break them down because isolating and investigating individual constructs allows positive psychologists to examine the way that different aspects of human functioning and the environment contribute to a the more holistic goal of a life well lived.

This is a particularly useful approach for resilience because, unlike a single emotion such as joy or happiness, resilience is a complex construct made up of multiple elements that need definitions of their own. A good definition is important because it determines what people measure. Agreement about definitions is essential to expanding our understanding and scholarship in the field. It doesn't help much if we all agree resilience is important but we're all measuring something different.

In this chapter, we will:

1. Explore definitions of resilience and some of the differing perspectives on the structure and process of resilience
2. Identify some of the key constructs in resilience: self-efficacy; cognitive appraisal and reframing; and emotional resilience and related constructs such as grit, persistence, and hardiness
3. Examine some of the ways that understanding resilience has been used in prevention and recovery from the impact of trauma, stress, and adversity

WHAT DOES IT MEAN TO BE RESILIENT?

In the 1950s, Timex introduced an advertising campaign with the now-iconic tagline "It takes a licking and keeps on ticking." This seems like a perfect example of what it means to be resilient. But consider the following stories:

The Little Engine That Could

A train full of toys broke down on the side of a steep hill. When larger engines wouldn't help, a small blue engine came forward, willing to take on the challenge of hauling the broken-down train over the hill. The little blue engine puffed his way into immortality by chugging out the words "I think I can . . ." over and over with each puff of smoke as he strained to haul the train of toys up the steep incline to the waiting children on the other side. Slowly at first, then faster and faster as he picked up speed, "I think I can, I think I can" turned into a triumphant "I thought I could, I thought I could" as the little engine reached the summit and jubilantly raced down the mountain, greeted by the cheering children below.

The Two Wolves

A Cherokee elder was teaching his grandchildren about the ways of the world. "Inside me," he said, "are two great wolves that fight all the time. One is made of fear, anger, regret, arrogance, pride and self-pity. The other is made of joy, love, hope, peace, humility, truth, honesty and friendship. These two wolves are battling inside you as well."

The children were silent, until one of them asked, "But grandfather, which one will win?"

The wise grandfather replied, "The one you feed."

The Carrot, Egg, and Cup of Coffee

A young woman went to visit her mother. Her life was full of challenges and troubles. She was tired and wanted to give up. Her mother went to the stove and put on three pots of water. In one pot she placed a carrot, in the second an egg, and in the third, some ground coffee. She set the pots to boil for 10 minutes and then set the carrot, the egg, and a cup of coffee on the table.

The woman then said to her daughter, "Each of these things has faced the same hardship of boiling water. Yet each has reacted differently. The carrot has become soft; the egg has become hard. But the coffee has changed the water. The very heat that caused the carrot to soften and lose its strength and the egg to become inflexible has released the fragrance and flavor of the coffee, becoming something better." So the woman asked her daughter, "Which are you?"

DEFINING RESILIENCE

From the Timex ad to the aforementioned folk stories, each describes something that we would call resilience, but each seems vastly different from one another. The straightforward Timex commercial tells us that being tough enough to survive being beaten up and "keep on ticking" is evidence of a successful outcome. *The Little Engine That Could* demonstrates perseverance and self-efficacy. The Cherokee grandfather is talking about self-regulation and choice. The mother is demonstrating the benefits of adaptability under stress.

These examples suggest that human resilience is considerably more complex than just keeping on ticking. Human resilience can include persistence, intentional effort, choice, perception, and adaptability. This complexity illustrates some of the differences in focus and perspectives among researchers and theorists as they attempt to measure and define the construct of "resilience." There is little debate as to the existence of such constructs. The dissension centers on whose theories and which definitions make the most difference in human functioning in order to set the standard.

BORN THIS WAY

Resilience was initially considered a personality trait. Researchers now agree that resilience is a complex and dynamic process describing someone who has the ability to achieve a good outcome in spite of significant adversity or threats that pose risks to normal development and adaptation. But consider. Once someone has been identified as resilient, two important judgments have been made. The first is that someone meets an expectation for positive adaptation and second, that the person has experienced something that can be defined as a significant threat. What is positive adaptation? Compared to what or whom? What constitutes a significant threat? Thus the construct of resilience implies certain assumptions about what constitutes both a good outcome and adversity. "Adversity" and "good" outcome are subjective components that must be clearly distinguished, operationalized, and measured to make sense out of what it means when someone is said to be resilient.

RISK

According to Ann Masten, one of the pioneers in resilience research, risk of adversity must be apparent, as people aren't considered to be resilient if they do not undergo some type of threat or trauma that could potentially disrupt the normal maturational process.

It is important to note that when researchers talk about risk, they are speaking of probabilities, not certainties. When looking at resilience, researchers examine a number of social, physical, and psychological risk factors that are related to poor outcomes across multiple domains, from psychosocial to mental and physical well-being. Defining risks presents challenges because of the wide range and nature of potential threats. Normal development and functioning can be disrupted by any number of things. This includes specific experiences such as acute trauma and chronic adversities as well as well-documented "risk factors" that predict later challenges in life, such as low birth weight.

Many risk factors have been studied enough to establish predictions of the specific problems or difficulties that are likely to result. For example, research has demonstrated that children who are physically, emotionally, or sexually abused have a higher risk of several types of problems in adolescence and adulthood, including violence, criminal behaviors, substance abuse, and mental disorders such as depression and anxiety.

Risk factors can have a cumulative effect over time and there is also the likelihood that more than one risk factor may occur at the same time. For example, children who have parents who are mentally ill also are more likely to live with limited financial resources and poor parental involvement and supervision. Longitudinal research studies, where investigators have been able to focus on childhood development in different populations over long periods of time, have identified many of these interrelated risk factors.

The goal of many such studies has been twofold. The first draws on psychology's traditional medical model and focuses on interventions to repair damage. The second embraces a positive psychology approach to create situations that promote resiliency. Research findings have helped psychologists and other professionals better understand the factors that contribute to detrimental outcomes in order to more readily identify problems and offer interventions in existing situations. Positive psychologists seek to identify common characteristics among those who manage to function well despite individual histories of adversity. The goal of positive psychology is to stop problems before they happen by helping people to cultivate skills and to create environments that will allow the promotion of resiliency. Research from positive psychology has shown that the combination of skill development and environmental change can better-equip individuals to handle life's serious setbacks.

POSITIVE OUTCOMES

Identifying risk of adversity is only half the equation. The second judgment inherent in defining and measuring resilience is establishing the outcome and specifying a clear and measurable interpretation of what it means to achieve "good" functioning. The approach to defining the outcome varies with the orientation of the investigators. Many researchers have relied on developmental and life span theories. These outline appropriate development tasks, competencies, and age-related expectations that researchers use to establish appropriate measures of successful functioning. Others use social and cultural expectations. These approaches define resilience as an adaptation that returns an individual to expected norms or baseline functioning. Good outcomes have also been defined in relation to pathology and mental illness. This approach views a positive outcome as the *lack* of problems, such as psychological or behavioral symptoms and impairment, rather than social, academic, or career achievements.

In 1962, Lois Murphy published the results of a study on coping and mastery in children. She wrote that living systems of all kinds can adapt in two ways: adapting to the environment or maintaining internal integration. Her work summarizes another debate in resilience research—whether positive adaptation is based solely on external measures, such as lack of delinquency, or whether positive outcomes need to include experience intrinsic to the individual, such as psychological well-being or lack of distress.

Compared to Murphy, Masten and Reed (2005) claimed the middle ground when they emphasized the capacity for successful adaptation. They distinguished among three types of resilient outcomes that we might think of as a "good, better, best" approach. These were: (1) good recovery from adversity and stress, (2) positive adaptation in spite of adverse circumstances, and (3) at-risk individuals with better than expected outcomes (A. Masten, 2001).

HISTORY OF RESILIENCE STUDY

Overcoming challenges and beating the odds are common themes throughout human history. The reluctant hero is at the center of Joseph Campbell's universal myth, commonly called "the hero's journey," and fairy tales and fables are replete with heroes overcoming great challenges. From Darwin's natural selection to Freud's interest in the ego overcoming adversity, how humans have adapted to their environment has been a subject of great interest. The development of psychology as a science reflects those concerns.

Early work on human resilience, however, was focused on the problems that resulted from exposure to dangerous environments and personal trauma rather than heroic journeys. However, researchers looking at maladaptive behaviors of severely disordered patients noticed an atypical and surprising subset that demonstrated adaptive behaviors and suffered much less severe courses of illness. This group was also reported to have various social competencies prior to the manifestation of their illness. These phenomena sparked researchers' interests for further study. In the 1960s, research into the roots of mental illness led to the study of childhood development, particularly focused on those who professionals believed would face problems as they matured due to their environments or genetic heritage. Investigators followed children of schizophrenics and children with premature births and environmental hazards, such as poverty and abuse. Once again, they noticed unexpected outcome differentials.

The systematic study of resilience began when clinical psychologists Norman Garmezy and Michael Rutter began looking for linkages between indications of good adaptation among children who succeeded in spite of their genetic or environmental risk among the offspring of schizophrenic parents. They noticed that some of the children who were expected to do poorly actually did well. This was an important discovery. Preoccupations with problems of trauma, parental mental illness, abuse, and other risk factors had inadvertently created biased assumptions among researchers that a poor outcome was inevitable for those who suffered from a variety of risk factors. The psychiatrists and psychologists who brought attention to the significance of children doing well sparked interest in researching this new and promising area called resilience. It also opened the door to studying people of all ages, not just children, who did well in the face of adversity.

Researchers began to pick apart the factors that contributed to the dynamic process of positive adaptation that allowed people to do well in face of risk. The idea of people doing well under terrible conditions was so contrary to expectations that the children from early studies who did well under adversity were sometimes referred to as "invulnerable" or "invincible," reflecting perceptions that anyone who could survive and thrive under threat or adversity was remarkable. An early article in a publication from the American Psychological Association referred to these children as "the invulnerables" as if they had extraordinary strength or inner capabilities. Masten notes that viewing resilience as a "super-trait" still persists, even in scholarly work. She cites a 1995 book review published in *Contemporary Psychology* on resilience in inner-city children. The name of the review was "Superkids of the Ghetto" (A. Masten & Reed, 2005).

Working concurrently, but separately from Rutter and Garmezy, another pioneer in resilience studies, Emmy Werner, began to question the usefulness of the whole concept of risk. Werner was concerned that using a term that originated in 19th-century England to insure against lost or damaged cargo on long sea voyages was now being applied to children. She felt the semantic influence might diminish the understanding of human experience.

Risk factors are not certainties. Children and teens from homes where parents were alcoholics, had little education, and a very low standard of living were all expected to do poorly but this wasn't the case. Werner and others began to conceptualize resilience as an adaptive process that changes over time, rather than a trait. People who are resilient, they reasoned, are able to successfully adapt to pressures and do so more or less successfully as the situations around them change. Young people, for example, may not have those same internal and external resources that they do later in life and sometimes vice versa. Werner believed that a single point in time was not indicative of resiliency across the life span and that the changes tend to be in a positive direction (Brendtro, 2012).

THE KAUAI LONGITUDINAL STUDY

Werner was the principal investigator on one of the few studies that have looked at resilience over a long period of human development. The well-known Kauai Longitudinal Study followed subjects from infancy into adulthood. The goal was twofold. The first was to explore the effect of a range of psychosocial and biological risk factors. The second was quite innovative. It was to identify protective influences and characteristics. The study participants were 698 children born in 1955 on the island of Kauai in Hawaii. The children were monitored at ages 1, 2, 10, 18, 32, and 40, believed to be significant growth-related markers. In developmental and life span theories, these ages are considered critical junctures in the development of fundamental human social and cognitive skills, such as autonomy, trust, productivity, intimacy, and generativity. The successful completion of each developmental hurdle defines positive development.

According to Werner, 30 percent of the participants in the study grew up under various forms of adversity, such as poverty, chronic family discord, or parents with less than eight years of formal education. While two-thirds of the "at-risk" population experienced academic or behavior problems by age 18, the remaining third did not. They were successful at home and competent in social life. They also set and achieved realistic education and career goals and expectations. They were employed and their achievements were equal or in some cases better than peers who had grown up in more economically and socially advantageous environments. Many of the participants that had experienced problems as teens had also "bounced back" as adults, overcoming earlier problems. In other words, the results of the Kauai study defied prevailing myths that adversity breaks people, that "at-risk" environments predestined people to failure, and that once a loser always a loser.

Decades of research, including the influential Kauai study, have upended the deficit models of development for children growing up in situations at high risk of adversity and trauma. Masten argues that the most extraordinary thing about resilience is, in fact, its ordinariness. Far from being a superhero skill, the ability to achieve positive outcomes in spite of high-risk and traumatic circumstances is part of our basic human adaptational system. These findings have been instrumental in ushering in a more positive perspective of human development and adaptability.

ASSETS

The results from the Kauai study, among many others, have isolated factors, or assets, that contribute to resiliency. Assets are the things that make a difference in one's ability to overcome adversity. Researchers break down identified assets into protective factors and protective processes in order to operationalize and examine the individual contributors to resilience.

Assets are the opposite of risk factors. Assets are measurable factors in an individual or the environment that predict better outcomes. Although the word "resources" is often used interchangeably with assets, resources generally refer to the more global factors, such as human, social, and material capital that contribute to successful adaptation. Protective factors are the characteristics and circumstances that have protective ability during high-risk situations. If a teacher mentors a child with a troubled home life, for example, this social support is considered a protective factor. Protective processes are the theoretical frameworks that describe how the protective factors work when healthy development is threatened. The social support supplied by the mentor, for example, may impact self-esteem, physical safety, and health, or the ability to develop competencies.

RESILIENCE MODELS

There are two major approaches behind the models of resilience: variable-focused and person-focused. Variable-focused methodologies look at the associations among individual characteristics, environmental factors, and life experiences, such as abuse or natural disasters, in order to determine what facilitates positive adjustment in the face of high risk or severe difficulties. A variable-approach method is used to isolate and test protective factors that benefit specific types of adaptation in discreet moments of time. A person-focused approach, conversely, looks at individuals over longer periods of development to compare the attributes and circumstances around those who exhibit resilience with others who experienced similar threats to healthy development and did not fare as well. This approach assumes a person to be adaptive over time and doing well in multiple domains, rather than isolating a narrow achievement set as is more common in variable-focused models. Person-focused models are applied to life span development studies across diverse individuals and cultures. We will discuss each of these models in greater detail.

Variable-Focused Models

Variable-focused approaches construct models as trying to capture how risks, such as poverty or trauma, and assets, such as intelligence or parental support, impact a person's development. There are different ways of conceptualizing the potential impact of risk and each approach raises issues about definitions and measurement. For example, we can define risks as having a direct impact, where each risk has its own effect on a person, independent of other factors. A direct risk, such as premature birth, has a negative impact if it occurs but no impact if it does not. Another way to evaluate risk is cumulatively recognizing that each additional risk may also influence the magnitude of impact of an existing risk. For example, taking a calculus exam can be challenging. There are many potential risk factors, such as poor training, not enough sleep, a case of the flu, and a diet of beer and pizza. Any of these factors would increase the risk that we might not do well on the exam. The more risks we face, such as a combination of no sleep and poor training, the more likely we will be to have a poor outcome. The effect of the risks adds up. Some risk factors, however, interact and increase the total impact beyond simple addition. For example, someone who both smokes and is obese has a higher risk of cardiovascular disease than if you added together the risk factors for cardiovascular disease from smoking or obesity individually. This occurs when the combination of things, in this case smoking and obesity, interacts in ways that amplify the impact of each, significantly increasing physical vulnerability to disease.

Risk factors also interact with strengths. In the calculus exam example, if we are especially talented mathematically, have an especially strong immune system, or have developed coping skills that allow us to stay calm under pressure, those assets may function to counteract the risks and increase our chances of passing the exam.

Obviously, real life presents people with a variety of much more serious and challenging situations than taking a calculus exam with no sleep. Multiple risk factors are described by risk gradient models, where the more challenges a person faces, the greater the likelihood of problems in life. An asset gradient similarly expresses how our strengths and skills can offset or compensate for the impact of high risks and decrease the probability of negative outcomes. Until positive psychology, however, the work on resilience focused on the negative end of the risk/asset gradient. Many researchers now believe that significant numbers of the low-risk children had unmeasured strengths.

Interactive models try to capture the complex and messy nature of human experience. They view the risks and assets as moderating the effects on outcome. In these models, risks and assets are conceptualized as vulnerabilities and protective influences that interact and influence how people face and overcome challenges. Researchers studying posttraumatic stress disorder (PTSD), for example, have examined a number of factors to better understand what combinations increase someone's vulnerability to trauma as well as what characteristics and strengths provide protective factors. Investigators hope that these types of research studies will isolate assets that can be strengthened through awareness, education, and practice to shift the balance in favor of providing more resilience against trauma.

Some believe that variable-focused models are of limited value in real-world situations because they focus on narrower definitions and dimensions of a positive outcome. Resilience, many researchers argue, is a lifelong adaptive pattern that doesn't always look the same. Therefore, variable-focused models tend to miss the holistic patterns and multidimensionality of resilience over the life span.

Person-Focused Models

Resilience studies from a person-centered perspective have taken three main routes: (1) case study research in which results from a detailed study of a single individual inspires larger research initiatives, (2) identifying and studying a resilient subgroup among high-risk individuals, and (3) developing full diagnostic models that classify children on a matrix of adversity versus competence to compare risk and asset factors in the outcome of different individuals. The person-focused models have produced notable results in the variation among the differences in assets of human and social capital that distinguish the lives of resilient versus maladaptive children from high-adversity environments.

In the Kauai study, approximately one-third of the children were identified as being resilient. The resilient children had many differences from an early age when compared to their peers in the high-risk group. In spite of shared adversity, resilient children had more outgoing personalities, received better care from parents or other adults, had higher self-esteem and intellectual functioning, and were more connected to social support. Interestingly, by the time these children reached their thirties, approximately 80 percent of the children in the study had "bounced back," able to overcome the adversity in their lives—even those who had developed significant life problems in childhood and adolescence. Common among their stories, however, was recollection of social support, whether a parent, relative, teacher, or other mentor, as being central to their success in overcoming early life challenges.

The full diagnostic model, designed to take advantage of both the person-focused and variable-focused analyses, locates people on a matrix between adversity level on one axis and competence, or successful adaptation, on the other dimension. Each section represents someone who has experienced some level of adversity and demonstrates their ability to adapt defined by competence. This model was used by Masten and her colleagues (1999) in the Project Competence study of resilience. They classified a group of urban students based on three areas: academic achievement, ability, and willingness to follow rules, and social skills with peers. Students who were rated high in all three were rated as *high competency*. Students were also rated for lifetime adversity by evaluating negative experiences beyond their control, such as home violence, severe health issues, or loss of a family member. Consistent with other studies, Masten and her colleagues found that upper left cell (*low adversity, low competency*) was nearly empty. They compared the students in the other quadrants and found that many students who were categorized as resilient shared the same lifetime adversity profiles as those who were considered maladaptive (as defined by negative outcomes). The resilient students, however, shared many of the assets with the students who were competent but not challenged by life's adversities. The shared assets were both personal, such as intelligence and an outgoing personality style, and social, such as community connections and effective parenting. This study indicated that there were common factors that were essential to normal development that also had protective qualities when an individual faced adversity.

Pathway Models

The full diagnostic models have led to an interest in pathway models that track behavioral patterns and experience over time. This approach emphasizes resilience as a process and maps experience and outcome longitudinally. It also draws on advances across multiple disciplines, both within psychology and from other fields, that emphasize the study of humans and their behavior as complex, dynamic systems.

Advances from the fields of neuroscience, molecular biology, and across the social sciences have contributed to our understanding of both adversity and resilience as processes that act over time. The American Academy of Pediatrics (AAP), for example, proposed using an ecobiodevelopmental framework (EBD) to better understand the impacts of adversity across multiple domains. Their intention was to examine the damaging effects of "toxic stress" as a by-product of adversity on brain development and potential origins of adult disease. They define toxic stress as extreme or chronic activation of the stress response systems without the safeguard from assets known to promote psychological resilience, such as social support.

Stress early in life has been repeatedly shown to interrupt positive development and undermine the development of adaptability and the coping skills necessary for handling difficulties later in life. Early life stressors often result in maladaptive coping patterns and unhealthy lifestyles. Stable and responsive social connections, for example, create a sense of safety that alleviates physiological stress. The EBD approach reinforces the emphasis on the absence of protective factors rather than the exposure to risk that predicts poor outcomes. The AAP argues that toxic stress creates biological memory increasing health risk and disease later in life. Childhood toxic stress has been linked to maladaptive behaviors that form an unhealthy lifestyle, such as drug abuse, poor food, and exercise choices, as well as perpetuating socioeconomic inequalities, such as lack of education, poor academic performance, economic hardships, and the resultant mental and physical problems such as depression, obesity, and cardiovascular disease.

PROTECTIVE FACTORS

There is a consistent set of individual and environmental elements that are reliably associated with good development in both normal and adverse conditions across many cultural contexts. While these elements were first identified in early studies, they have repeatedly emerged and been reaffirmed over nearly 40 years of resilience research.

The protective factors for psychosocial resilience have been broken down into three broad dimensions that exert influence over an individual's development and psychosocial functioning. These include personal characteristics, family, and social relationships, and the local environment such as community or workplace.

Individual

At the individual level, the most widely reported attributes consist of three domains: cognitive capabilities, such as effective problem solving, adaptability to stress, and critical thinking; self-beliefs, such as a positive sense of self-worth and self-efficacy; and social orientation, such as relationship skills and an outgoing nature.

Family

The qualities surrounding parenting and socioeconomic status are the most frequently reported family characteristics that act as protective factors to adversity. As you may surmise, many of the factors are interrelated. For example, a family with adequate financial and social resources may make many other factors, such as educational opportunities and good healthcare, more readily available. There are, however, many examples of parents without many socioeconomic resources who prioritize their children's education and moral development and provide a sense of security and belonging.

Local Environment

Beyond the family circle, the social, community, or work environments can play a critical role, providing structured and safe environments within which people can learn, connect, and grow. Community groups provide children with adult role models and adults with social support. Local organizations, churches, and gatherings can help support cultural values and spiritual growth.

As you look down the longer list of protective factors, you will see that many of them, such as self-efficacy, faith and meaning, humor, social connection, positive parenting, self-worth, and positive institutions, are areas that positive psychologists have isolated and explored individually and that we discuss in other areas of this book. As the resilience studies have shown, the assets that promote resiliency and the ability to bounce back from adversity in life are also those that promote happiness and what Seligman calls "a life well lived."

Protective factors:

- Individual characteristics

  - Good cognitive abilities, including problem-solving, critical thinking, and attentional skills
  - Positive social orientation; easy temperament in infancy; adaptable personality during development
  - Positive self-worth; belief in one's self-efficacy
  - Faith and a sense of meaning in life
  - Emotional and behavioral self-regulation
  - Talents valued by self and society
  - A sense of humor
  - General appeal or attractiveness to others

- Family and other relationships

  - Close relationships with caregiving adults
  - Authoritative parenting (high on warmth, structure/monitoring, and expectations)
  - Positive family climate; low conflict levels
  - Organized home environment
  - Postsecondary education of parents
  - Parents with the personal characteristics that benefit the child
  - Parents involved with child's education and life choices
  - Socioeconomic advantages
  - Close relationships to competent, prosocial, and supportive adults
  - Connections to prosocial and rule-abiding peers

- Environment

  - Effective schools and ties to prosocial organizations
  - Neighborhood with high "collective efficacy"
  - High levels of public safety
  - Good emergency social services
  - Good public health and health care availability
  - Positive work environments

(Adapted from A. Masten & Reed, 2005, p. 83)

RESILIENCE INTERVENTIONS

As Frederick Douglass (1817–1895) said, "It is easier to build strong children than to repair broken men."

This is the logic of the interventions and strategies for cultivating resilience in children and adults. Resilience comes in many forms, however, even in childhood. This complicates the efforts to design and test resilience interventions and programs.

Resilience training goals have targeted a number of issues across a wide range of phenomena. These include helping children avoid negative influences in high-risk environments and improving academic outcomes when families have intergenerational histories of school failure. Training goals also include building emotional resources, such as helping people regulate feelings when bullied or providing support to those experiencing traumatic disruption, such as acute loss of a loved one or a natural disaster.

Preventative initiatives, beginning with programs such as Head Start in the 1960s, have been, and continue to be, central to U.S. public policy. Programs have ranged from changing community ecologies such as housing to improving culture and attitudes in families, peer groups, and schools. Studies in resilience have demonstrated that there is no single cause of the many regrettable outcomes, from school failure and substance abuse to mental disorders. There are multiple pathways between risks and outcomes due to the range of differences among individuals even within a relatively narrow risk profile. In spite of this uncertainty, anecdotal experience continues to tell us that a person's level of resilience will determine who succeeds and who fails in life, whether it's recovering from illness or succeeding in business.

The research on resilience has led to a new approach to fostering resilience—focusing on cultivating positive goals starting with the individual. In developing programs and strategies for children and adults, psychologists now realize that promoting healthy development and competence, as suggested by Frederick Douglass, is as important, if not more important, than preventing problems because building strengths is not risk-dependent.

STRATEGIC APPROACHES TO BUILDING RESILIENCE

Strategic approaches to building resilience have taken three main forms: (1) risk-focused, (2) asset-focused, and (3) process-focused.

Risk-focused strategies are designed to reduce the likelihood of adversity and trauma in childhood. Risk-reducing programs include efforts to reduce homelessness, improve prenatal care, and provide community youth programs. The Oregon Health Authority examined the relationship between adverse experiences and wellness in their population and found that the cumulative effect of adverse experiences was significantly related to the number of mental and physical health issues suffered by their citizens, such as depression, suicidal thoughts, smoking, and overall health status. Since 2009, they have included surveys for adverse childhood experiences (ACEs) in the Oregon Behavioral Risk Factor Surveillance System (BRFSS) as promoted by the Centers for Disease Control and Prevention (CDC). The Oregon BRFSS now collects information to evaluative population risks and provide support services, such as home visiting, parenting classes, and life skills workshops, as well as therapeutic interventions.

Asset-focused strategies are approaches that increase access to socio-environmental resources and promote individual assets that support positive development. Some programs are designed to have direct effects, such as skill building and tutoring. The Boys and Girls Clubs of America, for example, offer a full range of programs offering a safe place to play, opportunities to form positive relationships with adults, and help with homework. Other approaches provide longer-term competence and knowledge. For example, the Search Institute and Capital One have collaborated to provide real-world financial literacy programs so that both children and parents can learn how to manage money, establish priorities and values, and develop responsible money management skills.

Process-focused strategies tend to be more comprehensive interventions that attempt to ameliorate problems by encouraging positive adaptation. Head Start and Early Head Start programs, administered by the U.S. Department of Health and Human Services, provide funds to organizations delivering Head Start services that support the social, emotional, physical, and mental growth of the child. The Devereux Center for Resilient Children is an organization that takes a holistic approach to fostering resilience, working with families, professionals, and organizations across the United States to develop systems that measure and promote social and emotional skills in children and adults. Researchers have found that impact of Early Head Start programs reaches beyond a children's cognitive and emotional development. Future generations also benefit. Parents who had been through the program as children reported engaging their own children with more emotional support, more language and learning activities such as reading, and spanked their children less.

RESILIENCE AND RECOVERY

Most people experience at least one life-threatening, violent, or traumatic event in their life. People cope differently. Some suffer acutely and never recover. Some seem to recover more quickly and then begin to have later difficulties, such as health or relationship problems. Others manage the disruption of loss or trauma without negatively impacting their close relationships, health, careers, or general functioning. Some researchers in the field make a distinction between *recovery* trajectories, in which a person works through a period of recovery to get back to healthy functioning, and *resilience* trajectories, in which an individual maintains healthy psychological and physical functioning. There are a number of distinct dimensions that researchers identify as potential contributors to both recovery and resilience trajectories.

COGNITIVE RESILIENCE

Resilience brings together topics from across the field of positive psychology. The core constructs that contribute to resilience don't just offset adversity but are critical parts of normal development and positive growth. The following sections explore several constructs considered to fall predominantly under the umbrella of cognitive resilience. These include self-efficacy, active and avoidant coping styles, cognitive reappraisal, benefit-finding, hardiness, per-severance, grit, self-enhancement, and repressive coping.

Self-Efficacy

The story of the "Little Engine That Could" from the beginning of the chapter describes important elements of resilience: self-efficacy and perseverance.

Self-efficacy is our belief in our ability to act and to produce positive results. Self-efficacy theory was introduced by Albert Bandura in 1977. The theory states that our perceptions of our self-efficacy have a direct effect on two very important things: our motivations to take action and our goals. Our goals are a reflection of what we believe we can accomplish because we predict the likelihood of our success. Therefore, self-efficacy influences how high, or low, we set our goals and aspirations. Our motivation to achieve those goals is determined by whether or not we believe we can succeed in reaching them.

Self-efficacy is not a personality trait nor is it trait-like. It is our belief in our ability to focus all our resources—skills, talents, attention, and any other available assets—to achieve a desired goal in the context of particular circumstances.

Self-efficacy comes from social cognitive theory. Social cognitive theory says that we are active participants in our lives, not passive bystanders. We have the ability to integrate and regulate our thoughts, feelings, motivation, and behavior. Social cognitive theory has four main premises.

1. We construct mental models of how the world works that we develop through observation of others and ourselves.

2. We interact with the world around us in a mutually influential way. The environment impacts us and we, in turn, act on the environment and make changes in it.

3. We exist in a social world, developing perceptions of others and ourselves in the context of social situations. Our sense of self is, therefore, developed through our interaction with others and is constantly changing.

4. We have the ability to self-regulate and make choices as we pursue our goals. As humans have the ability to project and plan, we develop assumptions and expectations about the future made up of our beliefs about the world, our beliefs about our past experiences and ourselves.

Self-efficacy is the "can do" attitude that reflects a sense of control over one's environment and, like the Little Engine in the story, creates a sense of optimism about what we can accomplish. Self-efficacy changes how people approach adversity. People with high levels of self-efficacy describe problems as challenges and experience less negative emotion and stress over life's demands.

Higher self-efficacy beliefs make the world seem more predictable, increasing both our feelings of safety and our willingness to take on risks. This makes us feel more able to meet challenges as they occur. It also enables our ability to form healthier relationships and enhances our willingness to seek out and undertake new opportunities.

**CASE STUDY: POSTTRAUMATIC GROWTH
AFTER HURRICANE KATRINA**

Hurricane Katrina (2005) was the deadliest hurricane to hit the United States in over seven decades. This natural disaster is often compared to the relief effort of the 9/11 terrorist attacks. Both were mentally, emotionally, and fiscally devastating to individuals and the United States as a nation. The efforts for 9/11, however, were more decisive, organized, and expedient than the effort for the Gulf Coast, in spite of the magnitude of damage left behind by Hurricane Katrina.

Marc Giudici PhD, NCC, was a first responder and actively involved in the massive recovery effort of Hurricane Katrina on the Mississippi Gulf Coast. He provided mental health services and, thanks to an earlier career, some construction consultation for the survivors of Hurricane Katrina—a handy combination of skills given the devastation.

The storm destroyed over 90,000 square miles, roughly the size of the entire UK. Thousands of residents from the Mississippi Gulf Coast were displaced by the storm, creating the largest population of internally displaced persons in the history of the United States. At one point, every state in the United States became a temporary home for Hurricane Katrina survivors.

For many of the survivors, the initial experience of living through Hurricane Katrina was filled with grief, fear, anxiety, and frustration. For some, it involved the loss or displacement of everything they held dear: their family, friends, community, culture, worldly possessions, and careers. Many survivors even lacked basic necessities, such as food, water, and electricity. With this destruction went personal identities. For many, it severely challenged their faith and spiritual foundations as people tried to imagine what life was going to be like after Katrina.

While media coverage is often positive, brining attention to social problems and people in need, this was not the case for the Mississippi Gulf Coast after Katrina. The initial emergency response was compromised by media coverage that focused on New Orleans at the expense of the rest of those in need. Inaccurate reporting molded the public's awareness of Hurricane Katrina so much so that Katrina became synonymous with the recovery effort and political missteps that occurred in New Orleans alone. This diverted the attention and much-needed resources away from the recovery efforts of thousands along other areas of the Gulf.

The initial relief response to Katrina was impressive. Many selfless individuals flocked to the Gulf, driven to provide comfort and aid to those affected. When the news coverage pulled out, however, many volunteer relief workers disappeared as well. The nonprofits that remained working in the region were sorely understaffed.

In traditional emergency response situations, the first teams' job is triage of the damage. Most first responders to Katrina came from a traditional

CASE STUDY (Continued)

medical model; therefore, assessments were done with a pathology or deficit focus. Giudici's work, however, was grounded in positive psychology. From triage onward, he focused on a strengths-based model, knowing that fostering individual strengths and assets would promote the resiliency that was essential to leading a productive life after such devastating trauma.

The development of positive characteristics in the face of trauma, such as identifying specific achievements and evidence of resilience and altruism, helps survivors manage with their psychological struggles. Giudici made multiple trips to the Gulf during this period, developing meaningful relationships with many of the survivors. In doing so, he saw firsthand the tremendous psychological growth of those who embraced meaning, faith, and hope on their path to recovery.

Giudici interviewed many survivors of Hurricane Katrina on the Mississippi Gulf Coast exploring the impact of a strengths-based approach to recovery. The respondents who had made the most positive recoveries reported that, post-Katrina, they had a renewed sense of meaning and purpose in their lives. Survivors who were able to shift their focus from loss and disadvantage to how they could contribute to others not only gained a more meaningful sense of existence but also had a much faster recovery. Embracing strengths and contributing to community kept the survivors from becoming stuck in victim mode, focusing on their problems and loss.

The survivors who demonstrated the highest measures of posttraumatic growth felt a new and deeper sense of purpose to their existence. They exhibited a strengths-based direction and were able to find meaning in the experience of surviving Hurricane Katrina. Some survivors said, "We can be better people because of our trauma." Others reported that finding meaning and working toward that goal stopped the downward spiral of emotions that would impede their recovery. Those who exhibited growth after trauma reported several benefits: they felt closer to loved ones, had developed more faith in their abilities to rebuild their lives, had become more spiritual and found deeper meaning and purpose in their lives, and, most powerfully, they had discovered an inner strength they didn't know they possessed.

Giudici reported that posttraumatic growth was accompanied by gratitude for newly built lives. Although people were nostalgic and had happy memories of life before the storm, they had settled into their new lives with a new awareness. While everyone vividly remembered the fear and challenges following Hurricane Katrina, a strengths-based recovery program had enabled them to transform that intense negative experience into a new appreciation of the importance of community, family, faith, and their own abilities, giving them a more powerful sense of purpose.

People lacking in self-efficacy tend to view obstacles as insurmountable and are more prone to psychological disorders such as anxiety and depression. Low self-efficacy can undermine people's perceptions of their coping skills in a number of domains. Self-efficacy beliefs have been shown to play a role in a number of health behaviors, such as smoking-cessation relapse, eating and weight control, pain management, success of recovery from heart attacks, and adherence to other health programs.

Self-efficacy beliefs impact our perception, decision making, and judgment. Our self-efficacy beliefs can determine whether we view challenges as opportunities or risks. People with positive self-efficacy beliefs are more likely to take on, rather than avoid, risks, viewing them as having potential for success. People with low self-efficacy beliefs have a tendency to avoid taking chances for fear of potential costs or failure. Success, as we know, often requires taking a risk. The more risks we are willing to take, the more likely we will experience success. Past experiences contribute to our beliefs. Successful actions from the past and how we interpret failure enhance our beliefs about our ability to conquer challenges in the future.

Coping Styles

When things don't go well, we have to cope. Coping styles are the behaviors, emotions, or thoughts that emerge in response to stressful events and determine our resultant physical and psychological functioning. These styles can be categorized as either avoidant coping or active coping (also called problem-focused coping). People who demonstrate resilience have hardiness qualities and strong efficacy beliefs and do not shy away from problems. They cope by actively finding solutions. Successful active coping increases our resilience. Every time we succeed, no matter how small the victory, it contributes to the upward spiral of psychological growth proposed by psychologist Barbara Fredrickson and gives us more confidence in our ability to overcome adversity. In contrast, avoidant coping, such as denying problems or refusing to think about them, has been shown to contribute to slower recovery from both emotional trauma and physical illness, and is associated with greater psychological distress.

Cognitive Reappraisal

One of the ways that self-efficacy influences resilience is through the ability to see adversity in more positive light. Cognitive reappraisal describes the mental process of shifting perceptions from threat to challenge. In other words, it's all in how you think about it. As you read when we discussed optimism and explanatory style, people differ in how they approach events and the meanings they attribute to them. Some people tend to see the glass half full rather than half empty. People with high self-efficacy, like those with high optimism baselines, tend to look at past events in a more positive light, often consciously reframing, or changing, the meaning as they think about it. Past mistakes become learning opportunities, not signs of personal failure. As the graduation speaker at Harvard in 2013, Oprah Winfrey was fresh off the initial flop of the Oprah Winfrey Network. She advised the graduates to expect failure. She said, "There is no such thing as failure. . . . Failure is just life trying to move us in another direction" (Winfrey, 2013, May 31, para. 7)

Winfrey was advocating a key tool for developing self-efficacy and resilience, reframing difficulty or failure to give you new direction.

Benefit-Finding

Benefit-finding is a form of cognitive appraisal linked to gratitude and post-traumatic growth (see discussion later). Benefit-finding is the ability to find the positive aspects in negative situations. In some instances, benefit-finding is an active cognitive activity to lessen the stress surrounding a trauma. In a study from the University of Miami, investigators found that cognitive-behavioral therapy (CBT) that emphasized benefit-finding reduced serum cortisol for women in early stages of breast cancer. Other studies on women with breast cancer have told a more complicated story, suggesting that seeing the benefit from suffering from a severe disease doesn't always improve quality of life. Surprisingly, in a study by Helgeson, Reynolds, and Tomich (2006) at Carnegie Mellon, benefit-finding was associated with a worse quality of life and worse mental functioning. Tomich notes that are stages in the coping process and where someone is in this process may influence the impact of finding benefits. For example, evidence suggests some instances of benefit-finding related to greater distress early in the coping process. Finding benefits later in the coping process, however, may facilitate more meaningful changes to perceptions of well-being and quality of life. In a separate study, the investigators found that benefit-finding early in the cancer experience played a positive role in the quality of psychosocial adjustment in later years. Part of the complication is that assessment of benefits comes from self-report survey completed by participants. To improve on the quality of information gathered, Helgeson and Tomich have developed a Benefit Finding Scale for Breast Cancer to expand the dimensions of perceived benefits to better capture the dynamics of potential impact.

Hardiness

There are considerable conceptual similarities among the constructs that are proposed to buffer adversity and promote healthy functioning. The construct of hardiness, viewed as a personality trait, comprises interrelated sub-constructs of commitment, control, and challenge. Individuals who exhibit hardiness have the ability to appraise circumstances in a way that transforms them into positive, growth-promoting challenges rather than something overwhelming, frightening, or painful.

Hardiness protects wellness and promotes effective functioning in the face of stressful circumstances. Evidence suggests that hardiness can be enhanced through training. In research comparing hardiness training with relaxation/meditation training, investigators report that hardiness was a more effective

buffer against stress. Stressful events trigger arousal reactions. Stress can esca-
late if multiple events, concurrently or over time, are perceived as stressful.
When stress reactions are significant or chronic, they undermine health and
impair behavioral ineffectiveness. Signs of health breakdown or behavioral
ineffectiveness can include a decreased sense of social support or diminished
job performance and satisfaction. While physical exercise, meditation and
relaxation, and healthy lifestyle choices are helpful in decreasing stress reactions, they do not decrease the stressfulness of the circumstances. Hardiness,
however, functions as a transformational coping process, like cognitive reappraisal. Hardiness impacts cognitive processing. It operates "behind the
scenes" like self-efficacy and gives us a broader perspectives and enables proactive behaviors that decrease stressfulness.

Perseverance and Grit

Why does someone keep trying? Perseverance has been shown to be a contributing characteristic to resilience and hardiness. Angela Duckworth and
colleagues (2007) examined the elements that make someone keep pushing
to accomplish their goals when others might give up. Duckworth called this
quality "grit," and defined grit as perseverance combined with a passion for
long-term goals. Multiple studies indicate that grit accounted for more variation in success than personality differentials, whether in cadets' accomplishments at West Point or young children competing in the National Spelling
Bee. Grit is another way to conceptualize resilience. It drills down to get after
a singular quality of not giving up, which turns out to be a better predictor of
lifetime success than GPA, good looks, or physical health.

Self-Enhancement

Self-enhancement, an overly positive bias of self, is among the dimensions
associated with resilience. Arguments from social psychologists in the 1980s
claimed that an unrealistic view of one's limitations could be adaptive and promote well-being. Self-enhancers score high on self-esteem but they also score
high on narcissism scales and tend to elicit negative response from others.
Studies on individual differences on self-enhancing biases compared citizens
in the United States suffering from personal loss with Bosnian citizens in Sara-
jevo after the Balkan civil war. In both populations, self-enhancers received
ratings as being better adjusted. Similarly people with self-enhancing biases
near the World Trade Center on 9/11 appear to have adjusted more easily. An
overly positive bias of self has its downsides, however. In the 1970s, a self-
esteem moment swept through the U.S. educational system. It was founded on
the theory that self-esteem needed to be encouraged as it provided protection
against stress, improved academic performance, and kept children out of trouble. Not so, says psychologist Roy Baumeister, who argues that the evidence

LIFE STRATEGY: DELAYED GRATIFICATION AND WELL-BEING

The *marshmallow test* was developed in the 1960s at Stanford University in which Walter Mischel (2014), a professor of psychology, examined how people exert self-control. For this particular study, Mischel and his colleagues would bring a four-year-old into a room where a marshmallow was presented as a treat. The child was told that he or she could have the marshmallow now, or wait 15 minutes when the tester returned and, if the marshmallow wasn't eaten, have two marshmallows instead.

Mischel and his colleagues tested over 600 four-year-olds. About one-third of those children decided to eat the marshmallow immediately, and two-thirds resisted the temptation and waited for the tester to return in order to receive double the reward.

These children were tracked over the course of many years and what the researchers found surprised them: those children who delayed gratification in the test had better outcomes in life, including academic test scores, physical health, and more education. The researchers concluded that mastery over one's impulses and the ability to wait now to enjoy gratification later reflects an important life skill.

Mischel went on to describe his results as reflecting a hot and cool emotional system that humans have. The cool system is our cognitive or thinking domain (the prefrontal cortex that is the most evolved region of the brain) in which we consider actions, goals, and feelings in making an assessment. This system was activated in the children who resisted eating the marshmallow immediately. The hot system reflects more of our primitive brain structure, which tends to be quick and impulsive to triggers in the environment. The hot system was engaged with the children who immediately ate the marshmallow.

A follow-up test was conducted at the University of Washington with 59 of the participants who are now adults. Those participants who immediately ate the marshmallow at age four continued to have self-control challenges as adults. When brain activity was measured using functional MRIs, individuals with low self-control had different brain patterns than those with high self-control. Those who had greater self-control had greater activity in the pre-frontal cortex.

Consider the marshmallow test the next time you are tempted to buy something impulsively online. Instead, put the item in your checkout cart or write it down and then step away from the temptation for a few days. Has your cool system overridden the hot system and found that the item is not so critical to purchase after all?

on self-esteem as a stress buffer is mixed unless self-esteem is grounded in other elements of resilience, such as a sense of competence and self-efficacy (Baumeister, Campbell, Krueger, & Vohs, 2003). He also notes that there is no evidence that self-esteem improves things like academic performance. The relationship is the opposite: high academic performance positively impacts self-esteem.

Repressive Coping

In spite of some evidence from studies on emotional coping, resilience to trauma and loss has been reported by people who used repressive coping styles. While hardiness, benefit-finding, cognitive reappraisal, and self-enhancement are cognitive approaches, repressive coping is cognitive intention that is believed to operate at an emotional level. Suppressing emotions, while linked with elevated blood pressure levels in some studies, was shown by psychologists George Bonanno and colleagues (2004) to be an adaptive response to extremely adverse events, such as the death of a spouse, with no residual mental or physical health issues. Additional studies by Bonanno and colleagues suggested that successful adaptation depends on the ability to be flexible in the expression or repression of emotion as the situation demands, where repression becomes a form of control rather than denial.

EMOTIONAL RESILIENCE

Research has shown repeatedly that adversity negatively impacts us through the stress response. Stress triggers a chemical loop that can negatively impact our brains and our bodies in a number of ways, such as diminished short-term memory, less cognitive flexibility, and impaired learning. Stress changes how we interpret things, interrupts our sleep and digestion, and narrows our emotions. Chronic stress from continued experience of trauma and adversity can have lasting effects. The power of coping skills such as cognitive reappraisal is that in reframing stressors, the physical effects are changed. Consider the difference between interpreting a stressful event as positive or negative. Both increase heart rate and breathing. However the ability to reframe stressful events decreases negative physical and emotional impact. Where negative stress decreases cardiac output and ventricular contraction, once you experience a stressful situation as exciting, you shift your emotions to positive stress, which can heighten performance and attention. The next time you have a paper to write or a job interview, tell yourself you're excited by the opportunity rather than dreading the assignment for a few days. Believe it or not, it makes a difference.

Resilience draws on our emotional capacity to stay positive and forward looking. Barbara Fredrickson has devoted her career to showing how positive emotions provide the "fuel" for resilience. Early work by psychologist Alice Isen broke new ground in examining the experience and potential of positive emotions (Masten & Reed, 2005). Among her findings, Isen showed that when we experience positive emotions, we behave differently. We are more likely to help others and we are more flexible and creative in our thinking and problem solving. Fredrickson extended Isen's work into a new theoretical framework, called the broaden-and-build model that describes the cognitive and social effects of positive emotions. As with the work by Isen, Fredrickson found that experiencing positive emotions expanded people's thinking and problem solving, which she calls the thought-action repertoire. Fredrickson also discovered that experiencing positive emotions helped people's autonomic system, including vasoconstriction, blood pressure, and heart rate, allowing them to return to normal more quickly after experiencing negative emotions such as anxiety, anger, or fear.

In response to the trauma of 9/11 and the World Trade Center bombing, Fredrickson and her colleagues (2003) found that positive emotions were central to the coping mechanisms of those who emotionally recovered most quickly. The ability to feel gratitude for survival and for their relationships with loved ones, for example, allowed people to more effectively overcome the emotional devastation of the crisis. Fredrickson argued that the positive emotions also supported their physical recovery from the impact of stress by allowing the bodies to replenish resources. The cognitive broadening of positive emotions enabled more ability for cognitive reappraisal and finding new meaning in the terrible situation—key factors in the positive adaption of resilience.

Fredrickson and her colleague Thomas Joiner also found that the effect of positive emotions builds resources as well. They found that initial levels of positive emotions predicted increases in overall problem solving and creativity. The experience of creativity and broadened thought predicted further increase in positive emotions. Positive coping ability predicted positive emotions, which in turn predicted more effective coping strategies. As mentioned earlier, Fredrickson refers to the way that positive emotions continually create more positive emotions and cognitive benefits as the upward spiral of positive emotions—one that leads to increased resilience.

Positive emotions are one of the keys to well-being across the life span. It has been associated with measures of successful aging, regardless of income. The most robust predictor of people on the happy-well end of the health spectrum was the extent to which they were able to employ emotion-focused coping styles such as altruism and humor in everyday life. A well-known study of the autobiographies of 180 Catholic nuns showed that positive emotional content in their writings was related to the length of their lives some 60 years later. The MacArthur Foundation Study of Successful Aging reported that three components were important: staying healthy, engaging with life, and maintaining physical and cognitive functioning (Rowe & Kahn, 1998). The research by Fredrickson and others suggests that positive emotions may be one of the central factors in the adaptability required of aging—positive emotions predict better physical and mental health and cognitive flexibility. James H. Fowler and Nicholas Christakis studied the spread of emotions across social networks. Their findings reinforce the organic development of emotion by demonstrating that happy people attract more happy people, creating happiness nodes that influence mood for periods up to a year.

Thus it may be, as Fredrickson suggests, that happy people are happier because they have developed the social and emotional resources for living well no matter what life brings, not just because they "feel good."

Optimism

Optimism is an attributional style that allows us to explain events in ways that support our longer-term well-being and resilience. The ability to internalize positive events builds self-efficacy. The tendency to externalize negative events, thinking of them as being caused by other events or people, seeing them as temporary rather than permanent and context-specific rather than global, increases resiliency by fostering hope and supporting beliefs of change. Optimism is related to cognitive reappraisal. The ability to see the positive in the negative turns threats into challenges, increasing resilience and diminishing negative emotions. Intentional positivity, a cognitive action, translates into true emotional experiences. Optimism reduces perceptions of helplessness and motivates people to change. Optimism also improves our ability to form meaningful relationships, expanding our social networks and social support, all critical to resilience in times of adversity. Hope, optimism, and faith were associated with fewer symptoms of anxiety and depression after the World Trade Center attacks on 9/11. In a meta-analysis of 83 studies, researchers determined that optimism had a significant impact on physical health, including longevity, survival from disease, cardiovascular health, pain tolerance, and pregnancy outcomes. Like the larger construct of resiliency, our levels of optimism can be improved just like our physical health, by exercise and practice (see the sidebar on developing optimism).

Emotional Regulation

People often refer to resilience as emotional resilience. Emotional resilience, like resilience, is the ability of someone to respond to adversity without longer-term difficulties or problems. It is a popular way of distinguishing between physical resilience and psychological resilience. Our physical resilience is, in large part, dependent upon our genetic makeup; however, we can improve our ability to withstand physical stress through lifestyle choices, such as diet and exercise. Our emotional resilience also has a genetic component. Individual differences in shyness, sensitivity, or intelligence have been shown to have biological bases. However, vast amounts of psychological research have shown that emotional resilience can be developed and improved by observing thought processes and learning new ways of coping.

There are several of the same characteristics common to resilient people: emotional awareness, perseverance, control, optimism, social connection, perspective taking, humor, and self-regulation. Here is a brief explanation of each:

- Emotional awareness is the ability to evaluate how feelings occur and the thought processes around them.

- Perseverance is the tendency to stay action-focused and not give up. It is related to self-efficacy—we are more likely to persevere if we believe we can succeed—and an element in hardiness.

- Similarly, our sense of control, also related to self-efficacy, is our sense that we can control our surroundings and ourselves in some capacity.

- Optimism, as we've discussed, is the ability to see positive aspects of situations and recognize opportunities even when things look bleak.

- Social connection is the sense that we have a network and that we are not alone in dealing with challenges and adversity. Social support is critical to many of these attributes that give us more strength to move forward.

- Perspective taking is another way of saying cognitive flexibility, or the ability to step aside from our initial beliefs and look for new points of view and explanations.

- Humor plays a role in emotional resilience in two ways. It acts on our bodies physically by triggering our relaxation and reward centers and provides us with some emotional detachment that encourages perspective taking.

- Finally, emotionally resilient people have learned self-regulation and have effective coping skills to handle negative emotions.

Humor and Laughter

We often hear that laughter is the best medicine. While historically, the use of positive emotion in averse situations was considered inappropriate, disrespectful or, in the presence of psychologists, a sign of unhealthy denial, research by Fredrickson and others has shown that positive emotions, such as induced by humor, reduce the level of distress by alleviating negative emotions and increasing the sense of social connection. Some researchers have demonstrated that the positive affect of laughter is enough to create the sense of social bonding without any conversational or verbal exchange.

Neuroimaging evidence shows that our brains show the difference in the quality of our laughter. Duchenne laughter, which is our natural, unforced and involuntary laughter, and non-Duchenne laugher, which is context-driven and voluntary, have different neural pathways, triggering different physical reactions. The spontaneous physical response of Duchenne laughter is behind laughter's contagion effect between people. Natural laughter is an intensely social phenomenon and has the ability to alleviate negative emotions and stress through the release of endorphins similar to physical exercise or massage. The act of laughing or the experience of positive emotions neutralizes anger, tension, and fear by triggering the autonomic system similar to taking a deep breath. These actions strengthen our immune system, lower blood pressure, and reduce levels of several stress-related neurotransmitters, such as epinephrine and cortisol. It also releases endorphins from the brain's reward system, which not only makes us feel better but also lowers our experience of both physical and social pain.

Humor provides psychological coping mechanisms for dealing with stress and trauma. The physiological humor-induced shift in our bodies allows us to feel stronger and more hopeful. Humor also allows us to distance ourselves from negative events and emotions, providing detachment from the trauma and creating a respite from emotional turmoil. Former president of the Boston Psychoanalytic Society and Institute Maurice Vanderpol reported that the use of humor provided Holocaust survivors with a critical sense of perspective. Psychologist Viktor Frankl, himself a Holocaust survivor, stated, "What helps people survive awful circumstances is their ability to detach and get beyond themselves. This is seen in heroism and humor."

POSTTRAUMATIC GROWTH

Resilience, as we've said, is the ability to survive adverse conditions; bounce back from setbacks, hardship, or adversity; continue to live purposefully; and be psychologically healthy despite difficult circumstances. But what about people who don't just bounce back, but find new meaning and growth as a result of negative experiences? Posttraumatic growth has elements of transformation that distinguish it from the concepts of resilience or hardiness. In posttraumatic growth, people who have been through adversity and suffered traumatic events report experiencing benefits and feel they have received something of value that would not have occurred if they had not been challenged.

Researchers have called this phenomenon a number of things, among them, *stress-related growth, transformational coping, strength from adversity*, and *benefit-finding*. Richard Tedeschi and Lawrence Calhoun (2004) used the term *posttraumatic growth* to capture the contradictions of experiencing positive growth and new meaning among those who struggled to recover from trauma and adversity.

Frankl, reflecting on his experience in Nazi internment camps, wrote about meaning as fundamental to human adaptation in his 1946 book *Man's Search for Meaning*. Frankl argued that people have the ability to choose their response to life circumstances and that finding meaning is essential to resilience and recovery.

Ronnie Janoff-Bulman (1989) studied the cognitive and emotional processes that trauma survivors used to reconstruct their understanding of the world. Her contention is that victimization and trauma result in the disruption of three core schema: belief in one's invulnerability, seeing the world as having meaning, and positive view of one's self. She has proposed that posttraumatic growth occurs when people attempt to restore what she calls "shattered assumptions." By evaluating the traumatic event and their own survival, survivors are often able to identify new strengths and characteristics, developing more adaptive beliefs that allow them to be more resilient in the future. Janoff-Bulman proposed three processes that facilitate the rebuilding of self-schema, recognizing strengths in suffering, developing a deeper appreciation of life, and, by virtue of having survived, feeling more prepared to face future adversity.

Tedeschi and Calhoun similarly argue that posttraumatic growth follows an experience of significant impact where the survivors must reevaluate their

---

LIFE STRATEGY: RESILIENCY CAN BE LEARNED

As we live our lives, we face unexpected challenges. Resiliency allows one to adapt to difficult situations and in fact even thrive under extreme experiences coming out on the other side wiser and stronger. Resilient people expect things to turn out for the best. This is a coping mechanism that is healthier than the victim or blaming role that others may choose to take.

A resilient person has the ability to bounce back from adverse situations. It is the ability to pick yourself up and try again and again that gets us through life the best. For those less able to do so, a sense of hopelessness or helplessness may set in contributing to depression, anxiety, or feelings of being "stuck." Resiliency can be learned. Everyone has set points that exist most likely through a combination of strong nature and some nurture. We can move within a certain margin of those set points and learn and incorporate traits of resiliency into our lives that may help us better navigate setbacks. Moving the needle to the right of your set point can make a great difference. There are a number of factors that researchers have found that make one more resilient. You can move toward becoming more resilient by addressing the following questions in your daily life.

- Do you have good relationships in your life?
- Have you learned how to be a creative problem solver?
- Are you able to communicate well with others?
- Do you often feel you are in control of a situation rather than being out of control?
- Do you actively seek out support or guidance in times of difficulty?
- Are you able to cope with stress in constructive ways (exercise, being with friends rather than using drugs or alcohol)?
- How often are you involved in helping others?
- Can you find healthy meaning in your life despite life's challenges?

The Resiliency Center Online provides a 20-question survey on one's level of resiliency. It can be found at: www.resiliencycenter.com/resiliencyquiz.shtml.

---

basic assumptions about life, such as who they are, their role in the world, their relationships with the people around them, and what the future holds. They have developed the Posttraumatic Growth Inventory (PTGI) that measures five domains derived from the research and extensive interviews with survivors of various types of adversity, from loss of a spouse and major disabilities to other life crises. The PTGI assesses across five domains common to posttraumatic growth: the appreciation of life and transformed sense of priorities; closer interpersonal relationships; a new recognition of individual strengths; increased awareness of opportunities and life choices; and spiritual growth and development.

Tedeschi and Calhoun note that trauma survivors repeatedly recount the paradox that loss could produce something of value. For example, researchers in Australia investigating patients who had suffered traumatic injury from car accidents found that, in spite of reduced social well-being and significant changes in professional and recreational activities after an injury, many patients had adopted new philosophy of life and expanded sense of self. Their accidents had, in fact, become springboards for growth enabling a new outlook on life.

Patrick Murphy and David Hevey (2013) investigated the relationship between the stigma related to HIV and posttraumatic growth among HIV-positive participants in Ireland in order to examine the role of additional distress from social marginalization on the potential for positive growth from trauma. They reported that perceptions of stigma diminished measures of positive growth, particularly in relationships with others, individual strengths, and new possibilities. This work provides valuable information for clinicians dealing with trauma overlaid with experiences of social marginalization.

Tedeschi and Richard McNally point out that there are some misconceptions about posttraumatic growth. For example, posttraumatic growth theory does not celebrate the trauma as a vehicle of change. The focus is on perceived benefits that come from the recovery process. Contrary to expectations, highly resilient people may experience less posttraumatic growth, not more. Stronger coping skills that are part of resiliency can reduce the need to struggle with the consequences of trauma. The cognitive processes are often where the reappraisal appears. They also note that clinicians often err in making posttraumatic growth a clinical goal of the recovery process, inadvertently creating shame. There should be no expectation that all trauma survivors must experience posttraumatic growth. Often, it is those who experience the most intense adversity and suffer intensely from symptoms of posttraumatic stress disorder who report positive growth.

Every path to recovery is different. Reports from former prisoners of war (POWs) in North Vietnam, who were imprisoned and tortured for years, found that 61 percent said that the experience had produced positive changes in their personalities, improving self-confidence and increasing their awareness of the important things in life. Those who suffered the worst treatment reported the highest levels of posttraumatic growth. A study by Israeli researchers examined veterans of the 1973 Yom Kippur War. Vets who had been POWs had both higher levels of PTSD and posttraumatic growth compared to peers who had been in combat but had not been captured (Tedeschi & McNally, 2011). For veterans of the Persian Gulf War, being in the combat zone was linked with higher scores on the appreciation for life domain of the PTGI. Social support upon discharge was the largest predictor of growth in the domains of personal strengths and warmer, more intimate relationships with others.

STRESS RESILIENCE IN THE REAL WORLD

The Comprehensive Soldier Fitness and Family Fitness (CSF2)

The U.S. Army, working with Seligman and the positive psychologists at the University of Pennsylvania, has embarked on a program of reliance training for solider and their families. While the army's traditional approach has been to treat soldiers when they develop problems after combat, they have now developed a series of preventative programs to teach the skills that build resilience and enhance critical thinking and performance in the field. The goals are to reduce combat-related emotional problems and support the overall emotional health of families having to deal with the stress of separation and knowing a loved one is exposed to danger. The Comprehensive Soldier Fitness and Family Fitness (CSF2) program includes assessment for soldiers and their families using the Global Assessment Tool (GAT) 2.0 to assess physical and psychological health along five domains identified as core to resilience: emotional, social, family, spiritual, and physical. The CSF2 program has multiple levels of resilience training, programs running online and in person, performance evaluations, and social connection to a larger community. Instituted in 2009, the program is not without detractors, who argue that empirical evidence from the training is limited. The purpose of the program, however, is to make inroads by broadening assessment and providing skills training for every member of the army family—soldiers and families alike. The army now recognizes that the development of human resilience includes psychological and social development that must be part of the army training programs.

Strength and Resilience for Children

Strength and resilience training programs for children and adolescents have been implemented around the world. Although not all studies have had rigorous use of empirical methodology, investigators in Canada found preliminary support for the effectiveness of strengths- and resilience-based interventions. The Positive Psychology Center at the University of Pennsylvania designed the Penn Resiliency Program as an intervention for late elementary and middle school children. Based on the cognitive behavioral theories of behavior and mood change, the program focuses on cognitive-behavioral approaches to behavior change and social problem-solving skills. To date, the program had been delivered to over 2,500 children. The program has been successful in lowering measures of depression and anxiety with results that endured over a two-year period.

The Stress Resilience in Virtual Environments Program (STRIVE)

The Institute for Creative Technologies at the University of Southern California (USC) used advanced media technologies to create virtual immersion therapy for the treatment of PTSD. Investigators Skip Rizzo and John Buckwalter (1997) evaluated the efficacy of virtual reality–based immersion to prepare users for

BARBARA FREDRICKSON AND POSITIVE EMOTIONS

Barbara Fredrickson is a social psychologist and a leading scholar in the study of positive emotions. She has spent more than 20 years studying the impact of the full range of emotions in order to understand the role that the positive end of the emotional spectrum has played in human evolution and, most importantly, how that matters for individuals today.

Many theories of emotion rely on the concept of specific-action tendencies. This concept says that the purpose of having emotions is to prepare the body psychologically and physically to take action. It's easy to see how negative emotions, such as anger and fear, are part of human evolution because they trigger behaviors that help us survive through fighting or fleeing. Fredrickson was intrigued by how positive emotions had withstood the evolutionary process. She researched positive emotions to unravel this mystery and found that positive emotions contribute to human survival by expanding an individual's "thought-action repertoire" or the range of responses that one has. Positive emotions give us a broader way of thinking that leads to new discoveries of skills, associations, and resources. Fredrickson called this the *broaden-and-build* theory of emotions.

Fredrickson's work is important as it shows how negative emotions make an individual focus narrowly on available resources, hence creating narrow cognition. This is the way that stress impacts our autonomic nervous system. Positive emotions, in contrast, not only have the opposite effect of expanding our thinking but their impact is cumulative. Even though emotions are fleeting, positive emotions increase positive traits, social bonds, and self-confidence into the future. Thus, Fredrickson's broaden-and-build theory reflects how positive emotions create an upward spiral by continually broadening the thought-action repertoire enabling continued positive growth.

In her most recent work, Fredrickson has further expanded her theory by developing a positivity ratio that is an indicator of an individual's "net positivity" at any given moment. By evaluating our thoughts using this ratio, we can become more aware of our emotional states and consciously cultivate positive emotions.

Fredrickson has a short quiz where you can monitor your positivity ratio at http://www.positivityratio.com/single.php.

---

the psychological challenges of combat before deployment. The research was based on two scientific principles. First, pre-exposure to traumatic events in a safe environment provides a degree of protection to subsequent exposure (also called *latent inhibition*). Second, resilience can be strengthened through systematic training.

The Stress Resilience in Virtual Environments Program (STRIVE) developed six virtual reality scenarios using advanced gaming software. Each scenario is based upon a trauma that is frequently reported as a source of PTSD rumination, such as witnessing the death of a fellow soldier or the death of a child. The resilience training focuses on several dimensions of resilience from the Headington Institute Resilience Inventory (HIRI). The STRIVE program has received attention for its innovation and was featured in the popular media on an episode of the TV show *Rizzoli and Isles* dealing with PTSD and vets.

The Headington Institute Resilience Scale (HIRI)

There are a number of assessment tools developed to measure resilience. For example, a 2011 article by Gill Windle, Kate Bennett, and Jane Noyes examined 15 of the best known measures. The evaluation process for any psychometric measure is technically difficult, as it includes many factors such as standardization and establishing validity and reliability. It is also conceptually difficult, as we've discussed. Developing an assessment tool requires precise definitions of constructs being measured and the theories of resilience and the pathways to resilience vary across scholars and researchers. Some assessment tools use checklists and scales, while others employ personal interviews. Still others focus on protective factors, such as strengths, self-efficacy, and coping styles rather than on outcomes. Additionally, assessment tools that are appropriate for adults may not be so for children. Scales developed for Western, English-speaking populations may not fit other cultures and languages. And some, while technically resilience tools, such as the PTGI developed by Tedeschi and Calhoun, measure constructs that target the capacity for positive growth rather than resilience.

The Headington Institute Resilience Scale (HIRI) is a widely tested scale. It is used by USC in their stress resilience training using virtual environments and assesses across multiple domains shown to be related to resilience. These include adaptability, emotional regulation, behavioral regulations, CBT Appraisal methods, social support, empathy, hardiness, and meaning in work. The HIRI was developed by the Headington Institute, whose primary focus is developing programs to cultivate resilience in the staffs and personnel of emergency responders and humanitarian and relief organizations to support their mental health and effectiveness in the field. The HIRI is under continual improvement as the institute's global clientele allows them to continually gather data around their world. The HIRI is designed to understand the protective factors central to resilience, stress, and trauma across cultures and languages.

CONCLUSION

Over four decades of research have shed light on how people recover, often well, from adversity and highlight important themes in positive psychology. Resilience research has helped refocus attention on understanding human potential by examining how human adaptive systems intersect with individual differences and environmental contexts to overcome adversity. Positive psychology, in turn, continues to drive researchers to a better understanding of the circumstances that promote, rather than undermine, positive growth and development across the life span and in multiple contexts.

Resilience is a complex construct that demands careful and specific conceptual and operational definitions. As many note, there are multiple pathways to resilience, often context-dependent and involving many different characteristics and processes that can change over time. In spite of the fact that resilience is something that is quite ordinary, occurring as a result of normal adaptive systems, Masten notes, "There are no magic bullets for producing resilience. . . . There are no invulnerable children" (A.S. Masten & Obradović, 2006, p. 23).

CHAPTER 5

Mindfulness

Mindfulness is a growing phenomenon around the world. Articles on mindfulness are appearing frequently in trend-spotting news sources like *Fast Company* and *Wired*. Mindfulness practices are embraced by NFL teams, and mindfulness sessions are filling the conference circuit. Mindfulness has been featured on *60 Minutes,* a search on Amazon books brings up over 8,000 titles, and a Google search returns over 29 million results. A 2012 U.S. National Institutes of Health (NIH) report estimates that approximately 18 million U.S. adults use meditative practices. The NIH has also funded over $100 million on research exploring the effectiveness of mindfulness on a range of issues, such as anxiety, depression, chronic pain, smoking cessation, and cardiovascular disease.

It's very clear that mindfulness is catching on, but what exactly is it? This turns out to be a good question because while there is a lot of academic literature surrounding mindfulness and mindfulness practices, there isn't complete agreement across academics and practitioners as to its definition. This may be due to the relative newness of the concept in Western society and the difficulty of operationalizing a contemplative experience. Creating a firm definition may be additionally challenging because many current approaches have appropriated practices and terms from long-standing meditative traditions, such as Buddhism, where the Buddhist scholars themselves continue to debate its meaning. Mindfulness is also a moving target. It has taken on new meanings and definitions as it has moved from one realm of practice to another. If this is confusing for researchers, it's worse for the general public where the marketing of "mindfulness" for everything from dieting to financial success is presented as a panacea with little explanation of theory.

This chapter will deconstruct the concept of mindfulness. In particular, the following four points will be emphasized: (1) definitions, history and theoretical roots of mindfulness; (2) the health and emotional benefits of cultivating mindfulness; (3) some of the key constructs related to mindfulness: acceptance, forgiveness, gratitude, empathy and authenticity; and (4) applying mindfulness exercises in daily life.

DEFINING THE EXPERIENCE OF BEING MINDFUL

Researchers view the construct of mindfulness primarily in three ways:

1. A mental trait displayed by those with mindfulness training.
2. A spiritual path with roots in the Buddhist tradition for cultivating meaning and well-being and to alleviate suffering. In this connotation, mindfulness refers both to the meditative process of holding the attention and the pursuit of a way of life.
3. A state of mind reflecting the cognitive processes and capacity for directed attention developed through mindfulness training.

The differences in definitional focus reflect the range of researchers' goals and theoretical orientations. Some are focused on understanding what subjective phenomenon makes up the experience of mindfulness, trying to understand what happens during the process of mindfulness meditation and training. Others are interested in examining how individual differences in personality and experience interact with mindfulness practices. Still others focus on identifying and measuring the impact, such as comparing the effects of different levels of mindfulness practices on the potential for transformation in everyday life. These studies typically compare people who have maintained long-term mindfulness practices, such as Buddhist monks, with people who have received short-term training and those who have no mindfulness experience. Positive psychologists in particular want to know if the reported benefits of mindfulness training and practice have sustainable effects that can increase well-being and, if so, for whom and under what circumstances.

Years of research have suggested a range of benefits of mindfulness in better performance and health, longer lives, more positive emotions, increased creativity, and less stress. Yet, as mentioned earlier, the research is uneven in quality and the results are often overstated in popular media. Researchers face multiple challenges in creating a standard definition of a subjective and private experience, while creating studies that adhere to empirically rigorous standards in mindfulness settings.

Like many positive psychology concepts like optimism, mindfulness can be cultivated. However, unlike other concepts, mindfulness is a practice-based skill embraced by positive psychology to achieve positive goals, rather than an innate quality within each of us that can be measured and encouraged. Therefore, it is important to remember that mindfulness is best understood through experience. It is something that you can undertake with no previous familiarity. It is a skill that can be learned but must be practiced to achieve results. Research suggests that more practice leads to more profound results. Also, there is no denying that mindfulness can become a philosophical approach to all aspects of life by those who truly embrace it. We encourage you to explore the mindfulness exercises throughout this chapter and experience mindfulness and the way it impacts your life.

HISTORY OF MINDFULNESS

The academic study of mindfulness comes from two theoretical orientations: one originating in the East and the other in the West. The Eastern perspective draws on ancient philosophies surrounding contemplative practices, while the Western perspective draws on cognitive and social psychology. Eastern philosophies and meditation practices are the best known. Mindfulness is often seen as a part of the "New Age" movement toward the adoption of meditation practices and other practices with an Eastern philosophical heritage, such as yoga. Adoption of Eastern philosophies into Western culture and contemporary psychology resulted in several variations in approaches to mindfulness: however, all Eastern-based characterizations share the commitment to (1) bringing one's attention to the present moment, (2) maintaining a nonjudgmental perspective, and (3) the integration of contemplative or meditative practices.

The Eastern approach to mindfulness in the West is frequently associated with the work of one of the most prominent mindfulness scholars and practitioners, Jon Kabat-Zinn. In the late 1970s, Kabat-Zinn (2003) developed a mindfulness practice that integrated aspects of Buddhist principles and Eastern meditation with Western psychology and clinical interventions that he applied in clinical practice. He describes mindfulness as an emerging awareness that comes from directing your attention to the present moment and to the experience of each moment as it unfolds. From his perspective, the act of being mindful describes the qualities of attention, the awareness of attention, and our interpretation of how and what we attend. It is a way of directing the attention that can be developed through practice.

Kabat-Zinn developed an eight-week program at University of Massachusetts called Mindfulness-Based Stress Reduction (MBSR). Since its inception, it has been attended by over 22,000 people and highlighted in the popular press on NBC's Dateline and CNN, and was featured in Bill Moyer's PBS Documentary *Healing and the Mind*. Kabat-Zinn's model brings together two distinct paths: the meditative practices of Buddhism with the methodologies of psychology, medicine, and science. Kabat-Zinn emphasizes intensive mindfulness practice based on the Dharma or Eastern meditative practices translated for Western culture. His Mindfulness-Based Stress Reduction program includes breathing practices, hatha yoga, and physical relaxation techniques.

Also in the 1970s, Harvard professor and psychologist Ellen Langer (1989/2014) approached mindfulness from a different theoretical direction. Langer, working from a social psychological and cognitive orientation, was initially focused on the concept of mindlessness. Mindlessness is the human tendency to function automatically, continually navigating by "autopilot" while making unconscious evaluations, social comparisons, and choices as we go through daily life. In looking at the prevalence of unattended reactions in daily life, she began to pursue the opposing construct, the focused attention of mindfulness, or "being in the moment."

While there are many experiential overlaps, the exclusion of meditative practices is a distinguishing feature between Langer's view of mindfulness and Eastern-based understandings. Langer's research examined the conscious shift from external reactivity to internally directed attention. She sees mindfulness as a human ability that does not need the augmentation of meditation. Langer's work has inspired researchers to examine mindfulness as a cognitive process achieved by focusing on the present, attending to changes of internal thoughts and feelings, noticing novel perspectives, and acknowledging multiple points of view. The basic precept is that when we are mindful, we are aware of the things that are around us, such as where we are and how things feel. In Langer's construct, mindfulness is a flexible state of mind that allows us to be open to new ways of seeing and experiencing. Rather than a meditative practice, mindfulness is the act of directing attention to avoid the automatic thinking of mindlessness. When one is mindless, one's behavior is controlled by habits and rules and trapped in an inflexible mind-set. Therefore we are not experiencing what is happening in and around us. Mindfulness is waking up from a life on automatic pilot and being sensitive to the newness in everyday experiences. Many spend time being mindless and don't even realize it because, as Langer notes, being aware of it would require being mindful.

Major contributions to what was to become the field of mindfulness also came from research on mind-body connections by Herbert Benson and Richard Davidson. Benson was an early proponent of the holistic relationship of the mind and body. He coined the term "Relaxation Response" and published a book by the same name in 1975 to demystify the concept of meditation to Western audiences. His research demonstrated that meditation could short-circuit the stress response, thereby preventing stress's negative impact on the body and emotions (Benson, 1975/2000).

Davidson is one of the world's experts on the effect of contemplative practices on the brain and has extensively studied relationship of emotions and brain activity. His interest in meditation originated during college during the 1980s. While completing his PhD in psychology, he traveled to India to study the meditation practices of Buddhist monks. Davidson has been instrumental in using neuroscience to study how meditation impacts gamma wave oscillations, an indicator of brain plasticity. His work has inspired further investigation into the potential of mindfulness skills learned through meditation as a pathway to neural change. This has the potential to impact emotional disorders, such as anxiety and depression, as well as developmental disorders such as autism. Results from Davidson's work have also shown that mindfulness training can target emotions in ways that provide sustained improvements in positivity and happiness (Davidson & Lutz, 2008).

These psychologists are not only major figures in the field of mindfulness but they are pioneers in the field of psychology. The very nature of mindfulness challenges many of the foundations in psychology—from how we conceptualize information processing and memory to individual identity and ego development. An important feature of mindfulness is the shift away from the reactive, instinctive evaluative nature of consciousness and attention. For example, our attention is engaged in response to stimulus. Commonly, our attention is engaged briefly as our brain evaluates the new information and then responds with an emotional or cognitive response. Stimuli that receive our attention are processed unconsciously as well as consciously. Our initial appraisal is part of our survival instinct, very basic and self-referential—safe, dangerous, good, and bad. We unconsciously make automatic judgments based on known patterns and experiences, processing information based on existing cognitive categories and schema. As Brown, Creswall, and Ryan (2007) note, this type of processing, while often expedient, means that we are never completely open and impartial in response to new sensory information. Mindfulness is a way of stepping outside our ways of knowing into experience.

While different schools of thought emphasize different elements, Brown and colleagues identify the following core concepts of mindfulness, often interrelated, as common among traditions that draw from Buddhist heritage.

Clarity

Mindfulness describes the perception of clear awareness of inner and outer experience and all that passes through them. This ability leads to increased receptivity and access to one's intuitive knowledge. Some therapeutic interventions use mindfulness to alleviate resistance to clarity where internal experiences are difficult or painful.

Non-Evaluative Awareness

Mindfulness awareness is observing without interference, judgment, or labeling.

Fluid Attention

Mindfulness attention is not the restriction of attention that we associate with concentration. It is a flexible and voluntary ability to move among states of attention and awareness.

Observable Experience

Mindfulness is the ability to experience fully and authentically, having direct contact with the present.

Presence in the Present

The human mind has the ability to time travel through memory and projecting into the future. This ability is valuable in many ways, such as crafting new self-narratives, but mindfulness is full awareness of the present.

Continued Attention

Mindfulness is steadiness of attention and the ability to sustain and notice what is present.

LIFE STRATEGY: BECOMING MINDFUL

To Increase Self-Acceptance

Open closed doors. Research has shown that self-labeling creates a mind-set of powerlessness. Every time you label something, you are closing a door to potential. When you notice that you are describing yourself in inflexible terms (e.g., "I am no good at drawing"), rephrase the sentence with the possible. Substitute "could be" and recognize that things change. The psychologist Carol Dweck (2006) demonstrated that when people believe their abilities can be developed through dedication and hard work, they are more motivated, productive, and successful. When you replace rigid words in your self-narrative (see Chapter 7), you open the door to possibility.

Find a new perspective. When you are stuck in a negative view of yourself or your situation, imagine you are looking at it from the perspective of different people, both ones you know and a total stranger looking in on your situation.

To Increase Gratitude

Increase awareness of what you have: Think about what you would miss in your life and then construct a "what I take for granted list."

Reframe frustration: Anytime someone or something irritates you, find a reason to be grateful. For example, if you get negative feedback on a project, be grateful you have the opportunity to learn from it. If someone makes you angry, be grateful for all the kind people you do know.

Recognize simple acts of others: Spend some time noticing the contributions of others around you doing things that make your life better. Who empties the trash, serves the food, or delivers your packages?

Pay it forward: Try to do one thing each day to make someone else's life a little better. As we discussed, even a smile is contagious and changes the neurochemistry of everyone "infected" by your smile.

Share your gratitude: Tell people what you appreciate about them and what they do for you. If it seems hard, start with just one person and work up from there. Try it in person, in a letter and on Facebook.

Take gratitude selfies: Put selfie-taking to positive use. Take a selfie when you are experiencing a moment of gratitude. Capturing image will allow you to re-experience the emotion of the moment every time you look at the picture.

Langer's conceptualization will also have many conceptual overlaps with mindfulness from an Eastern heritage. She believes that mindfulness is much easier than people often assume because it does not require hours of meditation. Rather, she argues that because people spend so much time not being "present" in their own lives, the simple process of noticing new things and learning to see the world with a more childlike excitement. Her research suggests that a focus on novelty and engagement is the simplest way to produce mindfulness in everyday life with many benefits. In 1979, Langer had eight older men live in an artificial environment constructed to give the experience of a time 20 years earlier. The participants' talked about news, politics, and sports of the previous period in the present tense as if they had traveled back in time. Langer found that the participants acted and felt younger. In 2014 the BBC replicated the experiment starring six well-loved British celebrities and achieved similar results. Langer's theory is based on the concept of mind-body unity and the impact of directed intention in mindfulness practices. The results from multiple studies on the placebo effect have lent support to Langer's hypothesis. The work by Italian neuroscientist Fabrizio Benedetti and colleagues (2011) have also shown evidence that the immune system responds to unconscious classical conditioning. In one study, Benedetti told healthy volunteers that any pain they experienced was beneficial to their bodies and found that the participants produced higher levels of natural painkillers.

MEASURING MINDFULNESS

Mindfulness may be as simple as an intentional shift in perspective that moves you from "doing" into "being." Assessing mindfulness, however, presents challenges. Researchers use a variety of self-report computer tests and other cognitive assessments measuring different cognitive abilities as well as qualitative interviews. While some have reported associations between mindfulness training and improvements in things like working memory and sustained attention, the reports have been mixed. At present, an objective test for mindfulness is still to be developed. Brain scans have examined long-term meditators and mindfulness practitioners and returned interesting results, but some argue that it is difficult to translate those findings to daily life.

Mindfulness scholar Ruth Baer (2010) underscores the importance of establishing the effects and mechanisms of change in mindfulness-based clinical interventions. As we have discussed, the subtle and individual experience of mindfulness makes it particularly difficult to operationalize and precisely define. There are several self-report measures of mindfulness that are currently considered to be the most accurate way of evaluating mindfulness. As with the definitions, these questionnaires vary in the aspects of mindfulness they capture. For example, the Freiburg Mindfulness Inventory assesses nonjudgmental, in-the-moment observation and susceptibility to negative thoughts. The Mindful Attention Awareness Scale measures awareness of being in the moment on a day-to-day basis. The Kentucky Inventory of Mindfulness Skills measures four elements of mindfulness: observing, describing, acting with awareness, and nonjudgmental awareness. The Cognitive and Affective Mindfulness Scale (Revised) measures attention, awareness, present-focus, and nonjudgmental acceptance of thoughts and feelings. The Southampton Mindfulness Questionnaire measures the elements of mindfulness related to negative thoughts and images, mindful awareness, thought releasing, and nonjudgment.

Baer combined the previous five instruments into the Five Facet Mindfulness Questionnaire to better capture the following five elements of mindfulness: observing, describing, awareness of action, and nonjudgmental and non-reactivity to inner experience. Examples of items on the questionnaires include: "I am open to the experience of the present moment," "I find myself doing things without paying attention," "When I have distressing thoughts or images, I am able to just notice them without reacting," and "When I'm walking, I deliberately notice the sensations of my body moving."

These measures have been applied in different contexts to evaluate the relevance of mindfulness to behavioral regulation, mental health, and relationship quality. While recognizing the potential limitations, published research provides encouraging confirmation that the assessment tools are reasonably valid and are consistent with theoretical expectations. Scores of most items are significantly correlated, suggesting that the researchers have similarly defined the terms and share an understanding of what it means to be mindful. Neuroimaging found a significant negative relationship between activity in the amygdala, the area of the brain that is associated with depression, and self-reports of mindfulness, suggesting that as reported mindfulness increases, brain activity related to depression decreases. A comparison of meditators and non-meditators found that the development of psychological well-being was associated with extent of meditation experience.

GETTING TO MINDFULNESS: STEPPING OFF THE TREADMILL

People have long referred to the pressures of life as a treadmill—or worse, the *daily grind*. The integration of digital technologies into our lives has created the potential for additional pressures, from the sense of immediacy, always on, need for a response to letting social comparison get the better of you, with FoMO (the fear-of-missing-out). This treadmill is just what Langer described as mindlessness—going about our daily lives automatically without paying attention, our minds racing with thoughts about what we have to do, what we should have done, what we did or didn't do to our satisfaction or someone else's. Those thoughts carry on seemingly without our help and can interrupt our ability to sleep well, function effectively, and care about others.

Mindlessness perpetuates our negative emotions and increases stress. A little stress may be motivating, but a lot of stress is just the opposite. Barbara Fredrickson and Christine Branigan and colleagues (2004) demonstrated how even the type of movie you watch influences what Fredrickson calls "action tendencies," the coordinated changes in people's thoughts, actions, and physical response to emotion. College students who watched humorous or positive movies reported more positive emotions and broader scopes of attention and cognition than those who watched movies from genres that commonly engendered anger, stress, or sadness. Fredrickson notes that while the emotions are not long-lived, the coordinated changes in thought and action brought on by the positive emotions can be.

Langer (1989/2014) demonstrated that our responses in a mindless state not only contribute to stress and negative emotions but also draw on our instincts, assumptions, and knee-jerk reactions. Langer and colleagues call these mind-lessly learned emotional responses "premature cognitive commitments." Our inability to separate our reactions from events means our responses are triggered and automatic, not thoughtful and intentional. A rigid state of mind increases the likelihood of rumination and circular thinking rather than creative problem solving, so our efforts to figure out why we're feeling unhappy or overwhelmed can make us feel worse, not better.

By contrast, mindfulness is the focusing of attention without judgment. It creates the emotional and cognitive foundation to deal with challenging events by creating a flexible cognitive state. It doesn't make all our problems disappear, but it better equips us to handle challenges by enabling a different mind-set that allows us to find new solutions.

THE BENEFITS OF MINDFULNESS

Mindfulness has been adopted in many situations, from businesses and sports teams to clinical settings. The majority of empirical research on mindfulness, however, has focused on clinical interventions using mindfulness-based therapies to deal with a wide range of psychological, behavioral, and physical issues.

Mindfulness-Based Stress Reduction (MBSR) developed by Kabat-Zinn initially was designed to relieve the suffering of medical patients. Even though MBSR made intensive use of meditation and Eastern practices such as hatha yoga, Kabat-Zinn's goal was to remove the cultural and religious associations with Buddhism and make the practices more accessible to a Western audience. In an eight-week course for outpatients, the goal was to enable people to take responsibility for their own well-being as well as reap the deeper benefits of mindfulness practices. At the time, the development of any in-hospital programs depended upon the success of the initial outpatient clinic program. The MBSR has been so successful that it has become a model for other hospitals and training centers and has been adapted to many situations where stress, emotional and physical pain, or illness and disease were concerns. A key to the MBSR programs' success is the attention they give to the format and trainers. The trainers are required to have extensive grounding in mindfulness practice. In Kabat-Zinn's perspective, instructors must be practicing mindfulness practices in their own lives in order to teach them to others with authenticity. The initial clinic program has also developed professional training programs to be able to deliver the model with integrity in the myriad of settings beyond hospitals now offer mindfulness training, such as schools, offices, prisons, and inner city health centers.

Early descriptive studies and anecdotal success stories have led to more rigorous, randomized trails. For example, Kabat-Zinn used the MBSR protocol on patients with moderate to severe psoriasis. The patients were randomized into one of two groups where one group received standard light treatment followed by guided mindfulness meditation. The meditations were delivered via audiotape in which they visualized the lights slowing down and stopping the rapidly growing skin cells. The other group received the light treatment with

LIFE STRATEGY: PRACTICING FORGIVENESS

Letting go and forgiving those who have wronged us reduces symptoms of depression, anxiety, and anger. In fact, those who practice forgiveness tend to feel happier, more optimistic, and have better relationships (Haupt, 2012).

Psychologist Robert Enright, a leader in forgiveness research and founder of the International Forgiveness Institute, argues, "Every human being on the planet has been injured by another's injustice, and how we respond to that can make all the difference . . . forgiveness helps quiet anger so it doesn't spill over onto innocent others" (Enright, 2012).

Enright and his colleagues argue that forgiveness is about choice and about letting go. Releasing negative thoughts and feelings and no longer harboring resentment has a positive impact on our physical and emotional health. It is important to remember, however, that forgiveness is not about forgetting or trying to act as if a hurtful and painful event never happened. The key to forgiveness is learning to let go of the pain associated with a grudge in order to improve one's own health and well-being.

Psychologist Sonja Lyubomirsky (2007) calls forgiveness a "shift in thinking" toward someone who has created harm or ill will. Forgiveness is not about forgetting, but rather acknowledging the wrong, reflecting and trying to understand it, and deciding how one wants to move forward in life.

Research supports that those who forgive are more likely than those who do not to:

- Have lower rates of depression
- Have lower rates of heart disease
- Have better immune functioning
- Have longer-lasting relationships
- Have a larger social network
- Have closer relationships
- Have fewer stress-related illnesses
- Be happy
- Be hopeful

From positive psychology researchers to physicians to religious leaders, there is a commonality that forgiveness is a way to live a better life. Following is a summary from the research on the essential steps to forgiveness practice:

- Acknowledge what took place. Do not withdraw or isolate yourself; rather, talk to someone about the pain.

LIFE STRATEGY (Continued)

- After having had time to experience the pain, start reflecting on the situation in a more rational way. Start trying to understand why the hurt and anger is so prevalent and see that holding on to it is toxic.

- Work toward regaining an equilibrium. Put the anger in perspective and focus on meditation, exercise, prayer, or talk therapy. Work on getting the poison out of your system.

- Return to the beginning of this loop until you move closer to moving away the harm or hurt.

---

no guided meditation tape. Although the sample size was small, the mindfulness group had four times the rate of skin clearing. This opened the door to explore treatment practices where medical treatments could be combined with psychological participation with many potential applications.

In a separate study by Richard Davidson and colleagues, employees at a biotechnology company were divided into two groups. One group received MBSR training for eight weeks and the other did not. Both groups were given flu vaccines at the end of the eight-week period. The employees with MBSR training not only had an increase in the area of the brain associated with positive emotions but also displayed a significant increase in flu antibodies compared to the waitlisted group.

The increasing interest in mindfulness has led to the development and testing of other approaches integrating mindfulness. These include Mindfulness-Based Cognitive Therapy (MBCT), Acceptance and Commitment Therapy (ACT), and Dialectical Behavior Therapy (DBT). There is a growing body of research supporting the successes of all these approaches; however, only MBSR uses meditative practices as the primary vehicle for change. The others have non-meditate exercises, both cognitive and experiential, to enhance mindfulness.

The research suggests that people receive many benefits from making this shift toward integrating mindfulness. Kabat-Zinn and Davidson demonstrated that mindfulness training enables people to establish a new happiness baseline through brain activation. Research results also suggest the potential for increasing trait mindfulness as well as state mindfulness. In other words, being in a mindful state is frequently associated with an increased disposition toward mindfulness behaviors. Trait mindfulness is correlated with increased well-being and life satisfaction. Other research studies have reported a relationship between sustained mindfulness practices and an increase in affect regulation—the ability to regulate and control emotions—a skill that is essential for mental health and adaptive functioning. Some of the benefits of mindfulness-related emotion regulation include clarity of awareness, acceptance of emotions, and greater ability to repair negative mood states.

Neuroscientists have corroborated these findings with fMRI research evaluating emotional reactivity and repair in response to threatening images. Participants with higher scores on the Mindful Attention Awareness Scale were less reactive to emotional stimuli, findings that are theoretically consistent with hypothesized relationships between mindfulness and brain activity

ACCEPTANCE

Acceptance is one of the related constructs that are both part of mindfulness and a by-product of mindfulness practices. In positive psychology, acceptance has many dimensions and interpretations. Acceptance is an element of mindfulness. The act of acknowledgement without engagement of the thoughts, feelings, and emotions experienced during mindfulness practice takes self-acceptance. Acceptance is also having compassion and tolerance for others. Acceptance is a component of well-being as well as a coping strategy. Acceptance, therefore, is multifaceted and can be seen as in three contexts: (1) self, as in self-acceptance; (2) other, acceptance through empathy; (3) situational, accepting what has happened or what is happening; and (4) existential, acceptance of our mortality and death.

Self-acceptance in the practice of mindfulness is seen as being able to acknowledge and release judgment rather than self-criticism to increase self-awareness and self-understanding. This encourages the ability to show compassion and empathy to whatever emotions, thoughts, or feelings we may have.

Other acceptance comes from the way that mindfulness facilitates our ability to have empathy for others by increasing our awareness of social context and interactions.

Situational acceptance comes from the way that mindfulness practices can increase our inner serenity and enable us to adapt and function in the face of things that cannot be changed. It allows us, as Langer demonstrated, to be more open and flexible to solutions and opportunities. By transforming the negative emotions associated with physical and emotional pain, mindfulness can lessen suffering by increasing our ability to acknowledge what is, whether painful or pleasurable.

Existential acceptance is the ability of mindfulness to assist us in finding meaning and affirming values in ways that give us the courage to face adversity.

The philosophical roots of mindfulness and acceptance are different—mindfulness came largely from Eastern practices and acceptance originated in empiricism. Both, however, emphasize a perceptual shift toward the nonjudgmental, tolerance of present experience. Mindfulness practices have been united with acceptance and acceptance-based interventions, such as ACT, which focus on the necessity of being fully present in one's experience. In contrast to the everyday interpretation of acceptance as containing a positive judgment, such as you've been accepted into this club, the psychological construct of acceptance is rooted in the nonjudgmental acceptance of internal and external events. Because of this, acceptance allows us to view reactions to events as understandable and temporary rather than unendurable or permanent.

Like mindfulness, the research on the impact of acceptance in the context of mindfulness comes from clinical applications and interventions in the treatment of psychological disorders. Acceptance-based skills are central to Kabat-Zinn's MBCT, ACT, and DBT. Clinicians have developed empirically based best practices for mindfulness- and acceptance-based interventions for personality disorders and mood disorders. They are now looking to validate the effectiveness with research aimed at improving posttraumatic functioning. These therapies apply experiential and cognitive exercises to challenge avoidance behaviors and reorient people toward their values. Trauma survivors, for example, are taught to focus on the present moment. This helps patients develop the strength to experience internal and external events and recognize that emotions can be transient in nature. This approach, combining mindfulness and cognitive reframing, allows them to override the automatic avoidance behaviors common in trauma survivors. Thus, mindfulness and acceptance have had success in relapse prevention of disorders triggered by exposure to traumatic events. Disorders such as substance abuse and depression commonly present as part of the avoidance behavior pattern that mindfulness and acceptance can break. Mindfulness and acceptance interventions also have been used with success to treat police officers exposed to trauma, Albanian civilian survivors of the Kosovo War, undergraduates with a history of interpersonal trauma, and gay males and lesbian women who experience episodes of sexual assault.

Sports psychologists, intrigued by evidence from Davidson's work suggesting that mindfulness and acceptance promoted neuroplasticity, have promoted mindfulness training as a means to improve an athlete's performance. Mindfulness offers advantages on a number of fronts for athletes because mindfulness training increases the ability to manage emotion and function effectively under stress. Sports psychologists were particularly interested in Davidson's work that showed a connection between mindfulness and cortical thickness from neuro-images that revealed increases in cortical thickness among Tibetan Buddhist monks with thousands of hours of meditation practice. Cortical thickness in certain areas of the brain is linked with high levels of motor skills, such as juggling and language learning. While not conclusive, these findings suggest a potential pathway for athletic improvement through the adoption of mindfulness practices.

Frank Gardner and Zella Moore (2012) reviewed the empirical research in sports psychology that incorporated traditional skills approaches, such as goal-setting, imagery, emotion regulation, arousal, and self-talk, with no definitive results. They hypothesized that while the mindfulness- and acceptance-based interventions are based on a completely different theoretical understanding of the mechanisms of behavior change, the other reported benefits of mindfulness practices were worth a try. Consequently, they undertook a mindfulness-acceptance-commitment (MAC) protocol to enhance athletic performance. After collecting data on the relationship between the MAC protocol cognitive processes and neural correlates over a 10-year period, the results showed that those who scored higher in mindfulness measures also had higher scores in skill balance, the merging of action and aware, goal clarity, and concentration. These measures, indicators that mindfulness enabled

LIFE STRATEGY: THE IMPORTANCE OF GRATITUDE

Cicero said, "Gratitude is not only the greatest of the virtues but the parent of all others." All world religions and historical philosophies speak about the importance of gratitude. Modern-day scientists confirm that gratitude, or being appreciative or thankful, leads to greater happiness and those who do not find a sense of gratitude in life tend to be less happy. Gratitude allows one to take a look at daily life and feel more appreciative and see that often the simpler aspects of life can provide a great deal of richness. Other researchers describe the power of gratitude as "an emotional muscle" that should be used and strengthened as this leads to an orientation of seeking out success in life and drawing success into life.

While many have a focus on what is wrong with life, practicing gratitude shifts our framework and increases one's overall satisfaction with life and promotes an optimistic explanatory style. One may take a proactive approach to cultivating gratitude through a number of ways, including:

- Reflect: Take time each day to review what you have appreciated, celebrated, or are thankful for having had included in that day. These do not have to be grand actions, and are often instead smaller actions such as the smile you received at the coffee shop, or the delicious cookie you treated yourself to for lunch.
- Journal: Others find the use of a gratitude journal helpful in moving toward recording appreciative experiences in the day.
- Talk: Sit down with a friend or a loved one and take time to review what is right in life rather than what is wrong. This activity can be catching and tends to lift everyone's mood.

Gratitude is not only a major factor in mental health, but also serves to reinforce prosocial behavior in those who receive your gratitude. One experiment examined the use of gratitude and post-sales responses with jewelry stores. Those customers who were called and thanked showed a subsequent 70 percent increase in purchases; those who were thanked and then told about an upcoming sale reflected a 30 percent increase in sales; and those customers who were not called did not show any increase in sales for the store.

Another study revealed that servers at restaurants who left a handwritten note of thanks on the bill received greater tips than those who did not write "thank you" on the bill. Gratitude pays off in more ways than one.

the development of Flow or being "in the zone," suggested that systematic mindfulness practice can facilitate the development of high-level athletic performance. In a study of 182 university student-athletes in Singapore, researchers found that higher levels of mindfulness measures were associated with higher propensity for dispositional flow or the character-based tendency to experience Flow. Similar indications of the ability of mindfulness training to achieve the flow state were found among 10 Olympic swimmers. Amy Gooding and Frank Gardner (2009) studied a group of U.S. NCAA Division I basketballs players and found that basketball experience, free throw shooting skill, and levels of mindfulness each predicted free throw shooting percentages where pregame routines did not. Among adult competitive archers, golfers and long-distance runners, mindfulness participants significantly increased overall trait mindfulness, sense of flow, and ability to focus. Runners also showed improved race times.

Mindfulness- and acceptance-based interventions are widely available to the public through a number of self-help resources. Studies have evaluated the effectiveness of Internet-based programs, books, and workbooks, as well as audio recordings designed to promote mindfulness and acceptance. The results from a meta-analysis from researchers out of the Universities of Sussex and Kent showed that people using self-help interventions that include mindfulness and acceptance components displayed significantly increased mindfulness and acceptance skills as well as lower levels of anxiety and depressive symptoms. There are, of course, many more books on the market than researchers have tested, but the research, though limited, indicates that regular self-study offers benefits if you commit to regular practice. The popularity of smartphones makes practice easy. Several mindfulness- and acceptance-based apps are available for mobile devices. Examples such as the ACT Companion Happiness Trap App and the ACT Coach provide exercises, tools, and guided mindfulness training. Both books and apps can be used alone or with the guidance of a coach or clinician. Working with trained mental health professional is always important when you face serious difficulties. Professional health care providers and coaches can also provide additional motivation and structure to less critical behavior change initiatives.

FORGIVENESS

Forgiveness is a logical extension from acceptance. Yet the human tendency to retaliate and seek revenge after being insulted or attacked runs deep. Anthropologists have proposed that revenge and retaliation were the primary means of social control in "pre-law" societies. Primatologists have even identified revenge patterns in chimpanzees and macaques. Not to be outdone by primates, we humans have legal systems built around making people "pay for their crimes." Throughout history, retribution and revenge have consistently appeared as primary themes in literature and entertainment, from *Homer* and the *Old Testament* to Hollywood blockbusters like *The Godfather*.

In spite of the centrality of forgiveness and retribution as the foundation of many human legal and moral systems, forgiveness has been studied very little. Since the late 20th century and concurrent with the emergence of positive psychology, social scientists have undertaken the study of forgiveness in earnest. While a lack of agreement on the definition of forgiveness has hampered a cohesive understanding of the benefits of forgiveness, aspects of forgiveness have been linked to health and well-being in a number of research studies.

Researchers such as Everett Worthington (2013) note that in the past 10 years, definitional agreement has made great strides, as much by agreement on what forgiveness is not, as to what it is. Scholars by and large agree that forgiveness is *not* letting someone off the hook, providing excuses, overlooking wrongs, or reconciliation. Forgiveness, however, does include the ability to let go of negative responses to an offense, such as the resentment-based emotions and cognitions of anger, desire for revenge, or grudge holding. As we discuss the components of forgiveness, you will see the direct links with the skills from mindfulness.

Forgiveness can be conceptualized as a coping mechanism that serves to reframe, neutralize, or remove negative emotions. Depending on the circumstances, forgiveness may be an internal process or it may involve interpersonal contact or negotiation. Forgiveness has been examined in relation to specific situations as well as a behavioral trait or tendency. Forgiveness can involve a number of targets, from self and others to events or God.

Forgiveness is of interest to positive psychologists because it involves positive growth—a prosocial shift in the victim's thoughts, emotions, and behaviors toward a transgressor. In all the definitions and conceptualizations of forgiveness, at the core people who forgive become more positive and less negative over time.

Researchers have isolated different types of forgiveness to better understand the psychological dynamics. Situational forgiveness can be decisional or emotional. Decisional forgiveness is the intentional decision to behave differently toward an offender. Emotional forgiveness is the ability to displace negative emotions with positive ones. Data from research looking at forgiveness and health support the importance of emotional forgiveness on well-being. One factor accounting for the psychophysiological impact may be link between positive emotions and the modulation of stress reactions. Decisional forgiveness, by contrast, appears to reduce outward hostility but it does not consistently relieve the stress response. Forgiveness of any kind can create a pathway toward well-being, no matter how someone is able to get to there. Psychologists agree that decisional forgiveness has the potential to lead to emotional forgiveness. All types of forgiveness have been shown to be important offsets to the negative emotions of unforgiveness. The inability to forgive, however, often amplifies negative emotion.

The ability to forgive has been examined as a personality trait that manifests in the tendency to forgive others across a variety of situations. In a telephone survey of over 1,400 respondents of all ages, people's self-rated evaluations of their physical health was related to their dispositional forgivingness—their general inclination to be forgiving. For younger people, positive perceptions of physical health were linked to their ability to be forgiving of their own transgressions—to be self-forgiving. In older people, however, positive perceptions of health were associated with the respondent's reported ability to be forgiving of others.

Forgiveness of self involves overcoming self-blame that can lead to depression and anxiety and undermine resilience. Low scores on the Forgiveness of Self scale were more strongly related to depression, anxiety, and low self-esteem, suggesting that people who had a tendency to forgive themselves were less likely to suffer psychological difficulties. The ability to forgive oneself, for example, has been associated with the ability of women to adjust more easily to a cancer diagnosis as well as the ability of students to adapt effectively to the demands of college.

Much of the forgiveness research studied the relationship of forgiveness to the reduction of negative emotions. The psychologists Kathleen Lawler-Row and Rachel Piferi (2006), however, were eager to understand the predisposition toward forgiveness, or the forgiving personality, and its association with the qualities of a life well lived. Self-report measures of the tendency to forgive were positively associated with mental health and well-being. Developmental psychologists such as George Valiant have argued that the ability to forgive contributes to successful aging; therefore, Lawler-Row and Piferi examined forgiveness as a resource for preserving social and emotional well-being. They examined the role of dispositional forgiveness on the health and well-being of older adults. More forgiving adults had lower levels of depression and stress, higher subjective well-being, and higher total psychological well-being across all six scales of the Ryff Scales of Psychological Wellbeing: autonomy, environmental mastery, personal relationships with others, purpose, personal growth, and self-acceptance. Lawler-Row and Piferi suggest that dispositional forgiveness may indicate a set of personal and interpersonal skills that allow people to develop and maintain critical relationships that enhance well-being.

Survey data from members of small groups indicate that group participation can enhance the ability of people to forgive themselves and others in ways that are related to measures of better mental health and higher levels of well-being. Groups that were formed specifically to address forgiveness reported significant results in the members' success overcoming addiction and guilt and the ability to perceive encouragement.

Forgiveness studies on physical health have focused primarily on the health-eroding processes of stress, hostility, and rumination and the importance of offsetting positive emotions. The negative emotions measured in psychophysiology studies on forgiveness indicated that unforgiving mind-sets are associated with higher blood pressures, muscle tension, and self-reported experiences of anger, fear, and sadness. Other researchers found cardiovascular benefits of both state and trait forgiveness. However, as implied by other research, participants who were high in dispositional forgiveness showed the least negative reactivity and the fastest recovery times.

Trying to explain the relationship between forgiveness and health, Worthington and colleagues (2007) proposed a theoretical model with forgiveness playing the central role in the positive impact on health. Social support and quality of interpersonal relationships were included as mediating variables, as proposed by the research on successful aging. Worthington had a professional and personal interest in the process of forgiveness. Nearly 20 years ago, he had just finished his first book on forgiveness when his elderly mother was violently murdered in a home robbery. The culprit has still not been found. Worthington's brother, who found his mother's body, was so distressed by the event that he committed suicide a few years after the event. Worthington found himself full of negative emotions—anger at the perpetrator and full of guilt for not being able to help his brother. He turned his professional research and his personal experience into a new life mission. He has spent the intervening years helping others lift the burden of self-blame and experience healing. For example, in his book *Moving Forward: Six Steps to Forgiving Yourself and Breaking Free from the Past*, Worthington (2013) integrates his years of research with a faith-based path to achieving forgiveness, creating the REACH method. This model has five steps, rooted in cultivating positive emotions. They include (1) recalling hurt (R), (2) replacing anger with empathy (E), (3) cultivating altruism to enable forgiveness (A), (4) commitment to the goal of forgiveness (C), and (5) holding onto persistence in the face of doubt (H).

While both forgiveness and mindfulness have been linked with multiple health and relational benefits, little empirical research has been done on the association of forgiveness and mindfulness together. As we have discussed, however, many of the characteristic of mindfulness practice promote core elements in forgiveness, such as promoting self-acceptance, perspective taking, empathy, nonreactivity, and the ability to suspend judgment.

GRATITUDE

A September 2015 article in the *London Daily Telegraph* proclaimed that "gratitude" was the new "mindfulness." The author cited everyone from Cicero to Oprah to validate the arrival of gratitude, claiming it would not only make you happier, but thinner and more successful, too. That's a pretty good deal, except it's a little misleading. In order to be grateful, you have to stop and think. In other words, you have to achieve a level of mindfulness to achieve gratitude. According to University of California at Davis psychologist Robert Emmons, one of the world's leading experts, gratitude comes from the recognition that you have received something of value, freely given, from someone or something else. Emmons's definition makes gratitude sound like a gift—and metaphorically it may be—but gratitude can come out of all kinds of events, even traumatic ones. Gratitude, by definition, taps in to our ability to appreciate and savor experience. You may be grateful you survived a car crash, came through a major medical procedure or you may wake up every day just glad to be alive no matter what the circumstances.

Practicing gratitude changes the glass from half empty to half full by replacing the "color" of the schema people use to evaluate the world. Gratitude practice shifts the lens from one of scarcity to abundance; it frames life as a gift instead of a burden and starts from a position of satisfaction rather than deprivation. Emmons and others have spent their time researching two main questions: (1) can gratitude be cultivated and (2) what are the effects of gratitude on health, happiness, and well-being?

Emmons and others have used journaling to explore the impact of gratitude (see the exercises at the end of this chapter). In one study, participants were divided into three groups. Group 1 recorded things for which they felt grateful. Group 2 wrote down things that bothered them. Group 3 wrote down neutral remarks. The gratitude group reported feeling more thankful for the upcoming week and felt better about their lives. The gratitude group also reported

JON KABAT-ZINN AND MINDFULNESS MEDITATION

Known for his bestseller, *Full Catastrophe Living*, Jon Kabat-Zinn brought meditation and mindfulness to the larger public. Zinn, a student of yoga and meditation, combined these practices with Western science into what he calls *mindfulness meditation*. Mindfulness meditation promotes a focus on the present moment rather than the hurts and angers of the past or the anxieties of the future. Maintaining this present orientation allows one to be more attentive to stimuli in the environment and to lessen one's negative interaction and to accept thoughts and feelings without judgment. When combined with the tenets of positive psychology, researchers are finding that mindfulness does indeed reduce stress and lead people to report a healthier life.

In fact, after eight-weeks of mindfulness training, a thickening in areas of the brain associated with learning, memory, decision making, and perspective taking are improved, which helps combat stress and pain. In addition, other regions of the brain get thinner, such as the amygdala, which reduces the fear and threat reaction.

In particular, mindfulness meditation has been clinically shown to:

- Improve the immune system
- Increase positive emotions and reduce negative emotions related to stress
- Help increase focus and attention
- Support better relationships
- Reduce anger, hostility, and mood disturbances
- Decrease levels of depression
- Decrease tendencies toward obesity

Kabat-Zinn's MBSR program was created in 1979 and since has been incorporated into keeping people healthy and supporting those with medical or psychological conditions to an improved state of well-being. He argues that mindfulness is about being compassionate and kind to oneself. He describes mindfulness as "wise and affectionate attention."

Says Kabat-Zinn: "Mindfulness is about coming to terms with things as they are." Therefore, mindfulness provides individuals a keener sense of what can and cannot be controlled and provides resiliency through wisdom rather than create a sense of learned hopelessness or helplessness.

Kabat-Zinn is a professor of Medicine at the University of Massachusetts, where he created the Stress Reduction Clinic and the Center for Mindfulness in Medicine, Health Care, and Society.

You can take the 16-question Mindful Attention Awareness Scale (MAAS) at www.ppc.sas.upenn.edu/mindfulnessscale.pdf to get an idea of how present you are with your thoughts and feelings and where you can go with your own mindfulness exercise using this online mindfulness scale.

being more alert, more determined and that they were making significantly more progress toward their goals, such as fitness, relationships, and school performance. In a similar three-week study, a group of patients with chronic neuromuscular conditions were assigned to either the gratitude journaling group or the control group. Those in the gratitude group slept more, felt more refreshed, reported less pain, and experienced better social connections. After six months, the difference between those in the gratitude and control groups were still significant on increased perceptions of life satisfaction, social connectedness, and less experienced pain. A similar gratitude journaling intervention with sixth- and seventh-grade children in an educational setting resulted in reports of increased optimism and overall life satisfaction both immediately at post-test and at the three-week follow-up. The teachers who participated reported less feelings of burnout and greater senses of accomplishment after the gratitude exercise.

Gratitude has physical as well as emotional impact. A 10-week gratitude-based intervention to treat hypertension in low-income, inner-city African American patients reported decreases in systolic blood pressures as well as an increase in perceptions of gratitude and a decrease in feelings of hostility among the gratitude group compared to controls.

Emmons notes that the most common misunderstandings about gratitude are that gratitude leads to complacency and takes away motivation to get things done. Gratitude, however, is an affirmative process that focuses on goals and facilitates achievement.

EMPATHY

Mindfulness means that you are able to take in and integrate information about both yourself and others. This makes you a more empathetic friend, partner, team member, and global citizen. Empathy is other-centered emotion, the ability to experience emotion that corresponds with what the other person feels. Empathy is considered a strength that can be cultivated. There is also evidence from neurophysiology of mirror neurons that many believe are the neural source of our ability to feel empathy.

The experimental psychologist Edward Titchener is credited with introducing the term "empathy" in 1909, a translation from the German *Einfühlung* (Stueber, 2014). Titchener described empathy as knowing enough about another person or situation to be able to imagine or project what he or she was feeling. The construct of empathy varied between an emphasis on cognition and an emphasis on emotion. In the 1930s, George Herbert Mead and Jean Piaget separately looked at the concept of empathy and both saw it as a predominantly cognitive, rather than emotional, experience (Hakansson, 2003). Mead, stressing the self-other component, emphasized our ability to take on another's role—to see the world through the eyes of someone else in order to understand his or her perspective. Piaget viewed empathy as the ability to step out of our own view and imagine the role of someone else.

The clinical psychologist Carl Rogers (1961) was one of the pioneers in the study of the experience of empathy from a more emotion-based perspective.

ROBERT EMMONS AND THE IMPORTANCE OF GRATITUDE

Robert Emmons is a leading expert on the psychology of gratitude and personal goals and how those interact with positive psychological processes of happiness, well-being, and personality integration. A professor of psychology at the University of California, Davis, he is also the founding editor in chief of *The Journal of Positive Psychology*. Emmons was a co-author of the *Satisfaction with Life Scale* (1985), alongside Ed Diener, Randy J. Larsen, and Sharon Griffin—a simple and quick survey that evaluates global life satisfaction.

According to Emmons, gratitude is a key factor in happiness because it not only improves the present and future but also lays the groundwork for healing the past. Gratitude enables the emotional reframing of past situations, lessening the negative emotions and memories, thus allowing people to manage and move beyond past pain.

Emmons argues that "without gratitude, life can be lonely, depressing, and impoverished." He believes that "people are moved, open, and humbled through expressions of gratitude."

One of Emmons's primary research interests is finding ways to encourage gratefulness in young people. He is a proponent of journaling and letter writing to record acts of gratitude and has found that journaling promotes reflecting thinking and well-being. His research results indicate that journaling has physical impact by increasing self-care behaviors, such as sleep and exercise. Emmons (2013) argues for gratitude as a lifestyle, not just a passing behavior. He argues that when gratitude training is begun at an early age, it positively impacts teen years by decreasing smoking and fighting, improving grades, and encouraging more satisfying relationships.

Emmons and his colleagues encourage one to reframe unpleasant experiences so that their negative impact is less on us. In particular, he suggests that one ask:

- What lessons did the experience teach me?
- Can I find ways to be thankful for what happened to me now even though I was not at the time it happened?
- What ability did the experience draw out of me that surprised me?
- How am I now more the person I want to be because of it?
- Has the experience removed a personal obstacle that previously prevented me from feeling grateful?

Rogers's believed that empathy, unconditional positive regard, and authenticity were the three critical elements in psychotherapy that were necessary for therapeutic change. Many believe that today's enthusiasm for empathy can be traced back to his phenomenological approach. Rogers believed that an individual's view of the world was the primary driver of behavior. Therefore, he saw the role of the therapist as developing empathy—the ability to understand how the client experienced the world. Echoing mindfulness's reliance on unconditional, nonjudgmental self-acceptance, Rogers felt the therapist must develop empathy to communicate a nonjudgmental and accepting attitude of the client's inner world.

Whether leaning toward the cognitive or the emotional, all researchers and authors agree that empathy involves acknowledging emotion appropriate to another's situation. Martin Hoffman (2000), whose interests centered on empathy and moral development in social and emotional development, argued that empathy was the root of other responses: sympathy, guilt, empathic anger, and feelings of injustice. In her research on empathy, Nancy Eisenberg (2000) became interested in differentiating between reactions of sympathy, empathy, and personal distress relative to another person's situation and how it was translated to their willingness to engage in prosocial behaviors, such as helping. Sympathy, while a feeling of care and concern for someone, does not imply shared experience. Personal distress, while triggered by another's situation, is a self-focused, rather than other-focused, negative emotional response.

Eisenberg and colleagues pioneered the use of psychophysiological measures in empathy research. Their research demonstrated that an arousal response was not necessarily a sign of empathy as had previously been assumed. In a group of children, those who registered physical distress on psychophysiological measures also reported the most psychological distress and were the least likely to help others. Based on multiple studies, Eisenberg concluded that reactions to others' situations were related to an individual's disposition toward emotionality and their ability to regulate emotion. Thus, she considered teaching emotion regulation to be a possible pathway to increasing empathy, altruism, and moral development.

Empathy, by all accounts, is a complex phenomenon. Daniel Batson (2010), who researches the motives of prosocial behavior and altruism, defines empathy narrowly as other-oriented emotion in response to another person's perceived welfare. To evaluate the motivations driving helping behaviors, Batson makes distinctions between empathy and several related concepts that are considered empathy by other scholars, such as knowing another's thoughts, motor mimicry, projective and imaginative empathy, and distress responses.

A number of research studies have provided evidence that experiencing empathy for someone by some measures increases altruistic motivation. There is, however, disagreement as to the primary motivational structure. Some argue that helping behavior is ego-based and self-serving rather than altruism defined as the disinterested and unselfish concern for the welfare of others. There are three types of potential self-benefits in helping behavior that have been hypothesized by empathy researchers. Helping behaviors may be motivated by an internal goal; for example, someone may be trying to avoid unpleasant emotions that arose in response to another's unpleasant situation. This is the logic behind years of starving children's images on fund-raising campaigns. Interestingly, Oxfam reports that these images have been so frequent that they have become perceived as inauthentic stereotypes. While these images are seen as depressing and hopeless, they are also seen as manipulative. When people feel manipulated or perceive an issue as hopeless, they are unlikely to lend support or donations. Another hypothesis as to why people engage in helping behaviors suggests that people may want to either avoid social recriminations or receive social benefits and self-reward, such as social validation from others or a sense of identity enhancement. In this line, evolutionary psychologists Mark van Vugt and Wendy Iredale (2013) argue that that altruism toward genetic strangers may have evolved because of the social benefits. For example, based on signaling theory, they suggest that those who signal altruism may increase others' perceptions of fitness through prestige or mating opportunities. They report that women show preferences toward mates who are altruistic.

Batson and colleagues (1981) argue that observing a helping relationship doesn't tell us much about underlying motivations or the ultimate goal of the behavior. In fact, it could be a combination of altruistic, egotistic, or both. Additional hypotheses as to the motivations behind altruism include the idea that the ultimate goal is to improve the welfare of the group or community as a whole or that an individual is acting in support of his or her moral principles. The most consistent findings, however, support the empathy-altruism hypothesis, where empathy has the power to evoke altruistic motivation.

Research on mindfulness and empathy has shown significant positive correlations between the two; increases in mindfulness are accompanied by increases in empathy and vice versa. As discussed, definitions of empathy places different emphasizes on the cognitive and emotional components, although both are considered to be involved. Empathy has been measured using the Interpersonal Reactivity Index (IRI) developed by Mark Davis in the 1980s. The IRI encompasses both cognitive and affective components in four subscales. Two are cognitive: fantasy and perspective taking. Two subscales are emotion-based: empathic concern and personal distress. Empathic concern and perspective taking are the most highly related to mindfulness. Researchers note that a surprising small number of studies have measured the impact of Kabat-Zinn's MBSR on self-compassion and empathy and the results have been mixed. In one study on medical and premedical studies, the MBSR training reduced stress and anxiety while increasing empathy. In another, nurses undergoing the MBSR training showed a decrease in stress, but no accompanying increase in empathy.

A study from the University of Calgary and Tom Baker Cancer Centre in Alberta, Canada, explored the impact of the MBSR on empathy and self-compassion on the 50 participants from a community sample. Researchers found that overall participation was beneficial and increases in mindfulness were related to increases in self-compassion. Aspects of self-compassion and empathy revealed strong associations with psychological functioning, and researchers felt that the study identified the more nuanced relationship between components of empathy and psychological functioning.

Self-compassion in multiple studies has been shown to mediate the relationship between mindfulness and aspects of empathy. Thus, researchers have concluded that self-compassion is a critical component in the ability to take on the perspective of others. Research out of Northeastern University examined empathy defined as taking action to help others. Their work revealed that meditative practices increase people's response to other's suffering. In one study staged in a crowded waiting room, only 16 percent of the participants from the control group were willing to give up their seat to a person on crutches compared to over 50 percent of those from the meditation group. Research by neuroscientist Tania Singer and the Buddhist monk Mathew Ricard demonstrated that meditation-based training reduced activation of brain networks associated with feelings of distress and activates those related to social affiliation. Buddhist scholar Thupten Jinpa believes that meditation-based training enables people to be more emotionally flexible, allowing them to move from the distress of seeing those in pain to the compassion of being able to act to help them.

Empathy has shown positive relationships with quality of life, social support, and marital satisfaction and personal accomplishment. It has also shown negative correlations with symptoms of depression, emotional exhaustion, depersonalization, burnout, and perceived stress. Many argue that a major benefit of mindfulness training will be in the manifestation of empathy—how we treat those around us. While not a scientific study controlled for extraneous influences, one middle school in a frequently violent neighborhood adopted a program of twice-daily meditation period. Over the four years the program ran, it coincided with a 79 percent drop in student suspensions.

As the Dalai Lama has said, we must have self-compassion before we can develop compassion for others.

AUTHENTICITY

Authenticity is an aspect of self-acceptance. It is the ability and willingness to allow others to see your true self without fear of judgment, applying nonjudgmental self-compassion to how you interact with the world. Multiple studies have shown that mindfulness and authenticity are highly correlated and mutually reinforcing.

Living mindfully means presenting your authentic self to the world. This, in turn, allows one to be fully engaged with others. When one is mindless, one acts as we think others think we should act, adopting "social scripts" that limit our behavior because when we're not authentic we can't adapt or be truly spontaneous because that would be violating the rules of the script. There are many reasons why people choose to hide their authentic self. Research has also shown that fear of criticism, self-doubt, expectations of praise, and protecting or inflating self-esteem are all motives for enhancing our self-presentation. Carson and Langer (2006) report that, ironically, when people behave authentically rather than mindlessly, they are seen as more charismatic and receiving praise for inauthentic behavior actually decreases self-esteem.

There is an important distinction between pretending to be what you're not and pretending to be what you hope to become. The difference is in the intention behind the actions. Behavior to win approval from others is inauthentic. Behaving "as if" for yourself, trying on new and desired behaviors is a mindfulness technique for behavior and attitude change.

CHAPTER 6

The Neuroscience of Positive Psychology

Positive psychology aims to make people happier by identifying and strengthening the factors that lead to a life well lived. This has led to the study of positive emotions, such as happiness and well-being, individual strengths, and personal meaning as components of what contribute to a life well lived. Just as psychology historically focused on human disease and pathology, much of neuroscience has been in pursuit of the malfunction in the human brain. Coincident with the pursuit of positive psychology's concerns, researchers have begun to explore the neural mechanisms and physiological implications that enhance our understanding and inform the interventions that enhance positive emotions and meaning and build our resilience to handle life's challenges more easily.

At the most fundamental level, the brain is the source of our emotions and intentions. Consequently, positive psychology interventions are attempting to change the way our brains work to enhance the quality of our lives. If our goal is to change our brains, it makes sense that we should understand a little bit about what's going on in there. In this chapter, we will look at the underlying mechanisms in the brain. In the process we will deconstruct the question "What's going on in the brain?" In particular, in this chapter the following will be examined:

1. The basic structures of the brain to get a frame of reference and some familiarity for frequent terms,

2. The definitions for concepts such as emotion versus affect so we know what the research is measuring, and

3. Examples of research that link the neural substrates with the interventions and concerns promoted by positive psychology.

A LONG-STANDING MYSTERY

History is full of philosophers and researchers attempting to decipher the workings of the brain. We continue to speculate on its structure and how that relates to experience and behavior and we poke and prod the brain with all manner of substances to see what it does and what it feels like. Some interesting highlights: As far back as 4000 BCE, Sumerians experimented with the brain-altering effects of substances, such as extracts from the poppy plant. Around 1700 BCE, the Egyptians produced the first written account of the brain's anatomy, although apparently they had a low opinion of this brain's value as it was discarded before mummification. The brain had gained greater respect by the time of Plato. The Ancient Greek philosopher believed that the brain was the seat of mental processes. In 1796, Franz Gall published a treatise on phrenology, claiming that specific brain areas had certain brain functions and that, therefore, you could understand someone's personality by "feeling" the skull. The idea of specialized functions in the brain turned out to be right, even if the rest of it was declared pseudoscience. By 1929, Cecile Vogt identified over 200 cortical areas.

The naturalist Charles Darwin relied on theories of the brain in forming his theory of evolution. According to historians, one of his notebooks suggests that he anticipated the concept of brain plasticity as a necessary part of evolution. Harbinger of things to come, Darwin believed the brain continually adapted to its environment, even over as short a period as individual's lifetime. Needless to say, the last 50 years of innovation in imaging technologies have led to an explosion of research, new levels of understanding and reaffirmed some earlier speculation.

While much of the brain still remains a mystery, two big lessons handed down from history are important for understanding the potential of positive psychology:

1. The Ancient Greeks were right: Our minds and body are connected.
2. Darwin was on the right track: The brain is plastic, and has the ability to grow and transform over time.

HOW DO WE LEARN ABOUT THE BRAIN?

The brain is studied in multiple ways. Some are structural, exploring the anatomy of the brain and how it communicates within itself and with the body. Other approaches to studying the brain are functional, aimed at understanding how it enables us to think, perceive, learn, and, perhaps most of all, have a sense of self. The goal of positive psychology bridges these two approaches. We want to better understand the structural and functional ramifications of positive psychology interventions by looking at the underlying neural systems as well as the emotional and behavioral outcomes that contribute to happiness, well-being, and the construction of meaning.

Until recently, learning about the brain presented obvious challenges. Most of the earliest observations came by treating people who had suffered brain damage or by dissecting cadavers. Technological advances in medical imaging technologies have opened up a wealth of opportunities by giving scientists the ability to see inside the brain without invasive procedures. Some examples include computerized axial tomography (CAT or CT) scans that illuminate the structure of the brain and positron emission tomography (PET) scans that display the brain's metabolic functioning at a cellular level by tracking the amount of glucose processed in different brain regains. Functional magnetic resonance imaging (fMRI) is another imaging technology in widespread use today. It allows researchers to link a subject's self-reported experience while monitoring the real-time blood flow activity through different regions of the brain. The findings have helped psychologists reframe their metaphors for approaching the brain, moving from the "brain as computer" legacy of the cognitive revolution to one of an integrated mind-body system.

THE BRAIN IN BRIEF

Before we talk about what the brain does, we'll touch on some of the main parts that will come up in the research we review. There are many excellent sources for anatomy. This is just a brief overview to provide some orientation.

The brain is the central command center that sends, receives, and communicates information throughout the body. The brain is about the size of a coconut and although only 2 percent of your body weight, it is metabolically expensive, drawing 20 percent of your total body's energy demands—more energy than any other organ in your body. The brain gets energy from glucose, carried in the blood vessels cross the blood-brain barrier. The brain uses glucose to produce adenosine triphosphate (ATP). ATP is the main source of energy for the brain's cells, supporting communication as well as growth. Research has shown that different parts of the brain have specializations, contributing to specific functions.

Cerebrum

The cerebrum or cerebral cortex is the largest part of the brain. It has four main sections: the temporal lobe, the frontal lobe, the parietal lobe, and the occipital lobe. The cerebrum is divided into left and right hemispheres that are connected by neurons that transmit messages between the two hemispheres. This is the origin of the concept of left and right brain thinking, which, however attractive, turns out to be metaphorically useful but structurally inaccurate.

- The temporal lobe is the center for visual and auditory memory and helps direct hearing and speech.
- The frontal lobe controls a range of functions, including creative thought, judgment, behavior, attention, abstract thinking, smell, and personality.
- The parietal lobe is predominantly concerned with comprehension, including visual functions, language, and reading and also sensory input.
- The occipital lobe is located at the rear of the brain and is associated with vision.

Cerebellum

The cerebellum is often referred to as the "little brain" and is responsible for balance, posture, and coordination. It monitors and coordinates your body movement and position so you can move properly.

Limbic System

The limbic system is often thought of as the seat of emotions, containing glands that help manage emotions and hormones. It includes the amygdala, hippocampus, hypothalamus, and pituitary gland. These glands are responsible for visceral functions and basic behavioral responses such as feeding, drinking, aggression, and pleasure. The amygdala responds to emotions, memories, and fear. The hippocampus contributes to learning and memory, including the coding of information for transfer between short-term and long-term storage, and supports the analysis of spatial relationships.

The hypothalamus controls hormonal processes and basic physical functions such as thirst and temperature. The thalamus keeps track of physical sensations and helps direct attention.

The brainstem, which is made up of the medulla, the pons, and the midbrain, is in charge of all basic life functions. It is, evolutionarily speaking, the oldest part of the brain and has much in common with other animals. It relays signals between the brain and spinal cord and controls automatic functions.

Nervous System

The nervous system is a complex network of interconnected, excitable cells that communicate chemically. The brain and the spinal cord make up the central nervous system. The peripheral nervous system is the bundle of nerves connecting the brain to other parts of the body outside the spinal column. The peripheral nervous system has two components: the somatic nervous system and the autonomic nervous system. The somatic nervous system controls the voluntary muscles in the body associated around the skeleton. The autonomic nervous system is also called the involuntary nervous system because it controls functions out of our conscious awareness. The autonomic nervous system has control over a variety of functions like heart rate, respiration, salivation, and sexual arousal. The autonomic nervous system is subdivided into two subsystems that may sound familiar: the parasympathetic nervous system is responsible for controlling activities that are primarily related to the body in a relaxed state, "rest and digest." The other division is the sympathetic nervous system that controls stimulating activities that we think of as "fight or flight."

The brain has two kinds of cells: neurons that perform communication and processing tasks and neuralgia that support and protect the neurons. It has about 100 billion neurons that gather and send electrochemical signals. A neuron communicates using electrochemicals called neurotransmitters.

Neurotransmitters

Neurotransmitters are the chemicals in the brain that allow the neurons to communicate. Neurotransmitters play a role in everyday functioning by delivering the signals that keep your heart beating and your lungs breathing as well as influence things like mood, sleep, and concentration. There is a junction, or space, called a synapse between the neurons. Neurotransmitters work by creating a chemical "bridge" across the synapse between two neurons to allow the electrical current to move forward. Communication can occur only when the neuron releases a neurotransmitter into the synapse and it binds with a matching receptor cell. We function best when our neurotransmitters are in balance. External factors like stress, diet, drugs, and exercise as well as disease and hereditary factors can influence our neurotransmitter function.

There are different types and classes of neurotransmitters and they have distinctive functions. Some are excitatory. They increase the likelihood that a neuron will fire. Others are inhibitory and their function is to lessen the likelihood of a neuron firing and can calm brain activity.

Some of most common neurotransmitters are as follows:

- Acetylcholine (ACh) is the transmitter at all neuromuscular junctions, stimulating all muscle contractions. It is also active throughout the brain, supporting memory, cognition, and motor control.
- Gamma-aminobutyric acid (GABA) functions in the body as an inhibitor to balance the over-firing of other neurons.
- Endorphins are involved in pain suppression, reward, and positive mood states.
- Serotonin contributes to mood stability and balances excesses of excitatory neurotransmitter activations. It contributes to feelings of well-being and happiness and regulates other processes such as sleep cycle, pain control, and digestions. Low serotonin is associated with diminished immune system function. Some antidepressants such as Prozac and Zoloft are a class called selective serotonin reuptake inhibitors (SSRIs) because they specifically target serotonin.
- Dopamine can be both excitatory and inhibitory. It is the main neurotransmitter behind attention and focus. It is active in the brain's perceptions of reward and pleasure. It allows us to recognize and move toward reward. It can also help regulate movement and emotional and hormonal responses. Stimulants such as ADD/ADHD medication increase the amount of dopamine in the synapse.
- Norepinephrine is the primary transmitter from the sympathetic half of the autonomic nervous system to the body's organs and glans. It is also in many brain areas involved in nervous system arousal, hunger, and mood control. A related neurotransmitter, epinephrine, is also an excitatory neurotransmitter related to stress and anxiety. Epinephrine regulates heart rate and blood pressure.
- Oxytocin is a hormone that also serves as a neurotransmitter. Oxytocin enhances bonding between mates and between mothers and newborns. It has been shown to increase the level of trust between people.
- Opioids are peptides that mimic neurotransmitters. They have pain-relieving qualities by flooding the brain's reward system with dopamine, but also play a role in a complex set of behaviors, such as physical attraction. Repeated availability of opioids can create a tolerance and lead to physical addiction (Carlson, 2012).

EVOLUTIONARY BRAIN MODELS APPLIED TO UNDERSTANDING BEHAVIOR

In spite of impressive advances, the brain remains one of the least under-stood parts of the human body, yet one of the most critical. It controls all the automatic functions like breathing and heart rate, is the source of our emotions and memories, and creates the conscious awareness that gives us the sense of who we are as human beings.

In the 17th century, the philosopher Descartes proposed the Cartesian the-ory of mind-body dualism, which stated that the mind and body were sepa-rate entities. Although long discredited, the model tends to permeate Western thinking.

Why Is It So Hard to Resist Chocolate?

In 1949, the neuroscientist and physician Paul MacLean published a paper in which he introduced the Triune Brain Model. MacLean wrote that brain evolution occurred in "quantum leaps," creating three separate structures. He believed that, in spite of vast neural interconnections, the brain could be viewed productively as three brains in one, the reptilian brain, the mammalian brain, and the neomammalian or new brain, each with different forms of information processing.

The reptilian brain was responsible for instinctive functions, such as breath-ing, heart rate, and vital functions, and primitive reflexive emotional reactions, such as seeking, fear, and sexuality. It is functionally related to the brainstem and middle brain structures.

The mammalian brain, also dubbed by MacLean as the limbic system, added social emotions and other mental non-reflexive activity. Neither the reptilian brain nor the mammalian brand had the neural circuits for verbal communication.

The neocortex, developed millions of years later, gave humans cognitive reasoning and the ability to assign meaning to sensory experiences, abstract thought, self-consciousness, and the evolutionary advantage of forward plan-ning. It created the executive functions that expand the repertoire of human emotions into evaluative emotions such as gratitude.

MacLean's neuroanatomical model is obviously simplistic relative to the brain's physical complexity and has, therefore, been the subject of criticism. However, this model has been adopted by an increasing number of neurosci-entists and across a number of fields, such as marketing, design, and leader-ship, because it provides a useful framework or heuristic for thinking about how humans react to and experience different events and emotions.

The neuroscientist Jaak Panksepp argues that MacLean's model provides a relevant perspective because it highlights how emotional responses serve an evolutionary purpose—our survival. He contends that we aren't used to thinking about our affective states as being part of an ancient structure that we share with other mammals.

MacLean's reptilian, mammalian, and new brains make it easier to visualize the difference between unconscious responses to perception and emotions and the "new" brain's conscious analytical, linear processing of information. This facilitates our self-understanding and increases our awareness of the complexity of emotions and behaviors, a useful step in making change.

The Triune brain theory is functionally similar to several other psychological theories of information processing. For example, the psychologist William James argued that awareness was made up of two elements: focused attention, or nucleus, and the unattended awareness, or fringe. This perspective is reflected in the Elaboration Likelihood Model (ELM) developed by psychologists Richard Petty and John Cacioppo. ELM is commonly applied today in marketing and media research. This model proposes multiple routes for message processing but not all information receives similar attention. Information received in the central route is given careful scrutiny and evaluation. Information coming via the peripheral route is not processed with conscious attention but can exert significant influence in surprising and unpredictable ways.

Similar to MacLean's theorizing, Panksepp's research has led him to define three affective networks that make up all emotions: (1) primary-process emotions that are basic-primordial affects in the subcortical area, (2) secondary-process emotions that emerge from simple learning via the basal ganglia, and (3) tertiary-process emotions that are the conscious cognitive executive functions. He summarizes his findings into seven basic emotional systems that operate on a continuum from positive to negative. The primary emotions are seeking, rage, fear, lust, care, grief, and play. All emotional systems, including abstract constructs, are experienced at the conscious level but all have roots in the subcortical emotional brain organization. Panksepp suggests a neurobiology of positive emotions must understand the primitive roots of emotions, not just the abstract manifestation.

In *Thinking, Fast and Slow*, the Nobel Prize–winning psychologist Daniel Kahneman captures a similar concept with his narrative model that characterizes two types of processing: System 1 as intuition and System 2 as conscious reason. Extending the ELM model, System 1 is unconscious, automatic, nonverbal, evolutionarily old and "fast." System 2 is intentional, language-based, explicit, conscious, judgmental, takes effort, and so is "slow." Kahneman describes System 2 as the person that thinks he's the star of the show, when it's really System 1 that calls most of the shots.

In the *Happiness Hypothesis*, social psychologist Jonathan Haidt provides another image to drive home this tug-of-war between our conscious intentions and our subconscious instincts, automatic behaviors, and desires. In Haidt's version, an elephant represents the primitive, sensory-driven unconscious brain and the elephant's rider is our conscious, rational brain. This metaphor visually illustrates the power struggle between the small rider's ability to control the attitudes, desires, and behavior of a large elephant when the two are at odds.

Thus when it comes to resisting chocolate or coveting a new smartphone, research suggests that the "reptilian" or instinctive brain (aka System 1 or the elephant) drives up to 95 percent of decision making through what happens in that initial preconscious processing. According to Panksepp's evolutionary perspective, that's because our natural reaction to people and events are initially influenced by the primitive responses. Primitive affective states are signals that let us know how we're doing in our quest to survive. Clearly, we need chocolate to survive.

However you visualize them, these models can provide you with insight about the sometimes-surprising behavior of different people—even ourselves. These models can help us develop different strategies for everything from dealing with roommates, and getting up early to exercise or forming new thought patterns of gratitude and appreciation that contribute to our sense of well-being.

STARTING WITH PLEASURE

In 1954, psychologists James Olds and Peter Milner made an exciting discovery. They found that when they implanted electrodes that stimulated an area of the limbic system in a rat's brain, the rats would repeatedly press a lever to continue receiving the electrical stimulation. Olds and Milner, along with many others, believed they had found the pleasure center of the brain. A nearby area was later identified as one of the principal regions where the neurotransmitter dopamine was released, causing researchers to declare dopamine to be the brain's "pleasure chemical." According to neuroscientists Berridge and Kringelbach (2011), this finding was embraced by hopeful psychologists who saw it as a cure for pain and suffering, if not the ability to spread euphoria to the masses.

The discovery of dopamine and the pleasure center, while a major milestone, turned out to be too good to be true. The impact of dopamine wasn't always positive. Dopamine has also been found to create sensations of "wanting" without the pleasure of "liking." Some researchers question whether or not Olds and Milner's electrical charges had caused "wanting" and the motivation to seek stimulation, not pleasure as originally thought. The search for a brain-based explanation for happiness had slipped away. As Stanford's David Lipton (2013) commiserates:

> We have come a long way from sticking a giant electrode in a rat brain and passing current. All of this technical mastery that we have access to today is absolutely necessary because it turns out that many of the circuits in the brain are so tightly intermingled and complex they require all the tools afforded by modern neuroscience.

EMOTIONS VERSUS AFFECT

Positive psychology researchers make distinctions between pleasure— hedonic happiness—and meaning—eudaimonic happiness—in order to have a construct they can accurately measure in order to understand the neural substrates of emotion. To do so, they separate primary level emotions where there are standard measures, such as rage, lust, and pleasure, from more abstract feelings that are more subjective to measure because they require learned response or cognitive appraisal to assign a positive or negative meaning.

For this same reason, researchers and theorists also discriminate between the terms "emotion" and "affect." In daily life, we're used to saying "emotion" to mean the full range of emotional experience—and most of us don't use the word "affect" at all in conversation. Most researchers define emotions and affective feelings as different constructs. Definitions matter when researchers operationalize constructs in order to do experiments for two reasons. First, experiments need to be standardized so someone can replicate them. Second, the reader needs to understand what the researcher is talking about for it to have any meaning. If a research study reports that taking a short walk every day improves your emotional outlook, we need to know what they are measuring.

Psychologist Barbara Fredrickson defines emotions as responses that happen over a short amount of time, beginning with the assessment of personal meaning, either consciously or unconsciously. Although not all agree, many scholars find it useful to categorize emotions and have created sorting schemes to identify what they consider primary emotions, such as fear, anger, love, or joy. Recently, researchers Saif Mohammad and Peter Turney (2010) used Amazon's online crowdsourcing service, Mechanical Turk, to create an emotional lexicon from the social web that makes an interesting comparison to long-standing academic models. Table 6.1 shows an established lexicon by well-known psychologists Keith Oatley and Phillip Johnson-Laird (2013), Mohammad and Turney's (2010) crowdsourced lexicon, and Panksepp's (2011) evolution-based primary-process emotions.

Table 6.1. Comparison of Major Emotional Lexicons

Oatley and Johnson-Laird	Mechanical Turk	Panksepp
Anger	Anger	Rage
Anticipation	Disgust	Seeking
Disgust	Fear	Fear
Fear	Happiness	Play
Joy	Sadness	Grief
Sadness		Lust
Surprise		Care
Trust		

Compared to categorizable and discreet emotions, the concept of "affect" is defined as a more general and free-floating experience, unrelated to a specific object and of indefinite time duration. Psychologist Ed Diener uses a two-dimensional conceptualization, where affect is evaluated in intensity from high to low and value, from positive or pleasant to unpleasant or negative.

We may find it most useful to look at emotions as complex structures that are part of the way we interact with the environment. They are our intuitive guides to the people and experiences around us. They also filter our understanding of new information.

There is an inclination to assume that only positive emotions are good, but there is adaptive value in both positive and negative emotions. Negative emotions serve as a warning signal. Humans are more natively responsive to negative emotions than positive ones. This is part of our survival instinct—things that threatened our safety were most important to identify to protect our existence. These instinctive responses, however, can turn an adaptive response into a problematic one. What used to serve us well on the Savannah of Africa hunting sabre-tooth tigers may not be as routinely useful in our day-to-day lives. The stress response was and is useful to keep you safe and can still play a role to keep you from stepping out in front of a taxi in New York City. There are plenty of situations, however, where the bodily changes from stress are counterproductive for the task at hand, such as the stress response generated when you're rushing to meet a deadline. In the case of stress before a deadline, the response means you work less effectively and creatively when stressed because all the blood is in your arms and legs ready to make a break for it. If you are under sustained stress, it can have longer-term negative health consequences. Sustained stress can lead to high blood pressure and clogged arteries.

Understanding a bit of neuroscience can help us recognize our biological and genetic predispositions. This insight can free us from unnecessary self-recriminations about willpower and allow us to intentionally move toward our inherent strengths and active exercises to short-circuit automatic reactions and function more intentionally, effectively, and happily.

PHYSICAL AND MENTAL BENEFITS OF POSITIVE EMOTIONS

Neuroscientists have examined a number of ways that positive psychology approaches can impact well-being and support quality of life, from keeping the brain healthy to improving mental and physical health. This section presents examples where neuroscience is shedding light on some of the underlying neurobiological mechanisms of positive psychology concerns.

Cognitive Support and Neuroplasticity

Happiness may bring to mind an image of skipping through a field of daisies or balloons and ice cream, but when you consider its impact on your body, happiness is not a frivolous emotion. As we said earlier, however, it's important to define our terms. When researchers talk about happiness, they're talking about the more substantive and enduring positive emotions, such as the happiness that comes from satisfaction or social connection, rather than the transitory pleasure from something like eating ice cream.

Positive emotions not only help you perform better; they keep you performing better throughout your lifetime. It wasn't long ago that scientists and doctors believed the cognitive decline due to aging was normal and irreversible. We now know that the human brain has neuroplasticity and neurogenerative properties and, as Darwin believed, adapts and grows in response to the environment. Employing a positive psychology perspective—cultivating positive emotions such as happiness, gratitude, and appreciation—can drive brain growth in positive directions by forming new neural connections, protecting it from damage and generating new brain cells.

Neuroplasticity enables you to change your brain through experience. The neuroscientist Richard Davidson and colleagues (2008) studied the brain function of Buddhist monks to explore the potential neuroplastic impact of positive emotions. He reasoned that the mental training of meditation was no different that the acquisition of other skills that cause changes in the brain. The fMRI imaging of brain activity during meditation by long-term practitioners confirmed that they had actually changed the structure and function of their brains. Activated areas were associated with sustained attention and lower emotional reactivity with minimal effort. In other studies comparing mindfulness, those who meditated had more gray matter concentration (density of neuronal cell bodies) in the hippocampus compared to those who did not meditate.

Some of the monks in Davidson's study had devoted as many as 19,000 hours to meditation practice. But it's not necessary to become a Buddhist monk to reap the positive physiological benefits of meditation. Britta Hölzel and colleagues (2011) at the Institute of Neuroimaging in Germany found that the stress-reducing effect was directly related to increased gray matter in the amygdala in as little as eight weeks. The temporoparietal junction also contained increases in gray matter for the meditators. This area has been linked to self-awareness of bodily states, or embodiment, which has been suggested to contribute to empathic responses.

In 2007, psychologist Sonya Lyubomirsky studied a group of healthy workers who were enrolled in an eight-week training program in mindfulness meditation. At the end of the training, participants showed increased brain asymmetry and more activation of the left prefrontal cortex, an area related to greater happiness and engagement. They also reported lower levels of anxiety and depression. After meditating for only eight weeks, the participants also showed a stronger response in their immune systems to a flu vaccination that had been administered at the start of the study.

New England Patriots quarterback Tom Brady is a real-life example of intentional activities to take advantage of neuroplasticity to maintain cognitive health. In the off-season, Brady looks for ways to sharpen his decision-making skills and maintain his mental acuity. Based on baseline scan of neurological functions, Brady and his coach designed a program to make his brain perform even better. After identifying areas where Brady's brain was deficient, they created exercises to get Brady back into what's defined as the median range. The exercises are geared toward speeding up visual processing, verbalization, and memory skills. Brady's coach also advocates brain training to help with brain resiliency to recover from the inevitable sacks.

GETTING ALONG WITH OTHERS

Human are social animals. According to recent advances in social neuroscience, a major portion of our brain is devoted to social processing. Research examining the "default" processing system—what we think about when we're not thinking about anything—fires up the same areas of the brain as when we're thinking about other people. This explains some of the irresistible nature of gossip, rubbernecking, and eavesdropping. According to social neuroscientists like Matthew Lieberman, our default state of social processing is a reflection our instinctive need for social connection. From an evolutionary perspective, we have always needed to be in groups for survival. Our ability to find shelter, food, and take care of our young relied on our ability to form tribes or collaborative groups with emotional bonds. It also contributed to our survival because being with others improves our physical defenses, but lowers the need for emotional defenses. We are more relaxed and this contributes to the emotional and physical health of the entire group.

Attachment

Attachment is the emotional bond that connects one person to another. Attachment theory is attributed to the 1958 work of London psychologist and psychiatrist John Bowlby. Bowlby (1982) treated emotionally disturbed children. This experience led him to focus on the importance of the caregiver–child relationship and how that emotional attachment influenced all aspects of a child's cognitive, emotional, social, and physical development. At the time, attachment theory was a groundbreaking perspective. It flew in the face of the widespread beliefs of the time that were based on behavioral theory. These credited feeding as the source of the child's attachment to the mother. In attachment theory, a healthy attachment develops due to interaction with a caregiver and caregiver responsiveness. Several theorists, including Bowlby, increasingly saw the caregiver–child attachment as an evolution-based adaptive behavior, deeply embedded into a child to enhance changes of survival.

Attachment bonds are not an "all-or-nothing" process. Individual differences in parent–child personalities, relationships, and context contributed to what child psychologist Mary Ainsworth (1979) identified as four primary attachment styles: secure, avoidance, resistance, and disorganized or disoriented. This model has been widely adopted both in and outside of clinical settings. Researchers and clinicians have identified the secure attachment style as most commonly associated with good psychological health, but more important, perhaps, are the relational patterns and emotions different styles signify in practical applications. Attachment styles have been a useful tool in understanding interpersonal dynamics at all ages and have been used as the theoretical basis for a wide range of applications, from relationship therapy and group dynamics to leadership coaching.

From a neurobiological perspective, forming bonds with others may start in childhood, but social bonds are a critical factor in well-being at all ages. Attachment styles can influence how we connect with others for social support, how we perceive social support and it contributes to our arsenal of coping strategies. Social support is one form of attachment that is widely researched. Social support comes in many kinds—a best friend, family, a group of friends, a group of people with similar interest or an online support group, or even fan forum. All have multiple positive benefits. Social support lowers stress, increases immune system strength, provides social validation, and enables personal growth. An online fan forum for Twilight fans provided social validation and normalized feelings of being "weird" for having an interest that their immediate family and friends didn't share. Lack of social connection is associated with depression, anxiety, and loneliness, all predictors of lower perceived quality of life. According to the Center for Aging Studies in Australia, older people with large groups of friends had a 22 percent chance of outliving those with only a few friends.

Neuropsychoanalyst Allan Schore (2001) studies the neurobiology of attachment connections and the impact on the evolution of structures in children's brains. He argues that, as Bowlby suggested, attachment theory is fundamentally a regulatory theory. Neuroimaging data confirm that the maturation of an area of the right front cortex is influenced by the interactions of the child and caregiver. As this area matures, a child's ability to self-regulate emotion improves. The ability to self-regulate is what enables us to calm ourselves down, create new habits, and generally exert control over our thoughts, feelings, and actions. In other words, it's self-regulation that gives us control over our reptilian impulses.

Shelley Taylor and colleagues (2007) looked at the health benefits of social support and social context. Taylor argues that in threatening times, people seek positive social relationships as a coping strategy for stress. Early nurturing experiences help shape a child's response to stress, such as giving the child emotional coping skills and the ability to control behavioral reactions. Like Schore (2001), Taylor looks at how a positive child–caregiver relationship and environment influences the development of the stress regulatory system that controls the hypothalamic-pituitary-adrenocortical (HPA) system triggered during a stress response. Lack of stress response regulation has been linked to a long list of physical and emotional problems, including metabolic syndrome, levels of C-reactive protein, hypertension, autoimmune disease, and affective disorders such as major depression (Snyder & Lopez, 2007).

Matthew Lieberman is one of the pioneers in the emerging field of social neuroscience. In *Social: Why Our Brains Are Wired to Connect*, he cites studies that have documented how our social intelligence uses different parts of the brain than general intelligence. The brain regions associated with social intelligence, such as thinking about what your friends are doing, light up the midline or medial regions of the brain. General intelligence, which includes things like working memory and reasoning, tends to shows up on the outer surface of the brain. This distinction between social and general intelligence makes sense to those of us who have had a friend who had "street smarts" but never did particularly well in school.

Our social intelligence is how we monitor group behaviors; recognize social norms, social validation, and affiliation; detect rejection; seek out social support; and maintain friendships and connections. Social connection is powerful. So powerful, in fact, that our brains don't discriminate between physical and social pain. The brain processes social pleasure, such as being loved, or experiencing social distress, such as being rejected, almost identically to the way it responds to physical pleasure and pain.

Why would the brain work this way? Some researchers suggest that the evolution of the brain and the importance of social bonds to survival the connection of social are the reasons that physical pleasure and pain neural mechanisms are connected to social behaviors. Evidence from one experiment showed that social support reduced sensitivity to physical pain and social rejection actually increased the experience of physical pain. In another experiment, subjects participated in a simulated ball tossing game where one participant was intentionally excluded while their brains were monitored using fMRI imagery. Results showed that experiencing social exclusion activated the somatosensory components of physical pain in the brain. In another series of experiments, the subject's friend was administered a mildly painful stimulus while the subject watched. Both the friend, who had actually felt the pain, and the subject, who empathized with the friend, registered activity in the sensory processing area associated with physical pain. In a reward-based experiment using computer activity, participants were monitored while they anticipated either a monetary award or social feedback in the form of friendly faces. For women, the brain's reward system in the ventral striatum reacted equally as strongly to social rewards as it did to financial rewards. The men reacted more to the financial reward than to the social reward, but both rewards shared the same neural basis. German researchers found that for individuals who used social media regularly, their reward system fired in response to positive online comments from friends. Twitter use has been shown to raise oxytocin in the blood, another indicator of the pleasure response.

Our socially oriented brains see social recognition and inclusion, like being acknowledged for your contribution on a project, getting a "like" on Facebook or being invited to a party, as valuable as cold hard cash. But rewards aren't always self-focused. Researchers also found that for participants who were offered money in an experiment, those who donated the money to charity rather than keeping it for themselves showed heightened activity in the brain's reward center. Altruistic behaviors, such as giving to others, trigger our reward mechanisms, hence the saying "It is better to give than receive."

The reward effect of giving applies to sharing online content as well. We experience increased brain activity when we think about sharing and who we'll share it with, suggesting that the reward buzz in our brains may also play a role in which videos go viral on YouTube.

But wait, as they say on late night TV, there's more. When the reward system is activated, it inhibits the alarm system in the amygdala, which is known for its role in the "fight or flight" response. In other words, the reward system offsets stress. Cues of social connection, indicating one is valued and cared for, reinforce the experience of social pleasure through the reward system. Scientists think that activation of the reward system helps encourage the reciprocal response of nurturing and connection. Our brains instinctively keep track of who is committed in a relationship by their willingness to fairly contribute. The reward center sends out "all's clear" safety messages that are related to reductions in autonomic and endocrine responses, alleviating both rapid heart rate and sweaty palms. The safety-related regions also can inhibit sympathetic responses, which we think of as the activation of fight and flight response, and promote parasympathetic responses or the signals to relax and repair. This ability can protect your health. When the reward center kicks in, the parasympathetic system responds by reducing heart rate, lowering cortisol (the stress hormone), and reducing the inflammation that contributes to things like hypertension and gastric ulcers.

Even thinking of one's social connections can trigger the "all's clear" neural mechanism and, therefore, have a positive impact on physical health. In a study by Eisenberger and Cole (2012), seeing a photograph of a romantic partner was linked with lower self-reports of physical pain, a reaction linked to the social bonding neuropeptides such as oxytocin and stress-reduction. This means there's real psychological benefit to keeping that picture of your loved ones on your home screen.

Your Empathic Brain

Imagine you're on your way to your high school reunion and you're looking forward to seeing your old friend Joey. You haven't seen him in about 10 years; you're Facebook friends but not really in touch. You remember him as a great guy. Charming, mellow, and athletically gifted. During high school and college, he was on the football team. During that time, he got knocked around on the field, sustaining several concussions over the course of his playing career. When you see him, you're surprised to learn that he just got fired from his job because he couldn't control his anger. His girlfriend left him telling him he was self-centered, intolerant, and obnoxious (no wonder he isn't posting on Facebook!). He confesses to you that he doesn't feel like himself. Everything, including him, feels out of control. What's going on?

Joey is suffering from traumatic brain injury (TBI). TBI is a painful illustration of how specific parts of the brain influence our ability to have and express emotions. In Joey's case, he has lost the ability to control his emotions. Because of this, he is unable to control his own emotions, such as anger, or feel empathy for those around him.

Research in social neuroscience has identified the pre-frontal and parietal cortices as integral to having capacity to mentalize, or form internal simulations about someone else's physical or mental state. When people like Joey lose the ability to judge other people's emotions from damage to areas of the brain, they have lost the skill that is crucial for empathy.

Our brains' networks are malleable and, thanks to neuroplasticity, continually change. Therefore our capacity for empathy and compassion can change as well. Even in the case of TBI, emerging research creates hope that damage isn't permanent given appropriate treatment to stimulate growth and restore cerebral function.

There is increasing evidence that mindfulness meditation, the intentional focusing of attention on the present moment, can influence brain structure and alter neural function, even in a relatively short period of time. The reports of gray matter growth (increased neural cell density) suggest that mindfulness practices may impact activity in the cortical centers, improving top-down control, and enhancing the ability to exercise self-regulation. Several reports suggest that regular mindfulness practices support brain health by decreasing the degeneration of neural tissues over time.

Using fMRI imagery, a group of neuroscientists recently demonstrated that it might be possible to train the brain to feel more empathy. Subjects developed personal anecdotes to capture different emotions, such as pride or affection or neutral emotions, such as daily activities. Similar to biofeedback studies, the researchers gave volunteers neurofeedback about their brain activity patterns in areas related to tenderness and affection when they recalled their anecdotes. The brains of subjects who had received earlier social feedback had significantly stronger activity in the areas associated with affection in earlier research in later trials, no matter what anecdotes they recalled.

BRAIN BENEFITS OF HUMOR

Humor and empathy are both related to healthy interpersonal relationships. To successfully appreciate humor means activating our ability to mentalize or view something from another person's perspective. Evidence suggests that there is a relationship between humor and emotional self-awareness, which is related to emotional intelligence. According to researchers at Stanford Medical School, humor activates the reward center, the same response as social pleasure. When we hear something funny, our subcortical network devoted to rewards and pleasure lights up. In 1989, researchers measured the impact of humor on neuroendocrine stress hormones from blood samples. After 60 minutes of a humorous videotape, five of the eight hormones known to react to stress significantly decreased.

As if that wasn't benefit enough, researchers Greengross and Miller (2011) suggest that a man's ability to make a woman laugh may make him more attractive as a mate. Based on activity in the reward center, humor is one of the most important predictors of mating success because it suggests intelligence, creativity, and "genetic fitness."

FORGIVE AND FORGET

Are you still harboring an old grudge? Do your brain and yourself a favor. Get over it. Forgiveness means getting over an injury to your sense of self. Realizing that you are identifying your "self" with the transgression can help. Anything from personal property to social affronts can trigger feelings of violation and disrespect. This is problematic from an evolutionary point of view, because it is your "self" that you are hardwired to protect. The sense of self is located in the frontal, parietal, and temporal lobes, linked to the sensory system of the emotional center in the limbic system. In other words, you were mad or hurt before you even knew it. The involvement of the limbic system makes us prone to resorting to primitive behaviors, such as revenge. We might intuitively understand the adaptive nature of retaliation when wronged because forgiveness means relinquishing the "right" to remedy a wrong.

Why would forgiveness be evolutionarily adaptive? Some theorists suggest that because insult triggers the stress response, sustained stress alters the neural structure and can damage the cardiovascular, nervous, and immune systems. Therefore, forgiveness improves your health by inhibiting the stress response. Forgiveness not only reduces stress from conflict but also increases social bonds when it triggers the reward neurochemicals that mediate the anger response. Positive feelings have more than an inward impact; they are also experienced externally. The renewal of goodwill generates positive actions toward the offender. In other words, the change in facial expression, voice tone, and body language sends signals beyond the words that others respond to. Both the forgiver and offender, when an apology is accepted, register neural activity in brain regions associated with empathy. Researchers found that areas in the brain related to emotional mirroring as well as mentalizing, or empathizing with the other person's feelings on a cognitive level, were involved. The behavioral ritual of apology-empathy-forgiving is viewed as a central process in preserving cohesiveness in damaged social relationships.

TAKING CARE OF YOUR BRAIN

Exercise

Once again, exercise may be the one positive psychology intervention that does it all. Studies show that exercise promotes brain health both inside and out by directly supporting the brain while giving it a healthier body to live in.

Researchers have documented a long and impressive list of benefits on physical and mental health from exercise. Exercise improves mood, lowers anxiety, boosts self-confidence, and enhances cognitive ability. Positive psychologist Sonya Lyubomirsky found that three 45-minute sessions of aerobic exercise a week for four months were just as effective at treating depression as the antidepressant medication Zoloft. Participants who participated in exercise as part of the treatment were also less likely to relapse.

Multiple studies have confirmed that exercise benefits brain health and function, particularly in aging populations. A large five-year study by Cotman, Berchtold, and Christie (2002) showed that exercise was related to lower rates of various types of cognitive decline, including Alzheimer's decease. Combined with data from animal research, evidence demonstrated that physical activity protects against brain injury and stimulates the production of new brain cells.

In the early 1990s, researchers assumed that the myriad of benefits from exercise was due to the improvements in general health. However, recently, studies have examined the possibility that exercise has direct benefits on the molecular systems of the brain itself. Some scientists have focused on neurotropic factors as likely candidates. Neurotrophic factors are groups of neuropeptides that promote the growth, function, and survival of neurons. According to Cotman and Berchtold, one brain-derived neurotrophic factor (BDNF) has promise as being a facilitator of neurons to communicate efficiently and adapt based on environmental demands. In one study using mice, the researchers expected any response to be restricted to the motor sensory systems; however, the results surprised them. They also saw positive impact in an area normally associated with higher cognitive function. Further research in this area has shown that BDNF and other growth factors are central to the benefits of exercise through dual pathways.

New theories view exercise as a mechanism that increases several growth factors impacting brain health directly and indirectly, just as it did for the mice. Diseases like hypertension, hyperglycemia, and insulin sensitivity are all part of a cluster of conditions called "metabolic syndrome." The common link among these features is inflammation. Consistent inflammation causing metabolic syndrome is linked to inflammation of the central nervous system and resulting cognitive decline. Exercise reduces inflammation that results in the improvement of conditions in metabolic syndrome, such as cardiac health, lipid-cholesterol balance, and insulin sensitivity.

Thus exercise improves brain health by two mechanisms. The central mechanism is by triggering growth factor cascades that directly support the brain—improved cognition, blood flow in the brain, and the ability of the brain to adapt and learn. The peripheral mechanism is through the physical benefits that decrease inflammation throughout the body that indirectly contribute to the health of the brain by reducing things like hypertension that are actively damaging to brain health.

We've been looking at the neural underpinnings of the benefits of exercise on physical and cognitive health. Many studies have also examined the specific relationship between exercise and the neural reward system, such as the release of endorphins for the "runner's high" as an approach to relieve depression and stress. To date, research is inconclusive and the mechanisms remain unclear. The impact of exercise on serotonin has also been examined as a means of understanding the relationship between exercise and mood. There are psychological factors at play, however, that may influence our perception of the experience. For example, undertaking regular exercise may increase self-esteem by improving self-perception. Increased strength, stamina, and coordination can improve the quality of our daily lives that also enhance our mood. Exercise can increase the sense of control and mastery, social validation, and reduce stress, all of which improve mood and self-esteem as well. And as shown by Cotman and Berchtold's model, physical activity has a myriad of effects that can be linked to a wide range of outcomes, from reducing the risk of cancer, diabetes, and hypertension to building stronger bones, muscles, and brain cells. The big question is—how can we motivate people to exercise regularly?

Building Resilience

Resilience is a dynamic process that enables you to overcome adversity and setbacks over the course of your life. One of the questions inspiring many positive psychologists is "why do some people recover quickly and easily from trauma and setbacks and why do others not?"

The neurobiology of resilience is related to the stress response and reward systems. Resilience in the face of adversity requires us to have the ability to regulate our response to stress and the feedback system that links the brain to our entire body. The Gene-by-Environment (GxE) concept has gained momentum drawing on data from human and animal studies. Recent studies have suggested that there are biological mechanisms that interact with the environment and influence our central nervous system's reactivity and adaptability.

Based on animal studies, researchers have shown how stressors in the psychosocial environment can influence gene expression and behavior during critical periods of development, underscoring the need for better understanding of the GxE interaction. For example, in one study mice were subjected to the "social defeat paradigm," in which they were subjected to hostile social situations (in other words, they were placed in a cage with a bully where they had no chance of winning the confrontation). This setup is one of the most successful experimental models for testing the impact of chronic and severe stress in mice. The typical results include anxiety and social withdrawal, accompanied by an extended rise in levels of corticosterone. In this experiment, all the mice came from the same gene pool and were exposed to the same stressors. However, not all of the mice displayed the expected social and physical reactions. Some demonstrated resilience by still behaving normally.

As we discussed earlier in this chapter, researchers have been looking at the impact of early childhood attachment on the GxE interaction. For example, a secure attachment stimulated by the caregiver facilitates the integration of sensory, emotional, and social experiences. Some researchers hypothesize that this experience of caregiver–child interaction integrates right and left hemisphere circuits, where maltreatment in early childhood interrupts the development of the brain structure linking both hemispheres.

Beyond the psychosocial skills of trust and love learned in early childhood, research suggests that positive emotions are important source of resilience, decreasing pain and pain-related rumination. Extensive research by Fredrickson and colleagues (2005) show that positive emotions contribute to multiple aspects of physical and psychological health. In one study, positive emotions were related to a faster recovery from cardiovascular reactivity. In another, positive emotions appeared to help resilient individuals cope with larger traumatic events, such as 9/11 attacks on the World Trade Center.

The U.S. Army, traditionally waiting to treat personnel when they develop problems, has embraced positive psychology to develop a proactive and preventative program to improve resilience. The Comprehensive Soldier Fitness program includes assessment of emotional and social fitness and support systems, individualized training, and formal resilience training.

A WELL-FUNCTIONING BRAIN

Cognitive Flexibility

Cognitive flexibility, which includes mental set shifting, cognitive shifting, and attention switching or shifting, is the ability to change what you're thinking about and how you think about it. A part of the executive function of the

LIFE STRATEGY: COGNITIVE REAPPRAISAL

Cognitive reappraisal, also called reframing, is the ability to change the way you think about any event that bothers you. Everyone has internal beliefs that influence how we think, even without our awareness. These beliefs become organizing principles, or schema, for how we see and interpret ourselves and the world around us. Cognitive appraisal is a way of looking at a situation from a different point of view. One can then recognize and change negative schema, shifting perceptions and emotions in more positive directions and increasing resiliency.

Reframing Guidelines

- Many tend to see things as right or wrong, black or white. Examine the situation for the middle ground. Imagine the situation from another person's point of view.
- Look for signs that you are setting unreasonable expectations for yourself. Listen for words like "should" or "have to." Try substituting "choose" and see how that feels.
- Make a conscious effort to see the positive side when you're upset. People often assume something is their fault or jump to negative conclusions when they react emotionally rather than rationally. When we're emotional, we tend to view things through that lens. When we feel bad, we tend to notice negative things and turn our feelings into facts.
- Bad things happen but that doesn't mean you're a bad person. People who generalize in this way corrode their self-efficacy. Do you blame yourself, rather than identify a situation or person as difficult?
- When we're tired, anxious, and stressed, it's easy to think something is worse than it is or anticipate a series of events that haven't even happened. Do a reality check.

brain, cognitive flexibility describes the ability to adjust your thinking and attention in response to what's happening around you or a change in your goals. It is the cognitive ability that allows you to apply old information to new problems or change your beliefs and attitudes with new information or new experience. It is essential to the ability to synthesize information and for the "thinking outside the box" ability driving creativity and innovation. Cognitive flexibility increases from childhood to adulthood with the development of maturing synaptic connection and the volume of the brain that increases from birth to the mid-twenties.

A considerable amount of research suggests that positive emotions increases cognitive flexibility. In fact, some of the most distinctive effects are on increased flexibility and creativity. Positive emotions also impact a number of related processes, such as problem solving, improving the ability to remember and recall material, and adapting strategies for decision making.

LIFE STRATEGY (Continued)

Exercise

Try this exercise and think about the different ways we can construct new perspectives:

1. Write down something that frustrates you or that you would like to change about yourself (be specific).

2. Write down four core beliefs that are behind the thing in step 1. Write down any negative thoughts that are behind it. (For example, if step 1 were "I procrastinate rather than do homework," step 2 might be thoughts like "I'm not smart enough to do it.")

3. Write down three opposing beliefs or observations that challenges each core belief from step 2. Do you have evidence that challenges the negative beliefs? Consider that what you see as a fault might be a strength.

4. Pick the most compelling of your opposing beliefs from each group in step 3.

5. Summarize the items from step 4 in a list.

6. Review. What is the conclusion from the new list? Does it give you a new perspective? Keep doing this until you get something that inspires you to think differently.

Dopamine Hypothesis

Why would positive emotions make your brain work better? Since positive emotions and the reward system in the brain are related, researchers have proposed that the influences on cognition of positive emotions may be influenced by the same neural systems that mediate reward. Dopamine is a neurotransmitter that helps control the reward and pleasure center, but it also interacts with number of other processes in the body. The Dopamine Theory of Positive Affect was developed to explain the link between positive emotion and broadened cognition. It originated from theorists extrapolating from research on the reward mechanism and cognitive performance, particularly focusing on the role of dopamine and how it facilitates tasks, learning, goal switching, and creative problem solving.

Multitasking and Life with Google

In spite of all the worries about the Internet destroying our ability to remember things, research shows that using Google doesn't make you stupid or mean you're going to lose the ability to remember things. Evidence does suggest, however, that the ability to use search engines changes how we remember things. Search engines have shifted the primary task to finding

ALBERT BANDURA AND SOCIAL LEARNING THEORY

Albert Bandura is a social psychologist and is considered the father of social learning theory. His research and studies on self-efficacy formed a cornerstone for positive psychology.

Social learning theory posits that human beings, as social animals, learn through imitation and modeling. For example, a monkey watching a parent, sibling, or member of the community peel a banana imitates the action. In some cases, one of these role models who has "expertise" in banana peeling may even provide some guidance and support for the novice monkey to master the challenge. Human beings are similar. We observe the world around us and how people navigate it and imitate it. Bandura's social learning theory emphasizes the interaction between actions, thoughts, and the environment.

Bandura's most famous study was the Bobo Doll experiment. Bandura created a film in which a person is shown hitting a Bobo doll (a popular inflatable toy with a sand base that would bounce back into place upon being hit) and using aggressive language. Children were shown the film and then placed in a room with a Bobo doll without being given any directions. The children immediately started imitating what they saw in the film, hitting the toy and using aggressive actions and language. The children imitated what they had observed, reinforcing Bandura's theory that we understand the world around us through observational learning.

Many researchers have cited this study as proof that violent television yields violent actions. What is not addressed is that the children in this experiment, after a period of imitating the action in the film, went back to a default way of behaving.

Bandura went beyond the notion that as human beings we simply respond to environmental stimuli. He felt it was too simplistic to reduce human behavior to a stimulus-response cycle. He expanded our understanding of interaction with the environment through observing, imitating, adopting, and eventually integrating the understanding. As children we encode this behavior into our own way of being. Therefore, parents, teachers, friends, and peers provide models or examples to observe and follow in some cases that are useful and other cases that may be antisocial.

Reinforcement plays an important role in the development of pro- and antisocial skill development. If a child is rewarded for certain behavior by the world around him or her, the behavior becomes strengthened. Negative reinforcement may lead to the extinguishing of the behavior. Hence, in the previous example, once the little monkey has mastered peeling a banana, he or she is reinforced by the reward of eating the fruit.

not remembering across all domains—whether it's hunting down an old classmate, finding the name of the actors in the *Rocky Horror Picture Show* or researching a paper. The evidence from four studies suggests that when people are able to access the Internet, they expect to be able to find the information again at a future time. Thus what they focus on is not the information

DANIEL KAHNEMAN, THE FATHER OF BEHAVIORAL ECONOMICS

Daniel Kahneman is a Nobel laureate for Economics (2002), a psychologist, and considered the father of behavioral economics. In his best-selling book, *Thinking, Fast and Slow* (2013), Kahneman makes the argument that we are not always the rational decision makers that we would like to think that we are. If humans were such rational thinkers, he argues, we would historically have made better decisions about individual and social challenges. Instead, we carry with us cognitive (thinking) biases that we try to verify by finding confirmation or validation for within our environment.

Kahneman argues economics is not a science but more about our psychology. Our brains have developed to be risk-averse. This aversion makes us instinctive beings rather than rational ones. Kahneman presented the dual-process model of the brain asserting that we understand the world in two opposite ways:

System 1 is the fast, intuitive, associative, automatic aspect of our brain's way of navigating. It is always on and cannot be switched off and is "the secret author of many of the choices and judgments that you make." System 2 is the slow thinking part of our brain that gets tired easily and accepts the alerts from System 1. Both systems may jump to conclusions, connect dots that may not be connectable, and be influenced by biases. These systems may create bad decision making and leads us into less than optimal ways of thinking.

When you think that you are being intelligent and confident, think again, according to Kahneman. We are all susceptible to what Kahneman calls the focusing illusion: "Nothing in life is as important as you think it is when you are thinking about it." In other words, whatever we focus upon at a given moment takes on a greater role in our lives than it actually is. The good news is that we can learn to be aware of these biases and reduce some of the blind spots in our lives.

itself, but where to locate the information when they need it later. The Internet has become an external memory where we can offload cognitive tasks. According to Gary Small, a neuroscientist at UCLA, the brain has specialized circuitry and repeating mental tasks strengthens some neural circuits and ignores others. So in this sense, Google is changing our brains; it's adapting them to fit current demands.

Internet use affects cognition as well as memory. In one of Small's (2009) studies on middle-aged and older adults, he compared those who were experienced Internet users to those who did not use the Internet. The Internet users showed higher-level decision-making skills, complex reasoning, and overall improved brain activity, suggesting that Web search activity may stimulate and improve brain function. Dutch researchers examined cognitive flexibility using first-person shooter video games that required subjects to react rapidly and switch frequently among different subtasks. They wanted to evaluate if experience with the games transferred to other cognitive-control tasks. Subjects with more videogame experience exhibited less cognitive "costs" when

SONJA LYUBOMIRSKY: DETERMINING HAPPINESS

Sonja Lyubomirsky is a professor of psychology at UC Riverside and author of the best-selling book *The How of Happiness* (2007). A leader in the field of positive psychology, Lyubomirsky's research is part of a body of work that is breaking down the determinants of happiness and systemically testing happiness interventions to explore the possibility of sustainable increases in well-being.

Lyubomirsky's research has focused on three critical questions: (1) What makes people happy? (2) Is happiness a good thing? and (3) How can we make people happier still?

Previous theories on happiness suggested that it wasn't possible to make someone sustainably happier. For example, the genetic set point theory says each person has a genetically determined level of happiness and the hedonic adaption or the hedonic treadmill theory says that no matter what joys or sorrows befall them, people will return to their happiness set point over time. However, in studying the differences in cognitive and motivational processes between happy and unhappy people, Lyubomirsky theorized that adaptation is influenced by how people create meaning around both positive and negative events. Circumstances and events are never completely objective. If events are evaluated, interpreted, and remembered differently, then people are actively, even if unconsciously, shaping their experiences to be positive or negative. Lyubomirsky began to explore several of these aspects, including how people compare themselves to others (social comparison), how people explain or justify their actions and choices (dissonance reduction), how people think about themselves (self-evaluation), and how people perceive and think about others (person perception).

Based on her research on these cognitive patterns and how they influence people's interpretation of events, she argues that people have the ability to determine their own happiness by introducing the intentional and persistent practice of specific activities. While acknowledging the role of genetics, circumstance and adaption, she suggests that up to 40 percent of each person's happiness is within their own control if they have the will and persistence to adopt purposeful activities to cultivate happiness.

Activities that impact happiness and well-being include expressing gratitude, avoiding overthinking and social comparison, investing in social connections, managing stress, and cultivating mindfulness and flow activities.

According to Lyubomirsky, it isn't enough just to do the exercises. Becoming happier requires motivated and diligence in the practice of happiness activities as well as being mindful of their purpose. In other words, her research shows that being motivated to becoming a happier person matters. Expressing gratitude and optimism, for example, did not generally increase well-being unless the person was aware of the exercise's purpose.

changing tasks. The researchers note that inexperienced players who were trained for several months showed significant improvement in tasks demanding spatial resolution and distribution of visual attention. They suggest that video game training may be an effective intervention to offset the decreased cognitive adaptability that comes with normal aging.

Multitasking May Not Be Contributing What You Think It Is

We all multitask and most of us assume we do it well. It may surprise you to know that in one study, subjects who identified as being "heavy media multitaskers" were actually worse at task switching than those who were light multitaskers. The difference came from the inability to filter out irrelevant stimuli. Heavy multitaskers had a more difficult time ignoring irrelevant information in memory and were less effective in task switching. This was surprising given that task switching is the central feature of multitasking. One study offers an explanation for the prevalence of multitasking beyond attributing it to the amount of media available. They argue that while cognitive goals may not be as effectively met, the participants may have some other needs that are being served, such as emotional or social. For example, watching TV or texting while studying makes studying less efficient but more pleasurable. This experience reinforces the desire to continue to multitask.

Spread the News

It may violate standard rules for journalism, but good news does spread. While we might think that memorable ideas—such as sex and violence—are the ones likely to be shared, surprisingly, that's not the case. Positive articles are more likely to be shared on social media. Fear may get our attention, but it's not what we want to share. A study out of the University of Pennsylvania reported that while high emotional content, both positive and negative, did get attention, positive content was more likely to be shared. Sharing requires action and high emotion creates an arousal state that facilities action. Ultimately it is articles that we find uplifting or awe-inspiring that we forward to our friends and that we want as a reflection of who we are.

Social neuroscience findings argue that our social cognition influences what we share. Our ability to mentalize—to anticipate what the receiver will find interesting—will be part of the decision-making process, whether conscious or not. Giving something of value triggers the reward center. Research also suggests that we may be becoming more aware of what we send as a reflection of ourselves. Sharing content becomes an implicit endorsement associated with us and reflects our identity, interests, and values.

NATURE VERSUS NURTURE

Genetics Underlying Strengths

A series of animal experiments have demonstrated that the ability to cope with extreme stress is partly genetic. While no one gene alone is responsible for resilience, genetic factors do come into play. As mentioned earlier, 30 percent of the mice subjected to social stress did not demonstrate negative impact of stress. Researchers believe that the response to acute social stress rests in the inability to mobilize reward and motivational systems. Investigators studied a transcription factor—a protein that binds to DNA and regulates bodily processes—and found higher levels in the brains of resilient mice. The transcription factor also appeared to facilitate more adaptive and flexible synaptic connections that supported higher motivation and more adaptive behavior. The good news is that this demonstration of resilience isn't a genetic anomaly— we all have it and we have the ability to become more resilient. Research on activities like mindfulness meditation, cognitive reappraisal, and aerobic exercise have shown that neurobiological systems can be strengthened to enable a more adaptive response to stress.

Genetics of Empathy

It's not just our genes that help us feel empathy for others; it's our ability to emotionally mirror what others are feeling. The discovery of mirror neurons by the neurophysiologist Giacomo Rizzolatti demonstrated that shared neural code from the cortical system and the limbic system links perception and emotion (Iacoboni & Lenzi, 2002). Unlike motor neurons, mirror neurons fire upon two conditions: (1) when planning movement and (2) when observing movement in others. While the discovery of mirror neurons has been a subject of some controversy among neuroscientists, they offer insight into understanding why we "feel" the actions and emotions we observe in others. Mirror neurons are helping scientists to expand the study of how we develop empathy for others. They are also opening opportunities for research into areas where people struggle disorders with such as autism and schizophrenia where one manifestation can be poor social interactions.

Mirror neurons are challenging many of our assumptions about empathy and understanding the emotions of another. In one study, participants in one group were asked to watch a person performing emotionally expressive postures. The participants in the second group were asked to physically mimic the expressive postures. The watchers from group 1 could identify all the emotions as accurately as the mimickers in groups 2 with only one exception. Embodying the emotions did not improve the participants' recognition accuracy of happy, sad, fearful, shameful, or surprised. Researchers are investigating how mirror neurons interact with mentalizing to empathize the intentions behind actions and emotions.

Our social interactions include full gestures and facial expressions to aid our communication. When we smile at someone, their ability to empathize generates a cascade of neural activity thanks to the mirror neurons. The physical act of moving our facial muscles into a smile sends message to the body that things are going well, thus stimulating the reward center. Smiles are so powerful that smiling can speed our discovery from stress. A study in Sweden found that it's almost impossible to frown when someone is smiling at you—in fact, subjects could not avoid producing a facial expression, either a smile or a frown, that matched the stimulus. If you're feeling down or stressed out, smile. Even a fake smile can help. Or watch silly cat videos on YouTube. Not only will you feel better, but you'll be paying it forward to anyone who's looking at you.

SPREADING HAPPINESS

As odd as it seems that you could "catch" positive emotions, think about the effect on your emotions when someone who is upbeat and full of energy comes into your room. Now picture that same room when someone drags in, throws himself or herself on your couch with a sour expression, and is full of complaints. It isn't your imagination that this second guy is a total energy suck.

Happiness is contagious. We are influenced by the emotions of those around us. Nicholas Christakis and James Fowler studied the impact of emotions on our social networks and tracked way that emotions spread across them. The happier people were more likely to be in the center of the network clusters, surrounded by other happy people. Looking at their data, they argued that happiness was a function of the group more than of individual experience. Happiness, they said, actually ripples through social networks, creating clusters of happiness and unhappiness. The impact of happiness had staying power, too. It could last up to a year.

Part of this may be explained by the evolutionary function of happiness behaviors—smiles and kindness tend to increase social bonds and approach behaviors. Our innate mirroring tendencies from mirror neurons mean that we tend to reflect back the happiness behaviors of others, further reinforcing social bonds and positive emotions. Unhappiness, while also contagious, doesn't spread as strongly, possibly because we don't have the same evolutionary incentives. The evidence showed that happiness had a "three degrees of influence rule"—the closer you are to a happy person, the more likely you are to be happy, too. Happiness was most contagious through frequent social contact rather than social connections, so neighbors who socialized with the happy person were more likely to be happy than a family member who never dropped by.

Keep this in mind the next time you're at a store or walking down the street. Grandma was right; good manners matter. Remember to pay it forward. You don't have to buy a Starbucks for the guy in line behind you, although that can be a nice thing to so. Think small and often. When you share a smile or take the time to interact pleasantly with someone, you are changing their brain chemistry for the better along with your own, increasingly the likelihood that the next person they encounter will receive some of that happiness. Everyone gets double rewards: the effect of smiling and the effect of doing for others. And so on and so on and so on.

MORAL BRAINS

Darwin argued that morality was integral to human nature and human evolution. In his writings, Darwin outlined several components that were necessary for the evolution and survival of communities. These included: (1) social attachment, the enjoyment of the company of others, and empathy for their concerns; (2) awareness and attention to community rules and norms accompanied by compliance through emotions such as guilt and shame; (3) ability to understand and compare the past with future goals and express dissatisfaction in lack of achievement; and (4) development of rituals and habits to promote cultural values. In Darwin's view, these moral features were hardwired into human development.

Darcia Narvaez (2008) proposes the Triune Ethics Theory that makes a case for connection between the neurobiological impact of early care and the moral behavior of people in adulthood. It is a "bottom up" theory that integrates neurobiology, affective neuroscience, and cognitive science with moral psychology. It focuses on the motivations that arise from instinctive emotional systems that cause people to respond and act without conscious intention. Narvaez's theory is informed by MacLean's (1990) Triune Brain Model, noting that research in affective neuroscience has validated the MacLean's general perspective surrounding the development of distinct, but interactive, functionalities that he designated as reptilian, old mammal, and new mammal (see the section on Evolutionary Brain Models). The Triune Ethics Theory identifies the different ethical behaviors triggered by activation of these three systems with the longer-range goal of better understanding the conditions for optimal human moral development.

The model describes three distinctive moral systems or "ethics" accompanying the development of the brain: the ethics of survival, the ethics of engagement, and the ethics of imagination. The ethics of security accompanies the formation of the "reptilian" brain and is based upon instincts that are related to physical survival, and keeps individuals focused on self-protective behaviors. The ethics of engagement centers on the role of attachment in the mammalians' emotional system that comes from harmony, play, and social connection. This relies on evidence of the critical nature of early childhood to establishing healthy emotional brain circuitry. Research has suggested that an infant's nervous system is much more vulnerable than previously thought. The healthy development of the brain, emotional regulation, and the neuroendocrine system not only govern resilience to stress but are critical to a child's ability to develop positive social interaction and to establish social bonds.

The ethics of imagination is related to the formation of the neocortex and related thalamic structure that are focused on the external world. This evolutionary development provides the capacity for problem solving and deliberate learning. It is this stage of cognitive development that is connected to fairness-related behaviors, the ability to see consequences and understand social values and norms.

The Triune Ethics Theory states that there is a neurobiological substrate to moral development. For example, research shows that a child's brain structures change in response to the effects of child–caregiver emotional interaction and the development of emotional regulation. Narvaez claims that morality is not about learning the rules, but is rooted in the learned physiological patterns over the life span, particularly during childhood. She argues that "not only do cognitive structures emerge from recurrent patterns of sensorimotor activity, but so do moral cognitive structures" (Narvaez, 2008).

Much of positive psychology raises ethical questions. We can't study quality of life, strengths, morals, and values without asking questions about how they arise and whose values they represent. The research emerging from neuroscience continues to test assumptions and paradigms. The early positive psychologists challenged the prevailing models about the focus of psychology. If we have indeed moved beyond Descartes mind-body dualism, Narvaez have to be willing to strengthen our understanding of the ethics of positive psychology and, indeed, moral psychology as a whole, with evidence from neurobiology and ethology.

The human brain is a complex and mysterious organ that has intrigued and baffled humans throughout recorded history. As we've seen, advances in neuroscience and the coupling of neuroscience with emotions and social behaviors have opened doors to thinking about the biological foundations for abstract concepts, such as well-being and quality of life. Central to quality of life is our physical and mental health. Happy people live longer because they are healthier. The reverse can also be true—that health contributes to our happiness. It may sound like a chicken and egg problem but we know that intentionally applying concepts from positive psychology can positively impact the way every part of our body functions.

In this chapter we looked at some main reasons why the brain–body connection is so powerful and integral to positive psychology. The brain:

- Has the ability to change
- Translates emotion into physically feelings
- Is influenced by social connections
- Allows us to cultivate empathy by understanding what other people experience
- Benefits from exercise

Our thoughts and emotions are a reciprocal cycle—around and around like watching a game of jump rope. What we think influences how we feel. How we feel influences how we think. Don't be shy. Jump in any time. Through intentional exercises like mindfulness, physical exercise, or cognitive reappraisal, we can change our brains and change the game. The next time someone says, "It's all in your head," you can be thankful that, yes, it is.

CHAPTER 7

Storytelling and Positive Psychology

What does storytelling have to do with positive psychology? Short answer: everything. Storytelling—or narrative—is fundamental to how we think and make meaning of the world. The influential cognitive psychologist Jerome Bruner (1986, 1991) has long argued that meaning should be the central concept in psychology because it is the most essential aspect of human existence. In his view, it is narrative—the stories we construct and tell—that bridge human subjective experience with action. In *Maps of Meaning*, Jordan Peterson (1999) examines multiple academic fields to show that connecting myths and beliefs with science is essential to fully understand how people make meaning. In positive psychology, meaning is a primary component of happiness and creating a life worth living, and therefore, our well-being is also a product of our narratives, myths, and culture.

Whether we realize it or not, stories are at the center of everything we do. How we tell our stories controls our mood, self-image, and the influence we have on others. Our stories can also dictate our future paths and successes. Therefore, understanding storytelling is not only key to how we feel about ourselves and how we interact with others but it also gives us valuable tools we can use to make change.

This chapter will cover three areas: (1) the basic structure of stories; (2) the personal side of stories where we look at how stories influence identity, cognitive patterns, emotions, and behavioral choices; and (3) the public side of storytelling where we examine the influence of stories we tell and share with others and how they can be used to make change around the world. In particular, we will explore how the emotional impact of personal and social storytelling influences beliefs and behaviors, making them a valuable tool for positive personal and social change.

WHAT IS A STORY?

People often equate stories with play. Stories are more fundamental than that. Human brains are literally wired for stories. Evidence from cognitive and social neuroscience suggests what narrative psychologists have long argued—that narrative is essentially a Theory of Mind. All Theory of Mind perspectives seek to explain how people understand others; exchange abstract concepts; and are able to mentalize, project, and attribute intentions and significance. According to some theorists, Theory of Mind approaches focus too much on the cognitive side at the expense of emotion. Narrative is an alternative for cognitive Theory of Mind views. It solves the problem of integrating cognition and emotion because stories are how humans make sense of the world across all senses. Like positive psychology, narrative takes a holistic approach where instinctive and emotional elements are integral to cognition and ultimately manifest in well-being.

Stories perform several functions. At their most simplistic, stories are the basis of knowledge acquisition and social interaction. Stories are how we make sense out of any experience because a narrative structure allows us to translate what happens around us into a series of linear events so that we can attribute meaning, such as causality, importance, and relevance, and whether something is positive or negative. Like the clothesline where we hang our clothes to dry, stories give us a place to attach information in relation to other events, feelings, images, and impressions. Narrative structure is how we encode multisensory experience into memory for later recall. New information is processed and evaluated in relation to the stories we already know. Stories are causal relationships and we use the ones we know to predict outcomes and make assumptions about people and events, from simple interactions to complex relationships.

Narrative enables us to mimic, mentalize, anticipate, and project. These abilities function as a training ground for social interaction. Think of all the times you ran a "mental simulation" for rehearsing a speech, asking someone out on a date, practicing a golf swing, or "preplanning" what to do on a trip. Far from wasting time, daydreaming about future events allows us to anticipate and solve problems and practice social behaviors ahead of time, easing our anxiety and improving our performance and experience.

Because stories have the potential to activate primal emotions and themes, they are able to bridge individual and cultural differences. We may not know what it's like to live in another culture. In fact, we may have no knowledge at all about the embedded social pressures, standards, norms, and values that someone who lives there understands. However, universal themes such as heroism, sacrifice, yearning, love, and loss transcend cultural differences. They are something that bridges our differences, even if your hero and mine aren't quite the same. These are the human truths we all share and these truths come from the stories we tell. As author Jonathan Gottschall (2012) writes:

> Humans are creatures of Neverland. . . . We are attracted to Neverland because, on the whole, it is good for us. It nourishes our imaginations; it reinforces moral

behavior; it gives us safe worlds to practice inside. Story is the glue of human social life—defining groups and holding them together. . . . Neverland is our nature. We are the storytelling animal.

STORYTELLING ON THE RISE

The practice of storytelling is documented throughout history. Anthropologists have found evidence of storytelling across all ancient cultures and scholars of literature, myth, and psychology have identified common patterns. Until recently, however, storytelling was considered primarily cultural rather than functional. Even in psychology, appreciation for storytelling was isolated until the 1980s. The use of story was limited to clinical practice, where psychoanalysts in the tradition of Sigmund Freud used dreams for exploring the psyche. Some clinicians used narrative-based assessment tools, such as the Rorschach Inkblot test, and asked patients to tell stories in response to visual cues to get insights about patients' personalities to evaluate problems in cognitive development, mental illness, or mental distress.

However, the last 50 years have ushered in a new era. Psychologists from multiple fields see a more central role for narrative as a primary meaning-making device, from cognitive processing to the role of narrative in identity formation. The proliferation of technology, and the attendant flood of information across multiple channels, have also sparked an interest in storytelling both in and out of academia. Always central to the arts and entertainment, the power of storytelling to engage emotions has made it a subject of intense interest in business and marketing communications and leadership training as well as reaffirmed its position as an item of interest in the social sciences. Psychologists and neuroscientists are using new tools, such as brain imaging, to understand more about the human propensity for narrative as a communication, engagement, and behavioral tool.

RESEARCHING STORY

While the new interest and tools are exciting, research demands clear definitions. Yet as simple as storytelling seems, no one definition of narrative is accepted across research communities. Researchers have used a broad range of definitions, often informed by their research questions and theoretical orientations. As interest in the power of narrative grew, people began not only to research different aspects about how stories are used and the impact they have but also to employ them as a research tool in their own right. Narrative research gathers qualitative, story-based data, rather than quantifiable measures with the intention of capturing the richness of human experience and emotion that stories contain.

In spite of these variations in application, definitions of story have common themes and key concepts. One of the most prominent is the role of time as an organizing principle to create meaning. Humans are unique in this capacity and stories are a distinctly human invention to share and gain understanding.

One piece of evidence of the human need to create stories to make meaning out of our environment comes from research on the human propensity to attribute meaning to abstract shapes and inanimate objects. In 1944, experimental psychologists Heider and Simmel demonstrated how people attributed causality, personalities, and intentionality to the movements of four black geometric shapes: a circle, two triangles, and a rectangle. After watching an animated film in which the shapes' positions changed on a white field, the majority of the viewers projected varying degrees of stories onto the shapes' movement. The animation showed a large triangle inside lines that create a large rectangular shape. A smaller triangle and circle were visible on the outside of the large rectangle. The large triangle moved out of the rectangle through a gap in the corner where the lines didn't meet. The large triangle then moved close to the small triangle and bumped it repeatedly. During this action, the circle moved through the gap in the lines to the inside of the rectangular shape. People routinely attributed aggression to the large triangle and described the circle as moving into the rectangle to get away because it was afraid. For some, the shapes took on larger proportions, becoming variations on an allegory for good and evil. Some participants assigned gender to the shapes (triangles were male; the circle was female) and saw the animation as a love triangle (no pun intended). Researchers have replicated this experiment several times over the years, documenting how the human brain identifies patterns of behavior and assigns causal meaning. See for yourself. It's on YouTube. Watch the video and try to describe it. You will see that that you have an innate inclination to describe the actions with words that have subjective interpretations of intentionality, such as the large triangle tried to *chase* the small triangle away or the small circle *hid* in the rectangle. This experiment was repeated recently at USC and while the human participants still saw stories, researchers reported that a computer running the simulation was unable to deliver a "storied" response.

INNATE STORYTELLING: PROJECTING ONTO INANIMATE OBJECTS

Since the human brain automatically makes a story out of a couple of moving triangles, it won't surprise you that the brain fills in blanks and creates meaning and attributes purpose to everything around us, from our computer or call to assumptions about why someone hasn't immediately answered a text message. It seems counterintuitive that we would attribute intentionality to inanimate objects, but how many times have you said something like, "You stupid computer!" or "Please start, car, I promise to take you in for service tomorrow!" It's all part of how the brain makes meaning and uses stories to make sense of situations. You can imagine, then, how the addition of details facilitates our interpretation.

One of the most important cognitive competencies we need to survive and thrive in our social world is the ability to identify and interpret the internal states, beliefs, and desires of others in our environment. We don't even need objects to have human properties. As with the Heider and Simmel experiment, human brains imposed a narrative pattern on observed movements of geometric shapes. As the cognitive and Gestalt psychologists discovered, the human brain innately sorts and categorizes information about everything from all five senses into patterns in order to give it meaning.

The ability to "mentalize," imagining the mental activities of others and perceiving human behavior as intentional states, means we are essentially telling stories—putting a narrative organization on what we perceive about others. This social storytelling ability is a capacity used all the time. It is essential to collaborate, teach, learn, and understand ourselves and others. People subconsciously construct each new story based on our existing "story bank"—the meanings we have assigned to previous experience. Positive change comes from increasing awareness of how we construct stories and identifying core elements that drive the themes in stories that we tell ourselves and use to make judgments of others.

In the next section, we break down the elements of story so we can get a better understanding of how the brains reacts to and interpret patterns that form our stories. This happens internally and externally. Internally, stories impact the way we think, feel, and behave without our conscious knowledge or intention. Awareness of this innate response allows us to become more aware of instinctive influences and enables us to anticipate them. Internal stories can lead to mindlessness, an automatic response to the world. Externally, stories can be used to influence and persuade others in ways that support well-being, human growth, and positive development. There are several elements of story that are important in these two contexts: basic structure, genre, characters, and common literary devices, such as archetypes and metaphors.

Basic Structure

Stories have a pattern. They are built on a story arc with basic elements. The simplest is the three-act structure, attributed to the Ancient Greek philosopher Aristotle. It consists of a beginning, middle, and an end. Each section plays an important role because a story is the depiction of a journey. The beginning, starting point, or exposition establishes critical information about the story—such as time, place, and major characters. The beginning also includes an inciting incident or adoption of a goal that introduces the conflict into the narrative. The middle is the rising action that leads to the conflict manifesting in confrontation. The end is the actualized or anticipated transformation and resolution. Some stories are much more complex, with multiple second acts of increasing intensity, but fundamentally all stories follow this pattern, called a story arc. Without our conscious awareness or any literary training, our brain interprets and organizes the events into story arcs, creating time sequences and causality in accordance with our lived experience.

All stories, whether it's the films we go see or how we explain our first romantic breakup or why we're running late this morning, follow this pattern of exposition, conflict, and resolution. Why do all stories have conflict? Conflict provides the tension and energy that propels the story forward and gives it meaning. Without some element of conflict, there is nothing that invites emotional engagement. From Winnie the Pooh stuck in a honey pot to Luke Skywalker fighting facing off against Darth Vader, every great story centers around a dilemma that needs solving.

Where stories are incomplete, such as in advertisements, our brains are so hungry for a story that they will supply the missing ingredients. A good advertisement gives you a clear goal, such as joy represented by sitting on a beautiful beach sipping cold beer, freedom signified by speeding down a highway feeling the wind in your hair or altruism exemplified by feeding a starving child. These stories are crafted so that the viewer can step into the story and take action to bring the resolution to fruition, whether you buy the product or donate to the cause.

Characters

Stories are populated with characters that also reflect patterns and trigger our innate understanding. As we discussed earlier, the psychologist Carl Jung identified that people across cultures have common understandings of universal archetypes. They represent distinct attributes and strengths. Archetypes provide bridges of understanding independent of our differences.

Every story, whether it's the recounting of events in our lives or enjoying a movie, has a protagonist (hero) and antagonist (villain). There are many other characters that can fill up the cast in a story, but the primary elements of hero and villain must be in place for the energy necessary to create a story. Every event in life, no matter how minor, is constructed as a story. In fact, if we look carefully each event has a hero and a villain, whether it's the guy who was too slow pulling out of a parking place or the wind that blows our papers away.

After studying cultures around the world, the mythologist Joseph Campbell identified a basic story pattern that he called "the hero's journey" populated with archetypal characters. In his book, *Hero with a Thousand Faces*, Campbell (2008/1949) argues for the universality of myths that appear throughout history independent of era, culture, or society. Campbell contends that the recurring themes in different mythologies lead him to the realization that these themes portray universal and eternal truths about mankind. Therefore, mythology in the form of public stories provides meaning and purpose that help us deal with the inherent conflicts and challenges of human existence. Campbell's Hero's Journey model describes the path of a reluctant hero, who undertakes a difficult journey, overcomes many challenges, and returns victorious and transformed. George Lucas, creator of the *Star Wars* epic, is a well-known example. Lucas was greatly influenced by Joseph Campbell's work and spent many hours interviewing Campbell to better understand the hero's journey and its archetypal underpinnings. The story of *Star Wars* has resonated so profoundly that it has become deeply embedded in American culture, literally across generations. We can see this in the multigenerational fan response to the continuing saga in the 2015 *Star Wars: The Force Awakens* with record-breaking ticket sales both as presales and at the box office.

Many popular films are based on the Hero's Journey, such as *Avatar, The Matrix, Lord of the Rings, Silence of the Lambs, Jaws,* and *Casablanca*, to name but a few. These films become cultural artifacts, providing a shorthand for our understanding of many positive psychology virtues, such as courage, persistence, loyalty, love, and hope. These stories resonate because they remind us of the importance of these qualities in achieving happiness in our own lives. But the Hero's Journey has another important message. It isn't just about the social stories we tell each other in movie theaters or on YouTube. We can apply the Hero's Journey to ourselves to make sense out of who we are, where we are on our journey, and how to make positive change.

THE PERSONAL SIDE OF STORYTELLING

Narrative psychology uses storytelling as the centerpiece for approaching human behavior. Rooted in social constructivist theory to understanding the formation of self and identity, the focus on narrative emphasizes the way that language and culture construct individual experience. It views stories as how we make sense of what we experience in life. Narrative psychologists such as Donald Polkinghorne (1988) have long argued that narratives provide the time and sequencing upon which experience is understood. They believe that our thoughts, beliefs, and behaviors are made according to narrative structures. The psychologist Theodore R. Sarbin (1986) maintains that each person's story is a symbolic representation of actions over time, and, in keeping with Aristotle's view, every life story, like any story, has a beginning, middle, and an end. What we think of as literary structure can be applied to life stories because they follow the same recognizable patterns of events that in fiction we call plots. Every story recounts some form of human predicaments and attempted resolutions.

Stories such as Campbell's myths are how meaning is found because these stories are driven by the fundamental values in pursuit of a life worth living. Just as cultures transmit knowledge of relational patterns, meanings, and moralities in their myths, fairy tales, and histories, we are doing the same each day in the stories we tell ourselves. Stories are the blueprint for how we see and interpret connections between events, people, and the world.

The notion of life stories describes a comprehensive grasp that brings together a series of events the author views as "mine." The philosopher Søren Kierkegaard argued that it is through the process of autobiographical selection that we become ethical beings and it is in the telling of life stories that we take responsibility for our lives (Rudd, 2012). Theorists like Roland Barthes argue that we are all authors writing life stories. Individuals are also editors (Barthes & Duisit, 1975). People add and eliminate the elements that are irrelevant or disruptive to the story that is being told. While life is messy, stories have implicit structure and define our identity through a series of events. We have big events and small ones, some are pivotal and transformative, some providing context and color. Individual choices of what to include or exclude, what to tell and what to hold back, determines the course of our life and how we allow others to understand who we are.

As stories are told, however, we are not just the teller but one of the listeners. These stories convince the self as well as others about our plans, goals, strengths, and weaknesses. It is a human tendency to believe the stories we hear that makes them powerful tools for increasing our happiness and well-being.

OUR LIVES AS STORIES

In the mid-1980s, psychologists from a number of subfields, such as cognitive, developmental, personality, and cultural psychologies, began to look for a broader and more integrated way to think about human behavior beyond the historical focus on a single trait or behavior.

The psychologist Dan P. McAdams (1993) has been central to the shift toward viewing narrative as a unifying principle of human development and behavior. McAdams developed a life story model of identity based on the theory that people construct internal and continually changing self-narratives. McAdams's view of the evolving nature of the life story was partially inspired by the work of developmental psychologist Erik Erikson in the 1960s and his stage theory of life span development.

Erikson developed a series of stages of psychosocial development that have been profoundly influential. Erikson's theories draw on his roots in psychoanalysis with an emphasis on the role of culture and society that he saw as key to the development of an individual's self-awareness and identity. Erikson conceptualized human development as a series of eight stages, each of which has specific developmental tasks that each person must accomplish. He saw these tasks as learning to resolve conflicting tensions between the ego (one's identity and sense of self) and the environment.

McAdams was particularly interested in the fifth of Erikson's eight stages, the ego identity development that occurs during late adolescence and young adulthood and focuses on the conflict between ego identity and role confusion—the questions of "Who am I?" and "How do I fit into the world?" During this stage, people begin to integrate different roles and beliefs as they create a sense of psychological unity and self-understanding. Contrary to many, McAdams did not believe identities were something that were created and then you were done. He proposed that people produce this sense of unity by creating self-defining stories that were internalized and continually evolving over the life span.

Developmental psychologists suggest that the ability to tell the story of the self starts around the age of two. Our stories become more complex as we mature. This capability coincides with the cognitive capabilities that grow in late adolescence as the brain develops. These include the increasing ability for formal operational thinking, such as thinking hypothetically, exercising deductive reasoning, and using logical thought processes. An important change in adolescence is the increase in social cognition, the emergence of a social self, and the ability to exercise perspective taking or reasoning about others' thoughts and feelings. These changes provide both the motivation and the ability to craft an integrated self-narrative essential to well-being.

McAdams believes that because emerging adults have the cognitive ability to create a life story, this was an essential step in becoming a self-reflective adult. Therefore, he sees this period as the start of a life story that began to integrate experiences and feelings into a culturally and socially meaningful story.

What does any of this have to do with positive psychology? Several things. First, understanding the evolution of life stories provides clues into how each one of us frames the world. The stories we create build upon the ones we began in adolescence. Second, life stories replicate literary patterns. Individuals are the heroes of their own stories. Stories have themes and characters, conflict, and the promise of resolution. Third, over time we believe the stories we tell. These stories influence the emotions and attributes that are so important to satisfaction in life. Finally, the ability to translate experience into stories that can be shared is a major mechanism for socialization, human connection, and social influence.

BUILDING LIFE STORIES

Starting in adolescence, people begin to construct causal narratives to explain how different events are linked together. People start describing traits, attitudes, beliefs, and preferences in terms of life events. One person might say, "My father encouraged me to do all kinds of projects and that's how I got my love of art." Another might say, "I couldn't stand the way people behaved in my neighborhood and that's why I rejected my parents' political views." We might look back on certain experiences and recognize them as pivotal moments in our life's trajectories.

Life stories are continually retold and remade because we have the ability to retell and reinterpret our autobiographical stories. We also have the capacity to make personal and social change by rewriting and retelling how we see our future selves. Our self-narratives become a guide, taking us through the story that connects us to our goals.

Chapter 2 emphasized the role of strengths and how we tap into archetypes in constructing emotional meaning. We experience these prototypes and archetypes as multisensory input. The prototypes and archetypal characters that we know, such as heroes, lovers, mothers, and villains, provide a framework of meaning for any new information. Archetypes link to larger models made up of universal narrative prototypes or genres. Each genre, such as romantic love, a heroic adventure, a tale of misfortune, or rise of an underdog, shows us a new way of being. The plots we, and the archetypal patterns we assume, draw from these models are fundamental to our well-being and effectiveness across all domains in our lives.

STORIES PUT THINGS IN PERSPECTIVE

Stories use time to organize information, events, and emotions. Sequencing and relating things according to when they occurred helps us establish causality and make meaning. Thus, stories essentially "put things in perspective" so we can think about them. Time is important as Western cultures often view it as a resource; time is something to be spent and can't be returned, like money. Think of all the metaphors we use to describe time "saving time," "wasting time," or "not having enough time." (According to several scholars, some Eastern beliefs see time as more circular.)

With the pace of modern life and the flows of information, many feel that there is not enough time to spend. Ironically, researchers found that people significantly underestimate the amount of free time they have by about half. Yet free time is one of the things that people cite as something that would make them happier. Thus, how we experience the concept of time impacts our sense of well-being and time is the organizing device at the heart of storytelling.

Like the three-act structure, social cognitive thinking, such as proposed by psychologist Albert Bandura's self-efficacy theory, proposes that time can be divided into three time perspectives—past, present, and future. Translating this into narrative, past experiences form the stories that influence our efficacy beliefs, or our belief in our abilities to take action and have an impact. These stories set the stage for how we make judgments about the present and the narratives we construct about future possibilities. Psychologists Philip Zimbardo and John Boyd (2015) have done extensive work on how time perspective influences well-being. Similar to the arguments about adopting a life span narrative rather than isolated traits, considering an individual's orientation to the full spectrum of time provides a more accurate and rich understanding of how someone sees the world. Zimbardo and colleagues say that individuals have a dominant time perspective in how they perceive the world. These time perspectives provide other clues to the stories that dominate our thinking and are linked with our sense of well-being. Not surprisingly, there isn't a "best" time perspective for well-being. Research shows that well-being is a combination of the meaning you make from past experiences and balancing your focus among what is learned from the past, what is enjoyed in the present, and what is planned for the future. The ability to view the past with a positive light and to tell stories that focus on the growth opportunities in challenges and trauma increases our ability to enjoy life in the present and have hope for the future. The facility to recognize the types and qualities of our stories will continue to be a theme in the next few sections.

STORIES TO CHANGE OURSELVES

The stories we tell ourselves are central to our well-being. There are many different types of stories that inform our lives and relationships. They come from the past, the present, and from our expectations of the future. Stories can belong to individuals, families, and communities. There can be stories about jobs, education, experiences, and relationships.

While "mental health" is sometimes seen as being in touch with "reality," psychologists know that there is no single reality. The way different people interpret and retell even the same experience can vary a great deal. The Innocence Project, an organization affiliated with the Yeshiva University Law School, uses DNA testing to review potential wrongful imprisonment cases. They report that nearly 75 percent of the situations where people were falsely convicted had been based on eyewitness testimony. Our stories are a constructed reality, a product of our environment, social interaction, and our internal interpretations and needs, such as mood, stress, or pressure from and perceived expectations of peers or authorities.

Narrative therapy emerged from the beliefs about the importance of this constructed reality within each of us. The premise behind narrative therapy is that the internalized stories act as the vehicle for access. Narrative therapy, like cognitive therapy, is based on the premise that these stories create filters that

CASE STUDY: CHILDREN'S TELEVISION AND
SID THE SCIENCE KID

Forty years ago, when Gerald Lesser, Joan Cooney Ganz, and their colleagues established *Sesame Street,* they were in the company of the only other existing educational television program, *Mr. Rogers' Neighborhood.* The Sesame Workshop, then known as the Children's Television Network, was established to provide educational scaffolding for underserved children. Today there are over 80 programs considered educational television for children spread across commercial networks and cable television, many with accompanying websites that add an extra level of interaction for the viewer.

Sesame Street found an audience that was much broader than its original target audience. *Sesame Street*, and its sibling for older children, *The Electric Company*, have pioneered a model of creating educational content and then developing compelling stories and characters around that content. Today, there are over 30 co-productions of *Sesame Street* in 140 countries around the world designed specifically for the needs and cultures in which the program is aired.

Much has changed since the inception of *Sesame Street*. The world of media has shifted tremendously in terms of technology, access to information, and models of edutainment. The BBC, for example, funded by a surcharge for television use in the United Kingdom, pioneered programming for children two and younger with *The Teletubbies*. BBC Children departed from the *Sesame Street* model and instead embraced (as commercial producers of educational television do) a model that focuses on first creating compelling characters and story lines with which children will engage followed by the creation of the educational content itself. It may seem to be a subtle difference, but it has been a successful strategy giving the Sesame Workshop's model a formidable challenge. In response, *Sesame Street* has changed its well-known introduction and has created a greater number of segments of shorter length, quick cuts, and fast changes to keep today's viewers engaged.

This includes cultural-specific story lines and characters for *Sesame Street*'s co-productions around the world. For example in 2003, South Africa's "Takalani Sesame" created the character of Kami, an HIV-positive puppet, to address the epidemic of AIDS, and in 2005 with the rising prevalence of childhood obesity, the Cookie Monster became the Veggie Monster encouraging kids to only eat cookies sometimes.

The authors of this book created the Media Psychology Research Center (with a focus on positive psychology) in Boston, where we worked collaboratively on the program *Sid the Science Kid* in conjunction with KCET Los Angeles, Henson Studios, and Fablevision. *Sid the Science Kid*, originally titled *What's the Big Idea,* was underwritten by a grant from Boeing. The leaders at Boeing wanted to increase an interest in science for children

CASE STUDY (Continued)

and to help adults model how to respond to the natural inquisitiveness of children. The character of Sid was designed to be a lively ethnically ambiguous boy who asked questions about the world around him. He carries a microphone with him as if he is both the interviewer and interviewee addressing questions about the physical world around him. Sid is meant to be a compelling and likeable character within an environment that children aged three to six could typically make associations, including a family life, a younger sibling, a loving older adult (his grandmother), a school setting including a classroom and playground, and friends with unique characteristics that when put together make a well-rounded person.

Other characters were carefully crafted to reflect a diversity of human qualities. They include Gabriella, who is an energetic, assertive "rock star scientist"; Gerald who has a very active imagination and pretends to be a tractor or a plane on the playground; May who quietly and calmly thinks of alternative approaches to a challenge; and Miss Susie, the schoolteacher that makes learning fun, with play and song.

We emphasized a science/practice model to test the story lines and characters as they were developed in order to provide immediate feedback to the practitioners/creators. Researchers across five sites within urban and suburban communities and all socioeconomic classes led focus groups of children aged three to six using a semi-structured interview format. The parents signed waivers to have their children's responses to the story, graphic stills, and TV clips recorded. The information was coded and sent to the lab for aggregation. The children provided consistent feedback about the program, characters, and educational content despite their varying backgrounds. Children had particular responses to the colors presented in the programming, including the color of the schoolhouse or the colors of the characters' hair. They engaged with appropriately humorous or fantastical story lines and diverted their attention to story lines that were strongly educational in content. With the accompanying website activities in which children could practice the scientific experiments they saw on the program, they found similarly certain activities entertaining and engaging, and others that led them to other forms of engagement (such as handheld gaming systems or other electronic games).

As a result, practitioners were able to refine, discard, or improve their approach with a minimal cost to the producers. This formative research approach provides a model for children's TV production, viewer engagement, and a product that can be constructively presented to children.

You can find out more about Sid and his friends whose lives were molded by positive psychology theory and practice at:

http://pbskids.org/sid/

www.mprcenter.org

influence how we understand new events and can even change our ability to process information.

McAdams notes that some self-narratives are full of hope and optimism while some are filled with resignation, mistrust, and doubt. A positive narrative tone implies an assumption about the world as being predictable and trustworthy. A pessimistic narrative tone is reflected when self-stories suggest that people don't get what they want or that they are unworthy. McAdams argues that this narrative tone reflects a worldview often acquired in childhood. Redecision Therapy, developed by Robert Goulding and Mary McClure Goulding (1979), is an approach to therapeutic change based on working with these childhood narratives. It is based on the premise that, as children, we make "decisions" or holistic assessments (e.g., I am not good enough, I can't trust people) from our negative experiences and messages. These form the core stories that we retell ourselves and use to filter new experience. The therapy employs experiential exercises drawing from Transactional Analysis and Gestalt Therapy to facilitate an active decision, or redecision in Redecision Therapy terms, to replace the original conclusion made in early life and shift from a negative to positive self-assessment that enables the "rewriting" of personal scripts and stories.

Similarly, narrative therapists want to learn about the narrative self. For narrative therapists, stories consist of events that are linked in sequence, across time and follow a plot. As seen from the discussion on literary structure and universal themes, stories follow patterns and without realizing it, we may impose a genre onto the stories to aid in the construction of meaning for ourselves and our audience. We begin our stories with clues about the pattern our story follows. Some are obvious. "Let me tell you a funny story" tells us to expect something funny. When seen through the lens of genre, we recognize that life is full of adventures, dramas, romance, thrillers, and comedies. Individuals often have a fondness for this particular type of delivery. For example, we're familiar with the stereotypes of "Class Clown" and "Drama Queen." These reflect the narrative quality of interaction and the needs of the story-teller as well as what it feels like to be the audience.

Narrative therapists are interested in all these aspects of our stories. They look at the genre and tone of dominant stories and how we selectively gather "evidence" to support and maintain them. For example: As a young boy, Michael was told he was bad at sports. As he grew, he began to define himself using "bad at sports" as one of his dominant stories, accumulating evidence of his lack of skill, overlooking conflicting times when things went well in an athletic event and avoiding situations where he feared he would not do well. Michael did not go out for a sports team at school, was uninterested in joining the community tennis club, and studiously avoided sports-related activities at work, such as playing on the office softball team or meeting colleagues for golf on the weekends. The negative story, which he has nurtured for years without realizing it, undermined Michael's self-value and made him pull back from some relationships and miss opportunities to expand his social and professional networks and expertise.

Conversely, Mary had good feedback on her writing as a child and was encouraged by teachers to develop this interest. She now describes herself as a great writer. She has developed a story about herself from the early experiences at school and successes at work continue to shape her story about herself as a competent writer. Because this is a dominant story for Mary, she discounts times when feedback on her writing was not very positive, viewing them as challenges and learning opportunities rather than a reflection on her core qualities. She is also more likely to take on new responsibilities where writing is a key feature of the requirements. Her level of self-competence, or self-efficacy, provides additional support by moderating negative emotions when she takes on related professional risks.

Positive psychologists now recognize that negative stories, such as Michael's, can cause problems in a number of ways. For example, researchers like McAdams have shown that the content of self-defining memories was related to emotional distress. For example, negative self-stories, such as recurring stories about disrupted relationships, predicted higher levels of distress. Self-stories that focused on feelings of stigma or inadequacy were related to higher levels of depression. Self-stories that generate depressive thoughts also create "depressive filters" for new information and the types of memories people recall. The downward spiral of negative emotions from pessimistic and fatalistic stories takes a toll on relationships and increases stress. Research by positive psychologist Barbara Fredrickson, among others, has shown that negative emotions adversely impact the immune system, creativity, resilience, optimism, and willingness to bear risk. The job of the therapist is to help people like Michael identify a negative or pessimistic story, challenge it with incompatible evidence, and find a new way of recasting the dominant story about him that supports positive outcomes.

POSITIVE ILLUSIONS AND OPTIMISM

Research studies demonstrate that redrafting experience from a different perspective can give people a new sense of their own self and purpose. How realistic does this have to be? Is there such a thing as being "too optimistic"? Possibly. In *Why Smart Executives Fail*, Sydney Finkelstein (2004) says that managers and salespeople who are ceaselessly positive are dangerous because they shut out critical information.

Being optimistic has benefits, but like most things, it's all about balance. Duke Finance professors Manju Puri and David Robinson (2007) found that that there are important differences between optimists and extreme optimists when it comes to lifestyles choices. Extreme optimists had shorter time horizons, in spite of the fact that they expected to live 20 years longer than average. They also had little continuity between present stories and future as manifested in lifestyle behaviors. The extreme optimists tended to have more irresponsible financial habits and little self-regulation on activities such as smoking and diet. Moderate optimists, by contrast, were surprisingly prudent, adopting a longer time perspective.

Psychologist Shelley Taylor (1989) has extensively researched "positive illusions" on well-being. She argues that a certain amount of optimistic self-deception allows us to cope better with adversity and more optimistically meet the challenges we face. The key is that the reality-optimism gap is not too extreme. In research on women with breast cancer, she identified three dominant themes among the women's self-stories: finding meaning, creating a sense of control, and building self-esteem. Although cancer is a complex disease with no isolatable cause, the women in the study crafted stories to explain why the disease had occurred. The explanations, such as heredity, diet or stress, were meaning-making devices. These stories often led to new behaviors to fight the disease, such as diet change or meditation practices. Making changes in these ways allowed them to construct stories about beating the illness and to gain more sense of control. The women also used additional self-narratives, such as focusing on what was going well, staying focused on positive images, and comparing themselves to others not doing as well as evidence that their actions had impact. Creating narratives that linked the disease to their personal stories enabled the women to create meaning and a perception of control that bolstered their sense of self. This type of optimistic bias can be a positive, adaptive approach because it is motivational and discourages apathy and inaction. In the case of disease, it promotes more positive emotions that support stronger immune systems, decreases stress, and lessens the amount of pain we feel.

CHANGE THE STORY, CHANGE THE EMOTION

To change our feelings, it is necessary to identify the story and to consciously retell the events by reframing the meanings. Without realizing it, we often tell ourselves future stories based upon internalized negative beliefs from the past. Researchers show that expectations have significant impact on the outcome of future events. For example, people entering cognitive-behavioral therapy who believe that it will work for them do about 40 percent better than those who enter therapy thinking they will fail.

Psychologist Timothy Wilson (2011) is a proponent of what he calls "redirection" to make personal and social change. He proposes three psychological interventions for people who get stuck in self-defeating story cycles. The first is "story-editing." Like it sounds, this is the act of editing, or reshaping, someone's narrative about themselves and the world. The second is "story-prompting." Wilson uses this technique to subtly redirect people toward a specific narrative to help them see possible alternative plots. Third, Wilson advocates the practice of "do good, be good," based on the theory that our attitudes and beliefs often follow our behaviors. (A version of this would be "fake it 'til you make it.") While narrative techniques are well known in clinical practice, Wilson applies the story-editing model to effect social change. For example, he has worked with frustrated parents at risk for child abuse to help them see new stories about why a baby cries. Wilson has also applied story-editing techniques with teens to help create new identity stories through engagement with volunteerism. His work has shown that by redefining themselves as caring for others decreases rates of teenage pregnancy and drug use.

EMOTIONAL STORYTELLING

Positive psychologists look for the ways to support positive emotions and improve well-being. Yet, everyone experiences stress or a loss at one time or

LIFE STRATEGY: PERSONAL STORYTELLING

Future Self Story

Telling the story of your future best possible self can increase positive emotions such as happiness and optimism, as well as improve coping skills. Most importantly, it raises positive expectations about the future. Your best possible self means imagining yourself in a future in which everything has turned out as well as possible. As you are describing your best possible self, connect it to your present self and make a personal story out of it.

- Take a moment to visualize the future time period. Be specific. Are you telling your story in one year, five years, or much further out, such as 10 or 50 years from now?

- Start by thinking of the goals you want to accomplish in that time frame in three areas: personal (psychological and physical skills), professional (achievements, occupation, and skills), and relational (relationships with family, friends, and social life).

- See yourself having worked hard and having realized your goals and dreams. Envision it as achieving development of all your best possible potentials. Be realistic, but aspirational.

- Imagine the scene in close detail, including how you have succeeded in reaching your goals or dreams. Describe your strengths that got you to this point. Describe some of the challenges you might have overcome to reach this point. Include the skills and goals that you would like to have in the future.

Developing Your Story Portfolio

A story portfolio can be a valuable tool throughout your life. It gives you a sense of growth and expands your storytelling repertoire. It can also give you insight as to how you see yourself and where you can make changes in how you think that will better support your goals. Start collecting stories and story notes in a journal.

Begin with some personal stories that you can use right away:

- What story do you tell to introduce yourself?

- What is your favorite story to tell about yourself?

- How does your story change with your audience? Is it a completely different story or a different way of telling? Consider your intentions for the story. What was your goal? What does the story say about you? Is this the story you want to be telling?

- How do your friends or colleagues introduce you? What stories do they tell about you regularly?

- Recall a story from the past few months that someone told about you. What was the reaction? How would you like the story to be told?

another. Not everyone, however, responds the same. Resilience, the ability to cope with difficult or traumatic events, varies because individuals adopt different strategies and approaches that enable or inhibit emotion regulation and meaning making.

Psychologists recognize that the facilitation of emotion regulation is one of the factors that is critical to resilience and moves people toward a positive outcome. Cognitive appraisal and the ability to understand and make meaning out of negative experiences are coping mechanisms that contribute to resilience. The narrative framework is another way of thinking about cognitive appraisal. In other words, how we tell the stories about events, such as what and why something happened and the perceived or expected outcome, forms the basis of resilience.

The psychologist Bernard Rimé and colleagues (1991) from the University Catholique de Louvain performed a series of studies indicating that emotion regulation is not a solitary activity. They claim that emotion regulation is a social process, accomplished through social sharing. Results indicated that 95 percent of emotional experiences were shared with others the same day they happen. This sharing occurred even after negative events, in spite of the fact that emotional memory can reactivate painful and difficult emotions. Rime's work also challenged a commonly held belief that expressing emotion has cathartic effects. His research demonstrated that "letting go," or venting, does not produce emotional relief. Sharing an emotional event did not change the original memory in any measurable way, nor was it related to recovery from a traumatic or difficult experience. In some cases, continued sharing of negative experiences actually impeded recovery.

There are, however, benefits from sharing stories of negative experiences under certain conditions. The difference lies in the meaning-making process of storytelling.

James W. Pennebaker at the University of Texas has spent more than 20 years studying the psychological value of emotional expression through writing. In multiple studies, Pennebaker and colleagues (1999) have examined how personal storytelling interacts with emotion suppression and expression. Pennebaker examined (1) the impact of suppressing negative emotions; (2) the effect of telling stories about emotional experiences, either verbally or in writing, on mental and physical health, and (3) the impact of writing as form of expression no matter what the content. His research has shown that even short-term writing, if it is focused on an event or period of emotional upheaval, may have a positive effect. His approach has provided benefits to a number of different populations, from people dealing with a serious illness and students adjusting to college life to victims of trauma.

In some studies, the immediate impact of the writing exercise about personal turmoil or trauma was highly emotional as participants revisited past experiences. The longer-term effect, however, was positive. Exploring highly charged emotional events on paper was found by most participants to be meaningful and valuable. In fact, most indicated that they would like to participate in the studies again. Being a part of the emotional writing experiment had an equally impressive impact on the participant's physical health with participants reporting significantly less visits to the doctor.

The studies by Pennebaker about the value of emotional writing are in direct contradiction to those by Rimes, who found that venting produced no psychological benefits. We also know that studies show that emotion inhibition as a coping mechanism doesn't alleviate the physical stress response. This would argue that "venting" should work as well as Pennebaker's journaling. What's the difference? Meaning creation.

Recent research results suggest that the interaction of inhibition and disclosure is not as simple as originally conceptualized. Emotional disclosure or "venting" isn't enough to explain the benefits from writing about trauma. The process includes both the reduction of arousal and the ability to understand the experience.

Pennebaker and colleagues drew on three theoretical perspectives in evaluating the impact of writing about emotions: inhibition and disclosure, cognitive processes, and social processes. In examining the participants' narratives, Pennebaker realized that it wasn't just the telling of the story that had impact; it was how the story was constructed. In some cases, Pennebaker had participants work on their writing over a few days. He notes that narratives started out disorganized and messy and became more structured and coherent over time. The ones who were able to make a coherent story out of the messiness of real life were able to make the experience more manageable cognitively and received the most psychological benefits.

Within the narratives, Pennebaker looked for words and sentence structures that were indicative of more complex thinking. An increase in specific prepositions and causal words suggested that the experience was becoming a clearer narrative. Even the choice of positive or negative words related to the physical impacts of the written narratives. The cognitive categories of the words used did the best job of explaining the relationship among the variables. For example, people who used more positive-emotion words or who constructed stories with causal relationships around the emotions had better health improvements. It wasn't just *having* a story; it was the act of *constructing* the story that was important. As we discussed, stories have a linear, causal format. When the storytellers went through the act of creation, they needed to construct explanations and perspectives that fit into a time perspective. This enabled new ways of understanding events and emotions. New perspectives and meanings allowed the storytellers to work through problems and achieve resolution.

The ability to translate our life story not only helps us achieve a new cognitive understanding that facilitates acceptance but also provides a vehicle for communication with others. Our willingness to be open and authentic connects us to a social world.

As Pennebaker and others have noted, stress and trauma are socially isolating. Through the exchange of stories, people convey more than just facts. They share emotion and meaning. Thus stories allow us to share experiences and establish more meaningful connections. Research studies from human development, such as the seminal work on early childhood attachment by John Bowlby and Mary Ainsworth, as well as Barbara Fredrickson's study of positive emotions in positive psychology, have repeatedly demonstrated the centrality of human connection to mental health and positive social development.

Social connections are maintained through social storytelling. By sharing stories, we share aspects of the self, including emotional state, values, and outlook. This information is embedded in the stories shared no matter what the content. These exchanges increase a sense of intimacy and trust. The cognitive load that comes from suppressing emotion and keeping secrets distances us from others in two important ways. First, because we are always preoccupied with monitoring our thoughts to withhold information, we are not able to be honest and authentic with our stories. Second, the cognitive load that comes from self-monitoring inhibits our ability to really listen to and feel empathy for others.

Pennebaker and colleagues found that both online and face-to-face social support had positive benefits and promoted positive change in health behaviors. Whether writing or talking, the translation and organization of events requires synthesis and integration into the nature and syntax of language. The processes that occurs lead to searching for meaning and understanding. There are instances where the disorganized and unintegrated nature of traumatic memories may lead to rumination rather than meaning making. Thus researchers speculate that the structural discipline of writing and talking provides a channel that leads to the release of painful experiences, whereas thinking can result in re-experience and rumination.

Since significant life events can be processed in a number of ways. Sonja Lyubomirsky and colleagues (2006) at the University of California, Riverside, explored the impact of writing, talking, and thinking on both negative and positive memories. Negative events challenge our sense of order and meaning in the world. The creation of new meaning is an adaptive method for positive coping in order to restore order. Research that examines writing positive narratives about best future selves, gratitude and peak experiences, and savoring positive experiences find that replaying and rehearsing positive moments is beneficial and related to greater well-being. However, Lyubomirsky examined positive experiences using a step-by-step analysis with a group of college students. She found that while analyzing negative experiences to construct new meaning had positive effects on well-being, breaking down positive experiences in this manner did not. She speculated that reviewing happy events with a noncritical eye helps retain the sense of joy and mystery about an event, whereas an analysis takes away some of the "magic" of the experience.

PUBLIC AND SOCIAL STORYTELLING

Stories are everywhere. We hear family stories, stories from friends, teachers, colleagues, and acquaintances. Stories are told about how things used to be, what happened yesterday, and what will happen in the future. We often hear children say: "When I grow up, I'm going to . . ." Whether the story ended with eating all the ice cream you wanted or becoming president of the United States, it was a story that came with emotions, images, and plot lines and established a tangible path for the future.

One of the biggest amplifiers for storytellers is media. From news, film, and television to YouTube and SnapChat, we hear stories all day long. Thanks to mobile Internet access, these stories travel everywhere. Adding together

HOW DO GAMES CREATE POSITIVE EMOTIONS?

For humans, playing is how we learn, experiment, and explore. It's also how we have fun and connect with others. From a very early age, humans transform play into games by creating rules. The rules of a game define its psychological and physical boundaries and context, what the Dutch historian Johan Huizinga termed the "magic circle," in his book *Homo Ludens*. The magic circle is a temporary world, separate from reality, where humans can play.

Games are, by definition, meant to be entertaining. Using the lens of positive psychology, however, we can understand what it is about games that attracts our attention, keeps us engaged, and creates positive emotional experiences.

Safety

The magic circle created by the game's boundaries creates a safe environment that empowers exploration and dreams—whether it's by assuming the role of a character or matching patterns and solving puzzles—and provides an escape from everyday problems and chores. Safety allows us to relax physically.

Agency and Self-Efficacy

In games, what we do matters. Our actions have consequences. As we continue to play, our skills develop and our confidence in our ability to take action and be successful increases. According to Bandura's social cognitive theory, increasing our sense of agency and self-efficacy increases resilience.

Social Connection

Many games are played with others. Even when games are played asynchronously, such as Facebook's Farmville, there is a sense of feeling connected to other players. Connectedness triggers reward systems in the brain, improving our mood.

Neuroscience

The human brain seeks out patterns and puzzles as part of its innate, hardwired functioning. We are intrinsically motivated to solve problems. Solving a puzzle or mystery triggers reward centers in the brain.

television, Internet, radio, newspaper, magazines, film, and outdoor media, like billboards and other signage, some estimate media consumption to be upward of eight hours per day. As media and technology become more prevalent and integrated into our lives, we will increasingly be in control of the media we create, consume, and distribute.

Self-stories influence thoughts, feelings, and behaviors, and telling stories allows us to connect with others. The ability to project, mentalize, and empathize is part of the neural structure and transcends physical presence. Thus, the experience of mediated narratives is a simulator of life, whether we're "lost in a good book," identifying with a protagonist in a film, or laughing at a baby video on YouTube. Our brains are wired so that we have the ability to empathize with others and create a sense of presence. These mental processes transport us psychologically into narratives no matter what the format.

Psychology is late to the game in considering the impact of public narratives produced by entertainment and news sources. The integration of social technologies works to amplify the impact of individual voices alongside traditional media sources.

Even before the power of social networks, however, public narratives have had the power to influence public opinion. Published in the early 1800s, Harriet Beecher Stowe's novel *Uncle Tom's Cabin* is credited by many as turning the tide in favor of the abolitionists due to her empathetic depictions of the lives of slaves. However unrealistic—and Stowe herself said she felt it did not accurately represent the slave experience as she avoided many of the harsh cruelties—it nevertheless created a new awareness among white northerners of the human side of slavery. Stowe's book was the best-selling fiction book of the 19th century second only to the Bible. Some argue that it contributed so greatly to public opinion that it ultimately influenced Lincoln's thinking in crafting the Emancipation Proclamation. Others, including Stowe herself, argued that the power of *Uncle Tom's Cabin* was in the ability of narrative to "go for the heart" in the face of a proliferation of facts and numbers in the tracts, pamphlets, and newspapers circulated by both sides.

Novels still have power. The *Harry Potter* series is credited by many for sparking a surge in the reading habits of kids, inspiring them to read for pleasure. However, with the Internet and social technologies, media channels have proliferated. There is no shortage of information, but there is limited attention to give. Consequently, more and more media messaging is story-based, recognizing the power of stories to integrate message, emotion, and intention in their most memorable and attention-getting form. There is a wealth of research as psychologists and other scholars explore the impact of media and technology. In the tradition of the medical model, much of it focuses on what's wrong. The following examples, however, highlight some of the ways that storytelling can be used for promoting positive change at a social level.

STORIES IN THE MEDIA AND MEDIA STORIES

Media stories often exemplify attributes and strengths. Cinematherapy is the use of commercial films that are "prescribed" by a therapist to a client to create opportunities for healing or growth. Films can be a powerful catalyst for inspiration, show examples of behaviors to emulate, communicate a new attitude or perspective, or trigger an experience of emotional release or understanding. They can also enable useful discussions either within or outside of

POSITIVE PSYCHOLOGY AND MEDIA CONSUMPTION

The average American consumes 8 hours of media per day, of which 5 of those hours are television viewing (Kaiser, 2010). If you consider multitasking, such as watching television and texting or surfing the Internet on your tablet or computer, the average amount of media consumption is 11 hours. Media, in this case, are defined as any sort of mediated communication. The use or exposure to such media can vary from the moment you get up in the morning and listen to the radio or watch television, to reading the newspaper, checking the Internet, texting your friend, viewing billboards on the way to work, and working 8 hours on your computer.

While the consumption of the Internet is quickly catching up to the hours spent viewing television, television still reigns supreme in the media we consume most. In fact, it may seem as if some people know more about characters on favorite television programs than they know about each other given television's popularity.

If you look at the literature on media today, much of it is dedicated to the harmful effects of television and in particular television violence. Watching television provides most people with a sense of relaxation. However, Mihaly Csikszentmihalyi and Robert Kubey (1996) found in their research that after a few hours of television viewing our mood decreases. Why? People tend to start making comparisons to our lives and the lives of television characters portrayed in television series. Often these characters are good-looking and have beautiful homes, great friends, fun lives, and very little challenges with daily reality. As a result we begin to feel worse about our lives. This is called an "upward comparison" and it often causes cognitive dissonance because we aspire to have that lifestyle and we begin to pay less attention to the lack of reality it represents. Hence, many of us move to doing "downward comparisons" to decrease the cognitive dissonance. We may watch programming that shows individuals and groups at their worst and say to ourselves, "at least my life is not as bad as that."

The overconsumption of media also takes one away from time with family or friends, or being outside doing something active. As with most things in life, moderation and good choices are smart ways to approach media consumption.

the therapeutic setting. The psychologists Ryan Niemiec and Danny Wedding, authors of *Positive Psychology at the Movies: Using Films to Build Virtues and Character Strengths*, report that character strengths are everywhere at the movies. They contend that the most common strengths found in films are bravery, perseverance, love, kindness, humor, hope, creativity, and spirituality. Films have the ability to target and portray dominant strengths, where in daily life, strengths are rarely manifested alone and may be harder to appreciate when they are part of strengths constellations or combinations. *The Wizard of Oz*, for example, has several characters that pursue a distinct virtue, such as the Cowardly Lion who longs to have courage.

Bibliotherapy is the use of literature in the same capacity. The narrative format allows a message to be delivered in a way that opens the door for the client to feel transported into the story and experience elements of the story with more impact. Research on narrative transportation suggests that when people emotionally identify with a character and feel part of the story's world, it lowers their resistance to persuasive messaging and makes the reader or viewer more open-minded and more amenable to cognitive change.

Bibliotherapy has been used to reorient the lives of adult offenders. Changing Lives through Literature (CLTL) is a program begun in 1991 based on the idea that literature has the power to transform. With the intention of finding alternatives to prison, select prisoners were given probation rather than prison sentences, on the condition that they attended reading groups. The groups included an instructor, probation officers, a judge, and students—a combination that was critical to the success of the program. Over the course of several weeks, the groups would read and discuss a series of literary fiction. For the men's program, this included titles such as *Animal Farm, Of Mice and Men,* and *Deliverance.* For the women's program, this included titles such as *The Bean Trees, Dinner at the Homesick Restaurant,* and *To Kill a Mockingbird.* A year-long study of the first group in the program found that 19 percent were reoffenders, compared to 42 percent in the control group.

The instructors used discussion and role-play to make the characters and the situations feel real for the participants. This experience enabled access to emotional expression and behavioral alternatives that expanded what Fredrickson calls our "thought-action repertoire." In one case, a former drug user was inspired to resist drugs by the Hemingway's character of Santiago in *The Old Man and the Sea.* The ability to hear Santiago's voice and experience Santiago's persistence in the face of adversity and frustration helped the participant to resist the other voices tempting him to return to drugs.

The program has successfully spread beyond Massachusetts. There are CLTL programs across the United States and a version of the program, called Stories Connect, is running in a number of prison and community centers for people with drug and alcohol problems.

NARRATIVE AND HEALTH BEHAVIOR CHANGE

There are many ways that narrative can be applied to promote health-related behaviors. Based on the premise that storytelling is the basic mode of human interaction, narrative is a comfortable and familiar way of exchanging information. As Bruner points out, there are two ways of knowing, paradigmatic and narrative. Health information is usually delivered in a paradigmatic way, full of statistics and other empirical evidence. This type of message is rational and logical; it engages our brains at a conscious and rational processing level. As we have discussed, narrative knowing includes emotion and the experience of life. Therefore, it engages our brains in multiple processing pathways and allows us to visualize the desired behaviors, thus allowing us to practice new ways of being. For example, studies have shown that narratives are perceived to be more accurate than statistical evidence in persuading women not to use tanning beds. The more participants identified with characters, the more they perceived the health message to be accurate, useful, and believable.

ENTERTAINMENT EDUCATION

The attempts to use media-based storytelling as a vehicle to educate and influence social behaviors based on psychological theory can be traced back to 1969 in Latin America when Peruvian television aired a melodramatic telenovela called *Simplemente Maria*. The plot for this entertainment series centered on the challenges and triumphs of a poor country girl named Maria. To escape the poverty of her village, Maria moves to the city to get work as a maid. She is molested by her boss's son, gets pregnant, and loses her job. Yet Maria is resourceful and persistent. Week by week, viewers watched Maria raise her child, learn to read and write, and buy a sewing machine to start her own business. The viewers accompanied Maria through challenges and victories for an entire season, living through her emotional path to ultimately achieve economic independence and find love. *Simplemente Maria* was so popular that, much to the producers' surprise, thousands of people showed up to watch the filming of the final episode in which Maria gets married. *Simplemente Maria* had other unexpected impact: it led to a significant increase in enrollment in literacy programs and a surge in the sale of Singer sewing machine.

A Televisa executive named Miguel Sabido, recognizing the potential of stories told as serial dramas to further social and economic growth, embarked on what was to become a successful career in what we now call Education Entertainment (Singhal, Cody, Rogers & Sabido, 2003). His approach, known as the Sabido Methodology, integrated a number of theories into his media development process drawing from narrative theory, psychology, and communications. These informed his approach to the entire project, from process and delivery to content. Sabido's methodology included:

1. A communications process models from Shannon and Weaver that reflected the circular nature of mass communications. Also emphasized by Albert Bandura, this emphasized the co-evolving nature of content and audience and even anticipated the shift to social technologies.

2. Sociologist Paul Lazarsfeld's two-step flow theory of communication, which highlighted and recognized the power of the minority of the audience who become fan-advocates and engage with program content beyond the on-air viewing. Based on similar-style programing in Ethiopia, the characters in the stories model ways to talk about sensitive or taboo subjects, facilitating discussion and social acceptance.

3. Bentley's model of dramatic theory, specifically employing the genre of melodrama with its exaggerated emotions that emphasizes the tension between the moral universes of good and evil.

4. Recognizing that the target audience does not identify with these polar positions, Sabido also introduced transitional characters who experience the emotional struggle in the middle. In this way, Sabido integrated Bandura's social learning and social cognitive theories. By providing realistic simulations, these characters model how to meet life's challenges and adopt new behavior and attitudes. Sabido also uses this vicarious learning by doling out rewards and punishments to emphasize the types of behaviors he wishes to impact.

5. To increase the audience's ability to identify deeply with the actors, Sabido based characters on archetypes drawn from the work by psychologist Carl Jung. Jung proposed that archetypes represent patterns that are part of the shared collective unconscious and are part of all cultures. The archetypal essence is a pattern recognized by us all. By portraying characters in these expressions, Sabido was able to represent social norms that would resonate with the audience and be culturally appropriate.

6. Being interested in the whole body experience and intent on engaging the audience at all levels of perception led Sabido to Paul MacLean's Triune Brain Theory and allowed him to operationalize his goal of integrating drama that would engage the emotions and primary human values as well as unconscious and primal instincts that are motivated by the human survival response. Sabido saw the conscious, thinking brain as a reinforcement of the messages delivered to the emotions and instincts.

Population Media Center

The Population Media Center has adopted the Sabido Methodology for storytelling in numerous serialized soap operas to promote social change (Barker, 2007). They initiate and partner to develop projects around the world. The sophistication of technology has enabled them to create multiple ways of intersecting with their audiences, from radio and television to social media. Among their many notable projects, *East Los High* was a serial drama aimed at preventing teen pregnancies among Latinas. With an all-Latino cast, it has consistently ranked as one of the most popular programs on the subscription video service Hulu. With several transmedia storytelling components, the audience was able to interact with the story on multiple channels beyond the main program, from video blogs, texting campaigns, and key character social media profiles. The website provided extensive resources used by more than 60 percent of the show's viewers. For example, more than 27,000 people used a Planned Parenthood widget on the *East Los High* website in the first month that the program was launched.

Sierra Leone, one of the poorest countries in Sub-Sharan Africa, is less than the size of South Carolina and only 6 percent of the women use any method of birth control. The population of 6.1 million is projected to double by 2050 without a significant change in behaviors. Shared technology such as radio is the most practical way to reach a population with so few resources. Serial dramas are an effective way to support behavior change because they deliver a narrative in a culture that relies on oral histories. The format and plots encourage retelling and sharing of program story lines and speculation about the characters. Population Media Center's program *Saliwansai* (Puppet on a String) was a compelling 208-episode serial radio drama aired in the local language of Krio. The show has multiple story lines to be relevant and meaningful to different audiences, such as the struggling farmer Abu with a wife who is weakened by multiple pregnancies and Hingrah who risks his scholarship with risky sexual behaviors. The programming addresses a number of issues around population growth and health, such as family planning, gender-based violence, early marriage, and reproductive health. Each broadcast also encourages listeners to call or text comments about characters, story line, and program content, further making them emotional stakeholders in the program. The results are compelling. Besides tackling previously taboo subjects, such as talking about condoms and AIDS on the radio, 57 percent of people seeking health services and 82 percent of those seeking family planning services cited *Saliwansai* as motivating them to do so.

StoryCenter

Where Population Media works on a large scale seeking distribution in mass media audiences, StoryCenter is a much more personal approach to storytelling as a vehicle for social change. They began in 1993 giving voice to individuals and groups by uniting storytelling with participatory media production methods. Their storytelling strategy is used in a number of ways, from education and individual development to community mobilization and advocacy. They facilitate the creation of short, first-person narratives that reflect a wide range of culturally and historically embedded stories. They believe in the transformative power of storytelling, based on the psychological benefits of sharing personal memories, and their capacity to unite people around common experience.

StoryCenter's first digital story was produced in 1993. Only 150 words, it presented a compelling look at the depth of friendship and how a parent who has AIDS provides for her children's care after she dies. StoryCenter focuses primarily on training groups to become digital storytellers. They believe that through the use of digital technologies, they can train people to tell stories in ways that redefine the role of personal voice as a vehicle for social change.

Many of the stories focus on facilitating coping, normalizing identities through sharing life experiences, and allowing voices to be heard. Projects such as *Silence Speaks* enable people to tell stories of courage, struggle, and change using participatory media, education, and testimony practices—the telling and witnessing of stories—to impact human rights issues. *Promundo* was a project designed to give voice to Brazilian youth promoting gender equity and to prevent violence against children, youth, and women in Brazil and around the world. The Christensen Fund used storytelling among members of indigenous communities to bring their voice to light in efforts to maintain their land, language, and cultural practice in the face of commercial development. The Marie Stopes International used StoryCenter's model to create *Youth Like Me*, showcasing the narratives of youth in Papua New Guinea and Ghana to improve adolescent sexual and reproductive health.

Changing Lives through Literature

Cognitive psychologists and neuroscientists recognize narrative as a bridge between individuals and the sociocultural environment where they live. Narratives derive their power from individual meaning as well as the shared social narratives embedded in culture.

Storytelling for Empowerment

The Storytelling for Empowerment Program combined cultural empowerment, cognitive skills, storytelling, and the arts in a school-based, bilingual intervention for substance abuse, HIV, and other problem behaviors. The program targets at-risk Latino/Latina youth. Through storytelling approaches, the program enhances the factors that strengthen youth resilience and protection against substance abuse. The program was designed around risk and resiliency models and integrated stories and symbols to develop a positive peer group, create and share positive cultural identities, and build emotional strength. The storytelling exercises include "Stories to Live or Die By," which taught facts and myths about popular street and club drugs. Storytelling for Empowerment facilitates discussion among children and parents through the use of fotonovelas, a comic book-like print medium popular in Mexico and Latin America. First implemented in 1995, measures from two groups in 1998 and 1999 showed that all participants reported decreased alcohol use and increased resistance to drug use by the final year of the program.

Storytelling to Encourage Empathy

The organization *Facing History and Ourselves* creates story-based educational experiences to encourage active engagement that creates empathy in historical narratives, rather than the traditional lecture approach to history curriculum. Their goal is to have children connect events in history to their own lives in meaningful ways. For example, a lesson on the 1938 Kristallnacht tells a real story about a wave of violent Nazi attacks on Jewish communities with little response from most German citizens. By engaging with the lesson in story form, children are able to shift perspectives by discussing what it means to be different characters in the story, such as the victim or the bystanders. They are encouraged to equate the experiences to something similar in their own lives, such as bullying, and what it means to stand up for someone. Students studying this lesson through story showed increased measures of empathy and increased likelihood of intervention when others around them were targets of bullying compared to a control group studying the lesson in a traditional way.

CHAPTER 8

Positive Psychology in the Real World

Issues at every level of society, from education to global unrest, remind us that the power of positive psychology is in our ability to take what we know and apply it in the real world to make things better. While we often think of psychology as the delivery of a mental health intervention, psychology is about human behavior and, therefore, fundamental to everything we do.

People have always been interested in finding out what is good about human lives, but the threads of thought have been disconnected across many fields and academic silos, with little impact on the "real world" until now. Positive psychology is providing a common language and collective identity that enables practitioners to apply positive psychology to make a powerful and important impact on how we work, play, learn, and change over time.

Psychology is applied in a myriad of ways that we may not even realize. Psychologists are involved in product design, organizational structure, educational planning and delivery, and job design and hiring, to name only a few. From the placement of the knobs on your car to the products appearing at the check-out stand of your grocery story, psychology was involved. As positive psychologists, of course, we see a great need more than "just psychology" to be considered. We believe that the psychology of well-being and optimal functioning should be considered in the decisions, too, because the implicit choices we make about all kinds of things, such as parenting style, game design, the color of the paint on our office wall, job choices, and what's shown on television, can influence our emotional well-being.

The tenets of positive psychology allow us to frame problems with a different intention, that of creating growth and prosocial outcomes. It is not, however, a specific prescription for a way of being. Positive psychology recognizes that things like happiness and optimal functioning are subjective and value-laden, heavily influenced by social and cultural context and individual differences. Yet, positive psychology provides a way of thinking, sensitive to these differences, that remains dedicated to the facilitation of individual and social goals.

In *Authentic Happiness*, Seligman (2002) articulates the basic assumptions behind positive psychology:

- There is human nature or character.
- Our character determines action.
- There are two forms of innate character—we have the capacity, by nature, to be both good and bad.

Positive psychology is applied in the real world to influence human capacity and provide opportunities to exercise what is good. As we continue to research and question, we expand our understanding of what works to achieve this goal and how to make more of it. As we will see, making life better for individuals makes it better for society as a whole as well.

This chapter's emphasis builds on the theoretical foundations of the previous chapters and discusses how these fundamentals of positive psychology interact with individuals as part of a social system that includes all of society. In particular, we are going to examine the application of positive psychology in different ways:

- Positive psychology as an ecological system
- Positive psychology as a framework for understanding enabling institutions, such as family, schools, and organizations
- The impact of applying positive psychology to the environments we inhabit

SYSTEMS OF INFLUENCE

Nothing happens in isolation. Ecological systems theory provides a compelling description of the need to think about the psychological impact of more than just our inner psyches. It also highlights why the potential for the application of positive psychology is so great.

A derivative of general systems theory, ecological systems theory was proposed by Russian-American psychologist Urie Bronfenbrenner (1994). Systems theory describes the dynamic interaction of the forces within a network and how even events beyond our control can contribute to how we experience and define our world. Like Facebook, YouTube, and other social networks, our family, schools, communities, and countries each forms a networked system. Like social media, they are all linked and interdependent. Our social interactions reverberate through a system, just like a viral video or an e-mail hoax.

A child psychologist, Bronfenbrenner developed ecological systems theory to accomplish two goals: (1) describe how people are embedded in multiple levels of dynamic, co-evolving social networks and (2) highlight the profound effect this interactivity has on human development. Bronfenbrenner saw that events introduced pressures into a system there were never isolated on a single level, such as how changes in the economic environment impact the family or how shifts in interpersonal relationships between parents impacted how the parents relate to others at work, how they interact with their children, and how their children then engage with their school environments. The impact of environmental factors on human interactions, relationships and development underscores the need for applying positive psychology to social structures to create positive influences and pathways.

According to Bronfenbrenner's ecological systems theory, each person's environment is divided into five levels: the microsystem, the mesosystem, the exosystem, the macrosystem, and the chronosystem. Bronfenbrenner proposed that each person is inseparable from this complex layering of social networks and is both the recipient and a participant in the system dynamics. These distinctions help us understand how and where different interactions affect the system and where the introduction of new behaviors and ideas can influence the network behaviors.

Bronfenbrenner's five levels are arranged in proximity to the individual:

1. The **microsystem** is the closest level and describes our direct contact, such as at home, school, or work. It represents the direct relationships we have with others. For example, the microsystem would be how a young girl, Karen Washington, interacts with her mother. It also includes a child's biology, such as innate temperament, that can influence how others treat her.

2. The **mesosystem** is made up of the interactions among the different parts of the microsystem. The mesosystem would describe how the girl's mother, Ms. Washington, interacts with Karen's teacher, Mr. Gomez. We don't often think of the ramifications of these external relationships on a child, but if Mr. Gomez is rude to Ms. Washington or if Ms. Washington misses her parent–teacher conferences, Karen may be the unintended recipient of their experiences. Mr. Gomez may assume that Ms. Washington doesn't care and, therefore, Karen won't be a good student. Ms. Washington might assume that Mr. Gomez is a bad teacher and inadvertently damages Karen's respect for Mr. Gomez.

3. Beyond these interpersonal relationships, the **exosystem** describes the larger social system that encompass the microsystem and the mesosystem. For example, if Ms. Washington has a job that demands travel, then the company's needs can impact Karen. Karen may feel anxious or afraid when her mother leaves, losing interest in her schoolwork or turning to peer groups for guidance.

4. Each system is further impacted by the more remote yet equally influential **macrosystem**, which includes the larger environment, such as the economy, cultural values, and political systems. If the economy does poorly, Ms. Washington may lose her job or be transferred.

5. The **chronosystem** articulates the transitions and shifts that occur across a life span, such as physiological aging, death of a parent, divorce, and other dimensions of time that influence the environment. If Ms. Washington is transferred, she and Karen will need to change homes and schools, make new friends, and generally develop new social and practical support systems.

Psychologists such as Susan Sheridan and Jennifer Burt (2011) have used this theory to understand childhood development and create programs based on a family-centered approach that focuses on strengths and the capacity for growth rather than on the resolution of problems or fixing shortcomings.

Family-centered positive psychology (FCPP) uses the ecological systems model to address the relationships among people, the situations, and the environment that are inseparable from a child's life. FCPP allows social support workers to help families by addressing their complex lives more realistically. By using a strengths-based approach to identify and support strengths and assets within the family system, they are able to promote more sustainable positive outcomes for the child and family. The goals of the family-centered services focus on (1) family empowerment, (2) increasing skills, (3) listening to the families to determine needs, (4) identifying strengths that can be developed, and (5) extending the family's available social support networks. Key to the process is resisting the temptation to "solve problems" and approach situations as collaborators rather than providing treatment in order to promote optimal growth and agency. This approach increases the development of assets and protective factors that enhance resilience.

Parental involvement is among the things believed to be a protective factor against stress for young children. In the previous example, encouraging Ms. Washington's strengths in her positive parenting skills could help her feel more confident about her ability to provide Karen a good sense of security when Ms. Washington needs to travel. Developing Karen's strengths could also make Karen feel more competent and less dependent, making her mother's travel seem less difficult and alleviating some of Ms. Washington's anxiety over necessary work travel and improve her performance in that domain. Developing Mr. Gomez's emotional intelligence would help him be more sensitive to the issues that working parents like Ms. Washington face. This could help him be less likely to make quick negative judgments and be able to be more openly supportive. This would alleviate Ms. Washington's defensiveness and improve her perceptions of the quality of Mr. Gomez as a teacher. This would benefit both her relationship with Mr. Gomez and Karen's. It would also change Mr. Gomez's perception of himself and reduce his stress. This would influence how he relates to his fellow teachers and his family. Like a stone tossed into a pond, the ripples continue in all directions.

As ecological systems theory suggests, positive psychology can make an impact far beyond individual behaviors. In one example, a group of psychologists from Stanford, Pennsylvania State, Columbia, and Yale Universities demonstrated how an entire classroom benefited when individual children received values-affirmations-based interventions to improve their school performance. A small group of students were given the assignment to write about their most important values, such as friendship, family, or creative ability, believing they were participating in a regular writing activity. In contrast, the control group wrote about their least important values. Confirming the researchers' hypotheses that psychological interventions can impact the way people perceive their environments and create lasting change, the findings showed that changed individuals also interacted differently with their environments. The study showed that the academic performance of the entire class improved after the positive interventions experienced by a few students. The density of the intervention was also significant. The greater the number of students participating in the values exercise, the greater the improvement in academic performance for the entire group. The exercise was most effective when delivered during the first part of the term. Previous research has shown that positive affirmation reduced stress and concerns about being labeled with a negative stereotype among African American students. Therefore, the researchers posited that the early intervention offset any downward spiral of self-doubt and negative beliefs because the greater the number of higher performing African American students in the class, the lower the stereotype threat that the other African American students in the classes experienced. Researchers also suggest that other dynamics that may contribute to the positive shift. For example, the reduction in the number of students doing poorly may free up time for teachers to invest in the remaining students who need help. There was also evidence that when a large number of students received the positive values affirmation, it created a stronger norm for cooperation, order, and success that benefited all students.

THREE PILLARS

Positive psychology has three pillars or domains. The first pillar is the study of happiness and well-being. The second is the study of individual traits and virtues, because without higher purpose and meaning that comes from the cultivation of qualities like integrity, intimacy, and wisdom, happiness is fleeting. The third pillar is the focus of this chapter. It is the study of positive institutions, such as governments, organizations, communities, and families—all the structural supports that encourage the development and sustainability of virtues and positive emotions. As the research shows, the pillars do not stand alone; they are interrelated. Influence flows in all directions. The previous example demonstrated how individual interventions on student attention to values influenced the entire classroom and that classroom performance influenced teacher behavior in attitude and the use of resources (energy and time.)

Consider, however, the continued effect as these benefits flow through different social systems. The students who perform better experience more positive feedback at school and at home, creating positive emotions for the both giver and receiver. Research by Nicholas Christakis and James Fowler demonstrated that positive emotions travel farther across networks and have more staying power. They also reported that positive emotions resulted in "happiness clusters." Positive emotions, therefore, build social capital. We know from network theorists, such as Mark Granovetter (1973) and his seminal paper "The Strength of Weak Ties," that social networks have such tremendous reach and power because of the social capital that comes from connectivity. Positive emotions increase the likelihood of sustainable social links. Thus, positive experiences from the students' individual interventions do not stop when students leave the classroom. They carry out into the rest of their worlds and subtly influence how they think about themselves, how they behave, and how others respond to them.

Creating a positive institution, in lieu of an individual intervention, offers the advantage of leverage. Positive institutions create multiple and replicable opportunities for positive experience that impact emotions, such as happiness, optimism, and hope, the development of strengths, such as courage and creativity, engagement, and a sense of purpose. Instead of impacting one person at a time, an institution can touch many. It is like throwing many pebbles into a pond at once. As illustrated in the classroom experiment, the greater the density of people who received the positive intervention, the greater positive impact on the group as a whole. Institutions allow us to amplify network effects.

ENABLING INSTITUTIONS

As Christopher Peterson points, our institutions are complex. No single institution is all positive or all negative. Peterson argues that it's more reasonable to consider whether an institution is, on net, enabling rather than positive. Using "enabling" as the criteria require that we define our goals—what is the purpose and what is our intention? Different context and situations provide the scaffold for different outcomes. For example, a strong family structure enables the well-being of children and a positive work environment encourages employee well-being and job satisfaction. Both are positive outcomes, yet we would build different structures to enable each specific outcome to best fit the needs of the population and to target different mix of skills, resources, and support.

In spite of the growth of positive psychology, there is little empirical research on enabling institutions. This is in part due to the difficulty in identifying appropriate institutions in order to isolate measurable variables—as Peterson says, none are perfect examples. It is also due to the complexity in measuring outcomes in large social systems with so many extraneous and confounding variables. The five main forms of enabling institutions identified in the literature draw primarily from microsystems and mesosystems: family, community, church, work, and school. From an ecological systems approach, however, we can see that these inquiries are not discreet and many informal systems, such as mentoring, as well as environmental and socioeconomic systems, such as culture, political systems, and policies, such as free speech, also have a significant influence on our daily experience, choice, and emotions.

Based on research comparisons across various social and commercial institutions, from the military, mass media, and justice system to small business, Peterson suggests that although traits are individual characteristics, enabling institutions do have certain traits or features in common that influence whether or not an institution "contributes to fulfillment."

Positive psychology is inseparable from moral values and is very subjective. Fulfillment varies across individuals and cultures. When looking at enabling institutions, it's important to define the terms—to question just what is meant when things like "Google is a great place to work" are said. When one hears about jobs at Google, the most common stories revolve around the tangible and hedonic perks: free breakfast, lunch, and dinner; coffee and juice bars; free commuter busses with Wi-Fi; massage "credits" for a free massage on campus; or the ability to bring your dog to work. But when one looks at the interviews with employees, the free food may be great on face value, but it is delivering important benefits beyond calories, such as helping to build relationships with colleagues. In fact, the social and intellectual capital of working at Google is behind nearly every hedonic pleasure that makes the list. At the core, Google as a great place to work comes from the meaning derived from being connected to people and feeling that you are valued. These are the drivers of satisfaction across all the businesses that regularly rank high in employee satisfaction. At Google, employees uniformly report being energized and inspired by great thinkers, new ideas, people who are driven and committed, the sharing of diverse experiences and expertise, and the emphasis on learning. Even the fitness facilities and generous benefits, like maternity leave and life insurance, give people a message that working at Google is a long-term relationship, not just free food. The psychological value of short-term self-benefits, or stomach-benefits, is limited.

Personal fulfillment differs for every person, but we can agree that it doesn't happen in isolation from our social environment. How we interact and connect with others plays an important role in our sense of motivation, meaning, and well-being, so enabling institutions are those that set up structures that allow people to exercise their strengths and feel valued for them. As the ecological systems theory models suggests, organizational experience is inextricable from interpersonal relationships. Each is a dynamic contributor to our sense of well-being and fulfillment. An enabling organization provides structures, models, and scaffolding to encourage the kind of interactions that promote positive growth.

Peterson believes that fulfillment comes from the pursuit of morally valued activities over time. He also notes that when we look at case studies of enabling institutions, we often confuse things like profitability or customer satisfaction with moral values of goodness. This is why he argues in favor of judging institutions on their ability to contribute to fulfillment. This clarifies the task of identifying the characteristics of an organization that succeeds in contributing to the fulfillment of its stakeholders and delivers a better understanding how institutional practices promote and enable moral excellence and personal fulfillment.

THE FAMILY

The family is one of the most important institutions across all cultures. The definition of a family, however, varies widely. With changes in birth rates, the prevalence of divorce and remarriage, and the rise of nontraditional families, the size and shape of families have changed considerably in the United States. In spite of these changes, the role of the parent or caretaker remains critical in a child's development. The parent–child interaction establishes a child's sense of attachment, a behavioral motivation system based on the parent–child emotional bond. According to developmental psychologists, the early childhood attachment establishes behavioral patterns that become neurologically rooted.

The types of attachment can be: (1) secure, (2) anxious, or (3) avoidant. Different styles of parenting have been linked with the different types of attachment. Each has implications for the child's development.

During the early 1960s, psychologist Diana Baumrind (1968) identified four dimensions of parenting that have become the basis for defining parenting styles, the psychological construct that describes the strategies a parent or caretaker uses in child rearing. Baumrind recorded four strategies exhibited by the caretaker: the disciplinary approaches, the warmth and ability to nurture, communication style, and the expectations for the child's maturity and self-regulation.

Based on these criteria, Baumrind identified three different parenting styles that represented the majority of caretakers in the United States, which she labeled authoritarian, permissive, and authoritative. Eleanor Maccoby and John Martin (1983) proposed the addition of a fourth parenting style: uninvolved.

1. **Authoritarian** parenting emphasizes stern discipline and exercising control over children. A common approach to punishment is the withdrawal of affection. Authoritarian parents do not encourage a child's independence.

2. **Permissive** parenting is emotionally warm but lenient. Permissive parents rarely set and enforce rules or provide firm guidance.

3. **Authoritative** parents exhibit a more balanced approach, setting limits but encouraging discussion and independence. Authoritative parents are better able to listen, validate a child's experience, and offer explanations about why the rules and behaviors matter in a larger context, such as values and longer-term goals.

4. **Uninvolved** parents provide food and shelter but little else; they do not set or enforce standards like the permissive parents, nor do they give emotional warmth.

While a child's temperament and cultural patterns play a role in how parents interact with children, the four parenting styles have been shown to be useful constructs in understanding how the parent–child relationship impacts a child's social development. Parenting style approaches have been applied around the world. While they don't always map onto local parenting methods, they provide a useful guideline in identifying the types of parenting strategies that produce the best results.

Children with authoritarian parents tend to be well behaved, submissive, and unhappy. They tend to suffer more from anxiety and poor self-esteem. Permissive parents tend to produce children who are sociable and outgoing, but irresponsible, immature, and impatient. These children have higher self-esteem, yet are more likely engage in problem behaviors, like drug use, and have lower levels of academic achievement. Children from uninvolved families tend to have the most social and personal problems.

After reading about positive psychology principles such as self-efficacy and authenticity, it won't be surprising to learn that authoritative parenting tends to be the most positive environment for child development. Children with this type of parenting are more friendly, responsible, and competent, performing better academically and having more social success. Authoritative parenting is a two-way exchange where parents or caretakers spend time explaining the "why" behind their behaviors and talk about goals and values. This accomplishes several goals congruent with positive psychology: (1) it reinforces values through discussion and rules, (2) it delivers love and caring through communication and mirroring, (3) it provides social validation that builds self-efficacy, the cornerstone of resilience, and (4) it builds strengths.

Children often have multiple caretakers or parents who don't always agree on parenting strategies. The lack of agreement doesn't undermine the impact of the authoritative parent. Fletcher, Steinberg, and Sellers (1999) found that children benefited from having at least one authoritative parent. It did not matter if the other parent was authoritarian, permissive, or uninvolved.

Parenting style alone doesn't determine how children develop. As we have seen, children grow up part of a larger network of social influences, including school and peer groups, as well as genetic predispositions. It is complex and the influences flow both ways. For example, research has suggested that a child's behavior can influence parenting style. In a study tracking 500 adolescent American girls, researchers found that high levels of misbehavior decreased a parent's attempts to enforce rules, suggesting that children who are more difficult to handle can promote bad parenting habits. As we discussed earlier, how people behave plays a role in how they are treated. Thus knowledge of the importance of positive parenting is an important tool for parents to override the inclination to pull away when times are tough.

A positive parenting program out of Australia breaks down the core parenting skills that comprise positive parenting, mirroring the authoritative parenting style. These include (Sanders, 1999):

1. Self and child behavioral monitoring
2. Parent–child relationship skill (spending time, talking, showing affection)
3. Teaching new skills and behaviors (appropriate goals, setting good examples)
4. Managing misbehavior (clear goals, logical consequences)
5. Preventing problems in high-risk situations (advance planning, discussing ground rules and consequences, holding follow-up discussions)
6. Self-regulation skills (practice, evaluating strengths and weaknesses, setting personal goals)
7. Mood management and coping skills (relaxation, mindfulness, planning)
8. Social support and communication (partner support, problem solving)

SCHOOLS AS ENABLING INSTITUTIONS

As research emerges on subjective well-being and schools, the most successful examples of schools as empowering institutions are those that encourage the development of psychosocial strengths in addition to academic learning. Positive psychology offers valuable approaches to educational institutions to reprioritize how they see the learning process by integrating role of emotions, social connection, and meaning with cognitive skills.

In evaluating Australian high school students, researchers Adrian Tomyn and Robert Cummins (2011) found that school satisfaction was a unique construct and meaningful contributor to measures of subjective well-being, adding significantly to empirical measures of satisfaction in school-aged children. They argue that school can improve a child's sense of personal control and help them develop self-efficacy because school provides an experimental environment where children can test and learn about different behaviors and outcomes. They note that school interventions and reforms that are targeting classrooms alone have been unsuccessful since so much of student's focus, perception of satisfaction, and developmental maturation centers on their relationships with peers, family, and other important people in their lives.

Like psychology in general, schools must move away from solving problems to promoting wellness and expanding the opportunities for children to demonstrate and explore their strengths, abilities, and interests. There are several key attributes of positive schools:

1. Positive academic environments recognize the importance of positive emotions to academic success. Thus rather than monitoring academic performance alone, they actively track subjective well-being, school satisfaction, and emotional health.

2. Positive schools take a strengths-based approach, looking for a fit between school experiences and student strengths, recognizing the range of individual differences in abilities, personality, and interests. This applies equally to at-risk, special needs, and "normal" students. This also involves a shift from the deficit model to one that views everyone as being inherently capable of growth. Students who are validated by the school experience, programs, staff, and teachers view themselves differently, creating the positive emotions necessary for what Barbara Fredrickson describes as an upward spiral of positive emotions.

3. Positive schools promote positive relationships among all groups—students, staff, teachers, parents, and community. Schoolwide policies on inclusion as well as organized events and processes to break down barriers and encourage responsible school citizenship help overcome traditional hierarchies and social obstacles.

4. Positive schools, like positive parents, provide clear rules and discipline that are fair and consistent, focusing on correction and skill-building, not punishment or shaming.

5. Positive school environments look for ways to individualize instruction to engage creativity and engagement, intrinsic motivation, and meaning. Curriculum is designed with thought to the link between course content and the things a student sees every day. Most academic programs presume that a student has the ability to see the value by abstracting and projecting into the future. We now know that many of those long-range planning skills are continuing to develop in the cerebral cortex until the mid-twenties. A positive school provides cognitive scaffolding or support to provide context to the content and prepares students to understand the value of learning to enable lifelong success.

EARLY LEARNING ENVIRONMENTS

Imagine 3-year-old Anthony coming into his new preschool room. His emotions are on high alert and he has lots of questions. Will I like it? Will I know what I'm supposed to do? Will I fit in? Will I have fun? Is it a nice place?

These questions don't just apply to Anthony at preschool. We all have similar questions going into a new environment. New things are both exciting and scary. The brain is on overdrive trying to get information from the environment to determine if we are safe and welcome. A lot of that information comes from people. If, for example, Anthony's teacher is warm and caring, Anthony can start to relax, facilitating his adjustment to a new environment and his ability to learn.

However, Anthony's adjustment is not resting on his interaction with the teacher. His brain also gets information from the physical environment. If the environment is inviting, friendly, and accessible, it helps support learning and creativity and supports his emotional, physical, and intellectual needs. A well-designed, developmentally appropriate environment will allow Anthony to maximize his potential, explore his strengths and interests, and will create a foundation for his developing emotional security.

Brain research shows that there are "windows of opportunity" during the early years, when several critical cognitive and emotional areas are developing, including language, logical thinking, emotional expression, and self-regulation. Positive psychology can inform the design choices to make sure that a classroom supports cognitive and emotional needs. For example, a rich visual environment has lots of things to explore, but there is also the potential for young children to be visually overwhelmed. Therefore, a positive visual environment shows organized displays of materials and work that can be changed to facilitate interest and exploration. A positive emotional environment also respects a young child's emotional needs by providing a safe place to collect valuable things and offers places to retreat if the child gets tired or overstimulated.

Comfortable Classrooms

Multiple studies indicate that classroom environments designed with the child's socioemotional growth in mind can help students feel safe, valued, and secure—all positive emotions that increase motivation, self-esteem, and improve learning experiences. In a qualitative study of 25 first-graders, researchers interviewed students before and after their classroom was changed to include display of student artwork, reading spaces, plants, and a class fish. The interviews showed that the students responded positively to the changes. The students reported feeling more relaxed, enjoying the subjects more, and expressed pride over the display of their artwork and other contributions. In another study, researchers Beth Daly and Suzanne Suggs (2010) confirmed these findings. For example, they reported that teachers across 75 classrooms believed that having pets in the classroom contributed to the development of empathy and socioemotional growth.

ORGANIZATIONS AND BUSINESSES

As important as classrooms are to growth and learning, human development doesn't stop when we enter the workforce. In one survey, adults in the United States spend, on average, 47 hours per week at work. Nearly 20 percent reported spending more than 60 hours per week at work. Given the amount of time the average American spends working, positive work environments and enabling institutions clearly play an important role in our well-being.

Positive institutions are those with clear values. These values function as a compass or North Star and drive the institution's culture, brand, communications, and relationships, both internally with employees and externally with customers and vendors. While there are lots of ways to make judgment about a company's success, from financial return to employee retention, we want to see if it fits our definition of an enabling institution. Does it encourage and support the development of virtues? Is it contributing to the positive growth and fulfillment of individuals and society?

For many businesses, giving back to the community is an essential part of their corporate DNA. By institutionalizing volunteerism, the Baltimore-based consulting firm entreQuest finds that not only are they making a difference in their community, but they are affording employees the opportunity to be part of something larger related to their work. EntreQuest finds that this lifts moral, creates company loyalty, and improves decision making when on the job. EntreQuest has "give back days" where employees spend time working on local housing through Habitat for Humanity, tutoring children through Big Brothers Big Sisters, or serving meals in a local soup kitchen. For entreQuest, this commitment to social responsibility extends to their clients and they encourage them to organize their own "give back days" as well.

Some businesses are designed to integrate social good in their original business plan. Companies like Patagonia and The Body Shop have long histories of linking their corporate goals to the way they do business. Patagonia, a privately held outdoor-clothing company started in 1972, has a near iconic reputation built equally on the strength of product quality and commitment to the environment. Founder Yvon Chouinard has been donating 1 percent of total sales to environmental organizations since 1985. He has continued to make changes in Patagonia's production process to increase the emphasis on sustainability and durability. Durability may not seem like an obvious solution to increasing sales, given that it means customers would need to purchase less. However, consumers responded to Patagonia's environmental consciousness and emphasis on durability through increased loyalty and word of mouth. Sales increased. A recent campaign urged customer to "Buy Less," suggesting they sell their used Patagonia gear through eBay or Patagonia's website rather than buy new products, earning them customer loyalty and wide media coverage emphasizing Patagonia's ideals.

Patagonia's mission is built around four core values that are the guiding principles for its operations. These are (1) pursuit of quality in everything they do; (2) relationships built on integrity and respect; (3) to act as a catalyst for personal and corporate action to protect the environment; and (4) recognition that success and fun lie in developing innovative solutions and not to be bound by convention. Patagonia's goals are not just for the marketing department. They walk the talk. The company believes employees should be out enjoying nature or home with children if they are sick; therefore, employees can take time off during the day to exercise, or deal with personal demands. Patagonia continues to expand ventures that promote sustainable business practices and improve the environment and is a consistent winner of awards for Corporate Responsibility and ethical business practices for remaining true to the corporate mission and values.

The Body Shop, a beauty products and lifestyle company founded in 1976 by Anita Roddick, is also value-based. One of the first companies to make a name for itself by putting "doing good" ahead of doing well, the corporate values since inception have been (1) opposing animal testing, (2) supporting community trade, (3) promoting self-esteem, (4) defending human rights, and (5) protecting the planet. The Body Shop has a distinctive culture. While inspired by the personality and goals of the founder, the culture has permeated its meteoric growth. Even since its merger into the L'Oréal portfolio, Roddick remained what BBC News called a "fierce guardian for the founding values." While many look at the acquisition of companies like The Body Shop by the giant L'Oréal as "selling out," many analysts argue that its influence is actually going the other way—multinationals are recognizing the importance of ethical business practice to create sustainable customer bases and profits.

Newer organizations have emerged that are redefining business models to support their values. TOMS Shoes, for example, was built around the concept of one for one, giving away a pair of shoes to a child in need for every pair purchased. SoapBox, which manufactures a line of health and beauty products, was founded on the idea that a bar of soap could save kids' lives. Working as a contractor for USAID, SoapBox CEO David Simnick realized that clean water aid wasn't being paired with hygiene items, so critical to health, and he wanted to bridge that gap. SoapBox Soaps was founded around the virtue of altruism and hope. Their mission, like TOMS', is to raise awareness of the potential for linking consumer purchases with social change. SoapBox's goal is to empower consumers to see the power and implications of thoughtful purchasing—a bottle of liquid soap from SoapBox buys a month of clean water through clean water organizations such as Splash.

These companies, whether new or old, model positive values and organizational behaviors and inspire others to adopt new approaches to how they do business. As more and more businesses like TOMS, The Body Shop, and SoapBox are showing, ethics and business actually help, rather than hinder, profitability.

CORPORATE SOCIAL RESPONSIBILITY

There is a common assumption that anything that raises costs and prices will lower profitability, but business gurus like Michael Porter have long been arguing that they are not necessarily at odds. Increasingly socially conscious employees and consumers apply pressure from both sides that is moving business to find new ways that capitalism can have positive impact. New terminology such as Michael Porter's "shared value capitalism," John Mackey's "conscious capitalism," and Marc Benioff's "compassionate capitalism" all point toward the movement to put positive values into business practices.

Even without adopting an entirely new philosophy, however, many businesses are moving toward integrating programs that have positive impact on local communities or society at large through corporate social responsibility (CSR) programs. CSR refers to programs and initiatives that a company undertakes to benefit society rather than profits. Increasingly large numbers of companies are adopting CSR programs in response to consumer awareness of and a concern about global and social issues. Technology and social media platforms, such as Twitter and Facebook, have opened a new window on the world, shining a light on problems that were once out of sight. Technology has also enabled advocacy and a brought awareness to issues that used to be local or largely unknown.

CSR has become an increasingly integral part of business practice over the few years. It is commonplace to see a section in annual reports and on corporate websites dedicated to company activities aimed at causes or community support. They are challenging the beliefs of those who argue that it's not possible to "do well doing good," or those who suggest that CSR is (1) is an inappropriate use of shareholder money, (2) that it detracts rather than adds to firm value, and (3) that it is an advertising ploy rather than a real contribution to society.

There is a wide range of CSR programs, varying in scope and content. A study out of the London Business School reported that CSR programs don't have uniformly positive or negative impact on company value. They report: (1) CSR activities can enhance firm value, particularly for those with high public awareness; however, the opposite occurs when there are questions about the nature of the CSR activities; (2) the impact of CSR on lesser well-known firms is either neutral or negative, and (3) advertising has a negative effect on contributions to firm value of CSR if the CSR is irrelevant or inconsistent with brand reputation and purpose. Thus CSR only adds value under certain conditions, and is largely dependent on the consumer's appreciation of the CSR efforts. Thus consumers respond favorably when the organizational culture and values are extended into a CSR project and negatively when the consumer believes that the CSR program is a marketing device, "tacked on" as window dressing. Even big companies don't always get it right. Shell Oil, Coca-Cola, and British American Tobacco have all experienced backlash for their CSR efforts.

Shell Oil, for example, had the slogan "Only by behaving responsibly can any company hope to operate profitably," yet the Christian Aid Report *Behind the Mask* reported that Shell allegedly left large oil spills unattended and their community development programs were little more than lip service in terms of impact.

On the other hand, Whole Foods, whose brand promise is sustainability with the slogan "Whole foods. Whole people. Whole plant," is consistent across their business practices. Whole Foods' CSR programs are integrated into every aspect of their business rather than as stand-alone projects taking place outside of daily operations. They are consistent with their values from how they treat employees (whom they call members) to how they select vendors and products. Whole Foods members are encouraged to participate in volunteer activities on company time and the company continually seeks to improve operations by raising standards, such as finding alternative energy sources for stores (Blomqvist & Posner, 2004).

The millennial generation in particular is helping fuel the drive toward more positive business practices. Millennials, having grown up with social connectivity, demonstrate a new understanding of the role of business in the context of a global community. According to the *Net Impact Survey of 2012*, 72 percent of millennial students and 53 percent of millennial workers agree that having a job where they can make an impact is important to their happiness. This is reflected both in their job choices and their purchase decisions. The *2015 Cone Communications Millennial CSR Study* shows that 91 percent of millennials would switch to a brand associated with a cause. While they are leading the charge, the rest of Americans are following close behind, where 85 percent of consumers of all ages would do the same. The writing is on the wall for organizations that it's time to think of themselves as citizens, not businesses.

CONSCIOUS CAPITALISM

Conscious capitalism is a philosophy that builds on the foundations of capitalism as essential to a healthy economy but incorporates positive psychology principles of trust, compassion, collaboration, and value creation into every aspect of business. The proponents of conscious capitalism propose that by focusing on a higher purpose, the business becomes what we have been calling an enabling institution—one that creates meaning and purpose by engaging, inspiring, and energizing its stakeholders. Every business has multiple stakeholders, including investors, management, employees, customers, vendors, the local environment, and neighbors. Conscious capitalism's focus on all stakeholders reminds us of the interrelated nature of our society and economy. It moves values to the forefront, making them the foundation of a culture that connects employees, customers, and investors to the larger community and the larger community to the processes that drive the business.

SOCIAL ENTREPRENEURSHIP

Social entrepreneurship is another example of positive psychology in action. Social entrepreneurs are people who tackle society's problems with innovative solutions, often drawing on business techniques. Social entrepreneurs, like entrepreneurs in business, change the face of society by finding solutions to social issues that can be implemented on a large scale. The Austrian economist Joseph Schumpeter (1951) described successful entrepreneurship as a change agent who sets off a chain reaction in the larger economy establishing a new equilibrium that is self-sustaining and spawns numerous imitators. If, as many argue, the meaning of work is inseparable from the meaning of life, we can see social entrepreneurship as a way of achieving what the positive psychologists call the "balanced worker," one where work is of central importance and allows the expression of creativity and personal meaning and meets economic needs.

Social entrepreneurship is not about profit. Yet, nonprofit doesn't mean no profits. In order to be sustainable, social entrepreneurs build social solutions that can succeed in the private sector and achieve the financial resources to further the founder's social goals.

A classic example of social entrepreneurship is the Grameen Bank. Muhammad Yunus founded the bank in response to the human suffering from the abject poverty he saw in Bangladesh. He recognized that the poor had no options for borrowing even very small amounts of money without paying exorbitantly high rates of interest to moneylenders and so had no way to break the cycle of poverty. His original capital investment was $27, loaned out in small increments to women in a small village. The women borrowed money to invest in their own ability to generate income, such as the purchase of sewing machines, goods to sell, or seed to plant. Yunus relied on the relationships among the loan recipients to enforce loan repayment through a combination of social support and peer pressure. He found that women in this system were very reliable customers and he had very few loan defaults. Yunus's Grameen Bank developed what is now known as microcredit and micro-lending. It has since spawned a global network of other organizations that have adapted his model to other countries and context and created a global microcredit industry. The success of Grameen Bank not only found a new way to provide loans to empower individuals but also challenged negative stereotypes of the creditworthiness of the very poor. The 2005 Grameen Foundation USA report states that research on microcredit in the intervening years has some compelling, even surprising, results:

> . . . two major studies strongly suggest that microfinance works better for the poorest than the less poor. Second, there is strong evidence that female clients are empowered, though the data on increased adoption of family planning is less clear. Third, society-wide benefits that go beyond clients' families are apparently significant—which is a tantalizing possibility when we hear that roughly 92 million families (composed of 450 million people) are now being reached, according to the Microcredit Summit's 2005 State of the Campaign Report. Fourth, even in cases when women take but do not use the loan themselves, they and their families benefit more than if the loan had gone directly to their husbands. (Goldberg, 2005)

Applying a positive psychology framework, we can see that the impact of a project like the Grameen Bank has a far reach beyond the lives of individual borrowers. For Yunus personally, it was a way to work with meaning and purpose. For the women who received the loans, the opportunity provided a means to exercise agency and increase self-efficacy and personal control. For the families of the women, they had a model of inspiration and industry, taking on challenges and achieving. For the villages, the economic outlook improved and the effort of the group benefited the whole psychologically and economically, as we saw in the classroom experience. At the larger level, bankers began to consider the viability of micro-lending schemes, readjusting their attitudes toward the rural poor as a market, enabling more loans. At the society-wide level, the Grameen Bank caught the attention of corporate and global leaders and created enthusiasm and support for microcredit for a means of breaking the poverty cycle that exists in so many communities around the world. It also inspired other entrepreneurs to innovate around the micro-lending process, such as the development of technology to exchange of funds by mobile devices to overcome the physical and geographical constraints of having to transact only in cash payments. Since the very poor seldom have things like bank accounts, the ability to send money by mobile device increased the speed of resources transfer. This transfer of funds spreads the economic benefits to more people at a greater speed, allowing for further investment. The results are not only increased standard of living, but economic success was accompanied by an increased demand for social services and education.

Yunus and the Grameen Bank were awarded the Nobel Peace Prize in 2006 for pioneering a solution to poverty. The Nobel Committee (2006) wrote,

> for their efforts to create economic and social development from below. Lasting peace can not be achieved unless large population groups find ways in which to break out of poverty. Micro-credit is one such means. Development from below also serves to advance democracy and human rights.

Other examples of social entrepreneurship, where purpose and meaning created a snowball effect of empowerment and efficacy, come from widely different domains and include actor and filmmaker Robert Redford and pharmaceutical scientist Victoria Hale.

Robert Redford established the nonprofit Sundance Institute to disrupt the Hollywood choke hold of cost and access on filmmaking that kept new filmmakers from being able to break into the business. Sundance is credited with creating the independent film movement and expanding the viewing options of the public.

Victoria Hale created OneWorld Health, the first nonprofit drug company. Her mission was to overcome the disparity between drug availability, cost, and the disadvantaged populations who needed them due to the demands placed on drug companies for profitability. OneWorld Health has since been acquired by the global health organization PATH, an international nonprofit that is working to develop and ensure access to safe and effective new medicines for diseases impacting people with limited resources.

POSITIVE TECHNOLOGY

Mobile technologies have the ability to create enabling social institutions, although not the kind with bricks and mortar, by giving people access to information and improving connectivity. In developing countries where few

CASE STUDY: THE TOMS SHOES STORY AND CARING CAPITALISM

Blake Mycoskie wanted to "Start Something that Matters" (the title of his book as well) while in Argentina and seeing that many children were without shoes. In 2006 he started TOMS with the business model of donating a set of shoes for every pair of shoes sold. His business model is imbued with entrepreneurship and philanthropy and has been tremendously successful branching to eyewear (for every pair of glasses sold, TOMS donates a pair of glasses to those in need) and to coffee (for every bag of coffee sold, a person will get one week's access to clean water).

The TOMS (which stands for Tomorrow's Shoes) model has been replicated today by a number of companies offering the donation of one item with the purchase of another. What Mycoskie created was a creative approach to social problems that allows for profits while benefiting others. In fact, according to the *New York Times* (Bansal, 2012), 80 percent of Americans are likely to switch brands (holding price and quality equal) if a social cause is supported. It allows individuals who may want to engage in social supports or altruistic behavior in the service of others to do so through the consumer choices that they make.

This newer business model examines how consumer items can be created so that those who are in impoverished or underserved parts of the world may benefit as well. We know from positive psychology that people are better able to connect with individual distress than with large-scale suffering. Hence, when watching the evening news about war and destruction, we often throw our hands up feeling powerless to do something. These business models provide people an opportunity to give back in a passive way but nonetheless feels good.

In 2006, TOMS donated over 2 million pairs of shoes to children in 40 developing countries (Bansal, 2012); more recently TOMS Shoes has donated 11 million shoes to children and, with their new vision donations, helped 200,000 children with vision correction.

The TOMS model has shown to have an upward spiral impact on those who receive the shoes. For example, in Ethiopia, children were not allowed to enter the classroom without shoes. Hence, one could say that TOMS' donations help to promote education.

This new philanthropic model has created a mechanism in which creative problem solving, doing good for others, and a positive impact on social groups are surfaced while still making profits. Is this the 21st-century model of capitalism emerging? Mycoskie says yes. Now that his company

social services exist in rural areas, mobile technologies have provided health care information, delivered literacy programs, opened economic opportunities, facilitated environmental improvements, such as water quality, and have reconnected families separated by hardship, crisis, or war. Mobile technologies can disrupt practices that perpetuate disadvantage. For example, the Manobi

CASE STUDY (Continued)

has grown so quickly, he wants to find out how to use the resources to provide even more for others in need.

Indeed, TOMS has attracted major brands to their product who have incorporated TOMS Shoes as part of their campaigns (saving TOMS marketing and advertising dollars). Mycoskie and TOMS Shoes have been included in promotions for ATT, Microsoft, American Greetings, and AOL.

The appeal of TOMS is the "storydoing" of the One for One movement. People readily appreciate the objectives of this business story and want to contribute to the story themselves by buying the shoes or being associated with the brand.

Others are being carefully optimistic about this model alleviating poverty and providing basic necessities to those in need. While initial results look promising, a longer-term view is needed to declare this model a key to social inequities.

TOMS has influenced the way organizations understand corporate social responsibility. Mycoskie has consulted with many such organizations to create genuine campaigns that contribute to the well-being of others. He asks all organizations to examine the impact they have on the world and to see how they can possibly reduce waste, be less impactful on the environment, or give back.

TOMS has worked to improve the well-being of the factory workers as well. For example, the organization has dedicated itself to increasing wages, providing meals for working mothers, financing ongoing education, and providing on-site preschool education.

TOMS is not without its detractors. The International Development Community asserted that TOMS is really about making consumers feel good rather than addressing issues of poverty. Some charities have urged TOMS to consider creating jobs that would better help those in need. Mycoskie listened to his detractors and decided to tweak his business model by moving shoe production from China to have the brand's shoes made in those countries receiving current show donations.

TOMS model is now being studied in business schools as a "caring capitalism" model. Mycoskie was not a business student, nor a fashion designer. His story is one of simply having an idea to contribute to the well-being of others while still creating a profitable business.

And as we know from positive psychology, people find greater happiness when less self-conscious and in the service of others. TOMS has integrated this into their business operations.

Development Foundation distributes current market prices to rural farmers in Senegal, so the middleman or broker no longer has unfair advantage over farmers who don't know the market value of their produce. The access to this information changed the income level of some villages by nearly 400 percent. The economic success inspired village development, such as the construction of village schools, setting the stage for further empowerment through literacy and the creation of new opportunities for a new generation.

Mobile technologies' ability to improve the profitability of trade make them in such demand that it inspired some rural village women to become micro-entrepreneurs. A Grameen Bank affiliate in Bangladesh, the Village Phone Program enables women to purchase phones to rent to other villagers.

POSITIVE ENVIRONMENTS

Place is a central aspect of human existence. Houses, buildings, neighborhoods, and cities are the physical building blocks of our world. Big and small, structures are not containers; they are where we live, work, learn, and play. Psychologists in the field of positive psychology have made a huge contribution in focusing on the things that facilitate positive emotional and psychological well-being. We know that well-being is linked with a host of positive outcomes, from good health and marital satisfaction to job productivity. Place is the backdrop where life happens, where we find partners, go to work, develop emotional connections, and live our lives. Yet place is only starting to get due consideration in the positive psychology research. Researchers suggest that there are basic qualities that are important how place contributes to our well-being:

1. basic needs—education, shelter, healthcare, transportation, and safety
2. community—social connection, community organizations, local government
3. stimulation—opportunities for activities or intellectual engagement
4. freedom—the ability to pursue dreams and interests and express identity

WORK SPACES

There is much debate over the optimal organization of workspaces. Open plan offices, assumed to allow more communication and better social connection, were assumed to increase workplace satisfaction as well as team coherence and productivity. However, open plan layouts have been shown to be more disruptive and to decrease privacy with negative psychological effects. In empirical analysis, enclosed private offices outperform open plan layouts in terms of productivity. People did not find the benefits of interaction ease to offset the aggravation of more noise and less privacy. Research in open office design has shown that open office design is linked to work's dissatisfaction with their work environment and perceptions of lower productivity.

Research from Iowa State University, however, argues that earlier work on the physical work environments had conflicting findings and that not all studies take the value of social interaction into account when evaluating workplace satisfaction. They confirm that on a personal level, individuals react negatively to increased office density and openness. However, the broader effects, such as friendship opportunities, as well as interpersonal work-related experiences, such as work collaboration and innovation, can be more positive.

LIFE STRATEGY: HANDLING NEGATIVE EMOTIONS

Emotions often catch us by surprise because they are unconscious reactions triggered by things around us and we react before we think. When emotions are negative, our reactions can be destructive to our real goals, getting in the way of relationships and undermining physical and mental performance. Even emotions such as boredom can cause problems if it means one cannot finish tasks deemed tedious. Stronger emotions, such as anger, can sometimes trigger more dangerous behaviors such as road rage or substance abuse.

Developing the ability to regulate emotions improves your relationships and performance by building hardiness and resilience. Here are a few steps you can try to keep from letting your emotions run away with you.

1. Recognize and name the emotion. Try to be objective.

2. Pay attention to how the emotion is affecting your body and your behavior. Did your voice get louder? Does your stomach hurt?

3. Use your brain. Emotions are transitory; they come and go. Remind yourself that how you feel right now will change.

4. Identify the cause. Avoid self-criticism. Be compassionate. Don't assume everything is your fault.

5. It's okay to feel emotions. Negative emotions are legitimate responses to many situations. Own it, but don't let it own you.

6. Take a new perspective. Imagine how it feels from a different point of view.

7. Take a deep breath for a minute or two. Deep breathing resets your autonomic nervous system and will release the knot in your stomach.

8. Use humor, laugh or at least smile. Like deep breathing, humor resets our autonomic system, and laughter and smiling trigger the neurotransmitters in our reward center. If you can't manage a smile, hold a pencil in your mouth to force the sides of your mouth up as if you were smiling. It actually works.

Two fundamental approaches can help control and manage, even release, negative emotions: one is active thinking and the other is active being. Active thinking is a cognitive approach in which you identify the emotion, the cause, the impact it's having and in general, being in the driver's seat of your thoughts. Cognitive approaches help you manage and control emotions by applying appraisal and perspective. Active being or mindfulness approaches like meditation employ techniques such as deep breathing and quieting the brain. They work by releasing negative emotions from your body. Since the mind and body are linked, techniques that release tension and anger from the body will impact how emotions are experienced consciously, putting things into a new perspective.

The researchers argue that it is essential for organizations to be transparent in communicating their goals in office design and acknowledge the trade-off between the benefits and the discomfort of any change so that employees can envision the office redesign as an investment in worker satisfaction in order to enhance organizational commitment.

Designing Interiors

Interior spaces include more than walls and cubicles. Many choices made in office design have the potential to influence the work experience. For example, something as simple as color choices can have a profound impact. Colors induce emotional responses and can be used to encourage various kinds of behavior. While color responses are culturally subjective, there are some basic generalities applicable to Western societies that can be useful in creating positive environments. Here are some interesting examples that suggest how colors can be linked to positive goals:

Research has shown that wall color changes how we perceive temperature. Warm colors will cause us to think a room is warmer than it actually is. Even thinking of a color can change perception. In a Harvard University study, three Tibetan practitioners of an advanced meditation practice known as Tum-mo yoga were able to increase their body temperature in their fingers and toes by as much as 14.9 degrees (F) by visualizing red hot embers or flames within their bodies.

Research has linked green with creativity and open-mindedness. Green often brings associations of nature and growth.

Red tends to reduce analytical thinking, increasing emotional arousal. Anthropologists at Durham University found that athletes who wore red were 60 percent more likely to defeat an opponent who was wearing a blue uniform during the 2004 Olympic wrestling matches. In a University of Rochester study, men looking at photos of women found the women in photographs with red backgrounds or wearing red to be more attractive. This did not, however, impact perceptions of intelligence or likability.

In a 2007 research project known as the cocktail party study, designers and scientists created a series of rooms set up like a cocktail lounge, each with a different color: red, blue, or yellow. Behaviors varied with each room color. People gravitated toward the yellow and red rooms, ate more in the yellow room, were more sociable in the red room, and stayed longer in the blue room. This study suggests that if you want your friends to hang about but not eat as much, paint your room blue.

Researchers at the University of British Columbia tested 600 people to evaluate the influence of color on cognitive performance. Participants performed tasks with words or images on brightly colored or neutral backgrounds. Attention and recall was better with the red group, whereas imagination and creative thinking, like inventing new uses for objects, was better in the blue group.

A meta-analysis of 40 studies on environmental color in classrooms and student residences confirms the impact of interior color on alertness and attention during learning activity, both key factors in a student's self-efficacy and motivation to learn.

LIVING ONLINE

Our real world is part digital. In spite of how one may refer to online as being separate from the "real" world, it is all real. Offline and online are just different parts of the continuum of our social experience. Therefore, a chapter about positive psychology in the real world would be remiss without addressing this place where much of our social world connects. Social media isn't inherently bad or good. Its impact is, like all tools, the result of how you use it. Self-awareness, self-understanding, self-regulation, and mindfulness are all positive psychology tools that can give you insight into the benefits and pitfalls of all activities, social media included. As with all things, balance is key.

Social media sites are structured to show you the people you know. One can spend a lot of time checking up on friends and looking at Suzie's last trip to Acapulco. A consistent concern about social media is the perception that time spent on social media sites such as Facebook result in negative mood, diminished self-esteem, and poor body image due to social comparison. Social comparison is, as it sounds, when we compare ourselves to others. For example, on Facebook one see others on better vacations, with better bodies, raising better children, getting better jobs, and attending better parties. There is a popular impression that, thanks to social media, we all suffer from FoMO (fear of missing out), envy, regret, or inadequacy. However, this view is not only one-sided; it neglects the important benefits of social comparison.

Social comparison theory originated in the 1950s by psychologist Leon Festinger (1957), who proposed that humans have a basic drive to evaluate the opinion and ability of others relative to themselves. He saw social comparison as an information-gathering activity that people used when more objective measures were not available. This turns out to be only part of the story. People are indeed driven to compare themselves to others and they do it whether or not objective measures are available. In fact, social comparison is pervasive and automatic. One continually compares oneself to those we see, whether we perceive them as better (upward comparison), worse (downward comparison), or about the same. If we are hardwired for social comparison, it makes sense that it has some evolutionary value.

In the 1970s, Philip Brickman and Ronnie Bulman (1977) explored the inherent dilemma in social comparisons. If we want to improve ourselves, we have to risk our self-esteem by comparing ourselves to someone who has skills and attributes we want to acquire. In other words, one has to be willing to endure some amount of a sense of inferiority to improve ourselves. If one wants to feel good about the self, people often look at someone worse off. Research suggests that if there is a sense of self-efficacy—the belief of attaining goals—then upward comparisons become inspirational, not depressing. Research on comparisons involving self-improvement goals show that observations we make for the purpose of observing our desired behavior and learning how we can improve our own skills are positive. The ability to see someone achieving

ASSESSMENT TOOLS IN POSITIVE PSYCHOLOGY

Assessments allow researchers to understand an individual or population. Assessments for anxiety or depression, for example, help a clinician develop a treatment plan to alleviate these experiences. In positive psychology, researchers use assessments to understand the thoughts, feelings, and levels of optimism and pessimism to make inferences about an individual or group of people. An assessment is a test of a certain characteristic or behavior and by itself does not always provide adequate information. Someone skilled at reviewing the results within context is critical to the use of assessment tools.

When utilizing assessment measures, it is important that the measure be reliable and validated. In statistics the term "reliable" refers to the degree to which an assessment tool provides stable and consistent results. For example, in assessing for reliability, researchers may give a group an assessment one week, and then the same assessment the following week to measure the stability of the scores over that period of time. Validity refers to how well the assessment tool measures what it has been designed to measure. An assessment tool needs to demonstrate both reliability and validity before it is used in the wider community of researchers and practitioners.

What follows are examples of measures often used in positive psychology:

Connor-Davidson Resilience Scale (CD-RISC; Connor & Davidson, 2003). This tool assesses personal characteristics that reflect resiliency. It contains 25 questions on a five-point scale.

Ego Resiliency Scale (Block & Kremen, 1996). This tool measures how an individual's level of ego control returns after a stressful situation. It has 14 questions on a four-point scale.

Life Orientation Test-Revised (LOT-R; Scheier, Carver, & Bridges, 1994). This 10-item tool assesses levels of optimism and pessimism.

Purpose of Life (Ryff & Keyes, 1995). This tools assesses how much one has belief that life has a meaning and purpose. This tool has nine questions based on a six-point scale.

Brief COPE (Carver, 1997). This tool consists of 28 questions to assess 14 types of coping strategies. This tool is based on a four-point scale.

Perceived Stress Scale (PSS, Cohen, Kamarck, & Mermelstein, 1983). This tool includes 10 questions that assess one's perceived levels of stress on a four-point scale.

helps us to visualize desired results and see how a path can be changed and how we can assimilate things we admire into our own behaviors and life story. Upward comparison is, in fact, at the core of mentorship and the benefit of role models throughout our lives.

Psychologist Michael Cohn (2012) argues that looking at people who outperform us in some way is important in helping us to achieve positive psychology goals, such as increasing optimism and resilience and improving our ability to adapt, provided it is done right.

What makes some upward comparison positive and others not? Two things: (1) the belief of being capable of growth and change and (2) the need to pay attention to specific qualities that are admired and aspired to.

People's belief in a mutable—changeable—self, rather than fixed self, has been explored in depth by psychologist Carol Dweck (2006). People who believe that things like intelligence or talent are fixed are less willing to take on challenges and are less persistent in the pursuit of goals. Thus, if we believe that we are capable of change and development, and we learn to pay attention to the right things about our heroes, we significantly increase the chances of being able to learn from them—or indeed from anyone who has positive characteristics that are admirable.

For example, if Janelle wants to be a better student, she can compare herself to Amy who gets better results. It's how she compares herself to Amy that will give her the results she desires. If Janelle believes Amy is just smarter than she is, then Janelle won't be able to learn from the behaviors she observes and she may feel discouraged and use this to reinforce beliefs about her inadequacies. If Janelle only focuses on Amy's grade point average, she will have no information about how Amy achieved her results. If, however, Janelle's self-image isn't fixed and she believes in her ability to improve, she will focus on behaviors and attitudes that contribute to school performance, such as how Amy takes notes or the amount of time Amy spends studying. Then she will find the comparison positive and instructive. Dweck's work has shown that the belief about our ability to change is more important to success than innate ability because that belief motivates persistence. Resilience, persistence, and grit are the most important determination of success in multiple domains. Talent helps, of course, but resilience and persistence reign supreme. A great example of this is the 2015 Under Amour advertising campaign "I will what I want" showing the dedication and determination of tennis star Serena Williams and prima ballerina Misty Copeland.

As we navigate through social media communities, keep in mind that social comparison is a normal phenomenon and can be beneficial if you focus on the "right things." The right things are goal-based and:

1. Make a difference to achieving our goals
2. Are something we have some control over
3. Are realistic
4. Are where we can build on our strengths

A bit of advice:

If you find yourself falling into a trap of comparing yourself to others using things that do not meet the criteria for self-improvement or inspiration, remind yourself that you are in charge. If you went to a party and didn't enjoy the people, you would leave. You have the same control online: if you can't redirect your attention in a positive way, then unfriend, unfollow, or log off.

POSITIVE PSYCHOLOGY CAREERS

While many people enter the field of psychology with the idea of working as a clinical psychologist, there are lots of important, and perhaps less obvious, ways that psychology, and positive psychology in particular, can make a difference in supporting positive emotions and helping people have happier, more satisfying, and more meaningful lives. These include, as we've discussed throughout, education and leadership, where strengths- and values-based approaches, positive emotions, and emotional intelligence have had profound positive effects. But consider also the following:

Marketing and Public Relations

Advertising, like psychology, has long focused on "what's wrong" with the consumer, or deficit marketing, to promote products and services. Applying positive psychology shifts your thinking toward content designed to empower consumers. Research shows that empowerment marketing speaks more authentically and is more effective with a media-savvy audience.

Entertainment

Entertainment content and design relies on basic psychology for its effectiveness. The ubiquity of media messaging creates mental models for how the world works. Understanding positive psychology enables different choices at decision points and can lead you to make choices that are affirming, model empowerment, or resilience; break stereotypes; or engage positive emotions. Positive psychologists can also play a role consulting with media producers so that they understand the power they have in encouraging positive emotions and role models. Examples that we have worked on include *Zebra Fish* and *Sid the Science Kid*.

User Experience and Design

Designers are faced with many choices in development of digital products for e-commerce, e-learning, and e-government that drive user acceptance and usability. Designing for flow, for example, allows users to become fully engrossed while using a product. While games are commonly studied in flow research, all technology can benefit from the application of flow and self-efficacy during all phases of product development.

There are many psychological factors that contribute to flow conditions that are dictated by design choices and impact our experience and satisfaction when using any product. For example, color choices have meaning (red for stop, green for go) as well as influence our ability to read quickly and understand. Brains are hardwired for pattern making and visual processing can facilitate experience or hinder it, leaving us either pleased with ourselves or frustrated and feeling dumb. Truly effective design experiences help the user enter the state of flow, where we become so engaged with what is happening,

THE ANTIDOTE TO FOMO (FEAR OF MISSING OUT)

The proliferation of social media and the ability to watch what everyone you know is doing 24/7 cause some people to suffer from what is popularly called FoMO, or the fear of missing out. FoMO is the fear that others are having a wonderful and rewarding experience but you are not.

Part of the fear associated with FoMO is the anxiety about being excluded from our social groups. We are all very sensitive to being rejected by others. Functional magnetic resonance imaging, or fMRI, shows that the human brain registers social exclusion in the same way it does physical pain. It genuinely hurts. Throughout history, humans have used social exclusion to punish others, from excommunication, ostracization, social snubbing, and the allegedly humane parental punishment called "time-out."

People have always experienced FoMO. Social media, however, gives us 24/7 access to information to what others are doing. Seeing others doing something that appears fun can trigger our primitive emotional response of exclusion. Without the ability to examine our feelings, we feel left out and undesirable.

Practicing mindfulness, on the other hand, increases your awareness of automatic, unthinking responses and allows you to make choices about what to do and, yes, even what to feel. You can develop behavioral strategies to counteract negative emotions. For example, if you find yourself continually feeling bad about friends' activities when you're on Facebook, you can limit your time on Facebook, have a list of family or friends to catch up with by phone, or do something else you love, like play with the dog or watch old movies and eat popcorn.

Positive psychologists note that it is important to realize that you do not *know* these people are having more fun—you *believe* they are. By believing you have created the reality for yourself. The fear of missing out exists only in your beliefs and there is, in reality, nothing to miss.

that we lose track of time and the things around us. When we're shopping on Amazon, playing World of Warcraft, writing a paper on Microsoft Word, or trying to pay bills online, we want to be focused on the task, not the software. Bad design results in confusing menus, software bugs, annoying pop-ups and error commands, and lack of sufficient information to get the task done. We either dislike the site or software or feel incompetent. Neither is the foundation for a good long-term relationship.

The experience with technology has the ability to influence mood. For example, repetitive, pattern-based games like Bejeweled II have demonstrated that users entered a state of flow that improved mood and decreased stress. The ability to design for flow is also relevant to website design as it lowers cognitive resistance and increases our susceptibility to online persuasion, creating a sense of trust in recommendation systems, like Yelp, and enhancing mobile media adoption.

Designers who understand flow can avoid many of the commonly seen design mistakes, such as the games, marketing software, and educational programs that obscure the task focus and goal clarity. These elements are essential to engage emotions, enhance empathy, and create the sense of presence, or the subjective sense of "being there" within a virtual or imagined environment. The same considerations are true for the narrative design. When aimed at enhancing flow, designers' decisions enhance persuasion, facilitate learning, and increase user satisfaction.

Corporate Programs

Corporations are scrambling to understand how to develop effective employee engagement and development and how to design corporate responsibility programs. These often overlap, as employees demand more sense of meaning in their work lives. Positive psychology lies at the heart of program design by focusing on meaning, authenticity, and strengths building.

CHAPTER 9

The Road to Happiness

There are scientifically proven approaches to being happy and all require a change in behavior and a movement out of one's "default way" of being. Many of these recommendations you may have heard before from parents, grandparents, or teachers. Sometimes everything old is new again. In this chapter, ways of concretely practicing positive psychology are outlined, including:

- Exercise: Taking time to move is consistently found to reduce depression and anxiety, therefore impacting happiness. Exercise is useful for the body, improves cognitive functioning, and gives one a boost of energy. Research reflects that as little as seven minutes of exercise per day can have an impact. Shawn Anchor (*The Happiness Advantage*, 2010) emphasizes this point in a study that followed 3 groups that were treated for depression for six months with 1) medication alone; 2) medication and exercise; and 3) exercise only. The researchers found that the exercisers had a 9 percent relapse of depression whereas the other two groups had relapses of 38 percent (medication only) and 31 percent (combination of medication and exercise).

- Sleep-in: For most Western cultures, individuals are suffering from sleep deprivation. Many people are trying to extend their days by waking early and going to bed late. The use of technology with blue light emitting screens further decreases good sleep as it tricks the brain into believing that it should wake up. In fact, the fastest growing and biggest selling product in the pharmaceutical realm is sleep-aid medication. Sleep is critical to the body as it rests and restores the body. In addition, our happiness is impacted as researchers find that sleep-deprived individuals have more difficulty recalling pleasant memories. Those who don't sleep enough tend to be more reactive to daily situations and express more negative emotions over the course of the day.

- Community: Human beings are social creatures and we need to have time to spend with family and friends. Study after study reflects that individual mood is higher when with a group of people. Daniel Gilbert, Harvard Professor and author of *Stumbling upon Happiness* writes (2007):

    We are happy when we have family, we are happy when we have friends, and almost all the other things we think make us happy are actually just ways of getting more family and friends.

For many it is difficult to believe that more money does not necessarily buy more happiness. After a certain level of income, incremental increases in income do not provide the same increments in happiness. Increasing social relationships, however, can. Moreover, it is in stepping outside of oneself and being of support and service to others that people report the greatest sense of well-being in social interactions. Humans are hardwired to ultimately take care of the tribe. Today our tribe includes friends, community, schools, and interest groups. Many cultures have traditions that promote the supporting of others. The Native Hawaiians, for example, use the word "Aloha" with an emphasis on exhaling air at the third syllable as a way of exchanging breath. Aloha International describes the deeper meaning of this word:

    Aloha is being a part of all, and all being a part of me. When there is pain—it is my pain. When there is joy—it is also mine. I respect all that is as part of the Universe and part of me. I will not willfully harm anyone or anything. When food is needed I will take only my need and explain why it is being taken.

Here are empirically verified approaches to increasing happiness that can be implemented easily in daily life:

- Being outside: Nature plays an important part in many people's well-being. Those who spend 20 minutes outside during the course of one day are happier than those who do not. To add to that, temperature does impact one's happiness. In 2011, a report by the American Meteorological Society found that a good temperature for a state of happiness is 57°F or 19°C. While that may not be always attainable unless you live in the Bay Area of California, being outdoors is helpful for fresh air, vitamin D, and bodily movement.

- Volunteer: Throughout this text, scientific research reflects the importance of getting outside of "oneself" in the service of others to increase happiness. Recent research reflects that giving as little as two hours a week in giving or helping others makes one feel significantly better. It minimizes self-consciousness and focuses on the needs of others. In fact, in a study in which participants were asked to spend money that they were given on themselves or on someone else, those who spent on others reported a greater sense of happiness and well-being. In fact, one immediate route to happiness is enacting "random acts of kindness."

- Look and think happy: The simple act of smiling can shift one's sense of happiness. It is even more useful when one connects the smile with an authentic memory or feeling of happiness. Those who overuse artificial smiles feel worse and more withdrawn after a period of time. Those who learned to smile authentically (and engage the 10 to 12 muscles it takes to do so) have greater cognitive capacity to address challenges, and found pain and stress reduced.

- Distract in a healthy way: Watch a favorite movie, have coffee with a friend, or plan a vacation (even if you don't plan to follow through). The *Journal of Applied Research in Quality of Life* found that individuals reported a spike in well-being when planning a vacation regardless of whether one went or not.

- Increase the quality of life by reducing your commute: The length of one's daily commute is directly proportional to one's sense of happiness. The longer the commute, the less happy people report that they are. A Swiss study found that those who compensated for long commutes with a large house or bigger car still did not find relief in comparison to a short commute.

- Aging: Believe it or not, the myth that younger people are happier and older people unhappier is just that, a myth. As we age we learn a greater sense of wisdom; how to face challenges, how to be more diplomatic, and where best to put our energy. This happens especially after middle age. At this age, scientists speculate and individuals put a greater emphasis on family, friends, and community, all pieces that are shown to improve happiness. In addition, many in this age bracket start to place less of a priority on what others think and move toward living in a way that is more authentically representative of who one is.

- Using media in moderation: On average Americans consume 10 hours of media per day (Kaiser Family Foundation, 2010) and this is often at the cost of doing other things such as exercising, meeting with friends, or going outside. Media in moderation is fine, but too much use of it in fact reduces one's mood. This is in part due to the images of people on television or Facebook having wonderful lives free of unhappiness and stress (in other words a picture that is not entirely reality) as well as advertisers promoting products that promise to make us better. Reducing advertising messages (of needing ever more) and balancing life with other activities is critical to happiness.

- Lifelong learning: Those who remain curious about life tend to be happier. Learning improves well-being as it exposes one to new ideas, and ways of thinking and seeing the world. In addition, expanding one's skills increase self-confidence and resilience. This can be achieved by taking a continuing education course, joining a club, taking on a new hobby, or learning to cook. Such pursuits can expand one's happiness and skills at the same time. Embracing something new or a unique path may not always be met with positive reactions but it is worth trying nonetheless. As Mark Twain wrote, "A person with a new idea is a crank until the idea succeeds."

- Cultivate support systems: Support systems come in many shapes and sizes, including friends, family, therapy, groups, spiritual or religious organizations, and hobbies such as sports or outdoor clubs. One needs to have someone check in with you should you be withdrawing or a sudden change emerges in one's behavior. As social creatures, human beings need social support for well-being.

- Take care of a pet: Individuals who have a pet such as a cat or dog to look after have lower blood pressure and report a greater sense of well-being. Not everyone's circumstances allow for the care of an animal, a commitment that should not be treated lightly. In such a case, volunteering at a shelter may bring you closer to caring for animals in need. Research shows that pets improve one's life and in particular those with depression, feelings of loneliness, or those who have medical conditions such as heart disease or HIV. Overall, scientists have found that pet owners were happier and healthier than non-owners and pets insulated individuals from feeling alone or depressed.

- Have a close relationship: Healthy relationships can create a sense of safety and security. They also provide a sense of buffering and support during times of stress and upset. One must first allow, however, the ability to be loved and to love. Past relational experiences may impede this ability and this is where the examination of not having relationships or having unhealthy relationships is critical. Healthy relationships include caring, understanding, support, celebration, fun, growth, and learning.

POSITIVE PSYCHOLOGY IN THE WORKPLACE

These are practical applications of positive psychology for individual well-being. Positive psychology is also being applied to organizations to improve organizational and employee functioning. Silicon Valley is leading this effort at high-technology companies such as Google, Zappos, Facebook, and Tesla. Many of these organizations now have a Chief Happiness Officer (CHO) who is integral to the functioning of the organization. In particular, organizations are realizing that not just the individual but also the family unit needs to be considered for well-being given the demands on parents working long days (and weekends). Workplace policies are in flux as modern work–life changes and as employees are demanding that some type of healthy work and life balance be considered. Work–life balance has been touted a great deal in the popular press and in research, but most researchers are coming to the conclusion that it really does not exist. Rather, life has its ebb and flow when work and life may take priority over another at different times. This is called work–life integration.

U.S. culture typically celebrates employees who prioritize work over family. This is not universal, however. European countries continue to have more generous policies that support the family system with paid paternal leave benefits, for example, now being offered in Scandinavian countries. Child care benefits are also more widely spread outside of the United States than within. Research demonstrates that having a child care facility on-site improves the functioning of not only the parents who are able to have their children on-site but also of the whole organization who enjoy seeing children in the building on a daily basis.

As employees ask for more family-friendly policies, some organizations are starting to shift their stance. Facebook now provides a $4,000 stipend to families of a newborn. Scandinavian countries are providing men and women leave when a newborn arrives in a family; and Japan recently is encouraging men to stay at home for a period of time to raise children as part of their efforts to increase Japan's population.

Mindfulness training is an integral part of the training and culture at Google. Other Silicon Valley companies are insisting employees go home at 5.30 p.m. to be with family or take care of oneself.

Most of all, employees are asking for worktime flexibility. The opportunity to have greater ownership over one's schedule and time does indeed improve a sense of well-being. Yet, most workers report feeling pressure to work weekends and evenings to demonstrate their commitment to an organization. Some organizations will include on-site dry cleaning or gyms, but this simply tends to encourage a life lived at the organization.

GOING WITH THE FLOW

As mentioned in Chapter 3, Flow is an activity in which challenges and skills are matched such that one has a set of clear goals, self-consciousness disappears, and one loses track of time. Stress relief is a major outcome of Flow experiences. Engaging opportunities for Flow are important to consider and cultivate. There are many ways to cultivate a sense of well-being and happiness while at the same time reducing stress. Here are some examples:

- Read: People across cultures report that reading can be a pleasurable and relaxing opportunity to learn and escape daily life's challenges. For some who engage in texts that are challenging, with the learning new and difficult, Flow can be engaged such that hours pass by and it seem like minutes.

- Exercise: Movement is important for the body physically and emotionally. Some people report experiencing Flow when training for a particular sport or trying to master a new type of exercise. Regardless of whether one reaches a Flow state, exercise releases endorphins that make one feel better.

- Cultivate a garden: Gardeners report that their keen sense of involvement and concentration promote Flow experiences while also nurturing plants and creating a beautiful environment.

- Find a hobby: Hobbies provide many rewards, including promoting one's mood and clarity of thinking. In fact, researchers at Temple University found that hobbies engage the nucleus accumbens of the brain that influences one's life perspective making one happier than sadder. Other research reflects how hobbies can improve self-confidence and self-regard by shifting away feelings of anxiety or depression. In fact, for some of the happiest people, moving a hobby into a profession has been the winning formula.

Connect with Others

As social animals it is important to be connected with other individuals or groups. Research shows time and time again that having good relationships contributes most to a long and happy life. Feeling a sense of alienation or isolation is considered as risky as smoking, being obese, or having chronic high blood pressure. Other interesting empirical facts include:

- Men live longer when in a long-term relationship or marriage. Men and women typically live three years longer with a life partner.

- Friends, family, and other social networks help to mitigate the impact of stress in daily life. Having someone in one's life to confide and speak with increases one's health and happiness. In fact, in one study, college students who reported having strong relationships were half as likely to catch a cold when exposed to the virus. And individuals tend to be healthier with healthier friends. Friends influence the decisions and behaviors in which one engages. In another study, non-obese people are more likely to have non-obese friends because of the influence of healthy habits in a social network.

- Those who have a more robust social support system benefit from lower rates of depression; improved immune systems, and lower blood pressure.

INSIGHT ON HAPPINESS FROM AROUND THE WORLD

One way to land yourself within a happy setting is to live in one of the world's happiest countries. In 2015, the third publication of *The World's Happiest Countries* was released from the Sustainable Development Solutions Network for the United Nations. Students of positive psychology will not be surprised to learn that countries that were ranked the happiest had the following qualities:

- Long life expectancy
- Strong social supports
- Experience generosity more on a daily basis
- Have the freedom to make choices on a daily basis
- Perceive lower levels of government and corporate corruption
- Have a higher gross domestic product per capita
- People who volunteer their time for social good

The purpose of this report is to encourage other governments to assess their populations' happiness and work toward promoting factors of happiness within their countries. The top five countries ranked for happiness (from highest) are Switzerland, Iceland, Denmark, Norway, and Canada. Two of the major defining factors for these five countries (and all countries listed in the top ten) reflected social support and a decent level of income (such that one has some essentials for safety and security such as shelter and access to food). Thus, governments can promote happiness by pursuing policies that emphasize trust, health, honesty, and fairness according to this report. The report emphasized the well-being of children who experience happiness in childhood through the experience of having a sense of safety and security that results in healthier, happier, and more productive adults, thereby perpetuating a sense of happiness both socially and economically.

The first *World Happiness Report* was released in 2012 as part of the United Nations High Level Meeting on Happiness and Well-Being. This report was intended to show social progress using data that could be compared across countries. It also brought the discipline of positive psychology to a global stage to demonstrate how the theories can be applied to influence public policy that in turn would improve the health and well-being of individuals around the world.

The report has six major areas that are assessed:

- Mental health
- If people are happier
- Ethics and their impact on social well being
- Research on how to use data for improved well being
- Subjective well-being measures
- Use of data to lead to positive outcomes

Embedded within these areas of assessment are the variables of social support, life expectancy, and income factors. Social support is critical to communities being held together in times of crisis, whether economic or natural. There is a quicker recovery when people work together in the times of crisis (such as when Hurricane Iniki, the deadliest hurricane in Hawaii's history, hit the Island of Kauai, Hawaii, in 1992 and neighbors helped each other in comparison to the looting that took place when other natural disasters hit other parts of the world in 1992).

Life expectancy is an important marker of health and well-being, often indicating access to health care resources and good food and water. While some nations may have these factors, modern diets and stress can lower life expectancy, indicating an issue of well-being that needs to be addressed.

Finally, as discussed in earlier chapters, individuals need to be able to have a livelihood in order to live and mobilize shelter, food, and other resources. After a certain level of income is achieved, science has shown that additional amounts of income do not make people proportionately happier. However, access to jobs and a level of living is essential to a society's well-being.

In just a few years, this annual report has created discussion about metrics to assess well-being on many levels such as access to education, clean water, unpolluted air, and immunizations. These factors, researchers as well as policy makers are finding, impact world happiness at a high level. Moreover, many countries are experimenting themselves with unique ways of measuring happiness and supporting people in living better lives.

As a result, leaders from Germany, South Korea, the United Kingdom, the United States, Canada, and the United Arab Emirates are giving greater emphasis to indicators of well-being for their nations that goes beyond past uses of simply the gross national product (GNP).

What Are Countries Doing to Improve Happiness?

The information collected in the past few years of this report focused on examining variance based on age and geographic region. Researchers assessed individuals for self-reports on positive factors such as happiness, smiling laughing, enjoyment, safety, rest, and engagement. They also assessed for negative factors such as anger, worry, sadness, depression, stress, and pain.

The United Kingdom has worked with government and nongovernment agencies to collect data over the years, which are being used to analyze national indicators of happiness and well-being as well as local needs. In fact, the United Kingdom created the "What Works Centre for Wellbeing" to demonstrate the government's commitment to establishing policy that benefits the citizens of her country.

The United Arab Emirates has taken this charge to including it as part of the National Agenda, which is to be the happiest of all nations. In particular, the Dubai plan includes a vision of Dubai as a "city of happy, creative, empowered people an inclusive and cohesive society; the preferred place to live, work and visit; a smart and sustainable city; a pivotal hub in the global economy; and a pioneering and excellent government."

Cities from Jalisco, Mexico, to Boston, Massachusetts, are placing efforts into public spaces as a way to increase well-being in urban areas. Parks, greenways, gardens, and other areas in which people can enjoy nature and congregate are a public good that are being rediscovered and reemphasized.

CONTINUING TO DEFINE WELL-BEING

The evaluation of individual well-being can be traced back to Aristotle's approach called "eudemonic" in which an individual assesses his or her sense of purpose, meaning, and overall quality of life (this is on the flip side of a "hedonic" assessment in which the amount of pleasure over pain in life is assessed). Scientists are now using the average of emotional or eudemonic reports in order to assess human happiness. This is not to say that in the future another means of assessment will surface, but for now it is what is used as a best practice.

Subjective well-being is evaluated on three axes: (1) self-evaluation of one's life, (2) positive emotions, and (3) negative emotions. So much of our well-being can be contextually based and thus one's own experience of well-being may be difficult to measure against another. For example, an increase in pay for a poor person may bring greater sense of well-being (less worry about bills, food, or shelter) than it would be to someone who is already well-off.

A life satisfaction scale is then administered to individuals across the world in large numbers that is on a 0 to 10 rating scale, with the worst possible life as 0 and the best possible life as 10.

Recent research reflects that six factors make up for 75 percent of the variance in reports of life satisfaction. They are:

- Social support—having an individual or group to turn to in times of trouble
- Generosity
- Freedom from corruption
- Freedom to make life choices
- Healthy life expectancy
- A country's gross domestic product per capita (people earning some level of livable wages and the purchasing power that comes with those wages)

The report affirms and reflects positive psychology therapy and practice (see the section on Seligman) in that the experience of positive emotions is much more important to well-being across cultures than the absence of negative ones.

Gender and Happiness

Overall men and women report feeling happy across nations at about the same level with some lower levels of happiness reported for women in Latin America and Western Europe and greater for women in South East Asia, the Middle East, and North Africa.

On average, women smile and laugh more often than men do but this overall drops significantly with age. There is also a downward trend of "enjoyment" with age overall in most countries. An interesting finding is that women tend to report greater enjoyment overall before the age of 40, and men report more enjoyment at above the age of 50.

When it comes to getting rest, there are great variations across geographic region, age, and gender. Men around the age of 30 tend to be the least well rested, whereas for women they are least well rested at age 50. In addition, men report greater engagement and involvement in learning than women.

For both men and women, negative experiences are shared with the exception of women feeling slightly more anger before the age of 30 than men. Anger tends to be higher in the Middle East and North Africa with the highest incidence of anger being reported in South Asia. In other world regions, anger is reported less with the exception of a slightly significant increase among older people.

Worry tends to be reported more across world regions than sadness. Women report sadness at an average rate that is 7 percent higher overall than men. This is something that research in psychology has historically found. Many researchers hypothesize that socialization in which women are allowed to show and discuss emotional challenges may account for this difference.

Attempted suicide globally is higher for women than men, but men are more successful globally in completing suicide.

Self-reports of depression and pain tend to go hand in hand. Reports of depression tend to be low before the age of 20 (relatively the same for both men and women) but then rise twice as fast for women as for men. Pain follows the same pattern, with women reporting greater pain with age. Chronic pain in particular causes depression and anxiety across geographic domains.

Men report higher stress than women in Western Europe and Latin America. This is particularly true of men between the ages of 20 and 50. The highest reports of stress are in Middle Eastern countries.

Social support and freedom to make life choices are reported present for 75 percent of the respondents. However, social support also seems to be on the decline internationally with fewer community-oriented venues or less cultural emphasis leading the way. Robert Putnam, in his well-known book *Bowling Alone* (2001), writes about the decline of bowling leagues in the United States. These flourished in the 1950s and created what Putnam refers to as social capital in which community networks and connections are made. With

CASE STUDY: THE ROLE OF THE CHIEF HAPPINESS OFFICER

What originated as a new position within the technology industry in Silicon Valley is now becoming more mainstream across organizations across the country and the world: the role of the Chief Happiness Officer. This position, right along with the Chief Financial Officer and Chief Executive Officer, is called upon to make sure employees are content and productive.

Chade-Meng Tan, the 107th employee at Google when it was a start-up, is largely credited with creating this role. He worked for eight years in the engineering group at Google before moving to the company's "People Development Team." He sees his work as to "enlighten minds, open hearts, and create world peace." Using Google's famous 20 percent plan in which employees can pursue projects of their own interest with 20 percent of their working time, Tan created a course on emotional intelligence and mindfulness to promote a sense of well-being. This led to a course titled "Search Inside Yourself," which has become enormously popular both within and without Google.

A Chief Happiness Officer (or, as Tan is called, the "Jolly Good Fellow") works toward adjusting workplace policy and culture to create the conditions for engagement and well-being. The officer may assess levels of contentment at work; lead workshops to improve communication, provide workshops on approaches to stress; promote meditation for greater peace and creativity; and improve working conditions for greater health and happiness.

Zappos (see "Case Study: Delivering Happiness at Zappos" in Chapter 1) uses a Happy Business Index to assess key points of unhappiness as well as key points of employee motivation and engagement in the workplace. The index also measures the level of employee progress, connection to company's values and goals, and the opportunity for employees to forward creative ideas.

Some argue, however, that while the idea of creating positive work environments is useful, assigning a role to promote positivity reflects an intrusion into the daily lives of employees. Critics argue that this hints too much of a "Big Brother" oversight adding to the already extensive review of tracking employee e-mail and online activity. For example, *The New York Times* published an article that revealed that many companies are implementing mandatory 15-minute coffee breaks after research demonstrated that increased social interaction increases productivity. Hence, the question of whether such positions are really for employee welfare or simply to maximize further profits arises.

Whichever side you may take, happiness is now a business strategy. Chief Happiness Officers are incorporating general and positive psychology to create happy employees as happy employees are better employees. Here are some of the themes that Chief Happiness Officers handle:

- Make the workplace a respectful environment. According to recent studies around the world, only 44 percent of employees feel valued or respected by their employer. Poor treatment of employees leads to turnover and

CASE STUDY (Continued)

hence business leaders are starting to put the same value on employees they have had on customers through not only words but also actions.

- Create an opportunity for employees to be successful. Rather than creating a punitive environment in which only mistakes are given attention, providing employees with a good salary, manageable workloads, and ongoing training is essential to creating a platform for employees to shine.

- Listen, listen, and listen. Too often organizational leaders do a lot of talking without hearing or listening to what is taking place in reality. Employees need to be heard and often have creative and valuable insight and ideas into improving and embracing opportunities for an organization. Creating a means of allowing employees to have a voice is a major priority for Chief Happiness Officers.

- Define, revise, and share organizational values. Values are the foundation by which individuals, groups, communities, and organizations live. Oftentimes, employees are not clear as to what the company's values are. Values provide a "North Star" when difficult decisions arise or conflicts need to be resolved.

- Embrace flexibility such as tele-community allowing for greater employee freedom. People are keen on having a sense of agency and to manage their time in the most productive ways possible. The senior vice president of people operations at Google argues that "if you give people freedom, they will amaze you."

- Engage employees by skills matching challenges (see section on Flow). To promote Flow in an organization, it is important to challenge and develop employee skills. Providing opportunities for employees to develop their skills and strengths benefits both the employee and the organization.

- Promote fun or leisure activities. These breaks freshen the brain and lighten people's moods. Allowing for creative release is important to individual health and well-being.

- And finally, Chief Happiness Officers know the importance of engaging various perspectives to solve challenges. They thus provide support and guidance on effective teamwork. Employees need to learn how to think and collaborate together to be more productive in various domains.

At Google, mindfulness meditation is taught across the company, and most meetings start with a few minutes of compassionate contemplation to promote a more constructive and creative time. Many employees at Google report having integrated this mindful approach into their daily lives, which has created very healthy and positive shifts for them. Ultimately, Chief Happiness Officers see their work as adding value to the bottom line of the organization and adding a sense of well-being to the employee.

the decline of this symbolic social structure, where church, volunteering, or Parent–Teacher Associations (PTA) are disappearing, there is a marked social change toward being more disconnected in society. This sense of alienation or isolation has undermined the possibility of a society that is happier, healthier, better educated, and safer.

Corruption and a Decrease in Well-Being

Around the world, 80 percent of the respondents see corruption in government and business as a leading cause of decreasing health and happiness in their respective countries. Women typically identify or perceive corruption's existence more than men do. Corruption diverts resources for the purposes of public goods (health, safety, infrastructure, education) to the hands of a few. For example, recently industrial countries such as Germany, the United States, and China have looked to Africa to buy vast amounts of natural resources to keep the machinery of industry moving forward. However, when country dictators lease their land for billions of dollars over many years and pocket the money or send it to Swiss bank accounts, the people of those countries receive no benefit and at the same time lose valuable natural resources that in many cases will be sold back in type of consumer or commercial product (this may include many types of technology that rely on dwindling resources of metals that are required for mobile phones or computer tablets). Various nongovernment agencies are working to step in to protect the rights of citizens in such situations, but government corruption is a difficult ship to turn around once it has set in.

The Positive Psychology of Social Capital

As mentioned earlier, Robert Putnam, a professor at the Harvard Kennedy School of Government, wrote a groundbreaking book on social capital titled *Bowling Alone*. He examined trends in community participation, including political, civic, religious, and community groups. He uses the example of the decline of participation in bowling leagues in the United States as people no longer coming together due to personal and professional expectations and demands of modern life. Yet more people voted for the American Idol finalist in 2012 than in the U.S. presidential elections (voters for the talent competition program can use technology such as texting to vote more easily, however, than going to a polling station).

Putnam examines membership and participation in organizations such as the NAACP, knitting circles, potluck parties, and PTAs and various volunteer groups, and has found that direct participation and other club meetings has declined since the 1960s. Unions, once a stronghold for workers and networking, have been disassembled by pressures from within and without, and recent policies are further disbanding these groups. This does not mean these organizations and contributions to them have disappeared. Rather many engage in checkbook volunteerism (writing a check for a cause) or mobilize resources and actions online. The major difference, according to Putnam, is

that social interaction and therefore social capital is less available. Many people in suburban parts of the world now drive into their attached garage and
collect their mail inside their home without crossing the path of neighbors.
In fact, in a 2013 study, one in two Americans did not know their neighbors'
names. This number was higher for those renting than owning; nonetheless
this supports Putnam's argument: if you don't know your neighbors, how
likely will you be to ask them to watch over your home while on vacation,
borrow a cup of sugar, or get help fixing the lawn mower? As societies see
a decrease in social capital, there is an uptick of the number of lawyers per
capita. Suing for issues of difference rather than discussion or negotiation
then often becomes the norm.

There has been an increase in the number of and participation in self-help
groups, including Alcoholics Anonymous and various weight reduction programs. In part, issues of mental illness are more openly discussed and in part
people are feeling a greater level of stress, anxiety, and alienation and need a
place to share thoughts, feelings, and ideas.

Many people look at social media as a proliferation of connection. While
the research is still inconclusive about the impact media have on individual
and group relationships and in particular, whether mediated connections
work the same way as immediate connections do, there is no question that
media have changed the way we work, think, and play. Hundreds of thousands of specialized groups exist that bring together people of particular
interest. Bars in many communities where people once met for social or dating purposes have closed as the popularity of online dating and "hook-up"
sites explode. More choice, however, doesn't always mean people are happier. In a study by Barry Schwartz, participants who had the choice of
8 types of jams rather than the 42 the average consumer is faced with were
much happier with their choice than those with a large number of variations.
The latter felt after the purchase that they may have chosen the wrong item.
The choice of products in a grocery store has skyrocketed and discerning a
product from the many choices available takes a great deal of mental effort
(Schwarz & Stone, 1998).

In parts of rural Canada where individuals are separated by expanses of
land, the reports of alienation and isolation as well as depression and anxiety
were very high. After the phone company in conjunction with a research partner installed Internet services for those in these remote regions, there was a
marked improvement in morbidity tallies. Those who were able to chat online
or connect with online groups felt a greater sense of connection and belonging
to the outside world.

Public Policy and Happiness

Public policy and those who shape it have a tremendous opportunity to
influence the quality of life and happiness around the world. As research and
practice within positive psychology has created ways of measuring levels
of happiness (as well as understanding how those levels vary between individuals and countries), public policy makers can assess the impact of their

LIFE STRATEGY: ALLEVIATING STRESS

Stress seems to be more and more part of life in the 21st century. In fact, 54 percent of U.S. citizens report that stress is becoming unmanageable in daily life. There is good stress and bad stress. Good stress helps us move toward our goals and complete projects. In nature, stress helps our bodies move quickly to react to danger in the environment. The cumulative impact of long-term stress, however, is physically and emotionally harmful to the human body.

The major categories of stress include:

- Stress that is related to the pressures of work, family, and daily challenges
- Stress that is due to an immediate negative change such as divorce or illness
- Traumatic stress such as being assaulted, involved in an accident, natural disaster, or involved in war

Chronic stress may manifest itself through depression, anxiety, or somatic illnesses such as headaches, sleeplessness, or digestive problems. Chronic stress impacts the immune system, therefore making an individual more prone to viral infections and other illnesses.

There are a number of coping strategies that one can incorporate into daily life to mitigate the impact of stress:

- Take a walk or be physically active in some capacity. Exercise reduces the pressures of stress and provides a greater clarity of thinking.

- Do some creative problem solving. By taking control of a situation and finding a solution, one gains a sense of control. Lack of control often leads to a sense of hopelessness or helplessness.

- Reach out and connect with people. Withdrawing from others, while a typical response under stress, is exactly the opposite of what one should do. Find friends, family, or support groups in which one has an opportunity to connect with others. Being with others and enjoying time together can immediately diffuse stress.

- Cultivate time for yourself or for hobbies. People are working longer and longer hours without even time for breaks or vacations. Taking a break is critical to refreshing the mind and body. Make time to meditate, reflect, or work on a hobby two or three times a week.

- Engage in healthy habits. Under stress it is easy to turn to alcohol, excessive coffee drinking, or smoking to address one's stress; however, these coping strategies have a negative impact on one's health and contribute to greater stress. Binge eating and television viewing may create an escape but do not improve one's physical or emotional well-being. Instead, engage in some of the other activities listed here.

- Accept that there are things in life that you cannot change. Trying to control outcomes often leads to greater frustration and more stress. Instead, try to focus on that which one can change.

interventions geared at creating happier societies. The cost-benefit analysis is applied to all types of economic matters and can be redrafted to measure amounts of happiness against the costs of achieving it. This is referred to as evidence-based policy making. This is not always an easy task especially when it comes to preventive approaches. For example, providing prenatal care to all women may increase the health and happiness of both mothers and the future child; instead, what is practiced is crisis or emergency-based medicine rather than preventive medicine. Hence resources are put into the children who are born prematurely or may suffer health consequences that may have been prevented with earlier care. It is often difficult to assess preventive measures. Immunizations have been a widely accepted public good; however, as some parents elected not to have their children immunized as a preventive measure to some diseases, there has been an uptick in the number of children contracting diseases that had been eliminated for many years through immunization. In other situations, public policy has difficulty dictating how people should live their lives.

Over 30 percent of U.S. citizens are morbidly obese (Witters, 2015). This means that an individual is 30 percent over his or her ideal body weight. The health and economic implications are tremendous for a society as obese individuals often have greater rates of morbidity (disease) that require more investment in health care dollars than those of a health weight. Are people happier choosing whatever they want to eat or having bad options limited for their "own health"?

Former New York mayor Bloomberg imposed a ban on oversized high-sugar soda drinks as sodas are a major vehicle for high calorie consumption. Public health officials rejoiced, but the American soft drink industry prevailed in New York courts. It took decades for the tide to turn on smoking with tobacco companies denying the health dangers and medicine demonstrating empirical evidence that smoking reflected increased rates in cancer through the 7,000 chemical compounds created when lighting the cigarette (70 of these compounds are known carcinogens). Certainly the health of non-smokers benefited by not being exposed to secondhand smoke and many gave up smoking as the price of cigarettes increased and the tide of social acceptance of smoking became negative.

Rethinking happiness as a goal of government public policy allows for the following:

- Government policy should include not only economic emphasis but also the happiness of people (with the intention of reducing factors of misery such as poverty, poor air quality, no access to health care or education).
- Include happiness as a measurable variable to be assessed through policy analysis.
- Have an agency, such as the one the United Kingdom has developed, that evaluates the impact of policy in an empirical manner to determine increases in happiness outcomes.
- Generate social factors of happiness for each country (such as access to education, job opportunity, clean water, or length of life).

MARTIN SELIGMAN AND LEARNED OPTIMISM

Martin Seligman, often considered the modern father of positive psychology, has done extensive research on the pursuit of happiness, and explanatory styles as either pessimistic or optimistic. He supported the movement of psychology away from the medical pathology model (the "what is wrong with you" approach) to examining that which is healthy in individuals.

Seligman likes to tell the story of when he was gardening with his five-year-old daughter. He was taking a directed, goal-oriented approach to the task while his daughter was dancing around him. He found himself yelling at her for not helping him with the gardening, to which she reminded him that she was able to quit whining as promised since her fifth birthday and if she could stop whining, he could stop being so grumpy. Seligman reflects that this was an important turning point for him both personally and professionally. He realized that his job with his daughter was not to focus on what she was doing wrong but to celebrate that which she was doing well and help her make those qualities virtues throughout her life.

Seligman introduced the concept of "learned optimism" to positive psychology. His studies demonstrated that those who had an optimistic explanatory style (a way of explaining daily events in your life through the stories you tell about yourself) tend to be more resilient and bounce back from life's challenges, including many health-related illnesses. A pessimistic learning style reflects someone more likely to give up in the face of adversity, which is often accompanied by depression. The good news is that we can move our explanatory styles toward optimism, which benefits one both physically and emotionally.

Seligman recently coined the acronym PERMA to designate the qualities of what his research reflects as a good life. These five elements are as follows:

- Positive emotion—examining daily what went well and that for which one is grateful
- Engagement—performing tasks for intrinsic purposes
- Relationships—interpersonal connections that may include family and friends
- Meaning—belonging to and serving something bigger than one's self
- Achievement—determination is known to count for more than IQ

You can find your own level of optimism through this 48-question assessment developed by Stanford University (adopted from Martin Seligman's text *Learned Optimism*) at www.stanfrod.edu/class/msande271/online tools/LearnedOpt.html. Remember, no matter what the final score, one can always learn to move to a more useful optimistic style.

The Frontier of Neuroscience

As outlined in Chapter 6, the neuroscience of happiness is rapidly providing insights into human happiness and well-being. Advances in technology allow scientists to peer into the brain via neuroimaging devices to see how the brain reacts to different stimuli and emotions. Thus, happiness or well-being can now be seen lighting up the brain with these modern-day instruments.

In this realm of positive psychology, neuroscientists define happiness as a "momentary or short-lived" experience versus well-being, which is considered longer lasting and more related to long-term satisfaction with life. The field is open to new researchers and practitioners interested in identifying how the brain processes positive and negative emotion.

Individuals whose brains are monitored via fMRI (which measures brain activity by measuring changes in blood flow to regions of the brain) reveal that positive images to which they were exposed lit up specific regions of the brain. Humans across cultures when exposed to something that reflects a positive state (young animals, people embracing, seeing a newborn) have greater prefrontal cortex activation. All of this work is in its infancy, and greater insight into the brain and its functioning takes place as technology advances ever more rapidly. For neuroscientists the brain is the final frontier of understanding how the human body works. And yes, scientists can confirm that by making you smile, your brain lights up in a way that reflects a sense of well-being.

Neuroscience is being utilized to develop new technologies that impact mood and increase well-being and energy. A start-up called Thync (www.thync.com) in Boston and San Francisco created a wearable device (an adhesive attached to the forehead) that changes the way users feel by either calming or energizing the user. The device uses electrical currents to stimulate parts of the brain associated with arousal. These impulses create waves that recreate the sensation of a massage for relaxation or having a cup of coffee for energy. This device is pioneering neuroscience consumer products, which will be proliferating in coming years.

Most recently scientists have confirmed the importance of social connections for human beings who are social creatures. Being isolated impacts regions of the brain associated with pain. Any type of behavior that increases connections is essential to human well-being and happiness. This includes giving someone a gift, connecting with friends and family, being empathetic or sympathetic to someone, engaging in gratitude, and being altruistic.

Human beings reflect emotional well-being of others like a mirror. As various studies show, watching someone being inflicted with pain impacts the brain the same way as if the viewer himself/herself is being inflicted with that pain. It is even more intense if the person in pain is a loved one. Those who recovered from the negative event more quickly tend to indicate a person who may be able to bounce back from adverse conditions in life. Those individuals who continued to experience the negative emotional stimulus may be less resilient and may test higher for neurotic behavioral traits. In fact, Richard Davidson and his colleagues at UW-Madison's Center

THE VALUES IN ACTION (VIA) SURVEY

How do you measure character? This is exactly the question that positive psychologists set out to answer by developing the VIA (Values in Action) survey. It is a psychological assessment tool that measures an individual's profile of character strengths. It was developed to operationalize the research led by two of the leading figures in positive psychology, Dr. Martin Seligman and Dr. Christopher Peterson, which was published in 1994 in the *Characters Strengths and Virtues Handbook*.

The handbook was the first time people's positive psychological traits had been identified and classified in order to provide a positive psychology counterpart to the medical model used in traditional psychology. Instead of focusing on human deficits, positive psychologists wanted to provide a comparable, empirically based framework for human strengths to encourage research, evaluation, and applications based on positive psychology principles.

The VIA Inventory of Strengths is a self-report survey that measures 24 character strengths. Drawing on the writings of moral philosophers and religious thinkers throughout history, the VIA divides character strengths into six core virtues. Each virtue is made up of measurable psychological strengths as listed next (see Table 9.1). For example, the virtue of courage can be achieved through strengths such as bravery, persistence, integrity, and vitality, or the display of energy in the face of things that may be difficult. These strengths are related—they all involve aspects of courage—yet they are also separate attributes. An individual can be considered to have a courageous character through the display of any one or more of these strengths.

Table 9.1.   Measuring Character

Virtues	Strengths
Knowledge/wisdom	Creativity
	Curiosity
	Love of learning
	Perspective
	Open-mindedness
Courage	Bravery
	Persistence
	Integrity
	Vitality

Table 9.1. (Continued)

Virtues	Strengths
Humanity/love	Capacity to love and receive love
	Kindness
	Social intelligence
Justice	Citizenship
	Fairness
	Leadership
Temperance	Forgiveness/mercy
	Modesty/humility
	Prudence
	Self-regulation
Transcendence	Appreciation of excellence and beauty
	Gratitude
	Hope
	Humor
	Spirituality

The VIA survey has been used in hundreds of research studies and taken by over 2.6 million people in over 190 countries. It has been applied in education to help students approach learning from positions of strength, in therapy to support personal growth, and in organizations to build more effective work teams. One of the benefits of using the VIA survey is that, unlike many assessment tools, people enjoy finding out what their strengths are.

The VIA Institute offers the VIA Adult and Youth Surveys for free at www .viasurvey.org. The results show a list of the 24 strengths from your strongest to weakest.

for Investigating Healthy Minds found that those individuals who identified with a strong purpose in life exhibited the best recovery from negative experiences.

Neuroscientists are also confirming the value of mindfulness training and the nurturance of compassion for individual well-being. Those who engage in mindfulness courses often gain greater insight into their own emotions and increased their emotional intelligence in being with others.

The discipline of positive psychology provides tangible and concrete steps to make individuals, groups, and societies healthier. Individual researchers and practitioners are needed to implement what is known about how social capital, for example, can be promoted through trust, reduction in business and government corruption, and public good services. Improved social capital promotes more pro-social behavior (decisions made for the public good rather than for individual benefit), leading to a healthier and happier society.

Distrust and dishonesty are the drivers toward making a society sick. The emphasis on social goods such as honesty, trust, cooperation, and support counters this sickness. It takes people from all backgrounds and all professions to move the needle to the healthier side of the scale. In particular, psychologists, social workers, public policy makers, public health practitioners, health care workers, and teachers (as examples) have an amount of immediate professional influence that can nudge the world in this direction.

Leaders and followers of positive psychology need to be the voice that asks about a citizenry's well-being when creating public policy; who understand the role that compassion, empathy, and sympathy play for a patient in the world of healthcare; to emphasize pro-social modeling in the classroom; and to enlighten individuals, groups, communities, and governments about the factors that promote a healthy society beyond the GNP. The time is ripe for people to engage in this world of positive psychology.

THE CHALLENGE

Much of Western culture is based on a crisis model of care rather than a preventive one. In other words, we often wait until people get sick in order to treat the illness rather than putting a greater emphasis on the prevention of illness before it strikes. For example, our health care system often puts more resources into treating premature babies than in providing prenatal care for mothers. On the other hand, vaccinations are provided for the public good of all in order to reduce and eliminate many infectious diseases, which until recently (when many parents elected not to have their children vaccinated) were a success.

This approach stems from a traditional medical pathology model of medicine. Therefore, if there is an injury or illness, it is treated. The promotion of health and prevention of disease has largely been left in the hands of public health practitioners.

Fortunately, there is incremental change taking place in the 21st century. As water reserves are depleted in places such as California, a more proactive and preventive approach to drought is taking place. New rules and regulations are being put into place to keep our air clean and waste reduced so that we do not get to a point in society where irreversible damage is done to the air or there is no longer space for waste.

We can understand positive psychology as a buffer to increased rates of mental illness in the 21st century, including depression, anxiety, and experiences of alienation and isolation. At the individual level, learning the theory of positive psychology and applying its practice into daily life may reduce the experience of mental illness. These skills also provide an opportunity to bounce back from life's challenges, which we are always guaranteed in life, in more effective or constructive ways.

On a social level, positive psychology is available to policy makers to move from a 20th-century approach to measuring well-being through outdated economic markers such as the GDP. Consider that the GDP in fact reflects reduced economic health when gas prices go down and does not include the economic output of software designers who provide applications free of charge. The 20th-century model of measuring manufacturing output as an indicator of how well the country is doing neglects aspects of cooperation, clean air and water, access to health care and education, and many human rights that contribute greatly to the healthy functioning of states and nations.

These changes will take place slowly, but they will take place with more people understanding what creates resiliency and the experience of happiness. To create change, one needs to include new and fresh perspectives at the table. With additional voices at the table who have a knowledge of positive psychology, the opportunity to contribute to a happier world is in future hands. Bringing this knowledge forward to the many jobs, communities, friends, families, policies, students, teachers, and fellow human beings is the key.

CHAPTER 10

Finding Your Place within the World of Positive Psychology

While the discipline of positive psychology is fairly new, the opportunities to apply the theory and practice are plentiful. Most individuals specialize in positive psychology at the master's degree level with a degree in positive psychology or an allied field.

Those who pursue a focus in positive psychology go in many directions with their degree. At the University of Pennsylvania's Positive Psychology Center, there have been 160 graduates between 2006 and 2011. These graduates have utilized the degree across the spectrum of job opportunities, including:

- Private psychotherapy practice
- Academia
- Entrepreneurship
- Sales
- Marketing
- Customer service
- Training
- Business
- Career counseling
- Writers
- Coaches
- Motivational speakers
- Nonprofit management
- Teaching
- Health clinics

- Religion
- U.S. Army (recruitment)

Overall, those who pursue further studies in positive psychology are examining how to create change and how to lead a good life. Change is difficult for individuals and groups because of the loss that comes with it. We tend to prefer a default way of being as it gives us a sense of the known even if that known is not always useful to one.

For example, according to the U.S. Centers for Disease Control (CDC) in 2014 over 36 percent of Americans were considered clinically obese (weighing more than 30 percent of one's ideal body weight). This leads to issues of heart disease, stroke, type 2 diabetes, and certain types of cancer. Moreover, the medical-related costs could soon reach $1 trillion ($1,000 billion). Overall, Americans know what it requires to lose weight: eat healthier and smaller portions and move more. Yet the rates of obesity are increasing (from 10% in the 1990s to over 35% currently). What is at issue? Change. In 2012, Americans spent $20 billion on weight loss products, including programs, pills, books, and exercise equipment. Technically people know what to do to lose weight. However, many turn to quick fixes that usually don't work. A celebrity-endorsed diet book doesn't work for everyone. If it did, the United States would be a very healthy country given how many books are sold on the subject of dieting each year. What instead needs to take place is a change in the individual's culture, attitudes, beliefs, and values. Thus, a person needs to buy different groceries, change his or her daily movement patterns, buy clothing in which to exercise, find a local pool in which to swim, and so forth. This is difficult because it is compelling to go back to regular routines of high-fat foods and couch viewing. Here is where positive psychologists of all types can help to intervene. In supporting human strengths such as courage, hope, and optimism, one can impact people's values, attitudes, beliefs, and culture, hence creating beneficial and long-lasting change. Positive psychology promotes such resiliency and adaptation.

Adaptation is critical in today's world. If you consider Charles Darwin's Theory of Evolution, an organism must adapt to its environment in order to survive. Say, for example, a creature is living happily in its environment when all of a sudden a meteor increases the temperature of her environment dramatically. The creature can continue along as if nothing happened and most likely die; or it can adapt by going into the ocean, finding another niche in the environment, or perhaps ridding itself of additional fat or fur. In a world in which we are facing faster and faster change coupled with environmental, political, social, and economic suffering, creative thinkers are needed to find new approaches to these challenges that mobilize the strengths of individuals and available resources to make useful change.

Many have heard of the following proverb (attributed to many people).

"Give a man a fish and you feed him for a day; teach a man to fish and you feed him for a lifetime."

What strengths as a positive psychologist can one draw forward to help individuals fish for themselves? Often people do not see their strengths, only their weaknesses. This is a limited view. By relying on others for a sense of resiliency, courage, hope, or optimism, the individual is robbed of developing the ability to internalize the experience. Thus, relying on others to fish for one is not as useful in the long term as learning with insight and support how to fish for oneself.

PUBLIC HEALTH

In the field of public health, it is widely known that the best way to make people or a population *sick* is to marginalize that group. In other words, if one looks historically at marginalized groups such as African Americans or the LGBT population, one finds higher rates of morbidity and mortality than with the group doing the marginalizing. This is in part due to the greater difficulty in securing health, safety, education, and equality that make one thrive. It is also due to the psychological toll that hopelessness and helplessness express. Recent community riots in the United States protesting police violence surface embedded hopelessness and helplessness. Some people express this with anger, self-destructive behavior, depression, and anxiety. In fact, Seligman and his colleagues (1991) have shown in studies that without a sense of control (even if it is only a perceived sense) one feels a sense of chaos and inability to work toward a goal. In studies conducted on hopelessness and helplessness, three groups of people were placed in three different rooms with a large button. One room was for control purposes (nothing happened); the other room had irritating static piped in but the individuals could control it with the button in the room, and the third group was also exposed to the static but no matter how they manipulated the button, nothing changed. Upon exiting the room and taking tests, the third group performed significantly worse than the other two groups.

A wonderful opportunity for those pursing an interest in positive psychology is to not only understand individual strengths but also to examine what makes groups stronger and healthier. In the previous example, the group that had a sense of control benefited from having had a sense of control in adjusting the noise to which that group was exposed. How can a culture of groups, organizations, and states promote health and well-being through the theories and practices of positive psychology? Bhutan created a Happiness Index that includes factors such as clean water, air, access to education, and vacation time to recharge; high-technology companies create Chief Happiness Officers; individuals take on hobbies.

There is continuing need for further examination of the 21st-century life from home, work, and community perspectives. In industrialized countries, people are reporting higher levels of stress, anxiety, depression, isolation, and alienation. In daily exchanges with people from all walks of life, one often hears and reads how stressed, burned out, and overcommitted they are. While the idea of working toward an ideal work–life balance is seductive, it does not seem realistic as life ebbs and flows and is never actually in balance. Stewart Friedman from the Wharton School of Business argues that rather than pursuing work–life balance, individuals will be happier if they focus on a work–life integration. He argues that by being authentic, creative, and whole is the path for oneself, leaders, and society to improve the coping ability within today's world. This theory needs to be empirically assessed but is worth considering for the future positive psychologist.

Positive psychologists and other practitioners can support movement toward integration with the following model for consideration.

Be authentic:

- Prioritize what is important to one.
- Make actions and values consistent with one another.
- Share your values through the stories you tell.

Be creative:

- Avoid default ways of being or thinking.
- Examine challenges with varying perspectives.
- Understand change comes with disequilibrium.
- Reduce conflicts, promotes creative problem solving.

Be whole:

- Support others.
- Create healthy networks.
- Manage boundaries well.
- Find retreat to recharge.
- Practice self-care.
- Do as you say.
- Cultivate friendships.

MEDIA PSYCHOLOGY

Media psychology examines the impact media have on individuals and groups. It is a rapidly growing field given the amount of media people around the globe consume. In the United States and Canada, the average person consumes eight hours of media per day. This includes radio, TV, Internet, video games, film, texting, and exposure to advertisements, including billboards on the road or within public transportation. It is everywhere. The research to date is not conclusive about either the long-term impact media have on people or whether mediated environments such as online gaming or virtual groups create the same sort of well-being for people who connect in person with others.

Media's impact is powerful. They persuade, influence, and shape thinking around the world.

PUBLIC POLICY

Public diplomacy is engaging principles of positive psychology within what Joseph Nye at the Harvard Kennedy School has coined as "soft power." Soft power is different from so-called hard power as it may inspire, attract, or ask for change. Hard power instead uses sticks and carrots (coercion and incentives) to achieve desired outcomes. This is often in the form of military or economic might.

Writes Nye:

> The basic concept of power is the ability to influence others to get what you want. There are three major ways to do that: threaten them with sticks, the second is to pay them with carrots; the third is to attract them or co-opt them, so that they want what you want. If you can get others to want what you want, it costs you much less in carrots and sticks.

Public diplomacy may use soft power to pull through wanted political, economic, social, or environmental change. In particular, soft power appeals to cultural values. For example, soft power may appeal to the youth of a country who buy into the technology, entertainment, or media of the United States. These young people may then find sympathy and support appeals for change the United States wants to create.

The buildup of military reserves is a form of soft power indicating military might. This is soft power that may dissuade others from attacking a country. When the military might is engaged, however, this becomes hard power.

While soft power may be considered a more humane approach to power, it is not an ethical construct. It is a policy one. It can be used for both constructive and destructive purposes. At times, hard power may be required for change as was seen in the U.S. Civil War after Lincoln directly and indirectly appealed for the abolition of slavery. When this attempt at change was foiled over and over, he moved to hard power. His assassination can best be understood as a leader who imposed change for many who preferred to maintain slavery. Often by removing the leader who makes change, the hope is that the change will stop. This was seen with many famous leaders such as Gandhi and Martin Luther King.

Soft power has been effective in promoting democracy and human rights. It has helped to win huge health strides in public health. Hard power was helpful in outlawing smoking but it was soft power that created a message that smoking was not sexy, healthy, or attractive (to counteract the messages created at the turn of the 20th century claiming just the opposite).

Hollywood and the entertainment industry have long held a powerful cultural influence across the world. This soft power has been utilized to promote democracy and mobilize resources during times of war or other difficulties. This certainly was the case when "loose lips sink ships" became an oft repeated phrase in the United States during World War II. Television, film, and radio broadcasting have long served as vehicles for the use of soft power to demonstrate alternative ways of living, thinking, and political allegiance. This persuasion ultimately can create allegiances with countries of similar values or move reform from within countries with disparate ideals.

Take, for example, the ability to be able to legally drive for women. In countries where women are forbidden to drive, there may be a popular demand to reconsider this policy given the images via the Internet, film, or TV showing women driving as part of daily life. Such images and stories have the ability to transform ideals, policies, ways of living, and alliances. They can inspire the cornerstones of positive psychology, namely, courage, hope, and optimism that mobilize people to come together, whether for a cause or for change. Stories that remind us of our strengths and our abilities to contribute to the world are a form of soft power that help leaders get what they want. For followers it is important to always assess whether hard or soft power is being used for good or bad purposes.

ORGANIZATIONAL PSYCHOLOGY

Organizational psychology's researchers and practitioners examine how to make work sites healthy and hence productive. Organizational psychologists assess the level of functioning at the individual, group, and divisional levels and look beneath the surface to understand dynamics that work and do not work. Their task under this model is to promote human potential, or fit, and thus create greater organizational success. Researchers have found the following factors from a positive psychology orientation to organizational psychology:

- Develop leaders: There is a difference between leaders and managers. Managers optimize the functioning of a division or organization; leaders mobilize resources for constructive change.

- Mentoring/coaching: Individuals across and up and down an organizational structure need time to reflect on how they are doing and what can be done differently. Coaches and or mentors help employees grow, learn, and engage more successfully in daily work (and personal) challenges.

- Optimize work and family integration: Organizations may say that they want to promote a work–life balance, but then require weekend hours and evening meetings. Many employees are forgoing vacations and time with family, friends, community, or hobbies because of the work demands placed upon them. An emphasis on people and profits is not mutually exclusive.

- Promote diversity: Diversity goes far beyond one's skin color. There is visible and hidden diversity that is rich and provides differing perspectives and understanding for organizational health. Diversity includes ethnic background, culture, sexual orientation, language ability, and differing intelligences (hobbies, communities, religions, foods, and ways of having fun).

- Emphasize wellness: Sitting 8+ hours a day in an office is not good for the human body. In order to maintain a healthy organization, physically and emotionally healthy individuals need to be found. Access to mental health services and the promotion of wellness programs that encourage being physically active, eating well, and having downtime are essential.

- Ongoing learning: People need to engage in lifelong learning to expand skill sets and face new challenges. Learning organizations continually examine how things can be done differently and more beneficially to inside and outside stakeholders. Learning organizations also provide opportunities for employees to expand their learning, whether through local course offerings or specialized training.

- Stakeholder buy-in: One can have the knowledge of what makes an organization healthy, but it needs to be translated into practice. Talented organizational psychologists can make this a reality by making sure buy-in for a positive organization, and its positive development takes place through the support of this culture by groups across the organization.

- Reducing organizational stress: Stressors in the workplace continue to exact an enormous toll on the physical and emotional well-being of employees. Turnover is often a symptom of too much stress. The opportunity to create healthier organizations exists, but corporate culture takes time to embrace changes to routine despite such changes benefiting individual as well as workforce productivity.

Organizational psychology is being applied to improving nonprofits, for-profits, educational institutions, government operations, health care, and NGOs, and is an open door for future application of positive psychology.

LEADERSHIP PSYCHOLOGY

Leadership psychology is a new field that examines how individuals from all walks of life and backgrounds mobilize resource for change. In this case, change for positive or constructive purposes (as from history we know there are good leaders and destructive leaders/dictators). In the past, many believed that certain traits and characteristics identified those most likely to be leaders. This has been shown not to be correct. If asked to name leaders, many people reference Gandhi, Lincoln, or Martin Luther King. All of these individuals brought together groups to create social change and did so in their unique ways under their unique circumstances. What is often overlooked is the everyday leader. Take, for example, the actual case of a woman in an impoverished part of El Salvador. She mobilized other women in her community to buy a sewing machine (through a microcredit loan scheme). She then bought fabric remnants from a nearby factory and brought her community together to sew and sell pajamas, robes, and quilts, which in turn raised the standard of living for everyone in the community. This woman is a leader under today's understanding of leadership and change. Leadership psychology examines leadership, and how it differs from not only management but also authoritarianism and dictatorship, as well as the importance of followership (without followers there are no leaders). Leaders for the 21st century that can effect constructive outcomes are needed more than ever given the many challenges of today's world. A new model of collaborative (rather than top-down) leadership is emerging, which allows followers and other stakeholders more opportunity to engage in the change needed.

OCCUPATIONAL HEALTH THERAPY

Today's workforce is more diverse and includes individuals across the life span of development with varying physical abilities and needs. Occupational health psychologists focus on workplace health and safety, applying principles of positive psychology to support employee wellness and productivity. The public issues impacting organizations in the past such as sanitation and disease transmission have shifted to a focus on diet, exercise, and exposure to chemicals as well as the prevention of injuries or accidents at the work site. Occupational health psychologists address issues of the modern workplace as well such as increased rates of anxiety, depression, and exhaustion. They take a public health approach by promoting health and reducing disease.

Occupational health therapists address workplace bullying, affirmative action issues, environmental assessments, employee stress, and risk factors for mortality and morbidity. This position is so critical as the well-being of an individual at work influences others at work as well as family and community. This position shifts the emphasis from a crisis-oriented response to a preventive approach that promotes the best in workplace functioning.

HUMAN FACTORS/USABILITY PSYCHOLOGY

Technology is integral to today's workforce, while some argue that it has made us less efficient with huge daily e-mail inboxes and the rapidity in which big data can be collected. Personal and workplace technology has exploded in the past 10 years and continues to move at an ever more rapid pace. Adopting technology is critical to maintaining a competitive advantage. Computers have become essential in the workplace and control everything from air control to subways. These complex systems that we rely on in the 21st century need to be easily used and understood by human workers. They need to be useful, safe, and reduce the risk of user error.

Human factors or usability that psychologists study show how individuals utilize websites and how many seconds it takes someone to leave a website when they do not find the information that they want (2 seconds). They examine how we interact, use, and understand technology, whether in design, interaction, or training of such technology.

In design, companies have embraced ergonomics to make interaction with technology easier, safer, and more secure creating a synergy between the worker and the technology being employed. Beyond ergonomics, these psychologists bring to the table an understanding of cognitive functioning and how individuals perceive information, process it, and then apply it. Many organizations have felt the pain of deploying new technology without having considered the user or the implementation process leaving expensive equipment sitting in storage.

TALENT MANAGEMENT

"Talent management" is the new term for human resources and acknowledges that employees bring with them a set of strengths (or talents) that need to be identified and supported for a mutually beneficial employment experience. Talent managers use the theories and practices of positive psychology to find the best employees within an organization, support their growth and development, and nurture their work and commitment to the organization.

CASE STUDY: GOOD BUSINESS, POSITIVE PSYCHOLOGY, AND THE BODY SHOP

Anita Roddick, founder of The Body Shop, was known to visit the cafeterias and bathrooms of companies with which she considered partnering. Her logic was that if the company treated their employees well with good food and clean restrooms, they would treat her well as a business partner. Many years later, Google focused on the quality of the food they had available for employees as they saw that good food made for good conversation and the sharing of ideas across divisions.

Positive psychology and good business go hand in hand. Roddick used her business acumen to create an international chain of stores that focused on fair trade and sustainable sourcing. Profits did not come before people, yet her company grew rapidly. She later used this business model to create a social entrepreneurship business program in partnership with the University of Bath in England.

Roddick had originally intended to pursue a career in drama. However, when her application to drama school was rejected, she decided to work for a time as a schoolteacher. When this became no longer interesting to her, she decided to travel the world to see Tahiti, Australia, and South Africa, where she carefully observed the customs of people, including the practices of using cocoa butter to make the skin emollient, and washing hair with mud. These approaches to body care became part of her offerings at The Body Shop.

Beyond The Body Shop, Roddick worked on behalf of a number of non-profits to demonstrate what she called "moral leadership." She supported the care of the rainforest, debt relief for developing countries, the protection of whales, voting rights, and gender and age equality, and supported an ethical approach to business. She is largely credited with moving forward the notion of "green consumerism."

According to Mihayli Csikszentmihalyi (1989), employees in the United States (and many other countries) live between boredom and anxiety. This means that some employees do tasks that are repetitive and do not engage the person; or the employee is doing the equivalent work of three to four people and is anxious all the time. He argues that individuals do best when there is a match between skills and challenges. This unleashes creativity and the best type of problem solving.

Examples of "good business" include auto companies reworking their assembly lines to better align employee challenges and skills (through additional training and rotation of assembly line responsibilities that increases productivity and decreases absenteeism), and technology companies creating spaces in which ideas can be shared and hierarchy is flattened. These models do not dismiss the importance of profits; they simply include an awareness of their impact on the environment, employees, and business partners.

CASE STUDY (Continued)

However, when employees report that they are bored or anxious, they are not necessarily able to be either creative or engaged in the work that they are doing. In order to be competitive in the global economy of today, business as usual is a prescription for extinction. Positive psychology helps organizations be more resilient and bounce back from setbacks; think about taking courageous steps and moving out of a default means of operating; and providing employees a sense of hope and support to get the work completed. Yet, many organizations continue to maintain a typical business model from the 20th century that is hierarchical and paternalistic.

Roddick proposed that first and foremost organizations needed to be responsible to employees, customers, and sellers. She also understood the importance of followers and how consumers and others within the public could use the power of public pressure to create change, forcing corporations to reevaluate their actions and the impact those actions have environmentally, socially, financially, and physically. Roddick's call to action was to expand the role and responsibility of entrepreneurs, and urge a review of business ethics. She died in 2007, a year before the Wall Street crash that many attribute to misguided ethical practices.

Roddick and organizations such as Google, Tesla, and Starbucks continue to provide examples of how to do business well, with a focus on creativity, sustainability, and support for the community.

Roddick said, "For me, good business is about putting forward solutions, not just opposing destructive practices or human rights abuses." She argued that in order to do good business, companies "must actively do good" and be "incubators of the human spirit." Using the tenets of positive psychology as well as her own passion and understanding of business opportunities, she altered how business can function in today's world.

The 21st century is ripe for alternative approaches that promote a sense of *community, creativity,* and *camaraderie* (we call it the 3 Cs of successful organizations). These include best practices such as:

- Embracing change (do not avoid change)
- Open to new approaches
- Focusing both internally and externally to promote best practices
- Fostering employee growth
- Promoting social responsibility
- Fostering flow work experiences
- Ongoing training and education
- Promoting a happy work environment
- Defining business roles and responsibilities in society
- Promoting health and wellness of employees
- Living the values and ethics to which the company adheres

Talent management expands the concept of human resources by promoting talent, retaining it, and developing it. Many organizations have found the hard way that by not paying attention to talent, performance and growth are hampered. Individuals need to have a sense of where they are before they know where they are going. Talent managers of the 21st century identify goals, objectives, and directions to success without a punitive or infantilizing approach. They ask how this person may not only fit in well with the organizational culture and mission but also how he or she can grow within that framework.

Additional responsibilities within talent management include:

- Talent alignment: Making sure that the best and brightest are in roles that optimize performance.

- Training and development: Such programs are taking the form of having a mentor for new recruits; many high-technology companies keep employees engaged and awake by creating rotational assignments where the individual is exposed to the work of the organization across job assignments, and creating corporate responsibility outreach in which employees can take time to volunteer at a nonprofit of their choosing to "give back" to the community.

- Identification and retention of talent: Talent managers make sure that valuable employees are satisfied with their work and have tools to integrate work and life requirements. Rather than a passive approach to employee dissatisfaction, today's talent managers are proactive in identifying employee engagement.

- Career development: Identifying career goals does not mean that an employee is looking to move onward and upward. Talent managers look with employees at career goals, employment objectives, and the tools to reach those goals. This includes a personal and professional growth and development plan.

Organizations are powerful in leading change in the world as well. Consider the movement toward people before profits. These are not mutually exclusive terms, but in the 20th century we saw a predominance of putting profits before the environment, fair trade, and many who were marginalized and used in creating corporate profits. While in the 21st century we are still working this focus to address the very human and environmental problems involved, there is at least discussion. These challenges will continue as the world invests more as a global economy and work crosses borders and cultures at an accelerated pace.

Talent management will continue to utilize the understanding from positive psychology to engage, retain, and create environments in which employees can contribute in a healthy manner so that the right person and right job can be ultimately combined.

LOOKING AHEAD

The world is changing rapidly and human beings are being asked more than ever to adapt to these changes. The human species has largely been successful on this planet by adapting over time to all types of geographic climates and conditions. Too much change too fast is overwhelming for many, however.

CENTENARIAN ADVICE

The pursuit of happiness is so much part of the U.S. culture that it is written in the U.S. Constitution, where U.S. citizens are guaranteed the right to "life, liberty, and the pursuit of happiness." Being happy has become an overriding focus in many of our lives, but as a society, we are not necessarily happier despite the consumption (and overconsumption) of self-help texts, medications, food, consumer items, and ever-increasing home sizes. In the last 50 years, rates of anxiety, depression, and divorce have increased.

Researchers turned to centenarians, those who have lived over 100 years and who have accumulated a great deal of wisdom, to give advice on how to live a good or happy life. They had a great deal to tell researchers. First and foremost, they said that being curious about the world was essential to their longevity. These groups of people were also lifelong learners enrolling in courses to learn something new or of interest. They also reported having a sense of purpose in their life often governed by a personal belief system. Health and well-being factored prominently into their responses, with the advice to manage stress with yoga or mediation; to eat whole foods instead of refined and processed foods; and to maintain weight. Finally they recommended that individuals make work more playful and play more purposeful.

As newer generations continue to live longer, understanding that which provides a sense of well-being for the long haul (as opposed to the hope that buying more makes us happier) is treasured insight and advice worth considering.

While we may not be able to slow the pace of such change, we can recalibrate the way we approach daily life in this modern world.

There is a promising new awareness about the food we eat, the energies we use, and the impact that a consumer culture has on the planet. Along with this awareness is action to move toward more locally grown foods, change to alternative energies, and to recycle what we consume. Similarly, there is a new awareness about the importance of mental health and proactively promoting health while also addressing pathology.

Positive psychology joins these exciting new shifts in the 21st century to better understand what happiness and well-being mean and how to implement them in daily life across the spectrum of life. New technologies enhance our life and provide connection and information like never before. Yet the consumption of these technologies should not replace the very inherent need humans have to be with each other and laugh, cry, and be with one another.

The focus on material acquisition as a marker of success is not making us happier. Never before have people had so much in terms of material items, and yet have found no enhancement of their happiness (after a certain level of stable income is reached). While many have been socialized to thinking and feeling that having more increases one's happiness, good science tells us that this is not the case.

Our definition of success needs to be re-crafted. Could success mean that which creates a better life such as clean water, access to education and health care, having time for friends and neighbors, and breathing fresh air?

We are at a critical juncture in environmental, political, social, and educational challenges that require new perspectives that incorporate new ways of thinking and acting. Injecting the knowledge and practice of positive psychology can contribute easily to any of these domains. Change comes slowly. Hopefulness to making constructive social change is the positive psychology message and catalyst to achieve such ends.

Students of psychology come from all different backgrounds. Similarly, the application of psychology is as varied as the people that study it. Human behavior is integral to all that one does in the world on a daily basis, whether for business, education, or managing one's life.

When one thinks of psychology, one typically thinks of psychologists in educational, clinical, counseling, or forensic realms. However fields such as health, occupational, and sports psychology are growing rapidly.

The key is the understanding of human behavior and patterns in differing situations. Those who pursue degrees in psychology may also find themselves consulting for marketing companies, teaching in schools, colleges, or universities, or within the realms of organizational development and talent management.

Some of the areas outside of the therapeutic/consulting roles that those who study psychology take include:

- Management
- Sales
- Personnel training
- Real estate
- Insurance
- Business consulting

Beyond the interesting content of the field are the important skills one can acquire for work and living in the 21st century. These include:

- Professional writing and communicating skills
- Critical thinking
- Knowledge of both individual and group behaviors
- Creative problem-solving skills

THE FUTURE OF POSITIVE PSYCHOLOGY

The future of psychology and mental health care as a whole is rapidly changing in part due to greater scientific understanding of human behavior, brain functioning, and the development of pharmaceuticals to treat mental

WHAT DO YOU WANT OUT OF LIFE?

A few years ago, *Forbes* magazine asked its readers what they consider "the good life." When the publisher aggregated the data, this is what their respondents reported:

- A primary residence of 4,000 square feet
- A second home in the country or by the beach
- Two luxury cars
- Dinner out at least once a week
- Three vacations per year
- Prep school as well as an Ivy League education for their children

While the readers of this magazine tend to skew to businesspeople who aspire to luxury, the desire to have more and more goods is driving most people to a frantic pace of life. In other words, one must work harder to possess goods and to also maintain, upgrade, replace, insure, and manage those goods. Do we own our goods or do our goods own us? The pursuit of materialism can become a vicious cycle in fact and is dubbed "Affluenza" by author John de Graaf and his colleagues (2014). They argue that a consumer-oriented economy creates insecurity and starts a quest for material wealth as we try to fill ourselves with more and more.

Barry Schwartz (2005) argues that more is not always better. In a study in which consumers were given the choice of 24 different types of jam versus only six types of jam, consumers felt more confident about their purchasing choice when fewer options were provided. In today's world of the choice of over 100 brands of cereals in the cereal aisle, consumers may be faced with "choice paralysis." Having an abundance of choice also makes the consumer have more buyer's remorse as the choice made often does not feel like the best one.

The economic collapse of 2008 changed this for many people who suffered tremendous economic hardship. People began to reassess this consumptive lifestyle and reflected on what gives meaning to their lives. A more recent study asked Americans across the country, "What do you want out of life?" People responded that they wanted less stress; more laughter; a greater sense of control over how their time is spent; fewer everyday details of our modern life (security codes, passwords, e-mails, phone calls); and, most of all, people in their lives that could really understand them. We know from research in positive psychology that people get their greatest sense of well-being from interaction with family, friends, and other loved ones. Human beings are social creatures and as much as we like our "things" it is nothing in comparison to the contact we have with others.

illness. Another great driver is the health care system itself and the attempt by providers and insurers (as well as consumers) to contain costs. Many health care practitioners report that the insurers are in fact calling the shots today about treatment, duration, and medication requirements. For example, psychotherapy practitioners are finding that the amount they are reimbursed for services is declining, while at the same time there is a push by some insurance providers to provide medication management rather than therapy (research reflects that the two in combination provide the most successful outcomes).

What is exciting is the development of new treatment modalities, which may turn what we know about the treatment of mental illness and health in a new direction. Take, for example, the treatment of tuberculosis (TB) in the middle of the 21st century. The prescription for treatment at the time was removing an individual for purposes of reducing transmission rates as well as rest and fresh mountain air. This was what science knew at the time for TB.

Today, scientists can assess for TB through clinical testing and treat and cure both latent and active forms of TB. This moved the care of TB to make it far less traumatic (being separated from family and friends) and improved positive outcomes greatly.

Similarly, historical approaches to mental illness have included some painful and misguided treatment approaches. If one was not being accused of being possessed by an evil spirit and branded a witch, warlock, or evil presence, one was often thrown into sanitariums where the conditions were fairly miserable. Sometimes husbands denounced wives in order to be divorced at the time, turning otherwise healthy women into institutionalized patients who quickly became physically and mentally ill.

In the 1960s with the passage of the federal Community Mental Health Act, many institutions that housed mentally ill people were disbanded. At that time, new drugs were introduced to reduce psychotic and manic symptoms. In addition, society moved toward more humane care for mentally ill people outside of clinics by bringing people home to family and communities. Finally, this further reduced taxpayer costs for such facilities.

Today it is clear that while the creators of this Act perhaps had the best intentions in mind, it ended up transferring care of mentally ill from clinical institutions to other facilities such as shelters, streets, and prisons or correctional facilities. This model, however, is not working for individuals in need of services, for states who foot the bill for services, and for the other institutions that are shouldering the responsibility for care for which they are not prepared.

This issue is a large and important one that is necessary for many in the United States and around the world to address. Leaving the problem of mental illness to the prison system has led to overcrowding, among other reasons, with mental health care not always the first priority for these prisoners.

Therefore, a large question remains about the future of mental health care for both those who can maintain daily life function with therapeutic supports and those who need more involved support services. How does society want to maintain the mental health of its citizens and address the needs of those who suffer from mental illness?

Deinstitutionalizing individuals whose needs for mental health care are great was intended to bring people back into their homes, communities, and daily lives. However, many people who suffer from mental illness may not or will not take their medications and may have breaks with reality that require more specialized care. The burden of this care is the responsibility of society. Otherwise, many such people end up homeless.

Supporting someone who has a severe mental illness or disorder is very exhausting as well. The supports are not always easily understood or available for these caretakers. As society moves away from extended family models, such people in need may fall through the cracks or end up in the streets or in places simply not suited for them. The cost both economically and socially for not addressing these issues continues to skyrocket.

The Future of Happiness

The topic of happiness has become very popular in recent years as individuals have examined what it takes to be happy in a consumer-oriented economy that promotes the notion that a product will be the solution to unhappiness. People have bought, consumed, eaten, and suffered the consequences of too much, especially when the most recent global recession hit. It often takes crises to move toward a new way of thinking and being. Many are reexamining what it means to be content and whether success is the large car and home (with a large mortgage) or whether it can be found in other forms easily available and attainable if we slow down to consider and implement certain practices.

The term "happy" can be a slippery one as it is a state of being that can mean different things to different people. We interchange the term "well-being" to expand the definition of happy and have avoided defining happiness as the absence of sadness. The challenge is that happiness comes and goes. We can create conditions to increase the likelihood of happier experiences, but the goal of being happy all the time is not realistic as the human condition is generally filled with both.

Pharmaceuticals are manufacturing more variations of antidepressants and antianxiety medication to fill the demand for these products, but the question remains whether these fairly new medications are indeed the answer to a society that is reporting feeling more depressed and anxious.

Industrialized countries have never had more wealth with larger house sizes and consumer items that provide entertainment and convenience. For many, an automobile is no longer a luxury, but a necessity to travel given the way many cities and suburbs have been created. In one Florida suburb, one has to drive one's car to the coffee shop one block away as there are no pedestrian paths or ways of crossing from gated communities to shopping areas. A large question for the happiness and well-being literature to continue to examine in the future is whether we have overlooked the simple aspects of life and instead substituted ever greater diversions in order for us to make us think we are happy and alive. It is shown in literature that children in poorer communities are able to engage themselves in activities more energetically than those from middle- and upper-class communities because they make up their own games and appreciate things differently than from children who rely on prepackaged entertainment and more sophisticated diversions for play.

Belief Systems

Understanding one's values and having a guiding philosophy in life can create stability in turbulent times. Organized religion provided a place of hopefulness and helpfulness for many for hundreds of years (and, of course, a great deal of death and destruction emerged about who held the actual "truth").

Today there is a remarkable shift among younger generations away from organized religion toward a self-created understanding of spirituality. This may include practices such as meditation and yoga to create a clear mind for reflection and relaxation. The new spiritual models of happiness and understanding continue to emerge, and their ability to provide "sanctuary" from the stressors and demands of daily life are redefining belief systems and creating alternatives for those seeking another perspective. Happiness is without question linked to meaning and meaning making. As social animals, human beings are natural storytellers. We understand our world and each other through the stories that emerge, change, or is rebuilt over time. For example, lightening was a phenomenon our early ancestors did not understand. As a result, cultures around the world created an explanation for what lightening was. Whether it was Gods playing with thunder bolts, or the heavens punishing man, it created sense out of something that felt unpredictable and mysterious. Today we have a scientific answer for this phenomenon, but this does not mean that the stories of today are the best and last. Science is often re-running experiments to understand the world the best way possible within the constraints of a time and technology.

Victor Frankl, the father of logo-therapy and existential analysis as well as a Holocaust survivor, wrote *Man's Search for Meaning* after his release in 1946 from three years at the Auschwitz concentration camp. In this book, he examines how to find meaning in the midst of the horror and harshness of a Nazi concentration camp.

In his book, he writes:

> Don't aim at success—the more you aim at it and make it a target, the more you are going to miss it. For success, like happiness, cannot be pursued; it must ensue, and it only does so as the unintended side-effect of one's dedication to a cause greater than oneself or as the by-product of one's surrender to a person other than oneself. Happiness must happen, and the same holds for success: you have to let it happen by not caring about it.

Frankl found that those fellow prisoners who no longer had any hope for life and had lost all sense of meaning soon lost their fortitude in the concentration camps and died. He attributed his survival to creating meaning for himself as a way to hold on to the only thing the Nazis left to him: his attitude. To Frankl, meaning (and happiness) came from meaningful work, love, and courage and the mindset that we bring to life.

Belief systems, whether of organized religion, personal philosophy, or some of the more modern ways of constructing understanding of the world, are essential to a sense of well-being. Schools of psychology, divinity, and social work continue to lead this charge. Medicine is stepping in as well as evidenced by the Schwartz Center for Compassionate Care at the Massachusetts General Hospital, which takes into account the many ways people understand and live in the world, which is so critical when facing morbidity or mortality. Moreover, as more people are dying in hospitals rather than at home in our current world, topics of death and dying are critical to the conversations that take place in such settings.

CONCLUSION

The cornerstones of positive psychology, courage, hope, optimism, and resiliency can be nurtured to improve a sense of hopefulness and helpfulness in society. Examining that which is good and strong in people, as opposed to just what is wrong, has led to a rich literature of scientific findings of what makes one happy across age, culture, gender, and ethnicity.

Understanding and pursuing happiness is part of the human experience. We seek it, try to hold on to it, and often find it appearing and reappearing but not a constant. This change is due to the unpredictability, in part, of the context in which we live. Change is a given and whether that is a change due to health, natural disaster, or other life circumstances it, creates disequilibrium, which impacts one's health and well-being with the hope that happiness may return upon equilibrium. Resiliency helps to move individuals back from dramatic changes in life and therefore helps to buffer one from shifts that occur. If change is part and parcel of life, then the answer is to nurture those aspects of life that help one get over the bumps and to maximize a sense of contentment in between. The notion that one needs to be happy all the time is incorrect. Humans are complex beings that feel happiness, sadness, boredom, anxiety, apprehension, hope, and the multitude of emotions that are part of the nature of life.

When we are too long within the realms of boredom, anxiety, and fear, for example, then one's mental and physical health deteriorates. Moving toward a healthier place of functioning and having the skills and tools to do so is at the heart of this book. Just try to take a moment to stop the sense of doing, rushing, dashing, finishing, and starting, and provide space for considering the strong and positive in oneself. Plant the seeds so that with some nurturance and insight, the psychology of health and well-being can be an integral part of one's life.

Glossary

Acceptance: An element of mindfulness; the act of acknowledgment without engagement of the thoughts, feelings, and emotions experienced during mindfulness, as well as a compassion and tolerance for others.

Acetylcholine (ACh): A neurotransmitter present at all the neuromuscular junctions, its primary function is to stimulate all muscle contractions.

Action Tendencies: The coordinated changes in people's thoughts, actions, and physical response to emotion.

Affect: A more general and "free-floating" experience of emotion, as opposed to categorizable and discreet emotion, unrelated to a specific object and of indefinite time duration.

Affirmative Bias: One of the three pillars of positive leadership according to Kim Cameron. *See also* **Confirmation Bias; Leadership for Good; Positive Deviance**.

"Affluenza": A term coined by John de Graaf that is defined by the pursuit of materialism and the vicious cycle that ensues trying to maintain that lifestyle.

Amygdala: A part of the limbic system of the brain whose central function is processing and regulating emotion.

Andon: Employee participation mechanism used in the automotive industry used to increase morale and feeling of value; employees are asked to detect defects, stop the assembly line, and help to correct the condition.

Archetype: A common concept in psychology where, according to Carl Jung, there are universal, mythic characters that exist within the collective unconscious of human beings, where these archetypes represent fundamental themes of experience. These figures include the Self, the Trickster, and the Shadow.

Assessment: A tool that allows researchers to better understand a specific characteristic of an individual or population.

Asset: Measurable factors in an individual or the environment that predict better outcomes.

Attachment: The emotional bond that connects one person to another.

Authenticity: The ability and willingness to allow others to see a true self without fear of judgment and applying nonjudgmental self-compassion to how one interacts with the world.

Autonomic Nervous System: A component of the peripheral nervous system, aka the involuntary nervous system, that controls functions outside of our conscious awareness and has control over functions such as heart rate, respiration, salivation, and sexual arousal. This is further divided into two subsystems: the sympathetic and parasympathetic nervous system.

Bibliotherapy: The use of literature selected by a mental health professional for a client to review in order to create opportunities for healing or growth.

Bobo Doll: A famous experiment conducted by social psychologist Albert Bandura in 1961 and 1963 that demonstrated a child's ability to imitate what he or she saw on a film.

Brainstem: A group of structures at the base of the brain that is in charge of all basic life functions, including regulation of cardiac muscle and breathing regulation. The structures include the medulla, pons, and the midbrain.

Broaden-and-Build Theory of Emotions: A theory coined by Barbara Fredrickson suggesting that positive emotions give us a broader way of thinking that leads to new discoveries of skills, associations, and resources.

Caring Capitalism: A philanthropic business model based on creative means to addressing social issues, famously reflected by the philanthropic need addressed by the company.

Cerebellum: A central part of the vestibular system of the brain that is responsible for balance, posture, and coordination of body movement and position.

Cerebrum: The largest part of the brain, divided into two hemispheres, left and right, and four lobes—the temporal lobe, frontal lobe, parietal lobe, and occipital lobe.

Chief Happiness Officer: A new executive position that has been recently developed, originating from the tech industry. This position integrates aspects of positive psychology into the workforce; the duties include adjusting workplace policy, culture, and even workshops to create the conditions for employee productivity and well-being.

Chronosystem: The "outermost" layer of the Ecological Systems Theory that articulates the transitions and shifts that occur across a life span that can influence an individual's environment.

Cinematherapy: The use of a commercial film selected by a mental health professional for a client to view to create opportunities for healing or growth.

Clifton StrengthsFinder: An assessment developed in 2013 that explores 34 different themes, such as Achiever and Belief, to see where an individual's strengths lie.

Cognitive Flexibility: The ability to change what one is thinking about how one thinks about it as well as the ability to adjust thinking and attention in response to what is happening in the environment.

Cognitive Reappraisal: The ability to change the way one thinks about any bothersome event.

Cognitive Dissonance: The state of having inconsistent thoughts, beliefs, or attitudes, especially as relating to behavioral decisions and attitude change.

Computerized Axial Tomography (CAT): A brain imaging technique that illuminates the structure of the brain.

Confirmation Bias: The tendency to interpret new evidence as confirmation of one's existing beliefs or theories.

Conscious Capitalism: A philosophy that not only builds on the foundations of capitalism but also incorporates positive psychology principles, such as trust, compassion, and collaboration, into every aspect of business.

Corporate Social Responsibility (CSR) Programs: Programs and initiatives that a company undertakes to benefit society rather than profits.

Courage: The capacity to manage fear and understand tolerance for risk or uncertainty. The five major aspects are vulnerability, surfacing fears, reframing your thinking, addressing the stress, and practice.

Creativity: Finding novel approaches and connections between ideas and ways to address challenges in work and life.

Dispositional Optimism: An individual's expected outcomes of an event; in the context of optimism, optimistic individuals will typically expect good outcomes, whereas pessimists will usually expect poor outcomes.

Dissonance Reduction: The attempt by an individual to minimize the gap between what exists and what one wants to believe, usually when an individual compares himself or herself to others.

Dopamine: An excitatory and inhibitory neurotransmitter behind attention and focus, active in the brain's perceptions of reward and pleasure.

Dopamine Theory of Positive Affect: A theory that produces a link between positive emotion and broadened cognition by focusing on the role of dopamine and how it facilitates tasks, learning, and creative problem solving.

Downward Comparison: The act of comparing reality to a reality that is portrayed (e.g., on a television show) as worse.

Dual-Process Brain Model: A model presented by Daniel Kahneman about how our brains process the world: One system is the fast, intuitive autonomic processing of our world, and the other system is the slow thinking part, believes what it sees and can jump to conclusions.

Ecological Systems Theory: Proposed by psychologist Urie Bronfenbrenner, this theory describes the dynamic interaction of forces from social or environmental factors within an individual's five leveled networks—the microsystem, the mesosystem, the exosystem, the microsystem, and the chronosystem (*see also* definitions).

Elaboration Likelihood Model (ELM): Pioneered by psychologists Richard Petty and John Cacioppo, this model proposes multiple routes—either central or peripheral—for message processing but not all information receives similar attention.

Emotion: The full range of emotional experience; defined by psychologist Barbara Fredrickson as responses that happen over a short amount of time, beginning with assessment of personal meaning, either consciously or unconsciously.

Empathy: Knowing enough about another person or situation to be able to imagine or project what the other person is feeling.

Enabling Institutions: Systems, either formal (family, community) or informal (mentoring, culture) that have certain features in common that define an institution as "[contributing] to fulfillment."

Endorphins: A neurotransmitter involved in pain suppression, reward, and positive mood states.

Exosystem: This layer of the Ecological Systems Theory describes the larger social system that encompasses the microsystem and mesosystem.

Experience Sampling Methodology (ESM): A research procedure that examines what people think, feel, and do in their daily lives by understanding the daily lived experiences of individuals; some examples are experience in living with a chronic disease or examining what makes a healthy relationship. Data are self-reported by the individual and can be used in a variety of contexts.

Extrinsic Motivation: Activities that are justified by consequent rewards such as prestige, power, and money.

Family: A nuclear social institution that is crucial for a child's development.

Family-Centered Positive Psychology (FCPP): A practice that empowers families by addressing the relationships among people, situations, and environments that are inseparable from a child's life using the Ecological Systems Model.

Fear of Missing Out (FoMO): The fear of missing out on social interactions and the rewarding experience that comes with it.

Federal Community Mental Health Act: Passed in the 1960s, this bill served to disband many institutions that housed mentally ill people.

Five Facet Mindfulness Questionnaire: Developed by mindfulness scholar Ruth Baer that combines five previous mindfulness self-reporting instruments and surveys.

Flow: A concept introduced by Mihaly Csikszentmihalyi; when one becomes very absorbed/immersed in the task that he or she is doing, an energized focus when his or her skills and challenges are balanced; this is akin to an athlete's "runner's high," where there is a match between high challenge and high skills.

Focusing Illusion: A term coined by Daniel Kahneman, stating that nothing in life is as important as you think it is when you are thinking about it.

Forgiveness: A coping mechanism that serves to reframe, neutralize, or remove negative emotions from an interpersonal conflict. Can be either decisional (intentional decision to behave differently toward offender) or emotional (ability to displace negative emotions with positive ones).

Frontal Lobe: The largest of the four lobes of the cerebral cortex, it controls higher-thought functions, including judgement, behavior, attention, abstract thinking, and personality.

Functional Magnetic Resource Imaging (fMRI): A brain imaging technique that allows for the link of self-reported experience while monitoring real-time blood flow activity through different regions of the brain, sometimes to associate functionality to different parts of the brain.

GABA (Gamma-Aminobutyric Acid): A neurotransmitter that functions in the body to serve as an inhibitor to balance over-firing of other neurons.

Genetic Set Point Theory: The theory that each person has a genetically determined level of happiness.

Gratitude: By the act of recognizing that one has received something of value, freely given, from something or someone else, it is a key factor in happiness and healing the past because it enables the emotional reframing of past situations, lessening negative emotions, and assisting in navigation through pain, according to Robert Emmons.

Gross Domestic Product (GDP): A term in economics that reflects the amount a country produces over a designated amount of time to determine the economic well-being of a country.

Happiness: Subjective well-being that reflects a person's own assessment of his or her life satisfaction, as well as having more positive than negative emotions.

Happiness Index: Created by the government of Bhutan, this is a tool to measure the health and well-being of a community with factors including quality of air, water, access to education, and vacation time allotted.

Happiness Scale: An assessment created by Dr. Sonja Lyubomirsky to measure an individual's subjective happiness using a four-question assessment based on a seven-point scale.

Happiness: Unlocking the Mysteries of Psychological Wealth: A book published in 2008 by psychologist Ed Diener listing four central qualities for a happy life: (1) Psychological wealth is more important than financial wealth. (2) Happiness not only makes one feel good but also contribute to daily well-being with friends, work, and one's health. (3) It is important to set realistic expectations about happiness and being happy is not the default way of being at all times. (4) Thinking in a happy framework helps to make one's daily life happier.

Happy Business Index: A tool used to assess key points of unhappiness, employee motivation and engagement in the workplace as well as the level of employee progress and connection to a company's values and goals.

Hard Power: Developed by positive psychologist Joseph Nye, this is an influential power that uses the tools of coercion and incentives to achieve desired outcomes. Antonym: *See* **Soft Power**.

Hedonic Adaption/Hedonic Treadmill Theory: People will return to their happiness set point at some point in time, no matter which hardships or sorrows they face.

Hippocampus: A part of the limbic system that contributes to learning and memory, including the coding of information for transfer between short- and long-term storage.

Hope: A cornerstone in positive psychology, realizing the goals, dreams, and objectives that one has in life.

Hot and Cold Emotional System: A theory developed by Walter Mischel describing different frames of emotional thinking; the former reflects the primitive structure that is quick and impulsive; the latter relates to the prefrontal structure that is based on conscious decisions and delayed gratification.

Interpersonal Reactivity Index (IRI): Used since the 1980s and established by Mark Davis, this tool is used to measure empathy level in individuals with cognitive and affective components.

Intrinsic Motivation: Referring to activities that are pursued because it is worthwhile to the individual and do not require any other external incentives.

Jikoda: Automation with a human touch.

Kaizen: An environment in which companies and employees proactively work to improve the manufacturing process to increase employee involvement and customer satisfaction.

Kauai Longitudinal Study: A study primarily run by scientist Emmy Warner, using 698 subjects to explore resilience over a long period of human development, as well as identify protective influences and characteristics.

Leadership for Good: One of three pillars of positive leadership according to Kim Cameron. Here, leaders have an opportunity to reveal the natural inclination of followers to do good work and happily contribute. *See also* **Affirmative Bias; Positive Deviance.**

Leadership Psychology: A new field that examines how individuals from all walks of life and backgrounds mobilize resource for change.

Learned Optimism: A learned skill to be able to focus on positive accomplishments and interactions instead of focusing on what goes wrong. *See also* **Martin Seligman.**

Life Orientation Test (LOT): Developed by Scheier and Carver in 1985, it is a tool to measure generalized outcome expectancies. It consists of a total of twelve items, four items reflecting a positive stance, four items reflecting a negative stance, and four filler items and a Likert Scale from 0 ("strongly disagree") to 4 ("strongly agree"), with negative items reversed prior to scoring.

Limbic system: The system of glands and brain organs that are considered the "seat" of human emotion, managing emotional response and hormones. Central parts include the amygdala, hippocampus, hypothalamus, and pituitary gland.

LOT-R: A revised version of the LOT developed in 1994 by Scheier, Carver, and Bridges to eliminate some of the content overlap. The new LOT-R is a 10-item instrument of dispositional optimism, including three positively worded items, three negatively worded items, and four filler items with the same Likert scale used.

Macrosystem: An "outer" layer of the Ecological Systems Theory that includes the larger environment—economy, cultural values, and so on—that impact the smaller layers and their networks.

Magic Circle: A term coined by the Dutch historian Johan Huizinga that pertains to a temporary world, separate from reality, where humans can play. It contains several elements such as safety, agency and self-efficacy, and social connection.

Marshmallow Test: Developed in the 1960s by Walter Mischel, this was a test that examined how people exerted self-control and delayed gratification.

Mesosystem: This layer of the Ecological Systems theory is made up of the interactions among the different parts of the microsystem. *See also* **Ecological Systems Theory; Microsystem.**

Microsystem: The "innermost" layer of the Ecological Systems Theory, which describes our direct contact and direct relationships one has with others. *See also* **Ecological Systems Theory.**

Mind-Body Dualism: A theory proposed by 17th-century philosopher Descartes denoting that the mind and the body were separate entities.

Mindfulness: (1) A state of mind reflecting the cognitive processes and capacity for directed attention developed through mindfulness training. (2) A practice-based skill that directs attention to the present moment.

Mindfulness-Based Stress Reduction (MBSR): Developed by Jon Kabat-Zinn, this is an eight-week model that integrates the meditative practices of Buddhism with the methodologies of psychology.

Mindfulness Meditation: Introduced by Jon Kabat-Zinn, promoting a focus on the present moment rather than anxieties of the future; maintaining a present orientation allows one to be more attentive to stimuli in one's environment. Has been shown to have clinical benefits.

Mindlessness: The human tendency to function automatically while making unconscious evaluations, social comparisons, and so on.

Mirror neurons: A specific kind of neuron likened to the neurological process of empathy; they fire when planning movement and when observing movement in others.

Narrative: A bridge between individuals and the sociocultural environment where they live.

National Happiness Index: Established by the former king of Bhutan Jigme Singye Wangchuck, this tool measures combined levels of citizen happiness by measuring things like access to clean water, air, and education to determine the health of a country.

Nervous system: A complex network of interconnected, excitable cells that communicate chemically. This system can be divided into a central nervous system, consisting of the brain and spinal cord, and a peripheral nervous system.

Neuron: The central cell type of the nervous system, consisting of a nucleus, axon, myelin sheath, and dendrites.

Neuroplasticity: The ability of the brain to change either through experience or as a repairing mechanism to rebuild neuronal connections.

Neurotransmitters: Chemicals in the brain that allow the neurons to communicate.

Norepinephrine: A neurotransmitter that is the primary transmitter from the sympathetic half of the autonomic nervous system to the body's organs and glands as well as nervous system arousal.

Occipital Lobe: Located at the rear of the cerebral cortex, this lobe is associated with vision.

Occupational Health Psychologist: A professional that focuses on workplace health and safety applying principles of positive psychology to support employee wellness and productivity.

Opioids: These are peptides that mimic neurotransmitters who have pain-relieving qualities by pushing the brain with dopamine, but also play a role in behaviors such as physical attraction.

Optimism: The perception that one can move toward one's goals.

Organizational Psychology: A field related to positive psychology that focuses on examining how to make work sites healthy and productive by assessing the level of functioning among different divisional levels of a company.

Oxytocin: A hormone that also serves as a neurotransmitter, enhancing boding between mates as well as mothers and newborns.

Parasympathetic Nervous System: A component of the autonomic nervous system that is responsible for controlling activities related to the body in a relaxed state.

Parenting Styles: Identified by psychologist Diana Baumrind, who identified four dimensions of parenting that have become the basis for defining parenting styles: Authoritarian, Permissive, Authoritative, and Uninvolved.

Parietal lobe: One of the sections of the cerebral cortex that predominately controls comprehension, including visual functions, language, and reading as well as sensory input.

Peripheral Nervous System: The bundle of nerves connecting the brain to other parts of the body outside the spinal column forms. This system has two components: Somatic Nervous System and Autonomic Nervous System.

Person-Focused Resilience Model: A methodology of resiliency that looks at individuals over longer periods of development to compare attributes around those who exhibit resilience with others who experienced similar threats and did not fare as well.

Person Perception: How people perceive and think about others.

Pessimism: The frame of thought that sees the worst aspect of things or a belief that the worst will happen in difficult situations.

Place: The physical area or structure, such as a school or neighborhood, where individuals live, work, learn, play, and so on, and is a cornerstone of human development and well-being.

Positive Coaching: A concept supported by Robert Biswas-Diener to help individuals to greater well-being; its steps include examine strengths, harness positivity, diagnose positively, and assess positively.

Positive Deviance: One of the three pillars of positive leadership according to positive psychologist Kim Cameron. This is when leaders want followers to move away from the norm and engage in approaches that bring greater energy; they facilitate moving away from default ways of thinking or doing. *See also* **Affirmative Bias; Leadership for Good**.

Positron Emission Tomography (PET): A brain imaging technique that displays the brain's metabolic functioning at a cellular level by tracking the amount of glucose processed in different brain regions.

Project Competence Study (1999): Led by Ann Masten and her colleagues using a sectioned diagram that represents someone who has experienced a combination of adversity and demonstrates ability to adapt, defined by competence, using a group of urban students as subjects.

Protective Factors: A set of individual and environmental elements that can contribute to psychosocial resiliency such as individual characteristics (positive self-worth), family and relationships (positive family dynamic), and environment and good school systems.

REACH Method: A tool for self-forgiveness outlined by Everett Worthington; structured by five steps: Recalling hurt (R), replacing anger with empathy (E), cultivating altruism to enable forgiveness (A), commitment to the goal of forgiveness (C), and holding onto persistence in the face of doubt (H).

Reflected Best Self Exercise: A program that allows individuals to examine their own strengths by having five to seven individuals from their friends and family to submit a story about the individual at their best.

Reliability: The degree to which an assessment tool provides stables and consistent results.

Resilience: Generally, the ability to recover from adversity and challenges in life. In positive psychology, one can approach resiliency from a multifaceted approach.

Risk: The probability of encountering a factor of adversity.

Risk Gradient Model: Mapping out multiple risk factors where the more challenges a person faces, the greater the likelihood of problems in life.

Self-Acceptance: The acknowledgement and release of judgment rather than self-criticism to increase self-awareness and self-understanding. *See also* **Acceptance; Mindfulness**.

Serotonin: A neurotransmitter with several different functions; it contributes to mood stability and balances excesses of excitatory neurotransmitter activations, contributing to feelings of well-being and happiness as well as regulating other processes such as the sleep cycle, pain control, and digestion.

Social Comparison: When individuals compare themselves to another, for example, through the medium of social media.

Social Comparison Theory: Proposed by psychologist Leon Festinger, where humans have a basic drive to evaluate the opinion and ability of others relative to themselves.

Social Entrepreneurship: Actions that require addressing issues of society with innovative solutions, including drawing from business techniques.

Social Intelligence: A set of processes that perceive how humans monitor group behaviors, recognize social norms and validation, seek out social support, and maintain friendships.

Social Learning Theory: Established by social psychologist Albert Bandura, this theory posits that human beings, as social animals, learn through imitation and modeling.

Soft Power: A term coined by positive psychologist Joseph Nye to delineate influential power that inspires, attracts, or asks for change. Antonym: *See* **Hard Power.**

Somatic Nervous System: A component of the peripheral nervous system that controls the voluntary muscles in the body associated around the skeleton.

Storytelling for Empowerment Program: A program created to combine cultural empowerment, cognitive skills, storytelling, and the arts in a school-based, bilingual intervention for substance abuse and other problem behaviors.

Strength: The ability of individuals to feel a sense of agency in their world. They can be classified into cross-cultural groups such as emotional, character, relationship, and educational.

Strengths-Based Education: Within an academic setting, this approach identifies academic, behavioral, and emotional indicators to discover strengths of the individual and other variables to provide a picture of academic success.

Strengths-Based Leadership: This is an approach that looks at what is working well or is an asset in a follower and capitalizes on it. This can lead to matching challenges and skills and creating diversity.

Strengths-Based Leadership Model: A study done by researchers Tom Rath and Barry Conchie that found four major domains of leadership strength, which they labeled *Executing, Influencing, Relationship Building*, and *Strategic Thinking*.

Strengths-Based Psychology: A field that is credited to Donald O. Clifton, focusing on identifying strengths of an individual and developing virtues and inherent talents, expanding on these strengths, and building strengths-based organizations.

Strengths-Based Recovery Model: The utilization of promoting positive strengths, characteristics, and overall psychological resilience to traumatized individuals to assist in recovery and psychological growth.

Subjective Well-Being (SWB): The theory that every individual has happiness "set point" that is 80 percent explained by heredity.

Sympathetic Nervous System: A component of the autonomic nervous system that controls stimulating activities.

Synapse: A space between the neurons that allows the electrical current to move forward.

Talent Management: A term used in Human Resources that acknowledges that employees bring with them a set of talents that need to be identified for a mutually beneficial experience between employee and employer.

Temporal Lobe: A section of the cerebral cortex that is the center for visual and auditory memory, as well as hearing and speech.

Theory of Mind: A concept that seeks to explain how people understand others, exchange abstract concepts, and are able to conceptualize intentions and beliefs that are different from one's own.

Total Productive Maintenance: A program used in the automotive industry to increase employee participation, in some cases mandatory, by promoting ongoing skill training, feedback from employees on how to improve equipment, and open communication between operators and engineers.

Triune Brain Model: Published by neuroscientist and physician Paul MacLean in 1949, describing how brain evolution occurred in "quantum leaps," creating three separate structures: the instinctive reptilian brain, the emotional mammalian brain, and the cognitive neocortex brain.

Upward Comparison: The act of comparing reality to a reality that is portrayed (e.g., on a television show) as better, which can cause cognitive dissonance. *See also* **Cognitive Dissonance**.

Usability Psychologist: A professional that studies how individuals utilize websites and how quickly they navigate through such technology.

Validity: How much an assessment tool actually measures what it has been diagnosed to measure.

Values in Action (VIA) Inventory of Strengths: A survey that was the first to assess an individual's major strengths, developed in 2001 by the VIA Institute on Character Strengths. It consists of six "virtue" categories and 24 specific strengths, which are Wisdom and Knowledge, Courage, Humanity, Justice, Temperance, and Transcendence.

Variable-Focused Resilience Model: A methodology of resilience that looks at the associations among individual characteristics, environmental factors, and life experiences to determine what facilitates a positive adjustment in the face of severe difficulties. *See also* **Person-Focused Resilience Model**.

References and Further Reading

BOOKS

Affleck, G., Tennen, H., & Apter, A. (2001). Optimism, Pessimism, and Daily Life with Chronic Illness. In E. C. Chang (Ed.), *Optimism and Pessimism: Implications for Theory, Research, and Practice*. Washington, DC: American Psychological Association.

Amabile, T. (1983). *The Social Psychology of Creativity*. New York: Springer-Verlag.

Amabile, T., & Carver, S. (2011). *The Progress Principle: Using Small Wins to Ignite Joy, Engagement, and Creativity at Work*. Boston, MA: Harvard Business Review Press.

Anchor, S. (2010). *The Happiness Advantage: The Seven Principles of Positive Psychology That Fuel Success and Performance at Work*. New York: Crown Business.

Baer, R. (2010). *Assessing Mindfulness and Acceptance Processes in Clients: Illuminating the Theory and Practice of Change*. Oakland, CA: New Harbinger Publications.

Batson, C. D. (2010). *Altruism in Humans*. Oxford: Oxford University Press.

Baum, F. (1900/1996). *The Wonderful Wizard of Oz*. New York: Dover Publication.

Benson, H. (1975/2000). *Herbert Benson*. New York: HarperTorch. Reprint edition.

Bowlby, J. (1982). *Attachment and Loss* (Vol. 1). New York: Basic Books (Originally published in 1969).

Bruner, J. (1986). *Actual Minds, Possible Worlds*. Cambridge, MA: Harvard University Press.

Bruner, J. (1991). The Narrative Construction of Reality. *Critical Inquiry*, 18.

Campbell, J. (2008/1949). *The Hero with a Thousand Faces* (*The Collected Works of Joseph Campbell*). Novato, CA: New World Library.

Carlson, N. R. (2012). *Physiology of Behavior* (11th ed.). Boston, MA: Allyn and Bacon.

Cohn, M. A. (2012). Rescuing Our Heroes: Positive Perspectives on Upward Comparisons in Relationships, Education and Work. In P. A. Linley & S. Joseph (Eds.), *Positive Psychology in Practice* (pp. 218–237). Hoboken, NJ: John Wiley & Sons.

Csikszentmihalyi, M. (1997). *Finding Flow: The Psychological of Engagement with Everyday Life*. New York: Basic Books.

DeVries, M. W. (Ed.). (1992). *The Experience of Psychopathology: Investigating Mental Disorders in Their Natural Settings*. Cambridge: Cambridge University Press.

Diener, E., & Diener, R. B. (2008). *Happiness: Unlocking the Mysteries of Psychological Wealth.* Malden, MA: Wiley-Blackwell.

Diener, R. E. (2011). *Positive Psychology as Social Change.* New York: Springer.

Dolan, P., & Kahneman, D. (2014). *Happiness by Design: Change What You Do, Not How You Think.* New York: Hudson Street Press.

Donaldson, S. I., & Bligh, M. C. (2006). Rewarding Careers Applying Positive Psychological Science to Improve Quality of Work Life and Organizational Effectiveness. In S. I. Donaldson, D. E. Berger, & K. Pezdek (Eds.), *Applied Psychology: New Frontiers and Rewarding Careers* (pp. 277–295). Mahwah, NJ: Lawrence Erlbaum Associates.

Dweck, C. (2006). *Mindset: The New Psychology of Success.* New York: Random House.

Emmons, R. A. (2013). *Gratitude Works! A 21-Day Program for Creating Emotional Prosperity* San Francisco, CA: Jossey-Bass.

Enright, R. (2012). *The Forgiving Life: A Pathway to Overcoming Resentment and Creating a Legacy of Love.* Washington, DC: American Psychological Association.

Festinger, L. (1957). *A Theory of Cognitive Dissonance.* Palo Alto, CA: Stanford University.

Finkelstein, S. (2004). *Why Smart Executives Fail: And What You Can Learn from Their Mistakes.* New York: Penguin.

Gottschall, J. (2012). *The Storytelling Animal: How Stories Make Us Human.* Boston: Houghton Mifflin.

Goulding, M. M., & Goulding, R. L. (1979). *Changing Lives through Redecision Therapy.* New York: Brunner/Mazel.

Graaf, J., & Wann, D. (2014). *Affluenza: How Overconsumption Is Killing Us and How to Fight Back.* San Francisco: Berrett-Koehler Publishers.

Gregory, E. (2012). Children Media Use: A Positive Psychology Approach. In K. E. Dill (Ed.), *Oxford Handbook of Media Psychology: Oxford Library of Psychology.* Oxford, UK: Oxford Press.

Hakansson, J. (2003). *Exploring the Phenomenon of Empathy.* PhD Dissertation, Stockholm University, Stockholm.

Hoffman, M. L. (2000). *Empathy and Moral Development*: *Implications for Caring and Justice.* New York: Cambridge University Press.

Kahneman, D. (2013). *Thinking, Fast and Slow* [Reprint edition]. New York: Farrar, Straus and Giroux.

Langer, E. (1989/2014). *Mindfulness.* Boston, MA: Da Capo Press. Reprint edition.

Lesser, G. S. (1975). *Children and Television: Lessons from Sesame Street.* New York: Random House.

Lieberman, M. D. (2013). *Social: Why Our Brains Are Wired to Connect.* New York: Crown Publishers.

Linley, P. A., & Joseph, S. (Eds.). (2004). *Positive Psychology in Practice.* Hoboken, NJ: John Wiley & Sons.

Maccoby, E. E., & Martin, J. A. (1983). Socialization in the Context of the Family: Parent-Child Interaction. In Paul H. Mussen (Ed.) *Handbook of Child Psychology: Formerly Carmichael's Manual of Child Psychology.* New York: John Wiley & Sons.

MacLean, Paul D. (1990). *The Triune Brain in Evolution.* New York: Plenum Press.

Martin, J. (2012). *The Jesuit Guide to (Almost) Everything: A Spirituality for Real Life.* New York: HarperCollins.

Masten, A., & Reed, M. G. (2005). Resilience in Development. In C. R. Snyder & S. J. Lopez (Eds.), *Handbook of Positive Psychology* (pp. 74–88). New York: Oxford University Press.

McAdams, D. P. (1993). *The Stories We Live By.* New York: Guilford Press.

Mischel, W. (2014). *The Marshmallow Test: Mastering Self-Control.* New York: Little, Brown and Company.

Mohammad, Saif M., & Turney, Peter D. (2010). Emotions Evoked by Common Words and Phrases: Using Mechanical Turk to Create an Emotion Lexicon. Proceedings of the NAACL HLT 2010 Workshop on Computational Approaches to Analysis and Generation of Emotion in Text.

Murphy, L. B. (1962). *The Widening World of Childhood: Paths toward Mastery*. New York: Basic Books.

Myers, D. G. (1992). *The Pursuit of Happiness*. New York: Avon Books.

Niemiec, R., & Wedding, D. (2013). *Positive Psychology at the Movies: Using Films to Build Virtues and Character Strengths*. Ashland, OH: Hogrefe & Huber Publishers.

Panksepp, J. (2011). The Primary Process Affects in Human Development, Happiness and Thriving. In K. M. Sheldon, T. B. Kashdan, & M. F. Steger (Eds.), *Designing Positive Psychology: Taking Stock and Moving Forward* (pp. 51–85). Oxford: Oxford University Press.

Peterson, C., & Seligman, M. (2004). *Character Strengths and Virtues: A Handbook and Classification*. New York: American Psychological Association and Oxford University Press.

Peterson, J. B. (1999). *Maps of Meaning: The Architecture of Belief*. London: Routledge.

Polkinghorne, D. E. (1988). *Narrative Knowing and the Human Sciences*. Albany, NY: State University of New York.

Putnam, R. (2001). *Bowling Alone: The Collapse and Revival of American Community*. New York: Touchstone Books (Simon and Schuster).

Rathunde, K. (1988). Optimal Experience and the Family Context. In I. S. Csikszentmihalyi & M. Csikszentmihalyi (Eds.), *Optimal Experience: Psychological Studies of Flow in Consciousness* (pp. 342–363). New York: Cambridge University Press.

Rogers, C. (1961). *On Becoming a Person*. New York: Houghton Mifflin.

Rowe, J. W., & Kahn, R. L. (1998). *Successful Aging: The Macarthur Foundation Study*. New York: Pantheon.

Sapolsky, R. (2004). *Why Zebras Don't Get Ulcers*. New York: Henry Holt & Company.

Sarbin, T. R. (Ed.). (1986). *Narrative Psychology: The Storied Nature of Human Conduct*. New York: Praeger.

Schor, J. B. (1998). *The Overspent American: Upscaling, Downshifting, and the New Consumer*. New York: Basic Books.

Schumpeter, J. A. (1951). *Essays: On Entrepreneurs, Innovations, Business Cycles, and the Evolution of Capitalism*. New Brunswick, NJ: Transaction Publishers.

Schwartz, B. (2005). *The Paradox of Choice: Why More Is Less*. New York: Harper Perennial.

Seligman, M. (2006). *Learned Optimism: How to Change Your Mind and Your Life*. New York: Vintage.

Seligman, M. E. P. (1991). *Learned Optimism: How to Change Your Mind and Your Life*. New York: A.A. Knopf.

Seligman, M. E. P. (2002). *Authentic Happiness*. New York: The Free Press.

Sheridan, S. M., & Burt, J. D. (2011). Family-Centered Positive Psychology. In C. R. Snyder & S. J. Lopez (Eds.), *Handbook of Positive Psychology* (pp. 551–559). Oxford, UK: Oxford University Press.

Snyder, C. R., & Lopez, S. J. (2007). *Positive Psychology: The Scientific and Practical Explorations of Human Strengths*. Thousand Oaks, CA: Sage Publications.

Stueber, K. (2014). Empathy. In E. N. Zalta (Ed.), *The Stanford Encyclopedia of Philosophy* (Winter 2014 ed.).

Tan, C., Goleman, D., & Kabat-Zinn, J. (2012). *Search Inside Yourself: The Unexpected Path to Achieving Success, Happiness and World Peace*. New York: HarperCollins Publishers.

Taylor, S. E. (1989). *Positive Illusions: Creative Self-Deception and the Healthy Mind*. New York: Basic Books.

Vicens-Ortiz, E. (n.d.). *Strength-Based Models of Counseling and Resiliency: Course Outline and Materials.* Miami, FL: University of Miami Behavioral Health.

Vygotsky, L. S. (1978). *Mind in Society.* Cambridge: Harvard University Press.

White, M., & Epston, D. (1990). *Narrative Means to Therapeutic Ends.* New York: W.W. Norton and Company.

Wilson, T. D. (2011). *Redirect: Changing the Stories We Live By.* New York: Back Bay Books/Little, Brown and Company.

Worthington, E. (2013). *Moving Forward: Six Steps to Forgiving Yourself and Breaking Free from the Past.* Colorado Springs, CO: WaterBrook Press.

Yalom, I. D. (1995). *The Theory and Practice of Group Psychotherapy* (4th ed.). New York: Basic Books.

Zimbardo, P. G., & Boyd, J. N. (2015). *Putting Time in Perspective: A Valid, Reliable Individual-Differences Metric Time Perspective Theory; Review, Research and Application* (pp. 17–55). London: Springer.

JOURNALS

Ainsworth, Mary D. S. (1979). Infant-Mother Attachment. *American Psychologist, 34,* 932–937.

Anderson, E. (Spring 2005). Strengths-Based Educating: A Concrete Way to Bring Out the Best in Students—And Yourself. *Educational Horizons, 83*(3), 180–189.

Bansal, S. (2012). Shopping for a Better World. *The New York Times,* May 9.

Barthes, R., & Duisit, L. (1975). An Introduction to the Structural Analysis of Narrative. *New Literary History: On Narrative and Narratives, 6*(2), 237–272.

Batson, C. D., Duncan, B. D., Ackerman, P., Buckley, T., & Birch, K. (1981). Is Empathic Emotion a Source of Altruistic Motivation? *Journal of Personal and Social Psychology, 40*(2), 290–302.

Baumeister, R. F., Campbell, J. D., Krueger, J. I., & Vohs, K. D. (2003). Does High Self-Esteem Cause Better Performance, Interpersonal Success, Happiness, or Healthier Lifestyles? *Psychological Science in the Public Interest, 4*(1), 1–44.

Baumrind, D. (1968). Authoritarian vs. Authoritative Parental Control. *Adolescence, 3*(11), 255–271.

Benedetti, F., Carlino, E., & Pollo, A. (2011). How Placebos Change the Patient's Brain. *Neuropsychopharmacology, 36*(1), 339–354.

Berridge, Kent C., & Kringelbach, Morten L. (2011). Building a Neuroscience of Pleasure and Well-Being. *Psychology of Well-Being, 1*(3), 1–26.

Berry, J., et al. (2001). Dispositional Forgivingness: Development and Construct Validity of the Transgression Narrative Test of Forgiveness (TNTF). *Personality and Social Psychology Bulletin, 27*(10), 1277–1290.

Block, J., & Kremen, A. M. (1996). IQ and Ego-Resiliency: Conceptual and Empirical Connections and Separateness. *Journal of Personality and Social Psychology, 70*(2), 349.

Blomqvist, K., & Posner, S. (Summer 2004). Three Strategies for Integrating CSR with Brand Marketing. *Market Leader,* 33–36.

Bonanno, G. A. (2004). Loss, Trauma, and Human Resilience: Have We Underestimated the Human Capacity to Thrive after Extremely Adverse Events? *American Psychologist, 59*(1), 20–28.

Brendtro, L. (2012). Risk, Resilience, and Recovery: Emmy Werner Interviewed by Larry Brendtro. *Reclaiming Children and Youth, 21*(1), 18–23.

Brickman, P., & Bulman, R. J. (1977). Pleasure and Pain in Social Comparison. *Social Comparison Processes: Theoretical and Empirical Perspectives, 149,* 186.

Brickman, P., Coates, D., & Janoff-Bulman, R. (1978). Lottery Winners and Accident Victims: Is Happiness Relative? *Journal of Personality and Social Psychology, 36*(8), 917.

Brown, K. W., Creswell, J. D., & Ryan, R. M. (2007). Mindfulness: Theoretical Foundations and Evidence for Its Salutary Effects. *Psychological Inquiry, 18*(4), 211–237.

Brownlee, K. R. E., & MacArthur, J. (2012). Implementation of a Strengths-Based Approach to Teaching in an Elementary School. *Journal of Teaching and Learning, 8*(1), 1–12.

Carson, S. H., & Langer, E. J. (2006). Mindfulness and Self-Acceptance. *Journal of Rational-Emotive & Cognitive-Behavior Therapy, 24*(1), 29–43.

Carver, C. S. (1997). You Want to Measure Coping but Your Protocol's Too Long: Consider the Brief Cope. *International Journal of Behavioral Medicine, 4*(1), 92–100.

Cohen, S., Kamarck, T., & Mermelstein, R. (1983). A Global Measure of Perceived Stress. *Journal of Health and Social Behavior*, 385–396.

Connor, K. M., & Davidson, J. R. (2003). Development of a New Resilience Scale: The Connor-Davidson Resilience Scale (CD-RISC). *Depression and Anxiety, 18*(2), 76–82.

Cotman, C. W., Berchtold, N. C., & Christie, L.-A. (2007). Exercise Builds Brain Health: Key Roles of Growth Factor Cascades and Inflammation. *Trends in Neurosciences, 30*(9), 464–472.

Csikszentmihalyi, M. (1989). Optimal Experience in Work and Leisure. *Journal of Personality and Social Psychology, 56*(5), 815–822.

Daly, B., & Suggs, S. (2010). Teachers' Experiences with Humane Education and Animals in the Elementary Classroom: Implications for Empathy Development. *Journal of Moral Education, 39*(1), 101–112.

Davidson, Richard J., & Lutz, Antoine. (2008). Buddha's Brain: Neuroplasticity and Meditation. *IEEE Signal Processing Magazine, 25*(1), 176.

Diener, E., Emmons, R. A., Larsen, R. J., & Griffin, S. (1985). The Satisfaction with Life Scale. *Journal of Personality Assessment, 49*, 71–75. Retrieved August 15, 2014, from APA PsychNet

Diener, E., Horwitz, J., & Emmons, R. A. (1985). Happiness of the Very Wealthy. *Social Indicators Research, 16*, 263–274.

Diener, E., Sandvik, E., Seidlitz, L., & Diener, M. (1993). The Relationship between Income and Subjective Well-Being: Relative or Absolute? *Social Indicators Research, 28*, 195–223.

Diener, E., Suh, E., Lucas, R. E., & Smith, H. L. (1999). Subjective Well-Being: Three Decades of Progress. *Psychological Bulletin, 125*(2), 276–302.

Duckworth, A. L., Peterson, C., Matthews, M. D., & Kelly, D. R. (2007). Grit: Perseverance and Passion for Long-Term Goals. *Journal of Personality and Social Psychology, 92*(6), 1087.

Eisenberg, N. (2000). Emotion, Regulation and Moral Development. *Annual Review of Psychology, 51*, 665–697.

Eisenberger, Naomi I., & Cole, Steve. (2012). Social Neuroscience and Health: Neurophysiological Mechanisms Linking Social Ties with Physical Health. *Nature Neuroscience, 15*(5), 1–6.

Emmons, R. A., & McCullough, M. E. (2003). Counting Blessings versus Burdens: An Experimental Investigation of Gratitude and Subjective Well-Being in Daily Life. *Journal of Personality and Social Psychology, 84*, 377–389. doi: 10.10 37/0022-3514.84.2.377

Fletcher, A. C., Steinberg, L., & Sellers, E. B. (1999). Adolescents' Well-Being as a Function of Perceived Interparental Consistency. *Journal of Marriage and the Family*, 599–610.

Fredrickson, B. L. (1998). What Good Are Positive Emotions. *Review of General Psychology, 2*(3), 300–319.

Fredrickson, B. L., & Losada, M. F. (2005). Positive Affect and the Complex Dynamics of Human Flourishing. *American Psychologist, 60*(7), 678–686.

Fredrickson, B. L., Mancuso, R. A., Branigan, C., & Tugade, M. M. (2004). The Undoing Effect of Positive Emotions. *Motivation and Emotion, 24* (4), 237–258.

Fredrickson, B. L., Tugade, M. M., Waugh, C. E., & Larkin, G. R. (2003). What Good Are Positive Emotions in Crisis? A Prospective Study of Resilience and Emotions Following the Terrorist Attacks on the United States on September 11, 2001. *Journal of Personality and Social Psychology, 84*(2), 365.

Gallagher, K., & Updegraff, J. (2012, February). Health Message Framing Effects on Attitudes, Intentions, and Behavior: A Meta-Analytic Review. *Annals of Behavioral Medicine, 43*(1), 101–116.

Gardner, F. L., & Moore, Z. E. (2012). Mindfulness and Acceptance Models in Sport Psychology: A Decade of Basic and Applied Scientific Advancements. *Canadian Psychology/Psychologie Canadienne, 53*(4), 309–318.

Gooding, A., & Gardner, F. L. (2009). An Investigation of the Relationship between Mindfulness, Preshot Routine, and Basketball Free Throw Percentage. *Journal of Clinical Sports Psychology, 4*, 303–319.

Granovetter, M. (1973). The Strength of Weak Ties. *American Journal of Sociology, 78*(6), 1360–1380.

Greengross, Gil, & Miller, Geoffrey. (2011). Humor Ability Reveals Intelligence, Predicts Mating Success, and Is Higher In Males. *Intelligence, 39*(4), 188–192.

Helgeson, V. S., Reynolds, K. A., & Tomich, P. L. (2006). A Meta-Analytic Review of Benefit Finding and Growth. *Journal of Consulting and Clinical Psychology, 74*(5), 797–816.

Helland, M. W. B. (2005). Towards a Deeper Understanding of Hope and Leadership. *Journal of Leadership and Organizational Studies, 12*(2), 42–52.

Hölzel, Britta K., Lazar, Sara W., Gard, Tim, Schuman-Olivier, Zev, Vago, David R., & Ott, Ulrich. (2011). How Does Mindfulness Meditation Work? Proposing Mechanisms of Action from a Conceptual and Neural Perspective. *Perspectives on Psychological Science, 6*(6), 537–559.

Iacoboni, M., & Lenzi, G. L. (2002). Mirror Neurons, the Insula, and Empathy. *Behavioral and Brain Sciences, 25*(01), 39–40. doi: 10.1017/S0140525X02420018

Jackson, S. (2012). Flow: The Mindful Edge in Sport and Performing Arts. *Australian Psychological Society*. Retrieved January 2, 2015, from http://www.psychology.org.au/

Janoff-Bulman, R. (1989). Assumptive Worlds and the Stress of Traumatic Events: Applications of the Schema Construct. *Social Cognition, 7*(2), 113–136.

Kabat-Zinn, J. (2003). Mindfulness-Based Interventions in Context: Past, Present, and Future. *Clinical Psychology Science and Practice, 10*(2), 144–156.

Key-Roberts, M. (March–April 2014). Strengths-Based Leadership Theory and Development of Subordinate Leaders. *Military Review, 94*(2), 4–13.

Kirchler, E. (1988). Marital Happiness and Interaction in Everyday Surroundings: A Time-Sample Diary Approach for Couples. *Journal of Social and Personal Relationship, 5*, 375–382.

Kubey, R., Larson, R., & Csikszentmihalyi, M. (1996). Experience Sampling Method Applications to Communication Research Questions. *Journal of Communication, 46*(2), 99–120.

Lawler-Row, K. A., & Piferi, R. L. (2006). The Forgiving Personality: Describing a Life Well Lived? *Personality and Individual Differences, 41*(6), 1009–1020.

Lemay, R., & Ghazal, H. (2001). Resilience and Positive Psychology: Finding Hope. *Child & Family, 5*(1), 10–21.

Lockwood, N. R. (2006). Talent Management: Driver for Organizational Success. *Society for Human Resources Research Quarterly, 51*(6), 1–11.

Lopez, S., & Louis, M. (2009). The Principles of Strengths-Based Education. *Journal of College and Character, 10*(4), 1–8.

Lykken, D., & Tellegen, A. (1996). Happiness Is a Stochastic Phenomenon. *Psychological Science, 7*(3), 186–189.

Lyubomirsky, S., Sousa, L., & Dickerhoof, R. (2006). The Costs and Benefits of Writing, Talking, and Thinking about Life's Triumphs and Defeats. *Journal of Personality and Social Psychology, 90*, 692–708.

Masten, A. (2001). Ordinary Magic: Resilience Processes in Development. *American Psychologist, 56*(3), 227–238.

Masten, A.S., & Obradović, J. (2006). Competence and Resilience in Development. *Annals of the New York Academy of Sciences, 1094*(1), 13–27.

Masten, A. S., Hubbard, J. J., Gest, S. D., Tellegen, A., Garmezy, N., & Ramirez, M. (1999). Competence in the Context of Adversity: Pathways to Resilience and Maladaptation from Childhood to Late Adolescence. *Development and Psychopathology, 11*(1), 143–169.

Murphy, P. J., & Hevey, D. (2013). The Relationship between Internalised HIV-Related Stigma and Posttraumatic Growth. *AIDS and Behavior, 17*(5), 1809–1818.

Myers, D.G., & Diener, E. (1995). Who Is happy? *Psychological Science, 6*, 10–19.

Narvaez, D. (2008). Triune Ethics: The Neurobiological Roots of Our Multiple Moralities. *New Ideas in Psychology, 26*(1), 95–119.

Parr, G. D., Montgomery, M., & DeBell, C. (1998). Flow Theory as a Model for Enhancing Student Resilience. *Professional School Counseling, 1*(5), 26–31.

Pennebaker, J. W., & Seagal, J. D. (1999). Forming a Story: The Health Benefits of Narrative. *Journal of Clinical Psychology, 55*(10), 1243–1254.

Puri, M., & Robinson, D. T. (2007). Optimism and Economic Choice. *Journal of Financial Economics, 86*(1), 71–99.

Rimé, B., Mesquita, B., Boca, S., & Philippot, P. (1991). Beyond the Emotional Event: Six Studies on the Social Sharing of Emotion. *Cognition & Emotion, 5*(5–6), 435–465.

Rizzo, A. A., & Buckwalter, J. G. (1997). Virtual Reality and Cognitive Assessment. *Virtual Reality in Neuro-Psycho-Physiology: Cognitive, Clinical and Methodological Issues in Assessment and Rehabilitation, 44*, 123.

Ryff, C. D., & Keyes, C. L. M. (1995). The Structure of Psychological Well-Being Revisited. *Journal of Personality and Social Psychology, 69*(4), 719.

Sanders, M. (1999). Triple P-Positive Parenting Program: Towards an Empirically Validated Multilevel Parenting and Family Support Strategy for the Prevention of Behavior and Emotional Problems in Children. *Clinical Child and Family Psychology Review, 2*(2), 71–90.

Scheier, M. F., Carver, C. S., & Bridges, M. W. (1994). Distinguishing Optimism from Neuroticism (and Trait Anxiety, Self-Mastery, and Self-Esteem): A Reevaluation of the Life Orientation Test. *Journal of Personality and Social Psychology, 67*(6), 1063–1078.

Schore, A. N. (2001). Effects of a Secure Attachment Relationship on Right Brain Development, Affect Regulation, and Infant Mental Health. *Infant Mental Health Journal, 22*(1–2), 7–66.

Schwarz, J. E., & Stone, A. (1998). Data Analysis for EMA Studies. *Health Psychology, 17*, 6–16.

Seligman, M.E.P., & Csikszentmihalyi, M. (2000). Positive Psychology: An Introduction. *American Psychologist, 55*(1), 5–14.

Sheldon, K.M., & King, L. (2001). Why Positive Psychology Is Necessary. *American Psychologist, 56*(3), 216–217.

Shernoff, D., et al. (2003). Student Engagement in High School Classrooms from the Perspective of Flow Theory. *School Psychology Quarterly, 18*(2), 158–176.

Shifren, K. (1996). Individual Differences in the Perception of Optimism and Disease Severity: A Study among Individuals with Parkinson's Disease. *Journal of Behavioral Medicine, 19*, 241–271.

Sinfield, J.M., Gustafson, T., & Hindo, B. (Winter 2014). The Discipline of Creativity. *MIT Sloan Management Review*, 24–26.

Small, Gary W., Moody, Teena D., Siddarth, Prabha, & Bookheimer, Susan Y. (2009). Your Brain on Google: Patterns of Cerebral Activation during Internet Searching. *The American Journal of Geriatric Psychiatry, 17*(2), 116–126.

Smith, B., et al. (2008). The Brief Resilience Scale: Assessing the Ability to Bounce Back. *International Journal of Behavioral Medicine, 15*, 194–200. doi: 10.1080/1070 5500802222972

Taylor, S. E., & Friedman, H. (2007). Social Support. *Foundations of Health Psychology*, 145–171.

Tedeschi, R. G., & Calhoun, L. G. (2004). Posttraumatic Growth: Conceptual Foundations and Empirical Evidence. *Psychological Inquiry, 15*(1), 1–18.

Tedeschi, R.G., & McNally, R.J. (2011). Can We Facilitate Post-Traumatic Growth in Combat Veterans? *American Psychologist, 66*(1), 19.

Tomyn, A. J., & Cummins, R. A. (2011). The Subjective Wellbeing of High-School Students: Validating the Personal Wellbeing Index—School Children. *Social Indicators Research, 101*(3), 405–418.

Van Vugt, M., & Iredale, W. (2013). Men Behaving Nicely: Public Goods as Peacock Tails. *British Journal of Psychology, 104*(1), 3–13.

Windle, G., Bennett, K. M., & Noyes, J. (2011). A Methodological Review of Resilience Measurement Scales. *Health and Quality of Life Outcomes, 9*(1), 1.

Worthington, E. L., Jr., Witvliet, C. V. O., Pietrini, P., & Miller, A. J. (2007). Forgiveness, Health, and Well-Being: A Review of Evidence for Emotional Versus Decisional Forgiveness, Dispositional Forgivingness, and Reduced Unforgiveness. *Journal of Behavioral Medicine, 30*(4), 291–302.

BLOGS AND POPULAR PRESS

Aiken, K. (April 2010). Superhero History: Using Comic Books to Teach U.S. History. *OAH Magazine of History, 24*(2), 41–46.

Andersen, E. (2013, November 27). How Feeling Grateful Can Make You More Successful. *Forbes.com*. Retrieved August 28, 2014, from http://www.forbes.com/sits/erikaandersen/2013/11/27/how-feeling-grateful-can-make-you-more-successful/

Barlow, T. (2011, May 26). Measuring the Good Life. *Forbes.com*. Retrieved August 11, 2014, from http://www.forbes.com/sites/tombarlow/2011/05/26/measuring-the-good-life/

Biali, S. (2013, October 23). 10 Secrets to Living a Vibrantly Happy, Healthy Life. *PsychologyToday.com*. Retrieved April 9, 2015, from http://www.psychologytoday.com/blog/prescriptions-life/201310/10-secrets-living-vibranly-happy-healthy-life

Bicknell, J. (June 2014). Why Music Moves Us. *PsychologyToday.com.* Retrieved January 2, 2015, from http://www.psychologytoday/com/blog/why-music-moves-us/201406/flow-states-among-pianists

Brantley, K. (2014, November 6). TV vs. Hobbies: Who Wins the "Flow" Challenge? *Intercollegiate Review.* Retrieved January 4, 2015, from http://www.intercollegiatereview/com/idex.php/2014/11/06/tv-vs-hobbies-who-wins-the-flow-challenge/

Carrick, R. (2013, April 19). The Music of "Flow". *NYTimes.com.* Retrieved January 2, 2015, from http://opinionator.blogs.nytimes.com/2013/04/19/the-music-of-flow/

Cherry, K. (n.d.). What Is Flow? *PsychologyToday.com.* Retrieved December 29, 2014, from http://psychology.about.com/od/positivepsychology/a/flow.htm

Cohen, A. (2004, October 1). Research on the Science of Forgiveness: An Annotated Bibliography. *Greater Good.* Retrieved August 29, 2014, from http://greatergood.berkeley.edu/article/the_science_of_forgiveness_an_annotated_bibliography

Coplan, J. H. (2009, February 12). How Positive Psychology Can Boost Your Business. *Bloomberg Businessweek.* Retrieved January 1, 2015, from http://www.businessweek.com/printer/articles/222826-how-positive-psychology-can-boost-your-business/

Dean, J. (2009). The Longevity Expedition: Dan Buettner's Search for the Fountain of Youth. *NationalGeographic.com.* Retrieved August 11, 2014, from http://adventure.nationalgeographic.com/print/2009/06/live-longer-dan-buettner-text

Edberg, H. (2013, September 29). Mark Twain's Top 9 Tips for Living a Good Life. *Daily Good.* Retrieved April 9, 2015, from http://www.dailygood.org/story/533/mark-twain-s-top-9-tips-for-living-a-good-life-henrik-edberg

Ellison, K. (2006, September 1). Mastering Your Own Mind. *PsychologyToday.com.* Retrieved January 3, 2015, from http://www.psychologytoday.com/articles/200608/mastering-your-own-mind

Friedman, R. (2014, December 9). Work-Life Balance Is Dead. *CNN.com.* Retrieved December 10, 2014, from http://www.cnn.com/2014/12/09/opinion/friedman-work-life-balance/index.html

Friedman, S. (September 2014). Work + Home + Community + Self. *Harvard Business Review.* Retrieved October 21, 2015, from https://hbr.org/2014/09/work-home-community-self

Goldberg, N. (2005). Measuring the Impact of Microfinance: Taking Stock of What We Know. *Grameen Foundation USA,* Retrieved from http://www.grameenfoundation.org/sites/default/files/resources/Measuring-Impact-of-Microfinance_Nathanael_Goldberg.pdf

Greenberg, M. (2012, February 22). The Mindful Self-Express. *PsychologyToday.com.* Retrieved January 3, 2015, from http://www.psychologytoday.com/blog/the-mindful-self-express/201202/nine-essential-qualities-mindfulness/

Haden, J. (n.d.). 10 Scientifically Proven Ways to Be Incredibly Happy. *Inc.com.* Retrieved April 9, 2015, from http://www.inc.com/jeff-haden/10-scientifically-proven-ways-to-be-incredibly-happy-wed.html

Haupt, A. (2012). How to Forgive, and Why You Should. *US News & World Report,* Retrieved August 29, from http://health.usnews.com/health-news/articles/2012/08/29/how-to-forgive-and-why-you-should

Holmes, S. (2014, October 13). Could Americans Be Happy? *CNN.com.* Retrieved June 3, 2015, from http://www.cnn.com/2014/10/13/politics/americans-optimistic-in-poll/index.html

Johnson, M. W. (2011, September 1). What's Your Joy Trigger? *HuffPost.com*. Retrieved July 6, 2015, from http://www.huffingtonpost.com/margaret-wheeler-johnson/joy-trigger-little-things- happiness_b_944661.html

Johnstone, C. (2013, October 14). Good News for Improving Your Relationships. *Positive News*. Retrieved April 9, 2015, from http://positivenews.org.uk/2013/blogs/positive-psychology-blogs/14002/good-news-improving-relationships/

Kotler, S. (2014, February 25). The Playing Field—Sport and Culture through the Lens of Science. *PsychologyToday.com*. Retrieved January 2, 2015, from http://www.psychologytoday.com/blog/the-playing-field/201402/flow-states-and-creativity

LeBlanc, G. (2012, October 12). Happy People: Joyful Things They Do. *The Oprah Magazine*. Retrieved March 3, 2015, from http://www.oprah.com/app/o-magazine.html

Linkner, J. (2013, August 27). 7 Habits of Highly Successful Startup Leaders. *Forbes.com*. Retrieved December 9, 2014, from http://www.forbes.com/sites/ekaterinawalter/2013/08/27/7-habits-of-highly-successful-startup-leaders/

Lipton, D. (2013). Olds & Milner, 1954: "Reward Centers" in the Brain and Lessons for Modern Neuroscience. *NeuroBlog*. Retrieved August 28, 2014, from http://www.neuwritewest.org/blog/3733

Marr, A. J. (n.d.). Commentary: In the Zone: A Biobehavioral Theory of the Flow Experience. *Athletic Insight*. Retrieved December 29, 2014, from http://www.athleticinsight.com/vol3lss1/commentary.htm

Martin, D. (2006). The Truth About Happiness May Surprise You. *CNN.COM*. Retrieved August 17, 2014, from http://www.cnn.com/2006/HEALTH/conditions/11/10/happiness.overview/index.html?iref=allsearch

Martin, M. (2016, February 21). Gross National Happiness: Bhutan's Unique Measurement. *National Public Radio*.

McConnell, A. (2011, July 11). Friends with Benefits: Pets Make Us Happier, Healthier. *PsychologyToday.com*. Retrieved April 9, 2015, from http://www.psychologytoday.com/blog/the-social-self/201107/friends-benefits-pets-make-us-happier-healthier

McGowan, K. (April 2014). The Second Coming of Sigmund Freud. *Discover Magazine*, 54–61.

Millar, B. (2013, April 24). Essential Tools of Talent Management. *Forbes.com*. Retrieved May 27, 2015, from http://www.forbes.com/sites/forbesinsights/2013/04/24/essential- tools-of-talent-management

Miller, C. (2015, April 7). Silicon Valley: Perks for Some Workers, Struggles for Parents. *nytimes.com*. Retrieved April 9, 2015, from http://www.nytimes.com/2015/04/08/upshot/silicon-valley-perks-for-some-workers-struggles-for-parents.html

Miller, W. C., & Miller, D. R. (2008). Spirituality: The Emerging Context for Business Leadership. *Global Dharma Center*. Retrieved April 24, 2016, from http://www.globaldharma.org

Moran, G. (2014). 6 Habits of Resilient People. *FastCompany.com*. Retrieved October 5, 2015, from http://www.fastcompany.com/3024368/6-habits-of-resilient-people

Mourdoukoutas, P. (2012, January 14). The Ten Golden Rules on Living the Good Life. *Forbes.com*. Retrieved April 9, 2015, from http://www.forbes.com/sites/panosmourdoukoutas/2012/01/14/the-ten-golden-rules-on-living-the-good-life/

Niemiec, R. (2013, June 11). What Matters Most? *PsychologyToday.com*. Retrieved January 2, 2015, from http://www.psychologytoday.com/blog/what-matters-most/201306/when-mindfulness-trumps-flow

Niemiec, R. (2013, August 5). 5 Lesser Known Tips for a Positive Relationship. *Psychology Today.com*. Retrieved April 9, 2015, from http://www.psychologytoday.com/blog/what-matters-most/201308/5-lesser-known-tips-positive-relationship

Nobel Committee. (2006). The Nobel Peace Prize for 2006. Retrieved January 8, 2016, from http://www.nobelprize.org/nobel_prizes/peace/laureates/2006/press.html

Noren, R. (2013, September 24). Music Maker: The Benefits of Keeping the Beats. *Psychology Today.com*. Retrieved September 26, 2013, from www.psychologytoday.com/blog/music-maker/201309/listen-bach-listen-life

Nye, Jr., J.S. (2006, February 23). Think Again: Soft Power. *Foreign Policy.* Retrieved July 10, 2015, from http://www.foreignpolicy.com/2006/02/23/think-again/soft-power/

Peterson, C. (2009, December 21). The Future of Positive Psychology: Science and Practice. *PsychologyToday.com*. Retrieved April 9, 2015, from http://www.psychologytoday.com/blog/the-good-life/200912/the-future-of-positive-psychology-science-and-pracitce/

Pierleoni, A. (2013, February 18). Do Self-Help Books Work? *Suntimes.com*. Retrieved August 16, 2014, from http://www.suntimes.com/lifestyles/mindbody/18103724-423/do-self-help-books-work.html

Popova, M. (2013, March 26). Victor Frankl on the Human Search for Meaning. Retrieved July 7, 2015, from www.brainpkcings.org/2013/03/26/vicktor-frankl-mans-search-for-meaning/

Prive, T. (2012, December 19). Top 10 Qualities That Make a Great Leader. *Forbes.com*. Retrieved December 10, 2014, from http://www.forbes.com/sites/tanyaprive/2012/12/19/top-10-qualities-that-make-a-great-leader/

Prouix, E. (2013, August 7). Three Insights from the Frontiers of Positive Psychology. *Greater Good.* Retrieved April 9, 2015, from http://greatergood.berkeley.edu/article/item/three_insights_from_the_frontiers_of_positive_psychology

Rath, T., & Conchie, B., reviewed by Gladis, S. (2008). *Strengths-Based Leadership.* New York: Gallup Press.

Riffkin, R. (2014, February 27). U.S. Obesity Rate Ticks Up to 27.1% in 2013. *Gallup Poll.* Retrieved June 17, 2015, from http://www.gallup.com/poll/167651/obesity-rate-ticks-2013/

Rossum, M.V. (2012, August 30). How to Be Truly Happy. *HuffPost.com*. Retrieved July 6, 2015, from http://www.huffingtonpost.com/melissa-van-rossum/how-to-be-truly-happy_b_1840581.html

Rubin, G. (2008). Happiness Interview with Ed Diener and Robert Biswas-Diener. *The Happiness Project.* Retrieved August 17, 2014, from http://www.gretchenrubin.com/happiness_project/2008/09/happiness-int-1-3/

Russo, F. (2013, August 16). The Key to Happy Relationships? It's Not All about Communication. *TIME.com*. Retrieved April 9, 2015, from http://healthland.time.com/2013/08/16/the-key-to-happy-relationships-its-not-all-about-communication/

Schneider, K. (2010). Toward a Humanistic Positive Psychology: Why Can't We Just Get Along? *PsychologyToday.com*. Retrieved April 9, 2015, from http://www.psychologytoday.com/blog/awakening-awe/201011/toward-humanistic-positive-psychology-why-cant-we-just-get-along

Sederer, L.I. (2014, April 21). The Future of Mental Health Care. *HuffPost.com*. Retrieved July 3, 2015, from http://www.huffingtonpost.com

Segal, G.Z. (2015). Anderson Cooper: Why "No Plan B" Is the Only Plan. In *Getting There: A Book of Mentors.* Retrieved October 21, 2015, from http://www.fastcompany.com/3046338/my-creative-life/anderson-cooper-why-no-plan-b-is-the-only-plan

Shay, J. (2000). Aristotle's *Rhetoric* as a Handbook of Leadership. Retrieved December 10, 2014, from http://www.dnipogo.org/fcs/aristotle.htm

Snowdon, G. (2010, February 12). What to Do with a Degree in Psychology. *The Guardian* Retrieved July 3, 2015, from http://www.theguardian.com/money/2010/feb/13/degree-in-pyschology-job-options

Stone, J. (2014, February 9). 5 Steps to a Clearer Mind. *PsychologyToday.com*. Retrieved January 3, 2015, from http://www.psychologytoday.com/blog/clear-organized-and-motivated/201402/5-steps-clearer-mind

Strawson, G. (2011). Thinking, Fast and Slow by Daniel Kahneman—Review. *The Guardian*. Retrieved August 18, 2014, from http://www.theguardian.com/books/2011/dec/13/thinking-fast-slow-daniel-kahneman

Thompson, D. (2013). How Did Work-Life Balance in the U.S. Get So Awful? *TheAtlantic.com*. Retrieved April 9, 2015, from http://www.theatlantic.com/business/print/2013/06/how-did-work-life-balance-in-the-us-get-so-awful/276336

Trulia. (2013, October 24). 1 in 2 Americans Don't Know Neighbors' Names. *Forbes.com*. Retrieved June 24, 2015, from http://www.forbes.com/sites/trulia/2013/10/24/neighbor-survey/

Valeo, T. (n.d.). Choosing to Be Happy—Strategies for Happiness: 7 Steps to Becoming a Happier Person. *webmd.com*. Retrieved April 9, 2015, from http://www.webmd.com/balance/guide/choosing-to-be-happy/

Vanderkam, L. (2015, March 6). Gone Is the Notion of Balance. Increasingly, Professionals Are Comfortable Blurring the Line between Work and Home. *Fortune.com*. Retrieved April 9, 2015, from http://fortune.com/2015/03/06/work-life-integration

Walter, E. (2013, August 27). Four Essentials of Strength-Based Leadership. *Forbes.com*. Retrieved December 9, 2014, from http://www.forbes.com/sites/ekaterinawalter/2013/08/27/four-essentials-of-strength-based-leadership/

Weissmann, J. (2014, September 11). Americans, Ever Hateful of Leisure, Are More Likely to Work Nights and Weekends. *Moneybox*. Retrieved April 24, 2016, from http://www.slate.com/blogs/moneybox/2014/09/11/u_s_work_life_balance_americans_are_more_likely_to_work_nights_and_weekends.html

Williamson, M., & King, V. (2014, November 3). Ten Easy Steps to Happier Living. *TheGuardian.com*. Retrieved April 9, 2015, from http://www.theguardian.com/lifeandstyle/2014/nov/03/ten-easy-steps-that-will-make-you-a-happier-person

Wilner, J. (2011). Do You Have a Positive Social Support System? *PsychCentral Blogs*. Retrieved April 9, 2015, from http://blogs.psychcentral.com/positive-psychology/2011/06/do-you-have-a-positive-social-support-system/

Winfrey, G. (2013, December 18). The Mistake That Turned Warby Parker into an Overnight Legend. *Inc.com*. Retrieved April 9, 2015, from http://www.inc.com/magazine/201505/graham-winfrey/neil-blumenthal-icons-of-entrepreneurship.html

Winfrey, O. (2013, May 31). Winfrey's Commencement Address. *Harvard Gazette*. Retrieved January 21, 2015, from http://news.harvard.edu/gazette/story/2013/05/winfreys commencement-address/

Witters, D. US Obesity Rate Climbs to Record Height in 2015. Retrieved November 1, 2015 from http://www.gallup.com/poll/189182/obesity-rate-climbs-record-high-2015.aspx

Ying, H. K., & John Wang, C. K. (2008). Relationships between Mindfulness, Flow Dispositions and Mental Skills Adoption: A Cluster Analytic Approach. *Psychology of Sport and Exercise, 9*, 393–411. doi: 10.1016/j.psychsport.2007.07.001

Zimmerman, E. (2007, December 2). Hobbies Are Rich in Psychic Rewards. *The New York Times*. Retrieved January 4, 2015, from http://www.nytimes.com/2007/12/02/jobs/02career.html

WEB RESOURCES

Affluenza Viewer's Guide. (1997, September 15). *pbs.org*. Retrieved September 11, 2015, from http://www.pbs.org/kcts/affluenza/treat/vguide/vguide.html

Headington Institute. Heading Institute Resilience Scale (HIRI). http://www.headington-institute.org

Heider, F., & Simmel, M. (1994). Experimental Study of Apparent Behavior. Retrieved August 12, 2015, from https://www.youtube.com/watch?v=n9TWwG4SFWQ

Kaiser Family Foundation. (2010). Daily Media Use among Children and Teens Up Dramatically from Five Years Ago. Retrieved from www.kff.org

Learned Optimism Test. (2015). *Stanford.edu*. Retrieved November 10, 2015, from http://www.stanford.edu/class/msande271/onlinetools/LearnedOpt.html

Manobi Development Foundation. http://www.manobi.sn/sites/foundation/website/

Population Media Center. http://www.populationmedia.org

Scheier and Carver Index. Life Orientation Test (LOT-R). Retrieved from http://www.psy.miami.edu/faculty/ccarver/sclLOT-R.html

Seibert, A. (n.d.). Resiliency Quiz—How Resilient Are You? Retrieved from http://resiliencyquiz.com/index.shtml

StoryCenter (Center for Digital Storytelling). http://www.storycenter.org

University of Pennsylvania. Authentic Happiness Questionnaire Center. https://www.authentichappiness.sas.upenn.edu/testcenter

University of Southern California. Stress Resilience in Virtual Environments Program (STRIVE). Retrieved from http://ict.usc.edu/prototypes/strive/

RECOMMENDATIONS FOR FURTHER READING

Ben-Shahar, T. (2007). *Happier: Learn the Secrets to Daily Joy and Lasting Fulfillment*. New York: McGraw-Hill.

Fowler, J., & Christakis, N. (2009). *Connected: The Surprising Power of Our Social Networks and How They Shape Our Lives—How Your Friends' Friends' Friends Affect Everything You Feel, Think, and Do*. New York: Little, Brown and Company.

Frankl, V. (2006). *Man's Search for Meaning*. Boston, MA: Beacon Press.

Gardner, H. (2006). *Multiple Intelligences: New Horizons in Theory and Practice*. New York: Basic Books.

Gardner, H. (2011). *Frames of Mind: The Theory of Multiple Intelligences*. New York: Basic Books.

Gilbert, D. (2007). *Stumbling on Happiness*. Visalia, CA: Vintage Press.

Goleman, D. (2013). *Primal Leadership: Unleashing the Power of Emotional Intelligence*. Cambridge, MA: Harvard Business Publishing.

Hanson, R. (2009). *Buddha's Brain: The Practical Neuroscience of Happiness, Love, and Wisdom*. Oakland, CA: New Harbinger Publications.

Hanson, R. (2013). *Hardwiring Happiness: The New Brain Science of Contentment, Calm, and Confidence*. Easton, PA: Harmony Press.

Lieberman, M. D. (2013). *Social: Why Our Brains Are Wired to Connect*. New York: Crown Publishers.

Lyubomirsky, S. (2007). *The How of Happiness: A New Approach to Getting the Life You Want*. New York: Penguin Books.

Oatley, K., Keltner, D., & Jenkins, J. M. (2013). *Understanding Emotions* (3rd ed.). Hoboken, NJ: Wiley.

Rubin, G. (2013). *The Happiness Project: Or, Why I Spent a Year Trying to Sing in the Morning, Clean My Closets, Fight Right, Read Aristotle, and Generally Have More Fun.* Harper Paperbacks.

Sapolsky, R. (2004). *Why Zebras Don't Get Ulcers.* New York: Henry Holt & Company.

Seligman, M. E. P. (2012). *Flourish: A Visionary New Understanding of Happiness and Well-Being.* New York: Atria Books.

Index

Adaptation, 8, 32; evolution, 231; happiness, 21; resilience, 71–73, 75, 94

Archetype: defined, 42; figures by Campbell, 43–44; figures by Jung, 42–43; in stories, 273–74; superheroes, 44, 45, 46, 47–48

Attachment: defined, 136; different types of bonds, 36; neurobiology, 137; social support, 137

Automotive industry and positive psychology, 36–37

Bandura, Albert: model of self-efficacy, 4, 5, 9, 83; sense of control, 54; social learning theory, 146

Baumrind, Diana: dimensions of parenting, 188

Belief systems, 246–47; as cornerstone, 7

Biswas-Diener, Robert, 18

Bowling Alone, 217, 220

Brain: ATP, 127; benefits of exercise, 141–42; brain training, 135; flow, 58–59; history of, 126; hobbies, 61; humor, 93; imaging, 126–27; mindfulness, 104–6, 108; structures, 127–28; the Triune Brain Model, 130–31; Triune Ethics Theory and morality, 152–53. *See also* Structures of the brain

Broaden and build theory of emotions, 98

Bronfenbrenner, Urie, 182–83. *See also* Ecological Systems Theory

Campbell, Joseph, 5, 39; *Hero with a Thousand Faces*, 41–42; journey of the hero, 73, 159

Careers in positive psychology, 230, 233; corporate programs, 208; entertainment, 206, 234; marketing/PR, 206; public health, 232; talent management, 237, 240; user experience/design, 206, 207–8

Chief Happiness Officer, 218–19

Clifton, Donald O.: strength-based psychology themes, 25; StrengthsFinder, 28, 40

Cognitive processing: attachment, 136–37; emotion versus affect, 132–33; empathy, 139–40; "fear of missing out", 203, 207; fMRI imaging, 112, 135, 138, 140, 225; forgiveness, 140–41; humor, 140; inclusion, 138; multitasking, 145, 146, 147, 149; pleasure/reward, 138–39, 142, 145; sharing ideas, 138, 149; social exclusion, 138; social intelligence, 137–38; the Social Learning Theory, 146

Cognitive resilience: benefit-finding, 87; cognitive flexibility, 143, 144; cognitive reappraisal, 86–87, 144, 145; coping styles, 86, 90; hardiness, 87–88; perseverance, 88; reframing, 113; self-enhancement, 88, 90. *See also* Self-efficacy

Community Mental Health Act, 244

Conscious capitalism, 195

Coping strategies: aging, 16; humor, 154–55; of optimists, 15; repressive coping, 90; resiliency, 170; stress, 222

Corporate social responsibility, 193–94, 198–99

Courage: as a cornerstone for positive psychology, 9–12; in the VIA Inventory of Strengths, 27, 226

Creativity: flow, 55, 60; hobbies, 60–61; promotion of, 62–63; in VIA Inventory of Strengths, 27, 226

Csikszentmihalyi, Mihaly: biography of, 66; employment, 238; flow, 49–50, 52, 59, 60–61; media consumption, 175; Seligman, 2; using Experience Sampling Method, 66

Diener, Ed, 13; affect, 133

Ecological systems theory, 182; subsystems, 183. *See also* Bronfenbrenner, Urie

Education: flow, 54–55; online learning, 55, 58; strengths-based, 38–39

Eisenberg, Nancy, 122

Emmons, Robert, 118; goals, 121; gratitude, 119–20

Emotional resilience, 90–92; emotional regulation, 92–93; humor, 93–94; optimism, 92

Empathy, 120, 121; acceptance, 122; fMRI, 140; genetics of, 150–51; humor, 140; mindfulness, 123; a study about, 122. *See also* Mindfulness

ESM (Experience Sampling Method): adolescents, 21–22; applications of, 56–57; definition of, 56; measuring happiness in teenagers with technology, 27; as a research tool, 107–10; self-reporting, 64; to study ongoing behavior, 109–10

Family: attachment theory, 187–88; child-caregiver relationship, 136; childhood attachment, 143; parenting styles, 188–89; as a protective factor, 79

Flow: athletes, 60; conditions for flow, 50; creativity, 62–63; in daily life, 67–68; definition, 49; education, 54–55; hobbies, 60–62; individual development in counseling, 51–52; magnetic resonance imaging, 58–59; meditation, 59; mindfulness, 63, 67; musicians, 59–60; neurotransmitters, 96; reasons to engage in flow, 54; stress reduction activities, 213. *See also* Meditation

fMRI: empathy, 140; meditation, 135; positive images, 225; social exclusion, 207. *See also* Cognitive processing; Empathy; Flow; Positive emotions

Forgiveness: age, 116; physical health, 117–18; reduction of negative emotions, 117; research interest, 116; types of forgiveness, 116

Fredrickson, Barbara: action tendencies, 108; broaden-and-build theory of emotion, 98; defining emotion, 133; humor, 93; negative emotion, 167; positive emotion, 143; resilience, 90, 91

Goals: defined, 41; flow, 50, 51, 66, 67; goal setting, 4; hope, 4; intrinsic versus extrinsic, 4–5; the Life Orientation Test, 14; perseverance, 88; personal storytelling, 169; self-efficacy, 83. *See also* Emmons, Robert

Gratitude, 118; benefit-finding, 87; happiness, 121; at home practice, 106; its impact, 120; importance of, 114; in VIA Inventory of Strengths, 27, 227. *See also* Emmons, Robert; Life strategy

Happiness, 148, 241; its activities, 210–11; central qualities of, 13; community, 354; as cornerstone of positive psychology, 20–21; ESM, 21–22; exercise, 209; gender, 217, 220; happiness in countries, 214, 215–16; happiness set point, 45; hendoic versus eudaimonic, 132; its meaning, 13; National Happiness

Index, 65; neuroscience, 134, 135, 225; optimism, 224; public policy, 221, 223; serotonin, 129; sleep, 209; society, 245; spirituality, 246; travel, 18; in the workplace, 212, 218–19. *See also* Emmons, Robert; Life strategy; Lyubomirsky, Sonja

Happy Business Index, 218

Hope: in belief systems, 7; as cornerstone of positive psychology, 3–4; cultural limitations, 7; its different aspects, 3–4; heroism, 5; high hope versus low hope, 4; Martin Luther King Jr., 9; strengths-based counseling, 32; strengths-based leadership, 28; in VIA Inventory of Strengths, 227

Hurricane Katrina, 84–85; media response, 84; recovery, 85

Kabat-Zinn, Jon: MBSR (Mindfulness-Based Stress Reduction), 109, 123; mindfulness, 63, 103, 109; mindfulness meditation, 119

Kahneman, Daniel: dual process model of the brain, 131; economics, 147

Kauai Longitudinal Study, 74–75

Leadership: important aspects of, 28; leadership psychology, 236; positive leadership, 30–31; positive leadership orientations, 29; strengths-based leadership qualities, 29–30; in VIA Inventory of Strengths, 227. *See also* Strengths-based leadership

Life strategy: alleviating stress, 222; becoming mindful, 106; cognitive reprisal, 144–45; cultivating your strengths, 40; delayed gratification and well-being, 89; handling negative emotions, 201; importance of gratitude, 114; personal storytelling, 169; practicing forgiveness, 110–11; resiliency can be learned, 95

Lyubomirsky, Sonja, 172; exercise, 141; forgiveness, 110; happiness, 45, 148; mindfulness meditation, 135

Media psychology, 233–35; the fun theory, 47; media consumption, 135

Meditation, 174–75; Buddhist monks, 104, 135; in companies, 218; flow, 52; meditation studies, 63, 67, 108, 124

Mindfulness: acceptance, 112–13; affect regulation, 111–12; authenticity, 124; as a cognitive state, 174–75, 176; core concepts of, 105; defined, 102; different areas of research in, 170–71; Eastern and Western approaches, 103–4; empathy, 120, 121, 122; flow, 63; gratitude, 118, 120; measurement of, 107–8; Mindfulness-Based Stress Reduction (MBSR), 103, 109, 111, 119, 123; sports psychology, 113; studies in, 106–7, 113. *See also* Empathy; Forgiveness

Mindfulness meditation, 119; brain structure, 140; Google, 219; MSBR, 109, 111; studies in, 115. *See also* Kabat-Zinn, Jon

Mindlessness, 103; automatic thinking, 104, 108; defined, in stories, 158

Motivation: as defined by, 4; extrinsic versus intrinsic, 52–53; flow, 53, 55; hope, 3; intrinsic, 50, 52, 53; intrinsic rewards, 53

Narrative structure: health, 176–77; narrative psychology, 160, 171; narrative therapy, 163, 166; as principle of human development, 158, 161; public narrative, 174; redirection, 168; role of, 155; self-narrative, 161, 162, 166, 172; social cognitive thinking, 163; understanding experience, 160

Nervous system: central and peripheral, 128; mirror neurons, 150, 151; neuralgia, 128; neurons, 127, 128; synapse, 129

Neuroplasticity: cognitive support, 134–35; sports psychology, 113

Neurotransmitters: common neurotransmitters, 129; definition and role, 129; dopamine, 129, 243

Obesity, 231

Occupational health therapy, 236–37

Optimism: abilities of, 150; as coping mechanism, 15, 16; as a cornerstone of positive psychology, 12, 15, 16, 17; the diary of Anne Frank, 17, 18, 19;

hope, 5; positive illusions, 167–68; practices for resiliency, 17
Organizational psychology, 235–36

Pessimism: coping tendencies, 15
Peterson, Christopher, 41; Clifton StrenghtsFinder, 25, 27–28; *Character Strengths and Virtues: A Handbook and Classification,* 26, 41, 226; fulfillment, 187; institutions, 186. *See also* Seligman, Martin
Positive emotions: benefits of, 62, 91; its contagion, 249; coping, 91; education, 190, 191; fMRI, 374; games, 173; laughter, 93; learned optimism, 224; a study in, 91. *See also* Frederickson, Barbara
Positive institutions: company examples, 192–93; corporate social responsibility programs, 194–95, 198; defined, 185; early learning environments, 191; enabling institutions, 186–87; family, 187–89; Google, 186–87; interior spaces, 200, 202–3; organizations, 191–92, 212–13, 238–39; schools, 189–90
Power: in historical contexts, 234; soft versus hard, 233–35
Putnam, Robert: *Bowling Alone,* 217, 220

Reflected Best Self Exercise, 78–79
Resiliency: as an adaptive process, 71, 74; its assets, 75; cognitive reappraisal, 82–83, 86–87; gene by environment concept (GxE), 143; genetics, 149–50; history of study, 73–74; interventions, 81; pathway models, 78–79; person-focused models, 77–78; post Hurricane Katrina, 84–85; posttraumatic growth, 94, 95, 96; posttraumatic stress disorder (PTSD), 96; protective factors of, 79–80; role of risk, 71–72, 73–74; strategies for building resilience, 81–82; studies with children, 72, 73–74; its subjective components, 119; the subjectivity of positive outcome, 72–73; variable-focused models, 76–77. *See also* Cognitive

resilience; Emotional resilience; Kauai Longitudinal Study; Self-efficacy
Rogers, Carl, 120, 121, 122

Scales and questionnaires: Brief COPE, 204; Connor-Davidson Resilience Scale, 204; Ego Resiliency Scale, 204; Interpersonal Reactivity Index (IRI), 123; Life Orientation Test Revised (LOT-R), 14, 204; Mindfulness and the Five Facet Mindfulness Questionnaire, 108; Optimism and Life Orientation Test (LOT), 14; Perceived Stress Scale, 204; Purpose of Life, 204; Resiliency and Headington Institute Resilience Scale (HIRI), 99; Ryff Scales of Psychological Well Being, 117; Satisfaction with Life Scale, 121; VIA Inventory of Strengths, 27, 226–27
Scientist-practitioner model, 2–3
Self-efficacy: agency, 173; as cognitive resilience, 83; defined, 83; self-efficacy theory, 83; social cognitive theory, 83. *See also* Cognitive resilience
Seligman, Martin: *Authentic Happiness,* 182; *Character Strengths and Virtues: A Handbook and Classification,* 26; Comprehensive Soldier Fitness and Family Fitness, 97; helplessness, 8, 232; lack of hope, 5; optimistic and pessimistic thoughts, 15; "PERMA," 224; theory of learned optimism, 12, 15, 224; VIA Survey, 27. *See also* Peterson, Christopher
Sesame Street, 164
Sid the Science Kid, 164
Social capital: decline in, 217, 220–21; positive emotions, 185. *See also* Putnam, Robert
Social comparison theory: defined, 203; theory, 203, 204; upward comparisons, 205
Social entrepreneurship, 195–96; introduction of microcredit, 196–97
Stories: basic structure, 158–59; bibliotherapy, 289; characters, 268–69; cinematherapy, 174–75; cultural implications, 155–56; development of the individual, 161; life stories, 160; making meaning out of environment,

157; narrative structure, 155; projection, 157–58; research, 156; self-stories, 167, 174; time, 162–63, 171. *See also* Narrative structure

Storytelling: clinical practice, 156; emotional expression, 168, 170–71; media, 172, 173; narrative psychology, 271; as a research tool, 265; social storytelling, 172. *See also* Empathy

Strengths: character virtues, 26–27; different types of, 25; strengths-based counseling, 32–34; strengths-based education, 38–39; strengths-based models and talents, 60; strengths-based psychology, 25; strengths-based teaching, 34–35; StrengthsFinder, 27–28; VIA Inventory of Strengths, 27. *See also* Clifton, Donald O.

Strengths-based leadership: book by the same title, 30; defined, 28; the military, 31–32; qualities of, 29–30. *See also* Leadership

Stress: adaptation, 121–22; alleviation, 381–83; coping, 89; cortisol, 93; effects of, 90, 134; flow, 50, 61, 63; forgiveness, 141; humor, 93–94; laughter, 93; MBSR, 103, 109, 123; meditation, 135; mindfulness, 67; mindlessness, 108, 109–10; in modern life, 13–14; resiliency, 21, 23, 97, 98, 99; social support, 137; a study with mice, 143, 149–50; "toxic" stress, 78–79; work-life balance, 232–33. *See also* Resiliency: posttraumatic stress disorder

Structures of the brain: amygdala, 215; brainstem, 215; cerebellum, 214; cerebrum and its lobes, 214; cortices, 236; hippocampus, 215; hypothalamus, 215; limbic system, 214–15; pituitary gland, 215

Subjective well-being (SWB): its axes, 216; corruption of, 220; defined, 13; forgiveness, 191; happiness, 20, 21; life satisfaction, 216–17; schools, 189–90

Theory of Mind, 155

Usability psychology, 237

Values in Action (VIA) Inventory of Strengths: categories and strengths, 27; survey, 226–27

World Happiness Report, 66, 214–15

Zappos, 6

About the Authors

ERIK M. GREGORY, PhD, is executive director of the Media Psychology Research Center in Boston, Massachusetts, and is a Director at Sidekicks International—a Cambridge-based start-up in Harvard Square. He serves as the resident psychotherapist for the Humanist Hub in Cambridge, Massachusetts. Gregory received degrees from Harvard University and the University of Wisconsin-Madison and was a visiting scholar at the University of Chicago. His published works include *Children's Media Use: A Positive Psychology Approach*, and he is a blogger for *Psychology Today*. Gregory serves on arts and animal-rights nonprofit boards. He established the world's first doctoral programs in media and leadership psychology.

PAMELA B. RUTLEDGE, PhD, is director of the Media Psychology Center in Boston and a faculty member at Fielding Graduate University, Santa Barbara, California, where she designed the Brand Psychology and Audience Engagement certificate program. Rutledge consults on a number of media and technology projects applying behavioral science with an emphasis on positive psychology to marketing and brand strategy. She has published both academic and popular work and authors "Positively Media" for *Psychology Today*. Rutledge sits on the advisory boards of the Legends of Orkney Transmedia Literacy Project and the Social Media Marketing Certificate program at the University of California, Irvine Extension.